Poverty and the Underclass

Poverty and the Underclass

Changing Perceptions of the Poor in America

William A. Kelso

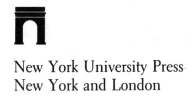

New York University Press
New York and London

NEW YORK UNIVERSITY PRESS
New York and London

Library of Congress Cataloging-in-Publication Data
Kelso, William Alton.
Poverty and the underclass : changing perceptions of the poor in
America / William A. Kelso.
    p.   cm.
Includes bibliographical references and index.
ISBN 0-8147-4658-6   ISBN 0-8147-4661-6 pbk.
1. Poor—United States.   2. Economic assistance, Domestic—United
States. 3. Poverty. I. Title.
HC110.P6K45 1994
305.5'69'0973—dc20   94-28203
                            CIP

New York University Press books are printed on acid-free paper,
and their binding materials are chosen for strength and durability.

Manufactured in the United States of America

10   9   8   7   6   5   4   3   2

Contents

Preface

Writing this book has been both a personal and an intellectual odyssey for me. Like many in my generation, I was hopeful that President Lyndon Johnson's "Great Society" would prove successful in promoting upward mobility and eliminating poverty in America. But once I began my career as a professor at the University of Florida I felt frustrated at the government's lack of success in helping indigents climb above the poverty line. As I became older I also began to have reservations about my previous belief in the ability of government programs to solve all of society's ills. When I began teaching a course on public policy, I finally had to face my doubts as my students kept asking me why the "war on poverty" has failed to work.

Over the last couple of years, excellent books on this question have appeared by William Julius Wilson, Christopher Jencks, David Ellwood, Lawrence Mead, and Charles Murray, among others. But for various reasons I have felt that they touched on only part of the story. In 1988 Isabel Sawhill wrote a very important article in the *Journal of Economic Literature* in which she suggested that previous research has failed to note that the intractable nature of poverty in this country is a result not of any one factor but of the interaction of a variety of causes. Building on Professor Sawhill's work, I have tried to analyze the many complex reasons, from the breakdown of the family to structural changes in the economy, that have contributed to society's failure to eradicate poverty. But what is more important, I have also tried to show how liberals, conservatives, and radicals have tried to deal with the failures of the war on poverty. Because too many analysts have become bogged down in minute discussions of individual programs, they have often failed to realize that a dramatic shift in the way the right and the left propose to tackle the problem of poverty has taken place. In the first and last chapters of this book I try to sketch out two alternative and sharply different political agendas that the political system can adopt to deal with the needs of indigents.

In writing this book, I have naturally accumulated a large number of debts. While many of my students may not have realized it, their excellent questions often caused me to rethink my position on a variety of issues. If any of them happen to read this book, I hope they will feel that I finally answered their questions more thoroughly in print than I may earlier have done in the classroom.

I also owe many thanks to a variety of student research assistants and faculty members for their help in putting this book together. Sybil Brown, Kim Murray, Philip Bonamo, Angie Ortega, Jordan Mertz, Kevin Hill, and David Gellen were excellent research analysts who helped me track down data from from the Census Bureau and the Department of Health and Human Resources. Tom Caswell, the documents librarian at the University of Florida, was also of great assistance in helping me locate "just one more government document."

Nobutaka Ike of Stanford University went out of his way to read and make valuable suggestions for improving the manuscript. His assistance went beyond the call of duty and is greatly appreciated. By constantly asking tough questions, Al Clubok, my colleague at the University of Florida, helped me to refine my arguments and improve the overall quality of the book. Another colleague, Bert Swanson, always generous with his time, made numerous suggestions for improving the organization of the manuscript. Likewise, Jim Button and Ken Wald, who also agreed to read the whole manuscript, helped me whip it into its final form. My longtime friend from high school, Roger Peterson, was instrumental in convincing me of the importance of entrepreneurship and workfare in enabling people to climb out of poverty. I also owe a special debt of gratitude to Niko Pfund of New York University Press. An author could not ask for a more helpful or insightful editor. I give thanks also to Gus Burns, Richard Scher, Shota Ike, Catherine Lee, Chris Schuetz, Mika Ike, Mary Gay Anderson, Kevin Kelso, Doug Harrison, Elizabeth Williams, Heather Schuetz, and Bharat Pateland for their assistance in helping me complete the manuscript. I should quickly add that not all of the above individuals necessarily agree with everything I have written.

Finally, I wish to thank my wife for all of her good will, support, and encouragement in writing this book. Despite her busy career as a lawyer, she has always patiently listened to me drone on and on about poverty. Like many an author, I often wondered if I would ever finish the manuscript. Her encouragement and support always made it easier for me to keep plugging away. Because of her love and devotion over many years, I gladly dedicate this book to her. I also know she has been looking forward to my finishing the manuscript for quite some time so that we could discuss some other topic besides poverty. Now that the book is finally published, I have agreed to mend my ways and talk about nothing but legal concepts for the next year. Already I am preparing myself for many fascinating legal discussions about hedge funds, the Securities Act of 1933, and the complexities of Regulation U. But on second thought, maybe I do have enough material left over for yet another book on poverty.

Poverty and the Underclass

PART ONE

The Poverty Debate

ONE

Doesn't Anything Work? Is a War against Poverty Really Feasible?

As Lyndon Johnson began his first full term as president of the United States in 1964, many liberal Democrats were optimistic and excited about his social agenda. Political pundits as well as the news media speculated that the country was finally going to take action to relieve the poverty and misery that seemed to afflict so many people in this land of plenty. After all, Johnson promised to initiate a "war on poverty" that would create a more just and humane society that all Americans could be proud of. In the heady days of the 1960s, the American political left sincerely believed that the plight of the poor would finally be eliminated by the government's attack on the causes of poverty.

But after three decades of experience with welfare programs, the sense of optimism that previously animated liberalism seems spent. By the late 1970s it was apparent that President Johnson's war on poverty had been a failure. Despite the billions of dollars spent on programs like compensatory education and CETA (Comprehensive Employment Training Act), government efforts to deal with the origins of poverty have met with minimal success at best. In light of these failures, an increasing number of liberals began to reassess their social agenda and started talking about treating the consequences rather than eliminating the causes of poverty: if the government could not help people become financially independent, its next best policy was to shield them from the hardships of limited income. But surprisingly enough, as the expectations of many liberals faded, conservatives started to argue that the government might be able to alleviate the origins of poverty after all. Over the last thirty years there has been a paradoxical shift in the attitudes of liberal Democrats, conservatives, and Marxists about the nagging problem of poverty. To appreciate this current state of affairs, it is important to understand how attitudes toward the poor have changed dramatically since the idea of the Great Society was first articulated thirty years ago.

In establishing his war on poverty, Johnson's goal had been to eliminate the causes rather than the consequences of poverty; or, as the president forcefully put it, his objective was to give people a hand rather than a handout. The Johnson administration rejected the policy of subsidizing he poor because it hoped to attack the origins of poverty by providing individuals with the training and skills necessary to earn their way out of a life of destitution.

To achieve that objective, the administration launched a multifaceted attack on the causes of low income. Some in the administration, such as Walter Heller, stressed the need to stimulate economic growth, while others emphasized the importance of eliminating racial barriers to upward mobility. But Johnson's main thrust was geared to upgrading the skills of the poor.[1] The Johnson presidency believed that even if indigents wanted to work, they lacked the appropriate training and skills necessary to compete in the labor market successfully. To correct these problems, the government launched a series of initiatives such as the Job Corps, the Manpower Development and Training Act, Head Start, Upward Bound, and the Elementary and Secondary Education Act.

However, governmental efforts to improve the education of the poor quickly proved to be ineffective in enabling people to climb out of poverty. The problem certainly was not from a lack of trying. From 1963 to 1985, the government spent over $282 billion (in 1986 dollars) on targeted education and training programs.[2] Yet during that same time, the percentage of people climbing out of poverty by securing decent jobs remained static, and the distribution of income in the United States became even more unequal. Even more disturbing was the growth of a large and often self-destructive underclass in our inner cities that seemed impervious to change. The government had offered a helping hand, but the vast majority of the poor seemed unable to grasp it.

As their hope for eradicating the causes of poverty turned sour, many liberals began to redefine the objectives of the welfare state. Instead of admitting that the government's war on poverty had failed, they insisted that the growth of government transfer programs had enabled millions of people to deal with the consequences of poverty. The metaphor of a war, with the implication that victory was possible, ceased to appear in discussions of the poverty problem. Instead of asking how to make people self-sufficient, government agencies began to focus on giving the less fortunate a handout in order to shield them from the financial insecurities of the marketplace.

The failure of Johnson's efforts to prepare people adequately for effective competition in the workplace convinced many liberals that they needed to focus their efforts on protecting people from the transformations occurring in the U.S. economy. By the end of the 1980s, the early rhetoric of enhancing the skills of the poor and promoting equal opportunity gave way to a new agenda that stressed entitlements, quotas, and equal results. If the government's efforts to help people help themselves had met with only mixed success, elected officials could at least make sure that those with low incomes received adequate subsidies to deal with the consequences of poverty. While many liberals became increasingly pessimistic about the efficacy of government programs and reluctantly became resigned to treating the effects as opposed to the causes of poverty, an increasing number of conservatives shook off their sense of despair and began to express exactly the opposite view.

In the early 1960s, academics on the right like Edward Banfield had insisted that the poor were afflicted by a "culture of poverty," which made it impossible for them to ever compete successfully in the workplace.[3] As conservatives watched the Great Society mushroom in size, they insisted that it would only prove to be a costly failure. What is even more important, they maintained that such programs would unjustifiably raise the expectations of the poor that things would get better, when in reality the plight of the poor would probably change very little. Because they believed the poor had little ability to improve their lot, conservatives thought it was futile for the government to try to solve the causes of poverty.

However, by the mid-1970s the view of many conservatives about poverty had changed dramatically. Beginning with Thomas Sowell, critics on the right began to write about the successes several ethnic groups had enjoyed in climbing out of poverty.[4] Instead of dwelling on the pathological culture of the poor, they identified ethnic groups such as West Indian blacks, Japanese, Chinese, and Jews who had come to this country poor but had achieved prosperity within a relatively short time. Many of these same ethnic groups had to deal with systematic racial discrimination and limited government assistance but had still managed to prosper. The critics thus suggested that maybe a war against poverty could be won after all: the success stories among ethnic Americans belied the claim that all the poor were permanently locked in a self-perpetuating poverty trap.

Similarly, other conservatives, such as Charles Murray, began to express hope that the poor could eventually become self-sufficient. In studying upward mobility in this country, Murray wanted to know if poverty rates had historically been constant or if they had declined over time.[5] To his amazement, he found that in the 1950s, when the government did little to assist the poor, the poverty rate dropped about 2 percent a year. Apparently, when people were left to their own devices, they seemed to be able to climb out of poverty on their own. But the picture began to change in the late 1960s, to the detriment of the poor. As the Great Society's efforts to combat poverty swung into action, the number of people escaping poverty on their own, that is, escaping what is now called "pretransfer poverty," leveled out and even began to decrease. Murray argued that well-meaning government transfer programs were in large part responsible for the poor "losing ground" in their fight against poverty.

Because Murray questioned the very raison d'être of the Great Society and suggested drastic cuts in the size of entitlement programs, he was harshly criticized by his liberal detractors. While its supporters recognized that the growth of the welfare state had proved ineffectual in eliminating the causes of poverty, they were determined to disprove the notion that their transfer programs created disincentives for low-income people to escape poverty. To concede that some public programs were ineffective was very different from accepting the proposition that government transfer programs were actually harmful to the poor.

In attacking Murray's pessimistic assessment, critics tended to overlook his rather optimistic assessment that the causes of poverty could be successfully overcome. Both Murray and Sowell suggested that, given the proper conditions, the poor could work their way out of poverty. Whether it was due to the entrepreneurial activities of ethnic groups or the trickle-down effects of economic growth, the number of people stuck in poverty had significantly declined in the 1950s and 1960s. If that progress had been halted in the 1970s, it could be restarted by a different set of policies. While conservatives in the 1960s had insisted that the pathological nature of lower-class culture rendered efforts to eliminate poverty an exercise in futility, they downplayed such sentiments in the 1980s and 1990s and optimistically suggested that the causes of poverty could be treated.

Simultaneously, many American Marxists also began to reevaluate their assessment of the welfare state. In the 1960s radicals like Francis Fox Piven and Robert Cloward had lambasted the war on poverty as a cynical effort to coopt and pacify the poor, but by the 1980s and 1990s they embraced the programs they had earlier criticized.[6] Marxists were initially critical of Johnson's poverty programs because they saw poverty as playing a functional role in a capitalist economy. In their eyes, the captains of industry needed a large pool of dispossessed indigents to maintain downward pressure on wages. If the working class ever became active and powerful enough to secure sizable increases in their wages, they would seriously eat away the profit margins of the country's corporations. Conversely, if there were millions of poor people waiting to fill any available openings at minimal wages, the leverage of trade unions would be broken and the threat to corporate profits would disappear. By playing the poor off against the working class, business interests could always neutralize the bargaining power of the working class. Given their perspective of the marketplace, Piven and Cloward saw poverty as essential to the workings of our capitalist system. People were poor not because they had a pathological culture or inadequate work skills. Poverty, in fact, had nothing to do with the characteristics of individuals at all. People were kept in poverty because it served the long-term functional needs of capitalism in general and the short-term profit needs of corporations in particular.

However, the poor often refused to play this docile role by periodically rioting and disrupting the peace and quiet of American cities. In order to stop this threat to political harmony, the political system tried to buy off the poor by temporarily expanding the scope of the welfare state. At the behest of the capitalist interests that allegedly dominated our government, public officials cynically placated the poor so that more meaningful reforms would not be required. Piven and Cloward contended that once the poor were pacified and the rioting in our cities had died down, politicians would begin to dismantle the enlargement of the welfare state. The expansion of the welfare state under Lyndon Johnson was thus part of a long-term cycle going back to the Great Depression. As the economy worsened, the government made cosmetic changes to pacify the poor and thus negate the need for dramatic and meaningful change.

Despite their wholesale condemnation of the war on poverty, Piven and Cloward were animated by a revolutionary belief that the riots sweeping American cities held out the potential for solving the poverty problem. If the government could be prevented from buying off the poor, there was hope for systematic change in our capitalist economy. In the early 1960s, American Marxists thus entertained a curious combination of both hope and despair that the causes of poverty could eventually be attacked. If only the poor could be made aware that the welfare state was part of the class struggle, they might resist its seductive nature and bring about meaningful economic change.

By the 1980s, the same Marxists who had condemned the war on poverty for coopting the poor vigorously defended those same programs against the budget cutters in the Reagan administration who wanted to contract the scope of the welfare state. They insisted that public relief had to be preserved intact in order to protect the financial well-being of those stuck at the bottom of the economic ladder. Instead of modifying capitalism and thus getting at the root causes of poverty, they seemed more intent on guaranteeing that transfer programs adequately insulated people from the vagaries of the market economy. Paradoxically, like liberals, Marxists had increasingly become preoccupied with treating the consequences rather than the causes of poverty.

WHY THE SHIFT IN ATTITUDES?

In less than a quarter of a century, attitudes toward poverty had been dramatically turned upside down. Why is it that many liberals, who had once hoped to win the war against poverty, now seemed resigned to treating its effects? Why did Marxists, who once condemned the welfare state as being harmful to the long-term interests of the poor, now embrace the programs they earlier saw as manipulative? Why did numerous conservatives, who once argued that the poor would always be burdened with low incomes, now argue that a sizable number of poor could permanently work their way out of poverty?

The answers to these issues are based on both changing perceptions of the causes of poverty as well as the political realities of American politics. Some Marxists insist that their opinions of the welfare state reflect the dialectical and contradictory nature of social change in general: while poverty programs may be functional to the needs of capitalist development, they may also simultaneously advance the class interests of the poor in their struggle to survive in a capitalist economy. However, in more practical terms, Piven and Cloward have probably altered their view of the welfare state out of a reluctance to lend any kind of support to conservatives who wish to curtail the growth of transfer programs. When Ronald Reagan raised serious questions about the welfare state in the 1980s, many radicals undoubtedly felt the need to respond to his attack. Even if ideologically they felt that the welfare state was manipulative, their hostility to the agenda of the right led them to embrace programs they had earlier dismissed. While their reversal of positions may have been of some tactical and strategic advantage, their credibility in offering a meaningful interpretation of the welfare state was called into question.

The dispute between conservatives and liberals, in contrast, was based more on empirical than strategic considerations. The changing perceptions of many on the left and the right as to whether or not the government could eliminate the causes of poverty reflected in turn their changing perceptions as to why people had become poor in the first place. As the government's efforts to effectively reduce poverty came to an end around the late 1960s, it was apparent to everyone that the government's original diagnosis of why poverty had occurred in this country was wrong. Since the proponents of Johnson's war on poverty maintained that poverty stemmed from a deficiency in educational and vocational skills, they could optimistically believe that a war on poverty could be won. But as liberals abandoned supply side theories of poverty and focused on structural conditions in the economy, their optimistic belief that they could eliminate the causes of poverty began to disappear. When the Japanese started to penetrate the U.S. marketplace in the 1970s, critics like William Julius Wilson raised fears that the industrial heartland of America would become a rust belt. As new jobs declined, the opportunities to escape poverty would also dry up, limiting the ability of government to treat the causes of poverty.[7] A very real danger thus existed that the economy would fragment into a series of high-paying and low-paying sectors. Rather than working in the industrial sector where prospects of upward mobility still existed, the poor now faced the bleak prospect of flipping hamburgers for minimum wages. In the same way that the war in Vietnam had not succeeded, the war on poverty also had been a misguided failure. In both cases the country had misdiagnosed the nature of the enemy. It made little sense to upgrade the skills of the poor when the manufacturing base of the U.S. economy had lost the capability to actually employ the poor. If these economic changes were permanent, it was obvious that protecting the poor from the changing world economy was the best substitute for victory the political system could achieve.

While liberals focused on structural changes in the economy, conservatives began to zero in on either government programs or the breakdown of traditional values to explain the persistence of poverty. They abandoned their belief of the 1960s that the poor were mired in poverty because of a pathological "culture of poverty." On the contrary, some analysts like Charles Murray insisted that the disincentives embedded in many government welfare programs as well as the philosophical underpinnings of many transfer programs had eroded the initiative and self-reliance of the poor. However, others, such as Myron Magnet, the author or the provocative book *The Dream and the Nightmare*, insisted that the problems of the poor reflected a breakdown in traditional values—such as a belief in self-restraint, hard work, and marital stability—in the larger society.[8] Once political and civic elites ceased upholding traditional beliefs in a clear and unambiguous fashion, many of the poor let go of traditional beliefs faster than the rest of society. As this phenomenon, which the famous French sociologist Emile Durkheim labeled "anomie," trickled down to the poor, a large and often destructive underclass began to appear in our inner cities. Despite their internal differences, analysts on the right increasingly believed that it was possible to eliminate the actual causes of poverty. While conservatives often espoused policies such as cutting back the size of the welfare state or the establishment of workfare, which generated considerable controversy, they remained optimistic that a war on poverty could eventually be won.

By the 1980s the political right and left had thus significantly revised their diagnosis of poverty as well as their solutions for dealing with the large poverty population in the country. As numerous liberals insisted that poverty was rooted in the changing nature of the economy, they increasingly became resigned to treating the effects of poverty while many conservatives, who blamed either governmental disincentives or the erosion of traditional values for the persistence of poverty, became hopeful that public officials could still eliminate the origins of poverty.

WHERE DOES THE DEBATE GO FROM HERE?

In light of the shifting political agenda by both the right and left, it is time for a reassessment of what kind of poverty policies the country should adopt. My main reason for choosing to write this book is to take a fresh look at the alleged causes of poverty. If we want an informed debate over what kind of poverty programs the government should adopt, we need to significantly rethink why poverty has become such a persistent problem in this country. As we have just seen, policy recommendations usually reflect people's perceptions as to why individuals became poor in the first place. As the debate over poverty and the underclass enters the 1990s, it is imperative that we reassess the alternative explanations that both the left and the right have embraced. Just as liberals and conservatives today claim that their predecessors had been incorrect in their diagnosis of poverty in the 1960s, it is very possible that their current reading of the poverty problem may be equally mistaken.

In the last thirty years, the debate over poverty has gone through a series of permutations and combinations. During the Johnson era, liberal, conservative, and Marxist opponents disagreed whether it was the lack of human capital, a specific culture of poverty, or capitalist exploitation that primarily explained the existence of poverty. Two decades later, they clashed over whether it was cyclical changes in the economy or the disincentives of government welfare programs that accounted for the persistence of poverty. By the late 1980s, the debate had become even more complex. Conservatives often advanced a diverse array of supply-side arguments that focused on the breakdown of values among the poor and the subsequent changes in their family patterns and work habits, while liberals focused on the collapse of the industrial sector and the structural transformation of the American economy to explain the persistence of poverty.

With the start of a new decade, it may be time for a reexamination of the various causes of poverty. The past tendency of many liberals and conservatives alike to collapse the discussion of the origins of poverty into opposing explanations often oversimplifies what is a very complex issue. Social critics need to recognize that the intractable nature of poverty is a result not of any one factor but of the interaction of a variety of subtle and often diverse causes. That is why the chapters to follow examine in greater detail the various explanations advanced to account for the government's failure to win the war against poverty.

At the end of the book, I offer a variety of recommendations for coping with the seemingly intractable nature of poverty in this country. Because our perceptions of why people have become indigents in the first place have obvious policy consequences, the analysis of the origins of poverty should suggest whether we can realistically hope to eliminate the causes of poverty or if we must be resigned to treating its effects.

In light of my belief that poverty is a multidimensional problem, there are grounds to believe that a war on poverty is potentially winnable. If the financial difficulties of the poor are a result of a multiplicity of factors, then policymakers may be able to intervene in society at a variety of points to attack the origins of poverty. For instance, if the working poor are suffering from low wages, government incentives to enhance productivity may lift thousands of indigents above the poverty line. However, the most controversial part of this book is its stress on the role culture plays in eliminating poverty. It is my contention that people's values, family ties, and their willingness to follow socially acceptable rules of conduct are the primary ingredients in determining whether they escape poverty or not. The unfortunate rise of the underclass in the 1960s may reflect the absence of these values or a growing sense of normlessness among the indigent population. The political system is likely to make little headway in combating the causes of poverty until it can successfully repair this breakdown of traditional mores by resocializing the poor into adopting more appropriate forms of behavior.

Given my assumption that a war on poverty can eventually prove to be successful, I have serious reservations about the tendency of post-1960 liberals to focus on ameliorating the consequences rather than trying to eradicate the actual sources of poverty. By constantly blaming structural factors such as the changing world economy for the country's checkered record in fighting poverty, too many liberals have become unduly pessimistic about what can be accomplished. Even more serious is the growing inclination of the left to advocate policies that stress equal results and entitlements rather than equal opportunity, which almost guarantees that the fight to eliminate poverty will be lost by default. Unless the poor are constantly encouraged, cajoled, or even required to become self-sufficient, the danger exists that the poor will become resigned to becoming permanent wards of the state.

While it is difficult to predict the future, there is hope that the Democratic party may eventually change its stand on poverty. President Clinton's suggestion that he will propose a welfare state based on the principles of the "new covenant" is a welcome sign that liberal Democrats may once more embrace and defend the principle of equal opportunity that they had unfortunately abandoned in the 1960s. It would thus be an ironic twist in the convoluted politics of poverty if Clinton, who proclaims that he is a new-style liberal Democrat, ends up adopting policies that partially mirror those of his predecessor, Lyndon Johnson.

But even more important, it is possible that Clinton's argument that the welfare state should reward only those individuals who play by "the rules of the game" might actually unite both the right and the left in developing a common agenda for fighting poverty. Many conservatives would undoubtedly support the stress on the work ethic in Clinton's proposals to revamp the welfare state. If the government enters into a "new covenant" with the poor that emphasizes their obligations as well as their rights, the growth of the underclass may one day reverse itself. Like the president, the political right believes that too many indigents are flouting socially desirable standards of conduct.

But the extent to which Clinton can convince his own party to rethink its views on poverty is still an unresolved question. Before we can realistically hope to alter the attitudes of the the underclass, we also need to alter the attitudes of liberal policymakers who often minimize the destructive behavior of the underclass. Too many liberal Democrats reject the idea that cultural values are important in explaining people's behavior and insist that to criticize the poor in any way is to "blame the victim" for his or her own plight. Thus they often dismiss the erratic work record of the poor, or the criminal activities of what Christopher Jencks has labeled the "violent underclass," as nothing more than a rational response to existing conditions in America. Daniel Patrick Moynihan has accurately pointed out that this tendency to minimize destructive behavior is nothing more than "defining deviance down." If we are going to eliminate poverty in this country, all sides of the political spectrum have to recognize the deviant and often pathological behavior of members of the underclass. But whether Clinton can persuade the left, which historically has been hostile to talk about duties and playing by "the rules of the game," to unite with the right in recognizing the urgency of such behavioral problems remains to be seen.

Because people's preconceptions make it hard for them to analyze the issue of poverty in an objective and dispassionate fashion, the debate between the right and the left over welfare policies has become highly partisan in nature. While too many on the right often fail clearly to appreciate some of the economic obstacles confronting both the working poor and the underclass, the left often makes the opposite mistake by ignoring the self-destructive behavior of the underclass while exaggerating the lack of upward mobility in society. The danger thus exists that the contentious nature of the subject matter may eventually doom any efforts to reduce the poverty rate in the 1990s. Even when we finally have an understanding of how to eliminate the causes of poverty, U.S. politicians may lack the public consensus and willpower necessary to act on that knowledge. The very real possibility exists that, instead of waging a successful war against poverty, America must resign itself to living with, as well as subsidizing, an intractable indigent population.

T W O

Poverty: How Serious Is the Problem?

Before analyzing the origins of poverty, it is essential to understand the magnitude of the problem. As any newspaper reader who looks at the yearly census count of indigents or scans information about the long-term dependency of welfare mothers or the violent crime of inner-city youths knows, millions of people still suffer from poverty. Despite the sense of optimism that animated the Johnson administration in the 1960s, there is a growing recognition that the country has failed in its efforts to eliminate poverty in two distinct ways. Today, on an aggregate basis, there are more poor people than when Johnson started his war against poverty, and, on a behavioral level, more indigents than ever before engage in self-destructive actions such as participating in criminal activity or dropping out of the work force. The tendency of the segment of the poor population that has been labeled the underclass to flout traditional norms of behavior has often destroyed any semblance of community life in the inner city.

DEFINING THE POOR

The failure of the war on poverty is reflected in the aggregate number of people who are classified as poor according to the federal government's official definition of poverty. Ironically, there was no national definition of poverty until the 1960s. Before the war on poverty began, welfare was primarily a state and local responsibility, and the federal government thus had no need to identify the poor. When Lyndon Johnson launched his war on poverty in the 1960s, the need for a definition of poverty quickly became apparent. The Council of Economic Advisors (the CEA) originally tried to come up with an acceptable definition, but its efforts met with limited

14

success. As a consequence, Mollie Orshansky of the Social Security Administration developed an alternative definition, which was eventually accepted as the official version of poverty in 1965.[1] What was remarkable about the government's conception of poverty was the way in which it was derived. In adopting Orshansky's definition, the government relied on a lower-level administrator to set the standards for determining the success of its poverty programs. Instead of establishing a blue-ribbon committee of experts to explore alternative ways of measuring and tracking the incidence of poverty, President Johnson, who had launched the war on poverty with much fanfare, seemed indifferent as to how the beneficiaries of his program were identified.

To fill this void, Orshansky argued that poverty was essentially a problem of absolute rather than relative deprivation. She believed that people should be considered poor if their income fell below some acceptable minimum dollar amount. In trying to identify what would be an acceptable cutoff point, Orshansky argued that a person needed sufficient money to purchase food for a nutritionally adequate diet. Accordingly, she took the Department of Agriculture's cost of an "economical" food plan for a family of a specified size and multiplied it by a factor of three. Orshansky derived this particular multiplier from a survey of American families which showed that the average expenditure on food by all families in the sample is one-third of their after-tax income. The resulting dollar amount became the official poverty line.

HOW UNSUCCESSFUL HAS THE WAR ON POVERTY BEEN?

In order to to tell if the government is making progress in fighting poverty, we need to (1) ask what its objectives are, and (2) decide in light of these objectives what resources available to low-income individuals should be counted in determining whether they fall above or below the poverty line. If the country's goal is to eliminate the causes of poverty, we need to focus on what poverty analysts call "pretransfer poverty." This indicator tells us if the income that individuals have earned on their own is sufficient to push them above Orshansky's absolute threshold point. However, if public officials are interested in treating only the consequences of poverty, then a more appropriate measure is either the official poverty rate or the net poverty rate. The government's official rate calculates how many poor people there are by adding together private income with the cash benefits provided by the government. If the combination of these two streams of income is not enough to push individuals over Orshansky's absolute level, we are talking about the official poor. Finally, net poverty figures merely modify the official rates by also including noncash benefits such as food stamps or public housing that

Figure 2.1

Rates of Poverty, 1950–1991

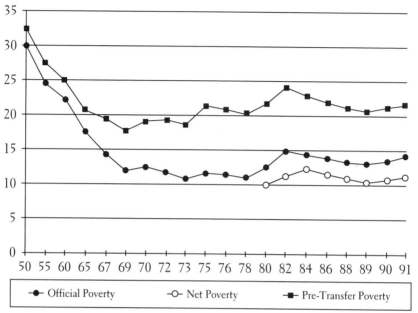

Sources: Official poverty rate is from House Committee on Ways and Means, *Green Book: The Overview of Entitlement Programs* (1991). Net poverty rates for 1980 to 1985 are from U.S. Bureau of the Census, *Estimates of Poverty Including the Value of Noncash Benefits,* Technical Paper 56 (Washington, D.C.: U.S. Government Printing Office, 1986). Net poverty rate for 1986 is from U.S. Bureau of the Census, *Estimates of Poverty Including the Value of Noncash Benefits 1986,* Technical Paper 57 (Washington, D.C.: U.S. Government Printing Office, 1987). Official net poverty rates for 1989 to 1990 are from U.S. Bureau of the Census, *Current Population Reports,* Series P-60, no. 176-RD, "Measuring the Effects of Benefits and Taxes on Income and Poverty, 1991." Pretransfer poverty rates for 1950 to 1984 are from Charles Murray, *Losing Ground* (New York: Basic Books, 1984). Pretransfer rates for 1986 to 1988 were obtained over the phone from the Institute of Poverty at the University of Wisconsin. The most recent data are from the House Committee on Ways and Means, *Green Book: The Overview of Entitlement Programs* (1991).

indigents receive from public transfer programs. This indicator tells us if the income that individuals have earned on their own together with the cash and noncash benefits they receive from government entitlement programs puts them above the poverty threshold point.

No matter which indicator we look at, it is obvious that the government's efforts to eliminate poverty have fallen far short of its goals. As figure 2.1 indicates, the percentage of people who are poor dropped steadily from the 1950s until the late 1960s, when it began a slow upturn. Because the official and net rates include resources from both the individual and the government, they provide no direct clues as to why poverty fluctuate upward or downward.

If the official rate declines, we cannot tell if it is because the government is stepping up its assistance to the poor, or because the poor are doing better on their own. By simultaneously comparing pretransfer poverty and the official measures of poverty, the reasons for the change in the level of poverty become clearer. When pretransfer rates of poverty increase while official rates either decline or grow at slower pace, then it is evident that the government has been more successful in treating the effects of poverty than in eliminating the causes of poverty.

Unfortunately, this scenario seems to be occurring in the United States. At the turn of the century, if one uses Mollie Orshansky's definition of poverty, probably around 40 to 45 percent of the population would have been considered poor. In contrast, in the immediate post-World War II period the official rate of poverty dropped steadily from around 30 percent in the 1950s to a little over 11 percent in 1973. For the rest of the 1970s, success in combating poverty leveled out, with the rate fluctuating between 11 and 13 percent. In the early 1980s the official rate began to rise once more, peaking in 1983 at 15.2 percent and then inching downward again to slightly more than 14 percent in 1991. For all intents and purposes, the country's success in eliminating poverty essentially stopped by the early 1970s.

A similar pattern emerges for pretransfer poverty but the decline occurred much earlier. By 1969 pretransfer poverty hit its lowest point of 17.7 percent, and then it began a slow rise to just under 22 percent by 1980. In the 1980s pretransfer poverty rose to a high of 24.2 percent and then dropped to around 22 percent in 1991. Despite Lyndon Johnson's efforts to give the poor a hand up rather than a handout, the number of people able to climb out of poverty on their own initiative actually decreased in the 1970s and '80s. When both types of poverty started to increase, the rise in pretransfer poverty was much sharper than the rise in the official or posttransfer measure of poverty. Pretransfer poverty rose 6.5 percentage points from its low point to its new high, while the official poverty rate rose slightly more than 4 points during the same period.

Both of these increases indicate that we have been losing the war against poverty since the end of the 1960s. But what is troubling is that the government seems to be doing a worse job in eliminating the causes of poverty than in treating its effects even though more money is being spent on public welfare programs. Although the government's cash and noncash benefits appear to compensate slightly for the worsening economic circumstances of many individuals, officials have yet to come up with effective programs that make more poor people financially self-reliant.

The same bleak situation is also apparent if we look at the social conditions in which the poor live. At present there is no single social indicator comparable to the Orshansky poverty index to measure the quality of life of the poor. In the following chapters, which look at indicators such as the number of poor people in college (chapter 4), the percentage of broken families among indigents (chapter 5), or the work record of the poor (chapter 7), it is readily apparent that the nature of poverty in this country has become more acute since the 1960s. The breakdown of the social fabric of everyday life is most evident among the poor of our inner cities. For this reason, the rise in the official poverty rate dramatically understates the severity of the problem. To use the language of economists, poverty is not a standardized or homogeneous good. We are seeing more and more people unable to escape poverty, and we are seeing an increase in the behavioral problems of the poor. In many respects, the growing pathological actions of the poor are as disturbing as the increasing number of people who cannot escape poverty on their own. As mentioned earlier, the government is losing the fight against poverty both qualitatively and qualitatively.

THE RISE OF THE UNDERCLASS: HOW PERSISTENT IS POVERTY?

But surprisingly enough, the willingness of poverty researchers to admit that things have changed for the worse over the last thirty years has generated a fair share of controversy. As we shall see, an attempt by Daniel Patrick Moynihan in the 1960s to describe the behavior of the poor stirred up so much hostility that many commentators chose to ignore the subject for the next two decades. However, by the 1980s there was a growing consensus that poverty had become a more intractable problem because of the rise of a large underclass. The fear was that poverty would increasingly become a persistent problem, with many people permanently trapped in a cycle of low income and limited mobility. To put this debate into historical perspective, it is important to note that academics have changed their view three different times over the last several decades with regard to the permanence of poverty. In the early 1960s, the Council of Economic Advisors pessimistically concluded "that the poor include a largely unchanging group of families."[2] However, the Council had data that indicated that almost one-third of the people who were indigents in 1962 had emerged from poverty by 1963: at this rate, very few people would be permanently stuck in poverty. But the consensus view was so strong that the Council chose either to ignore its own findings or not to believe them.

Michael Harrington also popularized a pessimistic view among the public at large in his widely read book, *The Other America*, in which he wrote "that the poor are caught in a vicious circle."*Harrington argued that the poor were a stable, unchanging group, "born to the wrong parents, in the wrong section of the country, in the wrong industry, or in the wrong racial or ethnic groups," and that "once that mistake has been made, they could have been paragons of will and morality, but most of them would never ever have had a chance to get out of the other America."𝑔 Besides echoing the conclusions of the Council of Economic Advisors about the present generation of poor people, Harrington also implied that poverty was a generational problem. If children were born to poor parents, it was unlikely that they would escape the hardships that had afflicted their parents. A variety of other studies in the 1960s seemed to confirm this rather ominous picture. Though the data were often sketchy, some reports indicated that approximately 40 percent of parents who received assistance from the federal government in the 1960s had themselves been children of welfare families.[4]

In the mid-1970s, a second and very different view of poverty began to emerge that revolutionized our understanding of the poor. This second picture grew out of research at the University of Michigan and was known as the Panel Study of Income Dynamics (PSID). Unlike most other research, which involved cross-sectional studies that in effect took a single picture of the poor at successive points in time, the Michigan study was an ambitious longitudinal study that followed the same five thousand people for successive years.[5] The Michigan researchers proposed two dramatic revisions of the portrait that Michael Harrington had popularized in the early 1960s. First, they found that a much larger percentage of the population seemed to float in and out of poverty. In one ten-year period in the 1970s, not quite 25 percent of the population experienced poverty for at least one year during that decade. While the official rates seemed to imply that there was a stable poor population that did not fluctuate much from year to year, the reality was very different. The poor seemed to consist of a large population that was constantly turning over. The finances of millions of people were evidently so fragile that any number of personal or economic events could push millions below the threshold level for poverty. Thus the PSID found that the poverty problem loomed much larger than was originally thought.[6]

However, the second finding of the Michigan study suggested that poverty was neither a long-term nor a permanent state of being for most people. If many individuals drifted in and out of poverty, most of their stays were for a limited time. The Michigan study discovered that of all the people who were poor one year, between a third and a half were able to escape poverty the next year.[7] Poverty was thus a difficult but generally temporary experience that lasted less than twelve months. Despite this relatively optimistic finding, the Michigan study did ascertain that a little over 2.5 percent of the population as a whole, or about 22 percent of the poor, seemed to suffer from bouts of persistent poverty that lasted nine years or more. Even though these figures tempered the overall conclusions of the panel studies, they suggested that long-term poverty was only a small part of the problem. The finding that only 22 percent of the poor were persistently poor was a far cry from Michael Harrington's picture of low-income individuals caught in a vicious cycle who would never escape the misery of the other America.

In the mid-1980s, however, two researchers at the Kennedy School of Government at Harvard, Mary Jo Bane and David Ellwood, suggested that some of the optimistic conclusions of the PSID were not fully warranted. They offered instead a third and more complex view as to whether poverty is a transitory or permanent phenomenon.[8] When most analysts of the Michigan data tried to calculate the number of the persistently poor, they used the relatively simple procedure of calculating how many people were poor for a specified number of years during the observation period. As Bane and Ellwood pointed out, this approach failed to take into account the fact that some people who appeared to experience a short spell of poverty might actually have been starting or ending a much longer bout. But because part of these spells fell outside the observation period, the nature of their poverty was incorrectly recorded. This problem of inadequate measurements because of incomplete sampling is known as "sample censoring." To adjust for this problem, Bane and Ellwood calculated exit probabilities for those with known beginning and exit points and then used these probabilities to estimate the length of poverty for people just beginning or ending a spell.

When Bane and Ellwood employed this methodology to determine the actual number of people who were were persistently poor, they confirmed the PSID conclusion that a substantial number suffered from only brief spells of poverty. But in a major revision of the Michigan findings, they also discovered that of all individuals below the poverty level at a given time, over 50 percent were in the midst of a poverty spell that would last a total of more than eight years. While most people who suffered a bout of poverty were indigent for a short period of time and received few resources from the government, a substantial number experienced long spells of poverty that consumed the lion's share of the government's entitlement programs.

Most scholars had failed to realize this point because they had overlooked the difference between a point-in-time estimate and an average estimate of welfare dependency. If we use the analogy of hospitalization, the differences between these two estimates will quickly become apparent.[9] Imagine that there is a thirteen-bed hospital in which twelve beds are occupied for an entire year by the same twelve chronically ill patients, while the remaining bed is used by fifty-two different patients who stay on average only one week. A patient count on any one day (a point-in-time study) would indicate that about 85 percent of all patients (12/13) suffer from a long period of illness. However, a study over a full year (an average time period) would reveal that short-term users are more prevalent than long-term users. In a twelve-month period, sixty-four patients use the hospital, which means that 52/64, or roughly 80 percent of all patients, spend only one week in the hospital. Because most studies preceding Bane and Ellwood's research had failed to distinguish between a point in time and an average time study, they had mistakenly concluded that most poor people experienced a relatively short spell of poverty.

Thus, in a twenty-five-year span, our perception of how long people were poor has swung back and forth like a pendulum. The initial belief that most of the poor were permanently stuck in poverty soon gave way to the optimistic belief that poverty was overwhelmingly a transitory matter. Bane and Ellwood's sophisticated reanalysis of the Michigan data revised both of these polar extremes and presented a much more complicated picture of the poor. They discovered that poverty is thus neither a totally temporary experience nor a vicious cycle from which few escape. Over a ten-year span we may see as many as a quarter of all Americans falling below the poverty level. But of those people who live in poverty at any one time, over 50 percent appear to be persistently poor. [10]

THE RISE OF THE UNDERCLASS: ARE THE POOR CAUGHT UP IN A TANGLE OF PATHOLOGY?

As troubling as the above data may be, the growing tendency of many indigents to engage in self-destructive behavior is even more disturbing. In the following chapters, we will see that the number of poor families who are working full time has dropped by 40 to 50 percent over the last thirty years. Not only do many indigents seem permanently mired in poverty, but when we look at their work record, penchant for crime, or marital behavior, they often appear unwilling to abide by conventional norms. These examples indicate that the poor may be fragmenting into several distinct groups. Besides the elderly poor and the working poor, there is a large underclass whose whose self-serving actions are undermining the sense of community in lower-income neighborhoods.

However, a variety of critics don't like to divide the poor into a series of separate and identifiable groups, such as the working poor and underclass, because they believe such labels are harmful. Historically, there are good reasons to appreciate their concern. During the Great Depression, there was a tendency to identify indigents as either members of the deserving or undeserving poor. Generally, the deserving label was applied to widows, the disabled, or men who were seeking but unable to find employment during the financially hard times of the 1930s. All other poor people were often summarily dismissed as lazy and thus undeserving of any kind of government assistance. The highly charged nature of these labels not only unduly stigmatized many low-income people, but the emotional nature of the terms "deserving" and "undeserving" often hindered rational analysis of the poverty issue.

In the early 1960s Michael Harrington proposed in *The Other America* another typology for classifying the behavior of the poor.[11] The language of the deserving and undeserving poor now gave way to his alternative terminology: the new and the old poor. The old poverty, he argued, included individuals who were financially strapped because of cyclical macroeconomic problems, while the new poverty described a wide assortment of individuals who appeared immune to economic progress. In a series of poignant chapters on the new poor, he described the plight of the migrant worker, the alcoholic in the Bowery of New York, and the hobo on skid row. (The term "skid row" incidentally comes from the docks of Seattle, where logs would come down on skids in their river journey. Since transient men would often look for work in this section of town, "skid row" became a generic term for a run-down, low-income area.) Harrington argued that the poverty of the 1930s reflected the imperfections of capitalism and its inability to generate full employment. But as the government's handling of fiscal and monetary policy improved and the crisis of capitalism gave way to renewed prosperity, the old poverty slowly faded away. The new poverty of the 1960s was thus "the other America," invisible pockets of misery in what was thought to be an affluent society. The key reason the improving economy seemed to bypass the new poor was because they lacked both the skills and the attitudes necessary to compete in a complex environment.

Despite the popularity of Harrington's book, the intellectual climate in Washington was extremely hostile to the idea of subpopulations of the poor. The single biggest factor that precipitated this reaction was the publication in 1965 of Patrick Moynihan's study of the black family.[12] Like Harrington, Moynihan chose to divide the poor, or in this case the black poor, into two distinct groups, a stable middle class and an "increasingly disorganized and disadvantaged lower-class" which he insisted was caught up in a "tangle of pathology."[13] Moynihan warned of the emergence of a class of poor blacks in which broken families, illegitimate children, and welfare dependency might eventually became the norm rather than the exception in our urban communities. As many commentators have noted, prominent black scholars such as Kenneth Clark and E. Franklin Frazier had often written about these issues before.[14] But by tying together in a systematic fashion previous disparate studies, Moynihan dramatized the fact that poverty was a diverse and heterogeneous phenomenon, especially among blacks. But even more importantly, he also suggested that what distinguished some elements of the black poor from the rest of the poverty population was their behavior. The black underclass, in his words, was a chaotic and "disorganized group" caught up in a pattern of pathological and socially undesirable behavior. In contrast to Harrington, Moynihan tended to place the blame for the breakup of the black family less on culture and more on racial prejudice and limited opportunities in society.

Whatever the merits of Moynihan's study, they were soon forgotten in the uproar following its publication.[15] A variety of liberals and civil rights groups unfairly impugned his motives and accused him of being racially biased. The whole controversy surrounding the release of the Moynihan study was certainly not one of the finer moments in the analysis of public policy. In retrospect, it is important to ask why Moynihan's report stirred up such a storm of protest. Part of the answer certainly lies in the fact that many of Moynihan's critics distorted his message and unfairly accused him of blaming blacks for their own plight. The majority of his detractors paid more attention to his rather bleak portrait of the black family than to his analysis of why the structure of the family in the ghetto was deteriorating in the first place. But why were his critics so hostile and inclined to distort his views? Perhaps given the nature of the times, it was inevitable that the reaction to Moynihan's analysis would be so biased and vitriolic. The civil rights movement was underway and many liberals were very sensitive to any studies that seemed to stigmatize blacks in particular and the poor in general. Likewise, Moynihan had the misfortune to publish his report at a time when part of the civil rights movement was also beginning to reject the idea of integration in favor of black separatism. Black intellectuals were thus very hostile to any studies that seemed critical of either the black family or the pattern of ghetto life.

In the aftermath of the negative reaction to Moynihan's monograph, there was an inevitable tendency among liberals to avoid describing the poor at all. In the late 1960s and early 1970s, few researchers developed typologies of the poor based on their behavioral characteristics. In many cases, the reluctance of researchers to distinguish between subgroups of the poor was based more on prudence than on merit. There were undoubtedly some analysts who justifiably believed that if they replicated studies such as Moynihan's, they would be accused of fostering racial stereotypes. Yet other critics on the left often disliked the "Christopher Columbus mentality" among researchers in the poverty field, to use James T. Patterson's phrase, who were always discovering new subgroups among the poor.[16]

But as the 1960s gave way to the 1970s, it was difficult to deny that life inside the ghetto was rapidly deteriorating. The breakup of the black family had now reached such epidemic proportions that it was impossible to ignore the gravity of the situation. Also, it appeared from statistics on crime, drug use, and out-of-wedlock births that the quality of life in the inner city had dramatically declined. As these alarming trends became more pronounced, the news media began to play up the deterioration of our urban centers. In contrast to Harrington's "new poverty" or Moynihan's "black poverty class," the press began to popularize the term "underclass" to describe some inner city residents. Finally, critics on the right such as Charles Murray started to describe the poor in pathological terms. Conservatives, who had always been skeptical of the expansion of government programs to assist the needy in the 1960s, were more than willing to point out that public assistance and the deterioration of conditions in the ghetto had gone hand in hand.

However, many researchers on the left still insisted that behavioral typologies of the poor denigrated the actions of the poor. For example, in his survey of social programs in America, Michael Katz passionately argued that the concept of an "underclass" is primarily a rhetorical device for a "war on welfare."[17] The very notion of an "underclass," he insisted, "justifies mean and punitive social policies" in that they imply that the working poor ought to take any job in order to slow their descent into the purgatory of the underclass.[18]

Katz's arguments are in many respects a restatement of the brilliant polemic developed in the early 1970s by William Ryan, who coined the phrase "blaming the victim."[19] In fashioning this slogan, Ryan, a psychology professor at Boston College, created an ideological battering ram that many liberals could use to silence their conservative opponents. Ryan maintained that even to talk about the behavioral problems of the poor was to suggest that the victims of poverty were somehow responsible for their own plight. Instead of studying whether the actions of some indigents were self-destructive in nature, Ryan insisted that all such inquiries into the behavior of the poor were tainted because they contained a hidden agenda for punishing the poor.

However, in spite of the intensity of these attacks, the liberal consensus on the underclass began to break down in the 1980s. In his highly regarded book *The Truly Disadvantaged,* William Julius Wilson, a prominent black sociologist, sharply criticized other liberals for summarily dismissing the notion of an "underclass."[20] He insisted that the breakdown of social norms in the inner city was so great that it did not make sense to pretend that the problem did not exist. He also maintained that conservatives had come to dominate the policymaking agenda in the 1980s because they at least recognized the gravity of the problems in the inner city. The hesitancy of liberals to write about the pathological nature of many of the poor because of the controversy surrounding the Moynihan report had created an intellectual vacuum which conservatives gladly filled. If liberals continued to deny the problems of the "underclass," they had to expect that their policy recommendations would be ignored.

But Wilson's main contribution to the debate over the identity of the poor consisted of his historical explanation for the rise of the "underclass." In contrast to many other liberals, he recognized that there was no necessary relationship between who the poor were and why they had become the victims of poverty. In fact, Wilson insisted that the emergence of the "underclass" paralleled the industrial decline of the manufacturing heartland of this country. Katz's notion that the concept of an "underclass" was a rhetorical device for attacking the welfare state was thus written off as verbal overkill.

In thirty years of studying poverty, our portrait of indigents had thus come almost full circle. After the initial efforts of Harrington and Moynihan to portray the poor as a heterogeneous group of people suffering from distinct social problems, writers like Katz chose to minimize the behavioral differences among the poor and stressed their economic similarities. But as the situation in urban areas seriously deteriorated in the 1970s, conservative and liberal critics alike began to recognize that poverty was made up of diverse and in some cases socially troubled groups. Over the years, the labels had changed from "the new poverty," to "the broken black family" to "the underclass." But tying these diverse phenomena together was the idea that poverty was as much a behavioral as an economic problem.

DEFINING THE UNDERCLASS

Among journalists and scholars who have looked at the underclass, there is a growing consensus that this population is itself made up of heterogeneous groups. However, all commentators agree that if there is any one trait that seems to characterize the underclass it is their willingness to flout the traditional norms of what society generally considers acceptable behavior. The perfect literary metaphor that sums up the attitudes of the underclass is to be found in the title of Albert Camus' well known novel *The Stranger,* which describes a rebellious and irresponsible individual who is strangely detached from his surrounding society.[21] The stranger, like members of the underclass, constantly shocks society by openly refusing to accept the rules of its games. Similarly, the public often finds the underclass to be strangers in the sense that they are at a loss for explaining their often self-destructive behavior.

At present, scholars are divided about how to classify the actions of the growing number of individuals who make up the ranks of the underclass. In most discussions of poverty, people tend to be either lumpers or splitters. Lumpers are those who tend to group members of the underclass into a single inclusive category. For instance, Isabel Sawhill has counted people as members of the underclass if they live in urban communities that have a large concentration of low-income people.[22] Sawhill has justified her position on the grounds that people who live in such areas are at risk of being influenced by the social dislocations of their neighborhoods. Because some individuals who live in areas with concentrated poverty are also chronic criminals or drug dealers, it is apparent that some socially deviant people are not poor at all. The underclass and the poor are thus two distinct groups that significantly overlap but whose profiles are not identical.

Splitters, in contrast to lumpers, argue that the underclass is made up of many heterogeneous groups with their own distinctive problems. They insist that studying the poor in this country is like examining a traditional Russian doll that contains its own separate and identifiable dolls. In the same way that the poverty population appears to be made up of internally diverse groups, so the underclass appears to have an equally complex structure. As we saw earlier, many of the scholars who write about the underclass stress very different traits. Harrington, for instance, emphasized the inability of the new poor to obtain work, and Moynihan stressed the increase in out-of-wedlock births and the breakup of the family, while Wilson saw the increase in crime and disorder among the poor as major factors. But perhaps the best-known splitter is Christopher Jencks, who insists there are several "types of underclass" which he respectively labels the impoverished underclass, the jobless underclass, the educational underclass, the violent underclass, and the reproductive underclass.[23]

The impoverished underclass are those who appear to be persistently poor. But in determining whether people fall into this category we need to ask if they "violate one or more widely shared social norms, such as the family head's failure to work regularly."[24] While lacking a job is a necessary condition for inclusion in this group, it is not a sufficient one. Long-term indigents are automatically excluded from the underclass if their poverty results from actions over which they have no control. The retired, the handicapped, or the merely long-term low-wage earners among the persistently poor are consequently not considered members of the underclass. But the disabled may qualify if their disability is due to drug or alcohol abuse, impairing their ability to work full time.

The jobless underclass, on the other hand, are classified by the source rather than the amount of their income. Just as many sociologists determine whether a person is upper or middle class by how they got their income, so they can use the same standard to determine membership in the underclass. If the upper class primarily obtains its income from interest payments and the middle class relies on wages, the jobless underclass gains its livelihood from welfare payments, erratic work, or illegal activities such as selling drugs. Long-term recipients of Aid to Families with Dependent Children (AFDC) are thus likely to qualify as members of the jobless underclass, as well as individuals who consistently break the law. Even the educational underclass may become identical with the jobless underclass if their lack of skills forces them to become long-term wards of the welfare state.

The violent underclass, in contrast, consists of those individuals who resort to force to achieve their objectives. As more and more young men and women have adopted the attitude of Camus' fictional character the stranger and ignored the injunctions of conventional morality, they have often destroyed the very fabric of life that once held together poor communities. In many urban centers it is not uncommon to hear about indigents preying on their neighbors, robbing local stores, and destroying in the process the civility and decorum of their local communities. What undoubtedly shocks most people is the random and often gratuitous nature of much of the violence that characterizes day-to-day living in low-income areas. From drive-by shootings to gang fights and fisticuffs in the public schools, poverty areas more often resemble war zones than residential centers. In major cities the largest cause of death among young black males is not disease but murder. To paraphrase Thomas Hobbes, life in the inner city has become increasingly short, nasty, and brutish.

The final segment of the underclass is the reproductive underclass, individuals who are often cavalier or indifferent about meeting their family responsibilities. The fact that many indigents are members of broken families is not necessarily a sufficient reason to count them as members of the underclass. The key issue is why they became members of nontraditional families in the first place. Before individuals start a family, they should be willing and able to care for their children. If young women choose to have children even when they lack the resources to provide adequately for them, they are acting in an irresponsible fashion that is not in the best interests of their children. When men refuse to provide their former spouses or lovers with the financial help needed to raise their children, they are likewise part of the reproductive underclass. Ethnographic data indicate that many indigent women refuse to stay married because they often view members of the opposite sex as amoral individuals who are more than willing to take advantage of women for sexual and financial gain. Aretha Franklin summed up this attitude of women toward such exploitation in her popular rhythm-and-blues song, "Who's Zoomin' Who." In one important survey in Chicago, inner-city men candidly boasted that when welfare time rolls around, they prefer to exploit their ex-girlfriends as "meal tickets" and hang out with their buddies rather than live up to any marital responsibilities. To be sure, such attitudes are not conducive to building a stable two-parent family.

To estimate the size of the underclass accurately, we would have to estimate what percentage of all its subgroups, including those unattached to the labor market, consistently on welfare, engaged in violent acts, indifferent about their families, or persistently poor, can be legitimately described as having serious behavioral problems. One solution is to identify the underclass as the "intersection of these various concepts—the able-bodied persistently poor who themselves are weakly attached to the labor force and live in areas characterized by high rates of male joblessness, crime, out-of-wedlock births, and welfare dependency."[25] Such an approach is an extremely conservative one and would predict that less than one percent of the poor are members of the underclass. The difficulties of sorting out these issues are so immense that estimates among scholars regarding the size of the underclass vary widely—from one percent to closer to 65 percent of the poor population. Those who focus on neighborhood effects or the intersection of different traits tend to cite the lower percentages, while those who focus on the duration of poverty are more likely to stress the larger figure. Given the advantages of both approaches, we shall take the middle ground and estimate that roughly 30 to 40 percent of the poor may be legitimately called the underclass. As will be discussed later, there is also some evidence that the absolute size of the underclass may have leveled off or even slightly shrunk by the end of the 1980s. But we also need to keep in mind that the percentage of indigents who are classified as the underclass will also reflect expansions and contractions in the economy. If the economy expands at a rapid rate, the percentage of the working poor will naturally decline, thus increasing the percentage of those in the underclass. Conversely, when economic times are harsh and jobs are hard to find, the opposite situation will occur as the rising ranks of the working poor will decrease the proportion of indigents who are members of the underclass.

In popular discussions of the underclass, a common misconception is that most of its members are black. But since roughly two thirds of all the poor in this country are white, and only around 30 percent are black, a substantial majority of the people who make up the underclass are Caucasians. This confusion over the racial makeup of the underclass stems from the fact the most people fail to recognize the difference between the incidence as opposed to the aggregate size of the underclass. While in aggregate terms most people in the underclass are white, more black indigents than whites are labeled as members of the underclass.

But more important, since the underclass are a small percentage of the *overall* white population and white neighborhoods are only moderately segregated by income, white poor are not likely to dominate many neighborhoods. Hence the white underclass is often relatively invisible to the larger public as well as to the press. Because the incidence of the underclass is much greater among blacks than whites, the underclass is more likely to make up a majority of residents in black neighborhoods. Their behavior can thus set the tone of interpersonal relations in a black area and adversely affect the quality of life in the inner city.[26] The unanswered issue, which we shall explore in later chapters, is why the incidence of the underclass varies so dramatically from one ethnic group to the next.

The troubling evidence cited above about the war on poverty naturally raises a host of difficult questions. If the country made slow but steady progress throughout the century in eliminating the causes of poverty, we need to know why that progress ended in the late 1960s or early 1970s. But even more importantly, we also need to ask why the social behavior of the poor has deteriorated so much over the same period. The destructive actions of the underclass, such as dropping out of the labor market, neglecting their family responsibilities or engaging in criminal behavior, have made poverty a much more brutal and pathological condition than it was during the early years of the war on poverty. How we answer these questions will shape the kinds of policies that should be adopted. It is important to know whether conditions in the future are likely to be a repetition of the past or whether they hold out the promise of significant improvement. In the remaining chapters, we shall look at (1) why the overall poverty rate has changed very little, (2) why the problems of the underclass have become so much more acute in the last couple of decades (see in particular chapters 7 through 9), and finally (3) why the incidence of poverty varies dramatically from one ethnic group to the next. Besides finding out why progress in lowering the country's overall poverty rate has become stymied, it is also important to know why some groups, such as Asian Americans, have been so successful in climbing out of poverty. We may find as many answers by examining those who have achieved upward mobility as by looking at those who remain mired in poverty.

THREE
What Is Causing the Problem?
An Overview

As the country's efforts to eliminate poverty ground to a halt in the late 1960s and early 1970s, researchers and government officials alike began to ask why the government's war on poverty had been such a failure. But the initial soul searching among poverty researchers over the lack of success in this war was often limited in scope and confined to policy issues. Instead of questioning the government's diagnosis of poverty, many researchers maintained that the government had been unimaginative in devising effective policies for attacking the then prevailing view of poverty. If, for example, inadequate income was a result of deficient educational skills, the government needed to be more creative in improving the training available to indigents. Other scholars, such as Michael Harrington, also stressed the underfunding of many welfare programs. In his mind, the battle against poverty had failed because the country was unwilling to spend enough resources to solve the problem.[1]

To test these propositions, the field of policy evaluation was born in the 1960s and 1970s. By studying variations in either the delivery of government services or the resources devoted to particular government activities, a variety of scholars hoped to identify policies that successfully reduced poverty. Unfortunately, most policy researchers came up empty-handed: they could identify few government programs in the educational and manpower field that seemed to work unequivocally.

In light of these inconclusive findings, both liberals and conservatives argued in the 1980s that efforts to eliminate poverty had failed because public officials had misdiagnosed its causes. It stood to reason that even the best-designed programs or ample resources would prove to be ineffectual if they were based on a faulty reading of the problem. In order for the government to understand why the fight against poverty began to lose steam by the late 1960s, it needed to go back to square one and ask why people became poor in the first place. If critics from the right and left were finally in agreement that this question was a priority, they were hopelessly divided about whom to blame for the persistence of poverty. The resolution of these issues was important because it would dictate what kinds of government programs should be adopted. The increasing divergence between liberals and conservatives was a reflection of their different explanations as to why so many individuals had become hopelessly trapped in poverty.

THE CAUSES OF POVERTY

The last thirty years have seen a proliferation of theories from the right and left over the alleged causes of poverty. Those who insist that poverty is primary a supply problem believe that the poor lack the skills or attitudes necessary to work their way out of poverty; but those who believe that poverty is essentially a demand problem blame the persistence of poverty on the economy's failure to generate enough "high-paying" jobs for the poor. While liberals in the 1960s took a supply approach to poverty and focused on the educational deficiencies of the poor, more recently they have pointed to demand conditions—such as the changing economy—as the primary reason for the war on poverty's failure. Conservatives, on the other hand, have insisted that supply conditions, especially the lack of adequate skills and motivation among indigents, is the major cause of poverty. This bewildering variety of approaches is due to disagreement among scholars about the plight of the poor: are they (1) unprepared and inadequately trained, (2) unmotivated, or (3) merely unable to find well-paying jobs?

When the government began to implement its war on poverty in the early 1960s, it assumed that the economic problems of the poor reflected primarily their poor training and lack of marketable skills. This approach, which came to be known as the "human capital" explanation of poverty, argued that a person's productivity on the job determined the level of wages he or she would earn. While this view fell out of favor in the 1970s, it is essential that the government improve the educational skills of indigents if it hopes to win the war against poverty. Since most low-income people have limited education and only elementary job skills, their poverty reflects their inability to exchange their labor for an attractive wage.[2]

The well-known conservative economist Thomas Sowell has also argued that the lack of appropriate skills has hampered the ability of many indigents to climb out of poverty. But Sowell, who has called attention to the unusual success of Asian Americans in this country, has insisted that those groups who had a knack for entrepreneurial activity were much more likely to escape poverty than those who shunned the give and take of the marketplace.[3] When Asians formed their own businesses, they could create a protected labor market to employ their relatives and thus circumvent many of the pay inequities and financial hardships that troubled other minority groups. While Sowell agreed with human capital advocates that individual training was important, he has correctly criticized them for focusing too narrowly on academic training and overlooking the importance of entrepreneurial skills in achieving upward mobility.

Finally, many scholars from the right and left also argued that poverty was such a difficult problem to eradicate because the number of single women with children in the population had dramatically increased. Because of the rise of out-of-wedlock births and the breakdown of the family, many young women were unable to acquire the educational skills necessary to secure adequately paying jobs in the labor market. Even more importantly, black children from broken families had a 70 percent greater chance of dropping out of school than their counterparts from intact families. The danger thus existed that the economic deprivation of single parents was being passed on from one generation to the next. In popular parlance, the growing difficulties of single mothers and their children became known as the "feminization of poverty."

With the rise of the underclass in the late 1960s, it was apparent that attitudes also explained whether or not people became mired in the ranks of the poor. The self-serving and even destructive actions of many white and black indigents, such as dropping out of the labor market, seemed to reflect a lack of motivation—rather than a lack of training or skills—to better themselves economically, though analysts were sharply divided over whether the motivational problems were basically cultural or economic in nature.

Edward Banfield achieved considerable notoriety in the 1960s when he argued that the problems of the poor stemmed from the fact that they had adopted a culture of poverty that embraced values differing substantially from those of mainstream society.[4] Given the pathological nature of this culture, which stressed instant gratification and living for the present, it became obvious why many of the poor had lost interest in becoming productive members of society. But more recently, Lawrence Mead has insisted that the poor in general and the underclass in particular are suffering from a general collapse of societal values and a lack of guidance as to how to regulate their behavior.[5] But Mead, unlike Banfield, blames more the libertarian nature of the welfare state rather than a separate culture of poverty for the often self-destructive actions of the poor. Since government transfer programs often don't expect expect much of the poor, it is understandable why many indigents have refused to abide by conventional norms of behavior such as holding down a job or staying out of trouble.

Finally, I contend that the attitudinal problems of the underclass are an outgrowth of a more pervasive transformation in cultural beliefs of American society as a whole. The problem with the underclass is that it has adopted an exaggerated version of our society's emancipated and increasingly anomic culture. After the relatively affluent condition of the 1950s and 1960s, the countercultural movement convinced many Americans that the old virtues of hard work, discipline, and the postponement of gratification should give way to a more permissive life-style. Unfortunately, public officials often failed to note that their endorsement of these beliefs often had self-destructive consequences for the poor. As soon as community leaders became ambivalent about administering rewards and sanctions to uphold traditional values, many of the poor, whose commitment to live up to those norms was weak to begin with, abandoned the values of self-restraint even more quickly than the rest of society. An unfortunate legacy of the Vietnam era and its hostility toward traditional values has been the growth of the underclass.

However, other students of poverty insist that the motivational problems of indigents are economic rather than cultural. For instance, as welfare programs became more generous in the late 1960s, it is possible that they created economic disincentives for the poor to achieve financial self-sufficiency. As already mentioned, Charles Murray raised the ire of liberals in his book *Losing Ground* by insisting that the war on poverty had made it economically irrational for many poor people to continue seeking work. He argued that as the government tried to improve the living conditions of the poor, it inadvertently may have made transfer payments competitive with entry-level jobs, often making the poor unmotivated to stay in the labor market. While this opinion may not be groundless, exactly how important welfare programs are in discouraging indigents from acquiring work remains an open question. When Congress lowered the "welfare tax" on indigent women entering the labor market in the 1960s its actions had little impact on the work record of AFDC recipients. The above data suggest that cultural beliefs rather than economic incentives may be the primary determinant of whether indigents participate in the work force or not.

Finally, many civil rights activists, who historically have tended to minimize any motivational difficulties of the poor, have insisted that the economic problems of indigents stem more from a lack of opportunities than a lack of motivation to find jobs that pay adequate wages. For instance, if minorities who constantly face racial discrimination are the last to be hired and the first to be fired, it stands to reason that a higher proportion of blacks than whites would be poor.[6] No matter how cohesive minority families are or how strongly they believe in an ethic of personal responsibility and hard work, they are unable to climb out of poverty as long as their employers actively discriminate against them. But as we shall soon see, the data in support of this argument are mixed to say the least. While many civil rights advocates insist that the inability of the poor to command decent salaries reflects the racial bias of society more than the deficiencies of those at the bottom of the social ladder, the abolishment of Jim Crow laws in the late 1960s has done little either to stem the growth of the black underclass or to integrate it into the work force.

Many people, however, may find themselves stuck in poverty for purely economic rather than racial reasons. In the 1970s, Alan Blinder and Rebecca Blank argued that the fortunes of intact families, or what Harrington would call the "old poor," depended on cyclical changes in the economy.[7] When business is booming and the GNP is expanding, many of the working poor can find jobs that enable them and their families to escape the misery of poverty. As the Michigan panel studies showed, the finances of such families are highly shaky and can easily shatter if the economy turns sour. When the business cycle matures and economic expansion is followed by a recession, as occurred in the 1970s, the ranks of the poor will naturally begin to swell. This thesis, which is known as the "trickle-down theory," was often advanced by liberals in the 1970s to discount Murray's arguments. While cyclical fluctuations appear to have played a major role in shaping the economic fortunes of the poor in the 1960s and to a lesser extent in the 1970s, they appear to have become less important since the 1980s. The numerous benefits of trickle-down economics have evidently trickled out.

In light of this unfortunate turn of events, many liberal analysts began to argue in the 1980s that structural changes rather than cyclical fluctuations in the economy had become the primary reason for the persistence of poverty in this country. As Joseph Schumpeter once argued, capitalist economies periodically go through what he called "periods of creative destruction" in which traditional companies and industries die out, only to be replaced by new technologies and more competitive companies. When these periods of major change occur, the opportunities available to the work force will naturally be altered, leaving many people financially worse off. While structural arguments take different forms, their basic contention is that the changing nature of American industry has severely limited the opportunities of the poor to escape poverty. One of the earliest structural arguments was developed by Michael Piore, who advanced what has become known as the "dual market theory" to explain the persistently low wages of many Americans.[8] Piore maintained that American industry had evolved into a set of primary industries, which were oligopolistic in structure, heavily capitalized, and had stable patterns of employment, and another group of secondary industries, which were fiercely competitive in nature and characteristically offered low salaries. Because of the restrictive hiring practices of businesses oligopolies, low-income people found it exceedingly difficult to secure stable employment with primary companies, forcing them to accept the inadequate wages and uncertain employment practices of secondary companies.

In a different version of this same theme, Barry Bluestone, Bennett Harrison, and Michael Harrington suggested that increased competition from abroad was the primary reason the working poor were having a hard time escaping poverty.[9] Since the 1980s, companies from the Pacific Rim have captured a large share of the American marketplace by producing higher-quality goods at a cheaper price than their American counterparts. In the process they have wiped out many of the high-paying industrial jobs on which upwardly mobile individuals had previously relied to escape poverty. According to William Julius Wilson, one of the consequences of the decline of work opportunities in the inner city has been the growth of the underclass. As the poor have become increasingly isolated from the rest of society, they have often dropped out of the labor market, abandoned their families, and engaged in criminal activity.

Finally, it is possible to argue that the economy has entered a new stage, which for lack of a better phrase we will label the "age of mass customization," in which companies are under constant pressure to provide high-quality and differentiated products that appeal to specialized market niches. Instead of eliminating well-paying jobs, more and more American firms may be reinventing and upskilling, rather than deskilling, the quality of work available in the economy. In contrast to Piore, Bluestone, and Wilson, I will argue that it is the growth of highly skilled jobs that pay fairly decent wages rather than the proliferation of "lousy work opportunities" that primarily accounts for the plight of the poor. As more and more U.S. companies reorganize their operations and upgrade the quality of work available in the labor market, they increasingly find that many prospective employees, but especially the poor, are unqualified to fill job vacancies. As Charles Schultze has aptly put it, the economy is presently facing a shortage of skilled workers rather than a shortage of skilled jobs. The lousy wages of indigent workers are a result of the workers' growing obsolescence in an economy that needs highly trained workers. The growing persistence of poverty in this country is thus a reflection of the growing mismatch between the attitudes and inadequate skills of the poor and the increasingly rigorous job demands of industry.

Finally, we shall look at the Marxist view, which holds that the presence of widespread poverty reflects more the needs of a capitalist society than the structural problems of a changing world economy. Contrary to my own thesis, Marxists insist that the poor are the modern version of what Marx once called the "industrial reserve army." Whenever it looks as if workers might become organized enough to secure a larger share of the economic pie, business interests rely on the availability of the poor to limit the wage demands of the working class. Marxists thus believe that poverty is an essential component of a capitalist society and not an unfortunate consequence of structural changes in the economy. But because of the changes occurring in the American economy, the economic problems of the poor may reflect the fact they they are increasingly superfluous rather than functional to the operations of modern-day capitalism.

THE PHILOSOPHICAL ASSUMPTIONS OF POVERTY ANALYSTS

Structural Theory

Besides their disagreement over the relative merits of individual, attitudinal, or institutional explanations of poverty, liberals, conservatives, and Marxists are also at odds about the philosophical assumptions that should underlie a successful explanation of poverty. For instance, as liberals increasingly have come to insist that the problems of the poor are a result of a lack of decent-paying jobs, they have tended to view poverty from a structuralist perspective. That is, they maintain that the makeup of the economy is the key variable in determining how much opportunity there is for upward mobility in society. Structuralists thus argue that policy analysts can for all theoretical purposes ignore the attitudes of people because their ability to act is severely restricted by external events. As Jon Elster once graphically put it, structuralists are more interested in describing the fence than what the cows do within it.[10] The most prevalent examples of structuralist explanations of poverty are studies of the economy that argue that the well-being of people is determined solely by institutional factors such as racism or the number of jobs available in the economy. As we shall see in chapters 10 through 13, all of these analyses tend to treat people in general and the poor in particular either as victims of society or as passive individuals who are incapable of offensive actions. Structuralists often seem to assume that people's behavior is automatically or even mechanically determined by economic practices or the prevailing prejudices of society. Thus they have trouble accounting for either the destructive behavior of the underclass or the innovative behavior of upwardly mobile Asian Americans. Their reasons for adopting this stance have both empirical and ideological roots. Because they believe that the alternatives open to people are limited, they think it is a waste of time to even consider people's motivations. However, more perniciously, many structuralists often unfairly downplay the importance of individual behavior because they think such arguments castigate the victim for his or her behavior. Rather than empirically investigating whether individual motives or values are important in determining upward mobility, they often rule out such a possibility for ideological reasons.

Exchange Theory

An alternative approach, which was popular during the development of Johnson's Great Society, is based on an exchange theory of poverty and argues that in the reciprocal relationships created by the division of labor, individuals must constantly bargain with one another over how the benefits of society will be divided. For example, if individuals elect to become better educated, they will naturally be able to extract more generous wage concessions from their employers. Exchange theorists thus argue that the willingness of the poor to become better trained depends on the economic payoffs of acquiring additional skills. The motivational problems of the poor are thus purely economic in nature. If individuals are basically rational economic actors constantly trying to maximize their self-interest, then it stands to reason that the behavior of the underclass is nothing more than a rational response to limited work opportunities.

The exchange theory of motivation is essentially a pulled-from-the-front view of human behavior.[11] It assumes that individuals will try to maximize their future rewards by choosing among the options open to them. The more generous the payoffs from a particular course of action, the more individuals will be pulled in that direction.

In spite of their emphasis on the actions of the individual, most exchange theories have trouble accounting for the creativity people often exhibit in achieving upward mobility. For instance, they are relatively silent as to why certain ethnic groups like Asian Americans have been so successful in acquiring entrepreneurial skills. All too often exchange theorists see people as passive actors whose major act of creativity involves responding to existing market prices. In some cases, when economists talk about people responding to market conditions, the exchange model often collapses into the structuralist model. Rational choice models are better at describing why individuals choose among the options open to them than in explaining why some individuals are so much more innovative than others in altering the choices available in the first place.[12] Or, to use Albert Hirschman's words, liberal exchange models are better at describing "exit" situations where people move from one alternative to the next than "voice" situations where people complain about the quality of the available options.[13] This deficiency occurs because most economic models assume that individual preferences are a given, or exogenous, variable, beyond the scope of their analysis. They consequently ignore much of the history and richness of the decisions that caused some people to escape poverty and others to become mired in it. This limitation of exchange theories will be most evident in chapters 5 and 7, where we will see that rational economic models provide little or no insight into why certain ethnic groups have left behind poverty and become entrepreneurs while others appear to be permanently trapped in the ranks of the underclass.

But the limitations of exchange models should not cause us to ignore their strengths. Many of the decisions that determine whether people will become poor are of the "exit" variety that involve choices among existing options. The eagerness of people to augment their income by investing in higher education, for instance, can be explained by the rate of return that students expect after a college education. The same motivation may also partially explain why government welfare programs adversely affect the willingness of indigents to seek employment.

Control Theory

A third and more fruitful explanation of poverty is based on control theory. While exchange theory has its roots in economics, control theory reflects the sociological tradition of Emile Durkheim, Talcott Parsons, and Thomas Merton. Control theorists, who are generally conservatives, argue that cultural values, and in some cases supervision and even coercion, are necessary to maintain the cohesion and smooth functioning of society.[14] They believe that if individuals and groups pursue only their self-interest in exchange relationships, the danger exists that the social fabric of society may be torn apart centrifugally. To function properly, society needs a coherent set of values to integrate and coordinate its diverse activities. Without any kind of cultural glue, organized life may spiral out of control and lead to destructive social behavior.

Since this book will analyze poverty from a control perspective, I will argue that the attitudinal problems of the poor and the growth of the underclass in the late 1960s may be more a symptom of a larger cultural problem than an isolated economic issue. The present explosion of crime, the fragile nature of family ties, and the increasingly pathological nature of poverty reflect cultural confusion in American life and the resulting breakdown in social cohesion.

Implicit in this view is the belief that individuals are primarily cultural and social animals rather than rational economic actors. Control theory sees people pushed from behind by their values rather than pulled from the front by the possibility of economic gain.[15] In trying to predict behavior, one must realize that people's actions are determined more by their internal gyroscopes than by their calculations of economic gain. If a community thus becomes confused and sends out no clear cultural signals as to what is appropriate behavior, it may inadvertently create an underclass in which individuals suffer from the breakdown of traditional norms. When cultural values become disorganized or the socialization process no longer works, people's behavior may become uncontrollable or destructive. This process, which Durkheim labeled "anomie," occurs when people lack values to regulate their behavior. Underneath the restrained actions of Homo Sociologicus, control advocates see Hobbesian tendencies that must be controlled if disorganized or pathological behavior is to be eliminated.

While conservatives have been the most categorical in advancing a cultural explanation of poverty, their reliance on concepts such as anomie has not been without its difficulties. In *Losing Ground*, Murray simultaneously uses both a socialized as well as a rational economic actor model to describe the poor. On the one hand, he argues that indigents have dropped out of the labor market because the government has culturally undermined the status of hard work; on the other hand, he maintains that the poor no longer work because they have rationally concluded that minimum wage jobs are not as attractive as welfare benefits. The fact that both accounts may help to explain the poverty problem still does not resolve the tension between them. Murray does not really clarify if it is the breakdown of values associated with the rise of the "entitlement state" or the economic disincentives of welfare programs that primarily explain the failure of government to win the war against poverty. Certainly, different policies are required to change the behavior of Homo Sociologicus as opposed to Homo Economicus.

Many liberals, in contrast, have a cultural aversion to using cultural explanations to account for the behavior of the poor. The most notable exception is William Julius Wilson, who has relied on cultural and social explanations (see chapters 7 and 9) as well as rational economic explanations to account for the conduct of the underclass. Wilson argues that the black family is disintegrating because poor black women are unable to find any economically "marriageable men." But he also maintains that the decline of civility in the inner city and the breakdown of marriage among poor blacks are a result of the growing cultural and social isolation of the ghetto. Like Murray, Wilson is silent as to how to reconcile this conflict in his work. We are never sure whether he believes that the poor are rational individuals making economically sensible decisions or culturally deprived people who have not been fully socialized into mainstream values. In our analysis of both Murray and Wilson's view of poverty we shall downplay their economic arguments while stressing instead how the fragmentation of traditional values has caused poverty to become such an intractable problem.

Conflict Theory

Finally, our last conception of poverty is based on what has become known as a "conflict theory of society." Conflict theory is an offshoot of the Marxist contention that capitalist society depends on the exploitation of the working class by the captains of industry. Advocates of conflict theory consequently downplay both the exchange relationships of the marketplace or the need for values to achieve social cohesion in society. They have traditionally believed that it is corporate and governmental coercion rather than the integrative role of cultural beliefs that contributes to the smooth functioning of society. But in the last thirty years, conflict theorists have argued that the capitalist state has become much more sophisticated in its ability to control and diffuse discontent in society.

American Marxists like Piven and Cloward believe that capitalists will try to divide and manipulate the working class rather than directly coerce it into accepting lower wages. By keeping a large reserve army of poor people available, corporations and the state can regulate the wages of workers. More recently, American and European Marxists, who have been influenced by the Frankfurt school in Germany, have argued that the capitalist state is not above using cultural values to make the public more docile.[16] The classic example is the tendency of capitalist societies to promote a cult of consumerism to dampen revolutionary activity. As individuals come to think of themselves as consumers rather than members of an exploited class, they tend to accept the nature of society as a given and thus become immune to calls for radical change. While the coercive nature of the capitalist state has remained

Table 3.1
Changing Views of Poverty: The 1960s to the 1990s

Liberals			
Explanations	Human capital	Cyclical changes in the economy	The revamping of the economy
Assumptions	Exchange	Structural	Structural
Conservatives			
Explanations	Culture of poverty	Welfare disincentives	Anomie
Assumptions	Control	Exchange	Control
Marxists			
Explanations	Exploitation	Exploitation	Exploitation
Assumptions	Conflict	Conflict	Conflict

unchanged, the government's tactical skill in dealing with dissent, including cooptation through welfare programs, has become more subtle and refined.

The assumptions about human motivation underlying this theory are less than flattering. Most conflict theorists see people more as manipulated individuals, subject to the lures of false consciousness, than as socialized citizens or rational economic actors who relentlessly pursue their self-interest. The political system, which acts like a puppeteer, can pull a variety of strings to insure that the public follows its prescribed routines. At the same time, very few Marxists appear to have abandoned hope that the lower strata of society will one day achieve true consciousness and push for a remaking of American society. Their contradictory view of human motivation explains both their pessimism about the present and their expectation that the poor can act differently in the future. But the ambivalence found among Marxists about the potential of workers to resist the coercion and manipulation of the state reflects the inadequacy of Marxist notions of human motivation. If most individuals are trapped by the ideological workings of the capitalist system, it is hard to explain either the destructive behavior of the underclass or the economic success of ethnic groups such as Japanese Americans.

ESCAPING POVERTY: IS THE PROBLEM THE RACE TRACK OR THE RACERS?

As we have seen above, dramatic shifts have taken place over the last thirty years in the way analysts have tried to explain poverty. While liberals and conservatives have come up with new theories about the failure of the war on poverty, they have also altered their philosophical assumptions about the makeup of human nature. In table 3.1 we see that when liberals decided to abandon human capital arguments in the early 1960s, they initially pointed to the dismal performance of the U.S. economy in the 1970s and finally to the disappearance of American manufacturing jobs in the 1980s as the main reasons for the country's failure to eradicate poverty. As they revised their explanations of poverty, they also began to shift from an exchange to a structural view of society. Increasingly, liberals have come to regard the poor less as rational economic actors advancing their self-interests and more as victims who are caught up in a changing world economy over which they have little control.

When conservatives lost interest in culture of poverty arguments in the 1960s, they focused on either the disincentives inherent in the welfare state or on the breakdown of cultural values in society to account for the growth of pre-transfer poverty. But in altering their explanations as to why people became poor, they have tended to fluctuate back and forth between a control, an exchange, and finally again a control view of human nature. Most conservatives who believe that the actions of the underclass reflect their sense of cultural estrangement from society fear that the structural assumptions of their liberal opponents too often excuse and even legitimize deviant behavior. They insist that until society stops "defining deviancy down" by blaming society for the often destructive actions of the poor, the problems of the underclass will never be held in check.

Only Marxists, surprisingly enough, still maintain that their original explanation of capitalist exploitation describes why so many people remain mired in poverty. While most Marxists have never jettisoned their belief that society manipulates and even coerces the poor for the benefit of capitalists, their politics have become less revolutionary with the passage of time. Instead of hoping the poor will one day rise up and overthrow the capitalist economy, they now appear content to treat the effects of poverty.

In spite of the shifting nature of the debate between right and left, conservatives and liberals remain sharply divided about the role that individual action as opposed to societal restraint plays in determining success in one's life. To use a sports metaphor to emphasize the differences, most liberals compare eliminating poverty to running a marathon race. But while the public focuses on the individual runners, liberals are like sports writers who maintain that the outcome of a race can be determined merely by observing structural factors such as the starting positions of the runners or the obstacles on the track. After viewing the lane assignments of the runners, most liberals would feel they could say who won the race even if they never actually witnessed it. They would argue that since the 1970s the conditions of the track (i.e., the declining competitiveness of U.S. industry as well as the rise of a competitive international economy) have deteriorated, thus making it extremely hard if not impossible for most of the poor to work their way out of poverty. Because they believe that the conditions of the raceway are so important, analysts on the left have generally downplayed altogether or dismissed the importance of studying attitudes and values as well. The strategy a runner uses to run a race may be unimportant if the conditions of the track make it almost impossible for him to run a competitive race.

Conservatives, in contrast, strongly believe that the motivation or the tactics runners use will be critical in determining who falls behind or who wins. As we know, many ethnic groups such as Asian Americans, who have suffered from intense racial prejudice, have enjoyed unusual economic success. The political right thus maintains that the major shift in the United States since the late 1960s is that many of the non-Asian poor have lost their motivation to become effective runners. It may not be the presence of obstacles per se, but how people deal with such obstacles that determines the overall incidence of poverty. In a marathon race, the conditioning and tactics of the runners may be more important than their starting point in determining who will win.

However divergent these arguments may be, it is possible that both of the above scenarios accurately describe events in the United States. It may be time for the poverty debate to enter a new phase in which we attempt to synthesize those views into a more comprehensive account of poverty. We may find that conservatives who insist that poverty is a supply problem as well as liberals who maintain that it is primarily a demand or structural problem are both correct. It is difficult to deny that over the last thirty years both the training and motivation of the poor as well as the structure of the economy have undergone tremendous changes. Because of competition from the Japanese, the U.S. economy is evolving into a new form of capitalism in which companies constantly have to upgrade and differentiate their products. To be competitive in this international marketplace, businesses will increasingly expect their workers to be highly motivated and well trained. But as the structural makeup of the economy has changed, the motivation and training of the poor have seriously deteriorated. While our economy has become more demanding of its work force, the poor have become less motivated as well as less able to respond to these demands. By focusing on either structural or motivational explanations, most liberals and conservatives have overlooked the dual nature of poverty.

In the remaining chapters we shall examine poverty from a variety of perspectives. If "everything" is responsible for the plight of the poor, then government proposals that improve the educational skills of indigents, shore up the family, or stimulate additional investment in plant and equipment, thereby enhancing worker productivity, should lead to higher-paying jobs for indigents. Because the plight of the poor is a multifaceted problem, we shall argue that government has a variety of options for alleviating its causes.

PART TWO

Explaining Poverty: Individual Explanations

As described in chapter 3, explanations of poverty tend to focus either on the poor's lack of training, motivation or appropriate work opportunities. Among students of poverty there is intense disagreement as to whether people are poor because they are (1) unprepared, (2) unmotivated and unwilling to improve their situation, or (3) unable to find the appropriate work opportunities to earn their way out of poverty.

The next three chapters will study in more detail the first set of arguments. By analyzing the educational, entrepreneurial, and family ties of the poor, we will look at the problem of poverty from a supply-side perspective. Among analysts who believe that the poor are unprepared for the workplace, there is sharp disagreement as to which skills or attributes are most likely to lead to upward mobility. Chapter 4 will examine the view of the Johnson administration that investment in education, or what is also called "human capital skills," may improve the fortunes of the poor. Chapter 5 will analyze the conservative belief that entrepreneurial skills may also facilitate upward advancement, and we will assume, as Lyndon Johnson did, that poverty is a supply problem that reflects the lack of marketable skills of the poor. In a competitive marketplace, the training and knowledge of workers will determine whether people climb out of poverty or stay mired at the bottom of the economic ladder. Finally, chapter 7 will explore how the family characteristics of the poor may influence their ability to prosper financially. As we shall see, when children are raised by poor single-parent families, the danger exists that they will inherit the poverty of their mothers.

FOUR
The Lack of Human Capital

In the the 1960s, the Johnson administration argued that the high incidence of poverty in this country was due to the poor training and lack of adequate skills of many of those in the labor market. If poverty was a result of too many individuals being ill-prepared and unqualified for the demands of the job market, the obvious solution to the problem was to improve their educational skills. As more people became better trained, the government could expect indigents to become more self-reliant.[1] This was especially the case with the 40 percent of the poor who were children under the age of eighteen. If the government could improve their educational skills, there was a real possibility that future generations would no longer be constrained to work in low-paying jobs. To implement this policy, the government invested billions of dollars in programs like Head Start, compensatory education, and occupational training to upgrade the skills of the poor. However, by the 1970s, numerous studies had raised so many disturbing questions about the effectiveness of such training programs that the optimism of the Johnson years was called into question. As liberals and Marxists became increasingly disenchanted with the idea that education was a viable means for overcoming poverty, supply-side approaches to poverty fell out of favor.

THE POPULARITY OF EDUCATION

In the beginning, the Johnson administration had strong political, historical, and economic reasons for emphasizing education as a means of eradicating poverty. In his fight to eliminate poverty, LBJ was eager to build a widespread coalition from all segments of society. His goal was to use the rhetoric of conciliation rather than class warfare to build a consensus for his efforts to help the poor. From a strictly political viewpoint, education was a policy that elicited support from across the political spectrum. Because it was a supply theory of combatting poverty, it focused on the inadequate skills of individuals rather than the defects of the political system or economy. Established institutions thus had no need to be wary of an activist role for government. By stressing the importance of investing in human beings, the Johnson administration could appeal to businesses that already understood the need to invest in capital equipment and physical assets. At the same time, liberals could enthusiastically support the program because it called for the public sector to play a prominent role. The government, rather than the business community, was to provide the leadership as well as the financial support to upgrade the skills of people so that they could escape from poverty.

Unfortunately, before the 1960s most economists who had been trained in the dominant tradition of neoclassical theory tended to downplay the importance of education in the operation of labor markets. Neoclassical theory, which was basically an exchange theory of society, argued that firms employed labor to produce goods and services while workers offered their labor at the prevailing labor rate.

As wage levels changed, the only question was how much labor the work force would supply businesses at different prices. Neoclassical economists, who had no theoretical reasons for supporting Johnson's war on poverty, assumed that individuals made this decision based on the utility they derived from the consumption of either leisure or consumer goods. They also viewed education as just another consumer good, and mistakenly overlooked the role education could play in enhancing labor productivity. They likewise made the assumption that firms faced a homogeneous supply of labor, in which all workers had comparable skills and levels of productivity.

In the late 1950s and early 1960s, three economists, Gary Becker, Theodore Schultz, and Jacob Mincer, revised these last two supply assumptions of neoclassical theory and developed a theoretical justification for LBJ's poverty policies which eventually became known as the "human capital movement."[2] They argued that their predecessors were wrong to believe that the labor force was homogeneous and that education was merely a form of consumption rather than a means of investment in human productivity. Instead, they insisted that businesses had the option of hiring workers from a heterogeneous labor force with varying levels of education. Holding everything else constant, those workers with more education were more productive than those with less. Since companies paid workers according to their marginal productivity, highly educated laborers could expect to earn significantly higher salaries than those with less education.

How much time an individual would invest in education would thus be determined by the costs and benefits of additional years of schooling. Individuals could achieve the optimal amount of "human capital" by acquiring or investing in additional units of education up to the point where the costs of further additions to human capital equaled the discounted value of the income generated by that investment. Or in simpler terms, the human capital school talked about the rates of return that people could expect to earn if they acquired more education.

However, the human capital school, which was eventually grafted onto neoclassical theory, recognized that many individuals would underinvest in education simply because of a lack of funding. Unlike businesses that borrow money to invest in physical capital such as factories, individuals cannot offer their "human capital" as collateral for a loan. Any labor contracts that as much as hinted at involuntary servitude would quickly be stricken down by the courts. Unless government assistance supplemented lending by private capital markets, individuals would not invest in the optimal amount of education. Such underinvestment in additional training would represent a significant loss to society as well as to the individual. Generally, Becker et al. found that the rates of return for education were excellent and usually equaled or exceeded those for more traditional investments such as physical assets.

The insights of Becker and Schultz significantly modified as well as greatly enhanced the explanatory power of neoclassical economics. They also provided neoclassical thought with a comprehensive and elegant explanation as well as a course of action for eliminating poverty: since the poor had not invested in their education and thus lacked highly developed verbal and cognitive skills, it stood to reason that they could not command the salaries earned by more productive workers. The obvious solution was for the government to launch a massive program to upgrade the skills or "human capital" of the poor in general and of those under age eighteen in particular.

THE POLICY IMPLICATIONS OF HUMAN CAPITAL

But upon reflection, the policy implications of the human capital movement were not always as obvious as they seemed. In fact, in some cases, the human capital/neoclassical approach suggested policies that even appeared counterintuitive. Public investment in education appeared to affect poverty in four separate and distinct ways.

First, if the government invested money in compensatory education for the poor, they would become more attractive to the labor market. As the 40 percent of the indigent population who were under eighteen became better trained, they would qualify for occupational opportunities that had been beyond the reach of their parents. But as many critics have pointed out, the human capital movement cannot guarantee that an increased supply of well-trained workers would automatically generate a demand for their services. If the number of skilled positions remained constant, government educational programs would alter only the incidence rather than the overall level of poverty. If the government changed the educational skills of the poor vis-à-vis other prospective employees in the labor market, it would merely reshuffle the people occupying the lowest rungs on the occupational ladder. While individuals who took advantage of compensatory education would achieve upward mobility, those who had failed to improve their skills would be left behind. If, in contrast, the government tried to improve the productivity skills of all workers, the relative advantage of people who were poor would not improve at all. As all employees became better trained, the poor would be unable to leapfrog over their competitors.

However, the human capital approach has minimized the above objections by pointing out that investing more money in education can also indirectly improve the well-being of the poor. The second advantage of Lyndon Johnson's educational programs was that if everyone upgraded their educational skills, the poor would benefit from working in a more productive society. Besides making workers more attractive in the labor market, education makes the labor force more efficient, which in turn means that the economy can pay employees higher wages. As a better trained labor force leads to an expanded economy, there is a good chance this affluence will trickle down to the poor and push them over Mollie Orshansky's poverty line.

Third, the advocates of human capital maintain that an increase in overall spending on education will also help reduce the size of the poverty population by equalizing income differences between the very affluent and the very poor. As increased educational opportunities decrease the overall supply of minimally educated workers, the give and take of supply and demand conditions in the marketplace will raise the wages of semiskilled laborers. Conversely, the increase of skilled workers will have the opposite impact on the earnings of the well trained. In the neoclassical view of the marketplace, changes in the supply of labor will result in wage competition. As the supply of highly trained employees increases, their wages will tend to drop as workers bid against one another in the labor market.

The policy implications of this last point are downright counterintuitive. The human capital model suggests that even if the poor did not receive any additional educational dollars, they would still prosper from increased government investment in education. As the supply of the well-educated increased and the numbers of the poorly educated decreased, Adam Smith's invisible hand would insure that the wages of the poor would rise substantially. All government educational programs, not only compensatory education, would eventually improve the well-being of the poor.

Either singularly or cumulatively, all three of the above consequences of education would benefit the poor. More spending on education would (1) facilitate upward mobility for better-trained workers, (2) increase productivity and thus expand the economic pie, and (3) narrow the income differences between those at the top and bottom by decreasing the supply of poorly educated workers. As a result, the poor would experience more occupational mobility, become more affluent, and reap the benefits of living in a society that is more egalitarian. Given the climate of the 1960s, these assumptions of neoclassical economics did not seem unreasonable or unwarranted.

The fourth but often unarticulated assumption of the human capital movement was that increased government investment in education would actually upgrade skills. As an article of faith, the Johnson administration assumed that if more money were invested in a wide array of programs, the quality of American schools would automatically improve. In keeping with this philosophy, the government allocated money for preschool programs (Head Start), compensatory education (Elementary and Secondary School Act, Title I), and vocational training (Manpower Development, Neighborhood Youth Corps, and Job Corps).

THE LOSS OF FAITH

Despite the initial popularity of the human capital approach to poverty, a wide array of critics soon began to attack the four educational and economic assumptions of the human capital movement. As already mentioned, the Johnson administration argued that in order to assist the poor the government needed to invest more money to improve the quality of the schools. In fact, the proposition seemed so self-evident that no one dared to question it. But at the end of the 1960s a whole string of reports seemed to suggest that the conventional wisdom was just plain wrong. The study that generated the most publicity was the Coleman report, which tried to determine, among other factors, if student performance on standardized tests was correlated with a school's educational resources. [3]

Coleman, then a sociologist at the Johns Hopkins University, caused a sensation with his research, which was funded by the Civil Rights Act of 1964. In a comprehensive study of thousands of students, he found that government spending on education seemed to have little or no impact on test scores. Whether a school had small or large classrooms, high- or low-paid teachers, or new or old classrooms seemed to make little difference in how well the students performed. The report found that it was family background and the social composition of one's peers that made the real difference. The implications of Coleman's report were rather stark. If family background was the most crucial factor determining a student's performance in school, the government's ability independently to upgrade the skills of poor students might be minimal indeed. More recently, Paul Barton has echoed that point by noting that it may not be the pupil-teacher ratio but the parent-teacher ratio that determines whether students do well in school. There is a strong correlation between the breakup of the family and the subsequent decline of student performance as measured by scores on standardized tests.

The importance of the Coleman report was that it raised questions as to whether government funding for programs such as compensatory education would prove to be successful in improving the human capital skills of low-income students. As other scholars started to evaluate the programs of the war on poverty, they often came up with contradictory and mixed assessments. In the often-cited Westinghouse study of Head Start, for instance, analysts found that any academic effects of the programs were limited and transitory. More recently, in a report prepared for the Department of Health and Human Services, researchers found that Head Start had no long-term beneficial impact on students.[4] Any gains in the intellectual skills or emotional development of students disappeared within two years of their graduating from the program. However, other researchers have found that some children in programs similar to Head Start do experience less delinquency, a higher graduation rate, lower pregnancy rates, and twice the employment rates of students in control groups.[5] The most frequently cited study to support this finding is a comparison of low-income black students in the Perry Preschool Program in Ypsilanti, Michigan, with a control group. But in this allegedly successful program, 40 percent of the control group flunked out of school while 35 percent in the Head Start program met with a similar fate. Likewise, while 22 percent of the students in the control group eventually became "serious" criminals, 19 percent of the Perry kids also turned into "serious" criminals. While the Perry program is considered an endorsement of the Head Start programs, its beneficial impact on low-income students appears to be marginal at best.

Similarly, evaluations of other Great Society programs such as Title I programs of the Elementary and Secondary Act and Job Corps were equally mixed. In one survey commissioned by the U.S. Office of Education, the evaluations of Title I's compensatory programs were generally negative. In most cases, students enrolled in these special classes showed little or no gain over students enrolled in traditional classes.[6] In contrast, the Job Corps, which provides training for unemployed young adults, has generally been judged the most successful of Lyndon Johnson's programs. But even then most studies indicate that women more than men have been the prime beneficiaries of the program. Their economic gains have occurred not because they obtained better jobs but primarily because they worked additional hours. The program's objective of helping male students escape poverty by finding well-paying jobs met with only modest success.[7] Other researchers, like Ken Auletta, have pointed out that when job programs try to rehabilitate individuals with serious problems, such as ex-convicts or high school dropouts who have been in trouble with the law, the record is even more grim. A variety of programs run by the Manpower Demonstration Research Corporation (MDRC) to help troubled students had no impact on their employment record, take-home pay, or level of criminal activity.[8]

But perhaps the most troubling evidence against the human capital approach was the fact that the billions of dollars spent on compensatory education and job training appeared to have little impact on the aggregate poverty level. Even when researchers could point to a specific study that indicated the effectiveness of a particular program, it was still impossible to find any evidence on a macro level that the cumulative effect of Johnson's educational programs had made a significant dent in the poverty rate. Like a military historian who loses sight of the objectives of a war, too many policy analysts had focused on the individual battles and not the outcome of LBJ's war on poverty. If roughly 40 percent of the poor were children under the age of eighteen, then two decades of specially designed educational programs to enhance the skills of low-income children should have led to a significant reduction in the overall poverty rate. Unfortunately, such a scenario failed to occur.

In spite of these findings, many analysts refused to accept Coleman's pessimistic conclusion that additional funding of educational programs might not be effective. However, when later analysts corrected many of the alleged methodological faults in Coleman's study, they were unable to rebut his findings that government spending on education would do little or nothing to improve the academic skills of students. In the most comprehensive and recent update of Coleman's study, Eric Hanushek surveyed the voluminous literature on education and concluded that "two decades of research into educational production functions have produced startling consistent results." Variations in expenditures on education seem to have no systematic impact on student performance.[9]

While Coleman found that government spending did not improve student performance in the 1960s, he could not have anticipated the growing evidence in the 1980s and early 1990s that government spending and student achievement actually appeared to be negatively correlated. By the late 1980s, school districts in the United States were spending nearly twice as much per student in real terms than in the mid-1960s, and nearly three times the level of the mid-1950s. In fact, even as funding for education improved, the quality of American education appeared to deteriorate. Whether one looked at falling Scholastic Aptitude Test (SAT) scores or the dismal record of American students in international competitions, it appeared that American schools were not succeeding in using their additional funds to improve education. In 1988, when the Educational Testing Service (ETS) compared the performance in mathematics and science of thirteen-year-olds in six countries, American students came in last in math and tied for last in science. Many critics, however, argued that the results were biased because foreign countries had tested their best students while America had tested a representative sample. When ETS corrected those sampling problems and repeated the test in 1992 with twenty different countries, American students once again ranked near the bottom in science and math. As further confirmation of Coleman's thesis on government spending, the countries that had the highest test scores in math and science, Taiwan and Korea, spent relatively little money on education. More recently, in an international comparison of Hungarian, Canadian, Japanese, and American students in math, our top students equaled only the mean score of students from Hungary and scored below that of those from Canada. Even more alarming, given the competition between the U.S. and Japan, only 2 to 3 percent of U.S. students could match the median score of the Japanese.[10]

The National Assessment of Educational Progress likewise found that only 5 percent of seventeen-year-old high school students could read well enough to use information in technical or historical documents. There is additional evidence that over a third of the forty million students presently enrolled in our elementary and secondary schools could be described as educationally deprived.[11] One task force that was established to study the quality of education in the mid-1980s was so distressed by the performance of American students that it entitled its report *A Nation at Risk.*

Education and Mobility

However pessimistic recent studies have been about the state of education in this country, these findings do not necessarily discredit the theory of human capital. In retrospect, all that Coleman and other analysts had done was to raise serious doubts about whether the government could do much to help low-income people narrow the educational gap that separated them from the middle class. The human capital/neoclassical argument that maintained that education was a vehicle for upward mobility remained intact.

By the 1970s, a variety of scholars began to question even this basic tenet of the human capital approach. In contrast to the optimism of the Johnson administration, many analysts began to doubt whether acquiring additional education would actually make the poor more attractive in existing labor markets or enable them to earn higher salaries. These critics, who often could not agree among themselves, raised four different and contradictory objections to the proposition that education leads to upward mobility.

First, a variety of economists maintained that education primarily recognized rather than produced occupational skills among workers. These scholars argued that the central role of schools is to act as a screening device for industry by identifying those individuals who have natural abilities. If that were the case, education would help individuals rise to the top who were naturally gifted to begin with and who would probably have achieved economic success on their own.

Second, Marxists, who had grown disillusioned with American institutions during the war in Vietnam, gained a fair amount of notoriety among policy analysts by arguing that the human capital approach was flawed because it failed to understand the purpose of education in this country. Unlike our first critics, Marxists argued that additional education did not identify but actually retarded the upward mobility of low-income students. In a sharp attack on supply-side theories of reform, Samuel Bowles and Herbert Gintis insisted that schools in a capitalist economy were designed not to promote equality but to promote social control and discipline among a potentially disruptive working class.[12] The emphasis in schools on punctuality, discipline, and the acceptance of authority had the effect of training lower-status people to accept their occupational roles without complaint. The purpose of the schools was to socialize the poor into accepting the existing order as legitimate rather than to educate them to achieve upward mobility.

Marxists argued that schools accomplished this goal through a variety of mechanisms. By stressing the ostensibly meritocratic nature of their system of grading, schools helped prepare lower-class students for failure. This process, which was known as "cooling out," occurred as schools assigned low grades to poor students.[13] As students start to doubt themselves, they lower their expectations for economic success later in life. When the economy subsequently turned sour, the "cooled out" working class or the poor would more likely blame themselves for their plight rather than the capitalist system or their employer. The constant exposure to failure in school had conditioned them to legitimize their low status in society.

Other reformers, however, minimized the speculative rhetoric of Marxists and their harsh attacks on capitalism but still found the school system ineffective in promoting upward mobility. The most celebrated example was Christopher Jencks, then a professor of education at Harvard, who claimed that existing empirical data also disproved the idea that education automatically led to higher salaries. Unlike Marxists who argued that public education deliberately tried to suppress the aspirations of low-income students, Jencks maintained that schools were merely ineffectual. In a highly publicized book, *Inequality: A Reassessment of the Effects of Family and Schooling in America*, Jencks argued that luck or personality rather than education primarily determined a person's financial and occupational success.[14] In a massive survey of numerous studies, Jencks found that only about 12 to 15 percent of the variation in income inequality could statistically be accounted for by a person's occupation, intelligence, family background, or education.

On the day of its release, Jencks's book became a media event that generated headlines across the country. As he readily admitted, he wrote the book to debunk the theoretical underpinnings of Lyndon Johnson's war on poverty. Jencks's study repeatedly stressed that even if the government could change the characteristics of individuals or groups, such policies would have few beneficial economic consequences. Unfortunately, Jencks's book was rather atheoretical, offering few clues as to why education was so ineffective in enabling individuals to achieve economic success. Because Jencks was more interested in policy questions than understanding the causes of poverty, he spent most of his time advocating a rethinking of the government's welfare policy. Like many social critics in the 1970s and 1980s, he implied that if public schools could not eliminate the causes of low income, then government agencies should treat the effects of poverty by directly redistributing income to those in need.

But the most obvious question is, how could Jencks's findings about education differ so radically from those of the human capital school? After all, Becker, Mincer, and other economists had demonstrated that there was a strong correlation between the amount of schooling a person receives and his or her subsequent income. The answer to this puzzle was found in the unique way he analyzed his data. While the human capital advocates have always tried to determine the impact of education by looking at income differences between individuals with varying levels of schooling, Jencks chose to look at income differences within groups. As one would expect, people in the same occupation with comparable years of schooling often receive very different salaries.

In publicizing this finding, Jencks often brushed aside problems with his unique style of analysis. Proponents of the human capital school readily concede that there is a considerable variation in income among people with the same level of education. They would merely argue that while income differences between different groups reflect variations in educational attainment, variations within groups reflect differences in ability or effort. After all, not all corporate executives or lawyers are equally intelligent, talented, or diligent in the pursuit of their business interests.

Jencks's conclusions also reflected his rather unorthodox procedures for controlling for other variables. If most scholars tried to determine the impact of education on earnings, they would undoubtedly control for a variety of other variables, including age or geographical region. Because Jencks wanted to prove that education and family background account for only a small proportion of the total variation in men's incomes, he deliberately abstained from adjusting his figures for other variables. As a result, Jencks's procedures led to some rather bizarre interpretations of the data. For example, if an attorney at age sixty earns more money than an attorney at age twenty-five, or a lawyer in New York has a higher income than a lawyer in Mississippi, we would not necessarily conclude that education had only a minimal impact on earnings. But because of the way Jencks structured his argument, he would be forced to argue the opposite. He would maintain that even if we equalized education in this country, there would still be other sources of variation in income. Unfortunately, these arguments fail to substantiate his claim that individuals cannot escape poverty by acquiring more education. However, in government circles Jencks's overall conclusion that "nothing works" overwhelmed and drowned out the critics' reservations about his data. By the 1970s, Jencks's message had become the conventional wisdom in Washington, and governmental optimism that education would enable the poor to escape poverty reached an all-time low.

Finally, if education were increasingly important for upward mobility, the rate of return on a college education should have remained steady or improved over time. But by the 1970s the opposite situation was occurring. Because the rates of return on acquiring higher education dropped significantly during the 1970s, even more analysts lost faith in the human capital approach to poverty. The architects of Johnson's welfare programs had to admit that in the years following the war on poverty the financial attractiveness of education was not what they thought it would be. Even if compensatory education had made the poor more attractive in the labor market

Table 4.1
Changes in Output per Hour
(Non-Farm Business Sector)

Period	Average Percentage Change in Output per Hour
1960–69	2.3
1970–79	1.3
1980–89	0.8
1990–91	0.2

Source: Economic Report of the President (Washington, D.C.: U.S. Government Printing Office, 1992), 349, table B-45.

than if they had remained less educated, the declining rate of return helped tarnish Johnson's belief that education was the key to upward mobility and higher salaries.

Education and Productivity

The questions about the efficacy of education as a cure for poverty were further magnified by the fact that in the 1970s many of the indirect benefits of education were hard to detect. As we saw earlier, human capital proponents maintained that increased spending on education should raise the productivity of the work force and lead to a rise in absolute wages. Before the war on poverty, productivity in the country had increased at a fairly substantial clip, and real wages and average family income in the United States had shown rapid growth. But, as table 4.1 indicates, within a few years after the establishment of Johnson's educational programs, the growth of American productivity and income per worker slowed down dramatically, which severely hurt the poor. When productivity grows rapidly, those at the bottom of the economic ladder can still enjoy an improvement in their standard of living. The fact that increased spending on education had not led to higher productivity and real income was especially hard on indigents, whose numbers began to increase in the mid-1970s.

Education and Equality

Finally, many critics abandoned the human capital approach to poverty when they noticed that increased government spending had not led to greater equality in the distribution of income. In fact, by the 1980s the income gap between the wealthiest and poorest segments of society had widened rather than narrowed. Even though Johnson's programs had dramatically increased the number of students with high school and college degrees, the problem of income inequality remained as intractable as ever. In the face of this evidence, economists sought to revise the human capital model in one of three different ways. First, analysts who believe there is a dual economy attacked the human capital argument that supply and demand conditions determine pay levels, maintaining instead that wages are determined more by the internal norms of primary and secondary industries than by Adam Smith's invisible hand.

However, other scholars, such as Barry Bluestone and William Wilson, implicitly voiced reservations about the human capital movement for failing to see that better-trained workers will not necessarily find better-paying jobs. Recent structural changes in the economy such as intensified competition from the Japanese and the emergence of a service economy have adversely altered the demand for well-educated workers, which in turn has led to the polarization of income in this country.

Finally, Lester Thurow has also criticized the human capital movement for failing to realize that changes in demand rather than supply conditions determine whether salaries become more equalized. Thurow insists that dramatic changes in the distribution of income may depend more on shifts in the cultural outlook of the country than on the available employment opportunities in society.[15] If we want to find a period in which income had become significantly more equal, we have to go back to the years of the Great Depression and World War II. Between 1929 and 1941 the bottom 40 percent of the population saw their share of national income jump from 12.5 to 13.6 percent. While the redistribution of income during the Depression occurred because many of the wealthy lost their fortunes, the greater equality that occurred during World War II represented a fundamental shift in public sentiment. Because the country as a whole believed that the burdens of financing the war should be shared by all, the government instituted a very progressive income tax and imposed wage and price controls on the business community that helped equalize market wages. The combination of these actions altered the rules of the game and changed people's conceptions of what constituted a "fair wage" for many positions.

The unusual nature of this situation suggests the difficulty of dramatically changing the overall distribution of income in America. Unlike most economists trained in exchange theory, Thurow suggests that only dramatic changes in cultural values would overcome structural rigidities in the economy, including the internal pay norms of companies, and create a significant degree of equality in this country. If that were the case, the prospects of achieving more equality in income by investing additional resources in the educational skills of the poor would be slim indeed.

THE REVIVAL OF HUMAN CAPITAL

However, as the 1970s came to an end, the deficiencies of the human capital movement seemed exaggerated, and the dismissal of education as a means of fighting poverty appeared premature. While the Johnson reformers had promised more than they could deliver in their war on poverty, their argument that education was a viable means for attacking poverty gained new life in the 1980s and 1990s. The reassessment of education began with a reanalysis of the quality of American high schools. In spite of the negative reports about the current state of education, there was growing evidence that the schools were proving to be effective at least with one ethnic group—the Asian Americans. It should be recalled that when Coleman undertook his study of public schools in the 1960s, he found that family background was the most important variable in determining the educational success of students. Undoubtedly, the phenomenal success of Asian Americans in general and Vietnamese students in particular reinforced his argument that family ties are crucial in explaining why some students excel academically. Children from families that stress the importance of education usually have impressive academic records. For instance, although the educational performance of most American students has declined in the last twenty years, Asian Americans have been taking more college preparatory classes, scoring higher on SATs, and generating more per capita admissions to elite universities than their white, Hispanic, or black counterparts. In the Vietnamese case, the majority of the students have achieved academic success despite the fact that they often had to attend schools in low-income districts with poor academic reputations.[16] This impressive record indicates that highly motivated students will always do well regardless of the quality of the schools they are forced to attend. If only policymakers in this country could convince more American families to take a similar interest in the education of their children, the deterioration of our public schools could be easily reversed.

But these examples do not necessarily mean there is nothing the schools can do to improve the educational performance of students. By the 1990s school reformers were advancing a variety of proposals for improving the quality of education. Surprisingly, in his powerful book *Savage Inequalities*, Jonathan Kozol has convinced many readers that indigent students do poorly in school because of the large inequities in funding between rich and low-

Table 4.2
Per Pupil Expenditures and Student Performance on SATs, 1992

High-Expenditure States			Low-Expenditure States		
State	*Expenditures*	*SAT Rank*	*State*	*Expenditures*	*SAT Rank*
New Jersey	$9,159	39	Iowa	$4,839	1
New York	8,500	42	North Dakota	3,685	2
Washington, D.C.	8,210	49	Utah	2,993	4

Source: Table is derived from data compiled by the Heritage Foundation. Reprinted with permission of the Heritage Foundation.

income school districts.[17] He thus suggests that until these funding differences are eliminated, low-income students will make little educational headway. While Kozol's normative argument that all students should be treated equally is persuasive, his assessment that more equal levels of spending will significantly improve the academic skills of indigents remains empirically suspect and highly problematic. As any summary of the educational literature shows, it is not clear how equalizing spending, without introducing reforms in the schools or more importantly shoring up low income families, will significantly improve the overall educational performance of students.

As a simple way of illustrating this proposition, it is interesting to note that states with very high per pupil expenditures do not necessarily turn out students with high SAT scores. For instance, New Jersey, which has the highest average per pupil expenditures of all states ($9,159) ranks only thirty-ninth in terms of how its students perform on the SAT. If we look at New York and the District of Columbia, which rank second and third in terms of per pupil expenditures, we find that their rankings on the SAT are 42 and an incredible 49, respectively. Kozol is correct when he argues that there are savage inequalities in the funding of education, but he fails to recognize that on a state level those who have benefited from more funding have not necessarily produced students who perform well on standardized tests. In light of his concern with the poor, the District of Columbia warrants more attention because it undoubtedly has the kind of well-funded school system Kozol would like to see established in the rest of the country. Yet despite such heavy funding, the district's students still have incredibly low test results. In fact, of the ten states with the highest per pupil expenditures, Wisconsin is the only state to make the list of the ten states with the highest SAT scores. Conversely, among the ten states with the lowest per pupil spending, four—Utah ($2,993), North Dakota ($3,685), South Dakota ($3,730), and Tennessee $3,707)—were among the ten states with the top

SAT scores. And Iowa, whose students had the highest SAT scores, spent only about half of what New Jersey did.

It thus appears that even those states that spend a lot of money on education still turn out students whose average test scores are mediocre. The key question is, why? The answer is possibly twofold. First, as Coleman suggested, the family background and culture of students may be more important than the actions of teachers in determining how well students perform on standardized tests. Even a cursory look at the above list indicates that states with relatively low divorce rates and stable families, rather than generous state funding, appear to do the best on the SATs. If that is the case, then raising taxes and investing more money in education (thus ending savage inequalities in the funding of American school districts) may have little real impact on academic performance. If students come from broken homes or neighborhoods that devalue education, their academic performance may be poor no matter how well funded their schools are, as is the case in Washington, D.C.

Secondly, even if students are highly motivated to learn, they may be attending schools that suffer from serious leadership problems. If the public schools are doing a bad job in educating students because they have terrible teachers and an inadequate curriculum, it is unclear why they would get any better simply because they received additional tax dollars. If teachers continue to perform as they have in the past, granting them a pay raise will merely reward poor teachers for continuing to do a bad job. In recognition of this point, most educational reformers, from both the right and the left, insist that Kozol and others asked the wrong questions. It may not be a school's level of funding but how it tries to educate children that determines whether or not it is successful. But among reformers there are three distinct proposals for altering our country's schools.

The first proposal, which is often advocated by conservative economists, sociologists, and political scientists, assumes that the poor quality of our public schools reflects their faulty organization. Since most public schools are monopolies, teachers and administrators have little financial incentive to improve their performance or to cut down on wasteful and unproductive procedures. These market-oriented reformers, who view education from an exchange perspective, believe that competition among schools will greatly enhance the quality of classroom teaching. When students or their families can vote with their feet and leave the schools they don't like, the schools can be held accountable for their actions. While Milton Friedman originally proposed this idea in the 1960s, the initial evidence indicating more "choice" would improve our schools came from a study by Coleman himself, who had originally popularized the belief that "schools do not matter." After analyzing the performance of over 58,000 students in two different school systems, Coleman concluded that private schools produced better cognitive outcomes among students than did public schools, even after controlling for family background.[18] More recently, John Chubb and Terry Moe, who analyzed an even larger data base than Coleman, have also concluded that a school system needs to offer parents and children more choice. They argue that when the educational system is under market rather than political constraints, the schools are more focused, better led, and consequently more effective in training students.[19] Many liberal academics, who intensely dislike the use of vouchers, have also called for more choice in public educations. But instead of relying on market incentives to promote more accountability, they would prefer greater reliance on magnet schools within the existing school district.

However, a second approach, proposed by many government officials and analysts in schools of education such as Diane Ravitch, Rita Kramer, and Chester Finn, argues that the problem of education requires a cultural shift in the attitudes of many public schools. These critics believe that the problems of public education can be traced back to the reform proposals of the Great Society. In her excellent survey of public education, *The Troubled Crusade*, Diane Ravitch laments what she feels was the "anti-intellectualism" that came to dominate the teaching profession in the 1960s.[20] In contrast to the post-Sputnik reformers of the 1950s who wanted a more demanding school curriculum that would improve the technical knowledge as well as the cognitive skills of students, the school reformers of the 1960s wanted to embrace the tenets of child-centered, life-adjustment education. While the Johnson administration wanted to improve the intellectual and hence productive skills of students, it failed to realize that the people implementing the government's policies might decide to promote a different agenda altogether. As Ravitch has pointed out, as the government increased the amount of money for compensatory education, a whole generation of social reformers appeared on the scene who were sharply critical of American society and American schools. Among other things, they implied that society's inordinate concern with excellence, competition, and order was partly to blame for the plight of the poor and the inability of schools to educate minority students. Instead of rigorously tutoring indigent students in math or science, the reformers of the 1960s called for a major restructuring of public education to deemphasize competition and academic excellence. But the adoption of such policies was only tangentially related to the human capital goals of enhancing labor productivity and improving the marketable skills of the poor. More recently, Rita Kramer has underscored this point by noting that our schools often fail in educating students because they downplay the importance of students mastering a subject matter.[21] All too often, they believe that "competition is distasteful, standards are elitist and the content of the curriculum is irrelevant."[22] Ravitch and Kramer thus suggest that merely investing more money in public education will not necessarily improve the performance of the schools in general nor the educational skills of the poor in particular. This is especially the case if the administrators or teachers running our schools do not share Lyndon Johnson's belief that the primary purpose of education is to improve the human capital skills of students. If teachers are hostile to principles of academic excellence and want to devote more time promoting social development than academic principles, it stands to reason that they are not going to prepare indigent children for the demands of the labor market.

Finally, many liberal proponents of educational reform have proposed changing the educational system by mandating the use of standardized testing in public schools. If there are cultural problems with not enough teachers insisting on rigorous academic standards, the problem can be addressed by holding teachers accountable for the academic performance of their students. Unlike the proponents of vouchers, the proponents of standardized tests hope to rely on administrative procedures rather than market incentives to induce teachers to improve their classroom performance.

Because all of the above reforms ignore the role of the family or the values of the larger society, it remains to be seen how successful they will be in improving classroom performance. But it is also clear that educational reform must accompany any increased spending on education. Whether we agree with the call for more standardized tests, or favor vouchers and other market-oriented reforms, or even advocate dramatic changes in the values of school-teachers and administrators, the above debate suggests that there is a renewed sense of hope that our schools can be improved dramatically. While "nothing seemed to work" in the 1960s, a wide array of reformers have suggested a variety of educational changes that may hold some promise of success in the latter part of the 1990s.

Education and Mobility

Similarly, evidence also indicates that individuals who are properly educated can indeed escape poverty and achieve higher wages. The counter argument of Marxists that education reinforces the status quo or Christopher Jencks's contention that schooling "does not matter" is simply not borne out by recent data, especially the 1980s figures on salaries of people with high school and college degrees. As noted earlier, monetary gains from a college degree declined during the 1970s to the lowest level on record, yet now they are higher than at any time during the past forty years. In the 1950s, the ratio of the median income of a twenty-five- to thirty-four-year-old with a college degree to that of a high school graduate with a comparable age was 1.3, which meant that the college graduate earned 30 percent more than the high school graduate. By the mid-1970s, that ratio had fallen to 1.2, raising questions about the value of a college degree. But in the 1980s the financial benefits of higher education dramatically improved as the income ratio between a college and a high school graduate reached 1.5.[23] The recession of 1990 and the efforts of companies to downsize have temporarily lowered the return on a college education. But as soon as the economy regains its momentum and businesses start hiring again, the financial rewards of a college education will again be apparent.

At the same time that the rate of return on a college education has increased, there has been a continuous and pronounced drop in the relative earnings of poorly educated men. Especially since 1979, the wages of un-skilled workers have fallen in relation to the wages of skilled workers. This dramatic drop in the wages of high school graduates and even sharper drop in the income of high school dropouts indicates that poorly educated workers do not have the skills or knowledge required by a modern, technologically oriented economy. For additional confirmation of this point, we need only look at the relationship between poverty levels and years of schooling. Rates of poverty dramatically decline with more years of education. For instance, among individuals who have completed fewer than eight years of schooling, the poverty rate is 28.3 percent, while high school graduates have a 9.3 percent rate and those who have finished at least one year of college have only a 3.7 percent rate.

Education and Equality

Finally, new data confirm the neoclassical belief that increased spending on education leads to greater equalization of wage income. As the supply of college graduates increases, their earnings should drop, and as the supply of poorly educated employees decreases, their wages should rise. However, the fact that the number of college graduates has significantly increased while the distribution of income has become more unequal in the past two decades

Table 4.3
Percentage Rates of Low-Income Students Enrolled in College,
Ages 16–24

	1976	1979	1982	1985	1988	1990	*(Percentage of Change)*
Blacks (low income)							
Men	37.2	36.1	23.0	29.0	23.0	17.9	−51.8
Women	41.7	32.9	34.2	27.1	35.6	22.1	−47.0
Whites (low income)							
Men	34.9	33.8	29.9	29.1	32.1	22.4	−35.8
Women	39.4	38.1	35.3	34.8	46.4	28.1	−28.6

Sources: Deborah Carter and Reginald Wilson, *Minorities in Higher Education* (American Council on Education, 1989), 39. Reprinted with permission of the American Council on Education. Data for 1990 are from U.S. Bureau of the Census, Series P-20, no. 460, "School Enrollment—Social and Economic Characteristics of Students."

has led many analysts to reach the opposite conclusion. Scholars fear that the growth of low-income jobs has canceled out the egalitarian effects of increasing the supply of well-educated workers.

While the above argument has received considerable attention in the media, it is not consistent with the available data on individual income. If the economy is disproportionately creating only low-skilled and low-wage jobs, the resulting demand for unskilled laborers should raise their wages and lower their unemployment rate relative to that of skilled employees. Presently, the opposite situation appears to be occurring. The wages and employment rate of low-skilled vis-à-vis well-trained workers have been deteriorating rather than improving throughout the 1980s and early 1990s.

In light of these data, a recent study from the Brookings Institute maintains that it is changes in the skill levels of workers that primarily account for the growing income inequality in this country.[24] While the supply of college graduates increased relative to the supply of high school dropouts and graduates in the 1970s and 1980s, the rate of that increase has slowed dramatically during the last decade. At present, we seem to be suffering from a growing undersupply of college-trained employees. What is most discouraging in terms of the nation's efforts to eliminate poverty is that the slowdown in college graduates is especially pronounced among minority children from poor to low-income families. Using census data, the American Council on Education has noted that between 1976 and 1990 there has been a 30 to 50 percent drop in the percentage of low-income students electing to enroll in college. As table 4.3 shows, the original objectives of the Johnson administration to significantly enhance the human capital skills of the poor and thereby to raise their wages are still far from being realized.

These figures are especially discouraging if we recall that the demand for highly trained employees appears to have accelerated during the 1980s. Instead of producing an overabundance of low-paying jobs, the economy appears to be generating an increasing demand for well-trained labor that is often unavailable in the marketplace. The economic premium for completing a college education is now at a forty-year high. Because fewer children from low-income families are attending college, they must compete with one another for the low-paying jobs that do exist. Unless these educational trends are reversed, there is little reason to believe that poverty rates will drop significantly in the next decade.

A puzzling question is why low-income individuals, especially black males, are less inclined to attend college than in the past. From an exchange point of view, if the poor were rational economic actors, they should be eager to acquire additional education in light of the high rates of return for a college education. It is possible that many college-age students are simply misinformed about the rewards of investing in additional education. But given the constant attention that is paid to the plight of the uneducated, this answer seems unsatisfactory. A second possibility is that the poor are rational and eager to attend college but lack the financial resources to do so. To support this point, it is a fact that Pell grants for disadvantaged students wishing to attend college reached their highest funding level in 1974 and have since been cut back. As the price of tuition at colleges dramatically escalated in the 1970s, the Carter administration and Congress began to offer college students loans, which must be paid back, rather than grants, which enabled students to attend school for free. It is possible that this alteration in the student aid program enabled more working and middle-class students to attend college but at the price of discouraging indigent students from acquiring a higher education.[25]

Finally, we cannot rule out the fact that changing academic standards or shifts in attitudes may also explain part of the drop off in college attendance by low-income students. As table 4.3 indicates, poor black males are the least likely to attend college. As schools in general and colleges in particular have come under pressure to promote academic excellence, it is possible that they have raised their admission standards and black males have had a harder time meeting the more stringent entrance requirements.

The decline in college attendance among low-income students is especially troubling because the United States does not have a strong tradition of vocational training programs to assist those who choose not to or can't afford to go to college. Even if students lack the financial resources to obtain an academic degree, they still might avoid the ranks of the poor if they could acquire industrial or vocational skills that industry and businesses need. The United States trails its major industrial competitors, such as Japan and Germany, in training people for readily available skilled jobs.[26] In Germany, for example, many students spend three years acquiring on-the-job training in formal apprenticeship programs that often lead to permanent jobs. The United States also lacks uniformly high-quality vocational or technical colleges for those who wish to learn a technical trade. To eliminate the real causes of poverty, it is imperative that Pell grants be made available for underprivileged youth and that we develop alternative forms of practical education. Only by implementing this dual approach to education will we be able to give low-income students the skills necessary to compete in a demanding and sophisticated international economy.

EDUCATION CAN MAKE A DIFFERENCE

In retrospect, the loss of faith in President Johnson's efforts to help the poor earn their way out of poverty appears to have been unwarranted. As we enter the 1990s, education still appears to be an effective policy to help combat the causes of low income. Since 40 percent of the poor are schoolchildren, educational programs ought to be able to whittle down the size of the poverty population by a comparable percentage. But that possibility assumes that school officials can develop adequate compensatory educational programs to train the children of indigent families with useful skills.

When the schools do succeed with low-income students, the prospects of reducing the size of the poverty population appear promising. If we look at the 3.7 percent rate of poverty among individuals who have attended one year of college, it is clear that additional years of schooling reduce the incidence of poverty dramatically. By assuming that government earns a certain rate of return on its investment, Isabel Sawhill has estimated that educational programs have lowered the overall poverty rate by 0.4 to 2.2 points.[27] But this estimate appears to be on the low side. While this range may be a good estimate of the effectiveness of education in filling available job openings, it overlooks the impact of education on both the absolute level of wages and the equalization of wage rates in this country. If the 40 percent of the population that is currently under the age of eighteen can improve their educational skills, there is a real possibility that the country can finally begin to lower the pretransfer poverty rate.

FIVE

The Lack of Entrepreneurial Skills

The doubts that surfaced about education in the 1970s eventually led analysts to search for alternative solutions to the poverty problem. Ironically, as liberals began to despair that the war on poverty would fail, conservatives became more optimistic that the causes of poverty could be eliminated. The catalyst for this renewed sense of hope was the observation by conservatives like Thomas Sowell that the incidence of poverty varied greatly from one ethnic group to the next.[1] Numerous ethnic groups who had suffered from intense discrimination, such as Jews, Japanese, Chinese, and West Indian blacks, have made unusual financial gains in this country. When Sowell tried to analyze why these groups were so successful, he pointed to their entrepreneurial skills as a crucial factor in accounting for their upward mobility. Like his human capital contemporaries, Sowell agreed that the traits people brought to the labor market were crucial in determining their ability to escape poverty. But instead of focusing exclusively on educational skills, he insisted that a group's proclivities to start businesses were of equal importance in achieving financial success.

THE OPTIONS

To appreciate Sowell's argument, it is necessary to realize that his conclusions have grown out of a comparative analysis of how different ethnic groups in the United States have escaped the hardships of poverty. There are at least three general patterns of upward mobility in America.

First, individuals or ethnic groups have advanced by investing in education and upgrading their occupational skills: employees may begin work in menial blue-collar jobs but, with additional training, advance into more demanding and prestigious positions.

Second, an ethnic group can achieve financial prominence by developing

71

entrepreneurial skills that enable them to operate a variety of successful businesses. Instead of, or in some cases in addition to, enhancing their educational skills, some ethnic groups have refined their marketing talents and focused their energies on developing businesses in a few key industries. The early German immigrants, Jews, Japanese, Chinese, West Indian blacks, and more recently the Koreans have chosen to pursue this route of upward mobility. Among ethnic groups that have pursued an entrepreneurial route, it is possible to identify in turn three different patterns of business activity.

First, Germans and Jews started businesses that eventually led to the development of whole new industries. For example, German Americans were successful entrepreneurs in electronics (Westinghouse and General Electric), beer (Pabst, Schlitz, Miller, Budweiser), autos (Buick, Chrysler, Packard, Studebaker), pianos (Steinway, Knable), paper (Weyerhaeuser), food (Heinz Corporation), oil (Rockefeller), and optics (Bausch and Lomb). American Jews, in contrast, were prominent in investment banking (Kuhn Loeb & Co.), retailing (Macy's, Gimbel's, Filene's, Sears, Rich's, Nieman Marcus, Bergdorf Goodman), clothing (Levi Strauss), newspapers (the *New York Times*), television (Sarnoff at NBC, Paley at CBS), and motion pictures (Paramount and M.G.M. and all other major studios except United Artists).

A second entrepreneurial pattern involves ethnic groups that develop small businesses that are often lucrative but occupy specialized niches in the larger economy. An example of this pattern is the ubiquitous Chinese laundry in the early twentieth century or the Japanese American truck farm or flower business in the years before World War II. More recent examples include data processing and specialized computer firms pioneered by Japanese and Chinese Americans in the 1980s as well as liquor stores, gas stations, and convenience stores operated by Korean immigrants in the inner city. Many scholars, usually of a Marxist orientation, further divide such ventures into traditional niche businesses that cater to small but lucrative segments of the marketplace, and so-called middleman businesses that act as go-betweens for large capitalist firms who want to sell products in low-income areas. The entrepreneurial activities of the Koreans, who often run franchises for corporations such as Seven-Eleven in the inner city, are examples of so-called middleman companies. In contrast, the high-tech data processing firms recently started by Asian Americans are traditional niche companies. These firms, which have striven hard to create their own identity, cater more to the affluent than to the poor, and have done well because they offer excellent service and competitive prices.

A third pattern of entrepreneurial activity consists of ethnic businesses that depend for their financial success on catering to the needs of their own ethnic constituency. Unlike the businesses in the first two categories, these so-called enclave companies play a minimal role in servicing the outside economy. Their focus is more parochial, consisting primarily of catering to the residents of their particular ethnic community. All ethnic groups have to some degree participated in this form of retail activity. But West Indian blacks and Chinese Americans, who have faced intense racial prejudice and were often forced to live in self-contained ghettos, are more likely to engage in this type of activity than their Japanese or Jewish counterparts.

Finally, instead of stressing entrepreneurial activities, an ethnic group can pursue a third avenue of upward mobility by seeking elected office, political power and career opportunities in government. Among the classic examples of this pattern of mobility are the Irish, who developed and ran political machines in many of our major American cities from the turn of the century to the post-World War II period. More recently, blacks have pursued a similar route by successfully gaining employment at all levels of government.[2]

In light of these diverse paths for achieving upward mobility, the crucial issue is whether Sowell and other conservatives are correct in suggesting that the entrepreneurial track is preferable to its governmental alternative. While any number of alternative occupational paths may enable people to escape poverty, some routes may be potentially more attractive than others.

THE DEFENSE OF THE ENTREPRENEURIAL ROUTE

The reason why small businesses appear attractive is because they benefit ethnic groups in four distinct ways. First, when individuals develop their entrepreneurial skills, there may be positive spillover effects for the rest of the ethnic community. The financial success of minority businessmen provides tangible evidence to other disadvantaged individuals that they can succeed if they work hard and improve their marketable skills. The tendency of some youth to engage in destructive social behavior or to deprecate the values of work can thus be checked if there is an active class of minority businessmen adopting and defending conventional values. In this sense, minority-owned businesses are social buffers that absorb the shock of economic hardship by upholding traditional norms and exposing disadvantaged young people to constructive forms of behavior.

Second, when groups have a flair for business and can identify untapped markets, they can generate jobs for their children and other relatives. Unlike the development of human capital skills, the acquisition of entrepreneurial traits not only enhances people's attractiveness in the labor market but also simultaneously creates employment opportunities for them. If the government invests money in general education, it must realize that increasing the supply of well-trained workers will not automatically generate a demand for their services. In contrast, the creation of business and the generation of employment opportunities are two sides of the same coin.

Third, small business activity has also worked to the advantage of minorities by enabling them to avoid occupations characterized by extreme inequalities in pay. As noted earlier, advocates of the dual market approach to economics insist that minorities are often unfairly limited to dead-end jobs in the peripheral sectors of the economy and denied job opportunities in primary companies where wages are high. This assessment, however, assumes that low-income individuals only have the option to work in a primary or secondary industry. If, in contrast, low-income ethnic groups have the opportunity to become entrepreneurs and "discover" economic niches where none existed before, their prospects for climbing out of poverty are much greater than liberal analysts would admit. This is not to suggest that all minority firms have been extremely profitable. First instance, early Asian immigrants often had businesses like restaurants or laundries where profit margins were extremely low. But in spite of these conditions, the first generation of Asian Americans was still able to earn a decent living by working long hours and by employing members of their immediate families. Even though their individual hourly compensation was often low, they could still enjoy financial success as part of a larger family unit. More recently, the grandchildren of these early Asian American merchants have prospered as entrepreneurs by using their educational skills (which their grandparents never possessed) to enter more technical and complex businesses where the profit margins are higher.

Similarly, entrepreneurial activity has also helped many minority groups to circumvent the pay inequities and financial hardships that often accompany racial discrimination. To illustrate this point we must look at one of the most commonly accepted institutional explanations of discrimination: the split-labor theory. According to this theory, white society discriminates against minorities because lower-class whites feel threatened by the presence of ethnic groups in the labor market. When Asian Americans or blacks can freely participate in the search for jobs, they increase the supply of labor, which in turn puts downward pressure on the wages of white laborers. To stop the downward drift of their wages and protect their economic self-interest, working-class whites will often support the adoption of discriminatory hiring practices which in effect will split the the labor market in two. While whites will dominate the main industries where wages are high, blacks and other ethnic groups will be limited to so-called colored or peripheral jobs where the pay is minimal.

Obviously, the fragmentation of the workplace into a split labor market seriously undermines the economic prospects of minorities. However, if ethnic groups pursue an entrepreneurial route, they may be able to take themselves out of direct competition with working-class whites. When Jews entered the retail trade and movie industry, when the Chinese opened laundries and restaurants, or when the Japanese started vegetable farms or, more recently, data processing businesses, they in effect discovered and entered economic niches where little or no competition from working-class whites existed. Since affirmative-action programs did not exist until the late 1960s, the most successful ethnic groups advanced by circumventing rather than by attacking head on the discriminatory practices of whites. While whites could prevent Jews or Japanese from finding employment in main-line industries, they could not stop these same groups from developing companies in which they would prosper by catering to specialized needs in the marketplace.

Fourth, entrepreneurial activity has also enabled minorities to avoid low-paying dead-end jobs and low wages by giving opportunities to the second generation to enter professions like law or medicine. Among both Asian Americans and Jews, we find that the first generation of immigrants, who became entrepreneurs, invested heavily in developing the educational skills of their children. The entrepreneurial success of the parents thus generated the resources that enabled the second generation to obtain the technical skills necessary to succeed in other occupations. By the 1980s many grandchildren of Asian immigrants had relied on their educational skills to start high-tech companies that could potentially be highly profitable. While first-generation Asian Americans were active entrepreneurs, and the second generation was successful in professional work, the third generation appears to be reviving the business traditions of its ancestors. The ability to combine their human capital skills with the entrepreneurial talents of their grandparents may enable even more Asian Americans to avoid the low-paying jobs that have often trapped other minority groups.

THE EMPIRICAL EVIDENCE

Census data show us that many enterprising ethnic groups who came to America and suffered from intense racial and ethnic discrimination have still managed to prosper financially (see table 5.1). In light of their mistreatment

Table 5.1
Relative Income of American Ethnic Groups
(Percentage of Median Family Income)

	1970	1980
Jews	n/a	138
Japanese	127	138
Asian Indians	n/a	127
Filipino	94	120
Chinese	108	115
Polish	118	115
Italians	112	111
Germans	105	108
Irish	101	105
Koreans	n/a	104
Whites	104	101
English	109	101
French	97	99
Cuban	85	93
West Indian	n/a	80
Hispanic	75	75
Mexican	72	75
Vietnamese	n/a	65
American Indian	59	64
Black	64	61
Puerto Rican	61	54

Sources: Data from the 1990 census were not available when the book went to press. The 1970 data are from the U.S. Bureau of the Census, *Current Population Reports*, Series P-20, no. 224, "Selected Characteristics of Persons and Families of Mexican, Puerto Rican, and Other Spanish Origin: March 1971"; U.S. Bureau of the Census, *Current Population Reports*, Series P-20, no. 249, "Characteristics of the Population by Ethnic Origin: March 1971 and 1972"; U.S. Bureau of the Census, *Census of the Population: 1970*, Subject Reports, Final Reports PC(2)-1G, "Japanese, Chinese and Filipinos in the United States"; PC(2)-1E, "Puerto Ricans in the United States" (Washington, D.C.: U.S. Government Printing Office, 1973). See also U.S. Bureau of the Census, *Census of the Population: 1980*, Vol. 1, Part 1, Chapter C, United States Summary, "General Social and Economic Characteristics," PC 70-1-C1 (Washington, D.C.: U.S. Government Printing Office, 1983). The data on Jews are from the National Opinion Research Center's General Social Survey as cited by Christopher Jencks in "Discrimination and Thomas Sowell," *New York Review of Books* 35 (October 1988): 34. The data on West Indians are from Reynolds Farley and Walter R. Allen, *The Color Line and the Quality of Life in America* (New York: Russell Sage Foundation, 1987), 403. Sowell found in his *Markets and Minorities* that West Indians averaged 94 percent of median white income. However, the recent influx of low-income Haitians has helped lower that ratio to 80 percent. The data for 1989 to 1990 are from National Opinion Research Center, Cumulative General Social Survey, 1972–1989, Chicago, distributed by Roper Public Opinion Research Center, Storrs, Connecticut.

Table 5.2
Poverty Rates for Select Ethnic
Groups

	1970	1980
Official rate	12.6%	13%
Blacks	33.5	32.5
Japanese	7.5	6.6
Chinese	13.3	13.3

Sources: The black poverty rate is from House Committee on Ways and Means, *Green Book: The Overview of Entitlement Programs* (Washington, D.C.: United States Government Printing Office, 1991). The data on Japanese and Chinese are from the U.S. Bureau of the Census, *Census of the Population: 1970*, Subject Reports, Final Reports, PC(2)-1G, "Japanese, Chinese and Filipinos in the United States." The data for 1980 are from U.S. Bureau of the Census, *Census of the Population: 1980*, Vol. 1, Part 1, Chapter C, United States Summary, "General Social and Economic Characteristics," PC 80-1-C1 (Washington, D.C.: U.S. Government Printing Office, 1983); and U.S. Bureau of the Census, *Census of the Population: 1980*, Subject Reports, Final Reports, PC80-21E, "Asian and Pacific Islander Populations in the United States" (Washington, D.C.: U.S. Government Printing Office, 1988).

by the U.S. government, the record of Japanese Americans is especially noteworthy. Even though many Japanese-Americans were financially ruined when the government forced them into relocation camps during World War II, their median income was 27 percent higher than that of the average American by 1970. Although the median income for the average American began to level off in the late 1970s, Japanese and Chinese Americans continued to prosper. By 1980 the Japanese family saw its income jump from 127 percent to 138 percent and the Chinese from 108 percent to 115 percent of median family income in America.

A look at the poverty rate among particular subgroups of Asian Americans shows an equally impressive record (table 5.2). By 1980, the poverty rate of 6.6 percent for Japanese Americans was less than half that of the population as a whole. While the country's overall success in fighting poverty had come to a halt by the 1970s, the Japanese experienced a 13 percent drop in the number of their poor. Despite the large influx of new immigrants, the Chinese poverty rate of 13.3 percent also matched that of the country as a whole in 1980. In the the 1970s, over 250,000 Chinese immigrants, primarily from Taiwan and mainland China, almost doubled the ranks of the 340,000 Chinese already present in America. The entrepreneurial tradition of both groups undoubtedly played a prominent role in helping the Japanese avoid the traumas of poverty and the Chinese to assimilate a large number of new immigrants.

However, we must be cautious about offering easy answers as to why some groups have enjoyed unusual upward mobility in this country. Asians differ from other Americans in that they participate more actively in the labor market, are more likely to live in states like California where wages are higher than the national average, have more intact families, and are better educated than their black or white counterparts.[3] Among males over the age of twenty-five, 35 percent of Japanese and close to 30 percent of Chinese have four-year college degrees, while only a little more than 21 percent of whites and roughly 8 percent of blacks have comparable levels of education. More than any other ethnic group in America, Asians seem to have successfully combined a human capital approach of heavily investing in education with an entrepreneurial tradition to achieve upward mobility.

While there is no one factor that accounts for the high median family income and low incidence of poverty among Asians in this country, it is clear that the entrepreneurial tradition of Asian Americans has played and continues to play a significant role in explaining their economic prosperity. For instance, from 1972 to 1982 the number of businesses operated by Japanese Americans increased by 174 percent, while the number of Chinese companies grew by 311 percent. The Census Bureau reports that from 1982 to 1987 (the most recent data available) Japanese firms rose almost 23 percent and Chinese companies almost 84 percent, while the total number of all new businesses in the United States rose only 14 percent.[4] Based on overall population figures, the Japanese are one and a third times more likely to start a business than we would predict on the basis of their population in this country. And the Chinese become entrepreneurs at roughly one and a half times what we would predict from their total population figures. While Sowell's praise of private initiative often seems excessive, the main thrust of his argument appears valid. Contrary to the claims of his critics that racial prejudice is often a crippling obstacle to upward mobility, the Japanese and other Asian Americans have convincingly demonstrated that individuals can circumvent racial discrimination and prosper by hard work, market acumen, and entrepreneurial skill.

SHOULD BLACKS PURSUE THE ENTREPRENEURIAL ROUTE?

In spite of the success of Asian Americans, Sowell's proposals for more black business activity have been extremely controversial. Because he has disagreed with the conventional wisdom that blacks should rely on politics and government assistance to achieve upward mobility, he has been harshly attacked by his critics, often in an ad hominem fashion. When the *New York Review of Books* reviews Sowell's writings, it often runs a cartoon depicting him as a blind and deaf individual who sees and hears no evil. Aside from attacking him personally, Sowell's critics have sought to discredit his ideas in one of three different ways. First, they have often asked if Sowell's call for more entrepreneurial activity among blacks is really a feasible option. If, as E. Franklin Frazier argued years ago, blacks have no tradition of small business activity, can we really expect the black community to achieve success as entrepreneurs? Second, even if the entrepreneurial route is feasible, we need to know whether it is also a desirable course to follow. Sowell's detractors have often suggested that neither the private sector nor the Asian American pattern of development is an appropriate normative model for the black population. Third, many of Sowell's critics insist that he has simply failed to realize that government assistance and employment may be an equally valid way for a minority to escape poverty. The fact that different ethnic groups choose alternative paths to escape the ghetto does not necessarily mean that one is superior to the other. The remaining sections of this chapter will look at each of these criticisms in more detail. In spite of the many attacks leveled against him, Sowell's contention that blacks would have a lower incidence of poverty if they developed a stronger entrepreneurial tradition has held up remarkably well.

The Feasibility of the Entrepreneurial Tradition: Why Blacks Can Imitate Their Asian Counterparts

The first criticism of Sowell is that it is impractical to believe that blacks can be successful in business since they lack an entrepreneurial tradition. As table 5.3 indicates, the propensity to become self-employed varies greatly from one ethnic group to the next. Unlike the Japanese, Koreans, or Chinese, blacks stand out in having a tradition that deemphasizes self-employment.

The aversion to business in the black community has deep historical roots. Since the end of the Civil War, three distinct groups have exercised leadership in the black community, and none of them has viewed entrepre-

Table 5.3
Percentage of Self-Employed Workers

	Employee of Own Corporation	Self-Employed Worker	Unpaid Family Worker
All persons	2.1	6.8	.5
Japanese	n/a	7.9	0.6
Chinese	n/a	7.2	1.0
Korean	n/a	11.9	1.6
Vietnamese	n/a	2.2	0.5
Mexican	n/a	3.5	0.3
Cuban	n/a	5.8	0.4
Puerto Rican	n/a	2.2	0.0
Irish	1.9	6.6	0.5
Italian	3.5	6.9	0.4
Polish	2.5	5.9	0.4
German	2.4	9.2	0.4
English	2.4	8.6	0.5
Black	n/a	2.4	0.1

Source: U.S. Bureau of the Census, *Census of the Population: 1980*, Vol. 1, Part 1, Chapter C, United States Summary, "General Social and Economic Characteristics," PC 80-1-C1 (Washington, D.C.: U.S. Government Printing Office, 1983).

neurial activity favorably. In the Reconstruction period, the elites who enjoyed the most prestige in black society were those who had the closest ties to their former white owners. This tradition reflected a continuation of the mores of the ante-bellum plantation period in which so-called house slaves had higher status than "field" slaves. If a freed black man had a menial occupation cutting hair, but his customers were prominent white businessmen, he was likely to enjoy the status that previously had accrued to "house" blacks under the old system of slavery.[5]

At the turn of the century, another elite took its turn at the pinnacle of black society. This elite, which was primarily made up of ministers, teachers, doctors, and other professionals, catered to the needs of a black clientele that was living in a rigidly segregated society. While there were a few undertakers and restaurateurs in this group, this emerging black middle class did not necessarily equate "money with status."[6] As Joel Garreau has noted, they often measured status in the same way the British aristocracy did: by a person's education and refinement of manner. "Being 'in trade' was considered declassé, even though this black middle class owed its position to a captive market."[7] But as the system of Jim Crow was dismantled and society became more integrated, this professional middle class eventually saw its influence and status slowly decline.

In its place, a third black elite emerged that was primarily made up of black politicians and government administrators. This third elite believed that if blacks acquired political power and created more government programs, they would create numerous opportunities for ambitious young blacks to achieve upward mobility. They consequently downplayed the importance of entrepreneurial activity and stressed political activism over personal initiative.

The result of this indifference, and in some cases outright hostility, to private business on the part of the black elite was that few African Americans became self-employed. For instance, in the 1980s the rate of business ownership (per 1,000 group members) was only 12.5 for blacks, 64.0 for the population as a whole, 68.5 for Japanese, 65.1 for Chinese, and an incredible 88.9 for Koreans.[8] But in spite of these data, some blacks enjoyed financial success operating enclave businesses in areas like mortuaries, cosmetics, and real estate.[9]

However, the overall record of black businesses has not been promising. In the most recent count by the Census Bureau, blacks, who make up roughly 12 percent of the population, owned only 3.1 percent of all businesses in the country, and black-owned businesses in turn accounted for only slightly more than one percent of the nation's gross receipts.[10] Despite repeated campaigns by black retailers to "buy black," African American business leaders complain about the lack of patronage by their own communities. In a study of black businesses after World War II, Joseph Pierce estimated that 90 percent of all money spent in the ghetto went to white-owned businesses.[11] *Black Enterprise* magazine has also stressed that point, reporting that 70 percent of black businessmen complained that the lack of community support was one of the most serious obstacles to operating a profitable company. In recent years, these trends have not appreciably changed. The largest black companies are still enclave companies primarily concerned with servicing their own population. In cities like Los Angeles and New York, Korean entrepreneurs are currently displacing black businesses by opening up a variety of companies such as liquor stores, gas stations, and convenience shops that cater to low-income blacks. Since the 1970s, a few black entrepreneurs have broken away from traditional enclave activities and opened firms that rely primarily on government contracts and set-asides for their financial health. Despite the promising nature of this development, this new group of government contractors has not appreciably altered the entrepreneurial traditions of the black community.

Thomas Sowell has repeatedly suggested that blacks need to alter this pattern of employment and duplicate the entrepreneurial success of Asians to achieve financial independence. But many critics suggest that creating an entrepreneurial tradition is not just a matter of willpower or choice. An ethnic group needs a tradition or culture of business activity to succeed in establishing new companies. It is thus naive to believe that the black community can imitate Asian Americans or Jews and achieve upward mobility through entrepreneurial activity. But if this argument is true, and I will shortly suggest that it is not, it is essential to know why Asians and Jews have been so successful in small businesses. As we will see, most commentators rely on one of four different arguments to explain the financial success of different ethnic groups in this country. Not surprisingly, they are often in sharp disagreement as to whether structural or control arguments best explain the unusual financial record of Asian Americans.

Business Activity and Opportunity Theory. The first major explanation for the rise of minority companies is a structural argument that insists that ethnic entrepreneurs are nothing more than victims of the societies in which they live. Minorities thus become merchants not because of any unique cultural traits or propensity for business, but because racial or religious hostility forces them to assume these roles. In a twist on traditional structural explanations, these commentators argue that it is the absence rather than the presence of traditional opportunities of mobility for minorities that explains why they become entrepreneurs. Ronald Takaki, for instance, insists that the Japanese and Chinese became businessmen because white society drove Asian Americans out of most other occupations.[12] Unfortunately, this argument explains both too much and too little. If Takaki were right, then blacks, who were also barred from many jobs, should be some of the most successful entrepreneurs in the country. But as we already saw, census data indicate that blacks are the least likely of all Americans to start a business. While discrimination may be a necessary condition for a group to become entrepreneurs, it is by no means a sufficient explanation.

Some critics have thus turned the above argument on its head and argued that blacks don't go into business because they have historically encountered more severe discrimination than Asian Americans. Harold Cruse, for instance, has argued that racial discrimination against blacks in the Deep South was so intense at the turn of the century that no black dared start his own business.[13] Stanley Lieberson has reinforced that argument by claiming that except on the West Coast, discrimination against Asians was not as blatant as that experienced by blacks.[14] He maintains that because immigration of Asians to America was cut off early, there were never enough Asian Americans to pose the same kind of threat to whites that blacks did.

While there is an element of truth in both Lieberson's and Cruse's claims, their arguments still seem wide of the mark. Both authors overlook the fact that West Indian blacks, as opposed to American-born blacks, have created a variety of successful businesses. In 1900, West Indians, who were 10 percent of the population of Harlem, owned over 20 percent of all black businesses in Manhattan and were known as the blacks Jews of New York City.[15] Since West Indian and American-born blacks were racially indistinguishable from one another, factors other than racial discrimination must be responsible for their success. Even if racial hostility was intense, societal discrimination should not have prevented blacks from developing their own enclave economy. Given the size of the black communities in the North, there were ample opportunities for many blacks to make a decent living catering to their own ethnic group.

In a similar vein, Lieberson's claim that Asian Americans suffered less than blacks may reflect his failure to distinguish carefully between prejudice and discrimination. Lieberson cites survey data from Princeton University in the 1930s indicating that whites often had a more favorable opinion of Japanese and Chinese than they did of blacks.[16] People's attitudes, which reflect their prejudices, are often a poor indicator of their behavior, which constitutes the essence of discrimination. While whites in the East who were not in competition with Asians may have had a benign attitude toward them, lower-class whites in direct competition with Chinese and Japanese on the West Coast often acted in a brutal and vicious manner towards Asians. Ronald Takaki observes that this was especially true when economic conditions worsened. During slow economic times, "Chinese were beaten and shot by white workers; they were herded to railroad stations and loaded on railroad cars."[17] Repeated occurrences of what became known as the "driving out" of Asians led to the development of so-called Chinatowns in large cities. The alleged difference in discrimination suffered by blacks and Asians may thus not be quite as stark as Cruse and Lieberson portray it. However, both authors are correct in pointing out that racial discrimination may cut both ways in either promoting or hindering the development of ethnic businesses. The very existence of racial discrimination may push minorities in the direction of becoming entrepreneurs. But if that discrimination becomes too violent, as in the post-bellum South, it may also stifle the ability of ethnic groups to start businesses.

Finally, some commentators insist that additional structural factors, such as the size of a particular ethnic group, may also play a role in determining whether or not a minority group can develop into successful entrepreneurs.[18] The large number of blacks in this country has made it nearly impossible for them to exploit economic niches like the Jews did in the film industry or the Japanese did in the produce business. But this argument ignores the fact that a sizable population did not prevent German Americans from becoming successful businessmen in the nineteenth and early part of the twentieth centuries. A large population may likewise facilitate the growth of enclave businesses. Even if sizable numbers are a disadvantage for an ethnic group trying to establish businesses that cater to the larger public, that same population is a decided advantage for a minority business that services its own population.

Cultural Theories. In light of the difficulties with structuralist explanations, many analysts have relied on a second explanation that uses cultural values to account for the success of minority businessmen. While external factors may initially stimulate a group to seek or shun a career in business, a group's internal beliefs, social ties, or unique circumstances may determine how successful they are managing their enterprises.

For example, Asians may have done well in business because they came to this country as sojourners or temporary migrants.[19] Unlike blacks, who were brought to this country against their will, many Chinese and Japanese came to America with the idea of staying a short time in order to earn money and then return to their homeland. Because of their "sojourner" status, many immigrants wanted to amass as much capital as possible. They were thus inclined to work hard, to be thrifty, and to take risks by opening their own businesses. When Asian Americans later decided to become permanent residents, they retained their immigrant business traditions, which were subsequently passed on to their children.

Other commentators, however, have argued that it was more their cultural traditions than their unique status as sojourners that explains the entrepreneurial success of Asians and Jews. For instance, the urban commercial background of many ethnic groups may explain their propensity to become entrepreneurs. But we must be careful not to exaggerate the commercial background of either Jews or Asian-Americans. As Arthur Hertzberg has noted, "American Jewish history is also the story of the poor."[20] Affluent and better educated Jews chose to stay in Europe, where they thought they could ride out the hostility directed toward them. The experience of Jews in Eastern Europe provided them with little training for their eventual success in developing new industries such as television and motion pictures. Similarly, the vast majority of Japanese and Chinese who immigrated to America were peasants who had little or no knowledge about the intricacies of running small businesses. More recently, studies indicate that the Korean immigrants who are prospering as merchants in the inner cities of New York and Los Angeles had minimal business experience in Korea.[21]

As a consequence, many scholars believe that it is the tendency of Chinese, Japanese, and Jewish immigrants to embrace the traditional values of their respective cultures which usually emphasized education, hard work, merit and discipline that enabled them to eventually prosper in the business world. But if such beliefs are responsible for the success of these ethnic groups today, it is imperative to ask why many of these same ethnic groups were not successful entrepreneurs in their own countries. At best the above traits may have contained latent beliefs that one day would enable ethnic groups to succeed at business. Because these latent abilities were often suppressed or diverted into noncommercial activities by other traditional beliefs such as Confucianism, which placed a low value on commercial activity, or by the policies of czarist Russia, which limited opportunities available to Jews, many ethnic groups were able to show little entrepreneurial talent in their native lands.

In light of these difficulties, a second and radically different explanation of the behavior of Japanese Americans has recently been advanced by Harry Kitano, who maintains that the cultural willingness of groups such as Asians to adopt the work ethic and entrepreneurial values of their adopted country explains their unusual financial success in America.[22] In Kitano's view, instead of traditional Asian values explaining the financial accomplishments of the Japanese and Chinese, their eagerness to adopt the values of their chosen country explains their unusual propensity to start their own businesses. Ethnic groups who did well in America were minority groups who worked hard at becoming more American than the Americans. While outwardly they clung to the traditions of their homelands, internally they adopted the American faith that hard work and business activity would eventually lead to upward mobility. Rather than a separate cultural identity, it was their internalization of traditional American entrepreneurial values that propelled them to become innovative businessmen.

However divergent these two explanations may at first appear, it is possible that both are right. The unusual financial success of Asian Americans and Jews may be a result of their ability to fuse their traditional beliefs of hard work and self-restraint with American cultural values that place a high premium on business activity. In imperial China, pre-Meiji Japan, or czarist Russia, society may have suppressed or channeled the intense work ethic of Jews and Asians into nonentrepreneurial activities. When these groups subsequently arrived in America, they found a country that neither bureaucratically suppressed business activity nor culturally denigrated entrepreneurial creativity. In the liberating atmosphere of America, Asians and Jews were able to synthesize a new culture that combined elements from both their traditional societies and their new homeland.[23] As most Asians and Jews willingly adopted American values, their simultaneous belief in traditional principles from their native cultures—such as hard work, education, merit, and discipline—enabled them to succeed in business.

Social/Cultural Explanations. Even if cultural beliefs are the primary reason why minority groups have done well in business, social ties also are responsible for ethnic entrepreneurial success. A third factor that has undoubtedly contributed to the business traditions of Asian Americans is their involvement in what Ivan Light has called rotating credit associations.[24] In this informal system of ethnic financial cooperation, members agreed to make regular contributions to a fund, which in turn would be distributed in whole or in part to the contributors on a rotational basis. These associations, which were called *hui* or *ko* among the Chinese, *tanomoshi* or *mujin* among the Japanese, and *esusu* among blacks in Africa and the West Indies, provided the start-up capital that enabled immigrants to begin business operations and weather financial storms. Without this kind of financial assistance, very few minorities could have started businesses. As Light has pointed out, white-dominated banks were often reluctant to lend money to minorities to finance new companies.*

---

* If Light is correct, it is important to know why West Indian blacks but not American blacks used rotating credit associations in their development of small businesses. If informal financial arrangements existed in Africa, why did the descendants of black slaves in the Antilles but not America use that tradition to create a viable business community? The answer appears to lie in the two different patterns of slavery that evolved in the Caribbean and the United States. In the West Indies, unlike in America, slave plantations were large enterprises often run by absentee owners whose main concern was to maximize their short-term profits. To increase production, the overseers who ran the plantations often treated their black hands harshly, resulting in a large death rate. To insure an adequate supply of labor, West Indian planters constantly imported new slaves to replace those who died. With the continual arrival of people from Africa, blacks were able to retain more of their heritage and keep alive their traditions from the old country. Similarly, in the Antilles the black population easily outnumbered their Caucasian masters. The resulting lack of whites meant that the plantation often had to encourage blacks to establish a separate slave economy to feed and provision the plantation. With the passage of time, West Indian blacks were able to develop practical experience in producing goods and exchanging them under quasi-market conditions. Their experience with informal credit associations facilitated such business activities.

In America, however, slavery was practiced more often on small plantations in a diversified economy, where live-in owners tended to act more paternalistically toward their slaves. Because they were less brutal, plantation overseers could satisfy their labor needs through the internal reproduction of their slave population rather than the buying of new slaves from abroad. Given the resources of the area, American slave owners also had no need to encourage their wards to

The absence of rotating credit associations among blacks was symptomatic of a much larger problem facing the black community in the United States. Among the social factors that distinguished American blacks from Asians and to a lesser extent from West Indians was the absence of a well-organized and cohesive community life. The Japanese and Chinese were highly disciplined ethnic groups with a multiplicity or organizations.[25] Because they had cohesive and stable family lives, they often prospered because they could always rely on the assistance of their spouses and children in operating their family businesses. In addition, an overlap of kinship relationships, territorial organizations, and trade associations in Asian American communities heavily regulated their economic behavior. Given this kind of paternalistic system, members of the Asian community often engaged in a variety of self-help projects, such as apprenticeship programs for new immigrants. When Japanese arrived in this country, they could often count on jobs with their *kenjin* or relatives, who would later help them in establishing their own businesses. Various Asian associations also practiced price fixing so that firms would not underbid one another, and they specified the geographical spacing of companies so that each business would serve a specific territory.

Black Americans, in contrast, had to rely on voluntary organizations rather than ethnic connections to structure their relationships with one another. Because slave owners wanted to minimize the potential for revolts, they deliberately reshuffled their slaves so that few people would share common ascriptive ties. Individuals from different blood lines, tribes, and jurisdictions often found themselves in America working in the company of complete strangers with whom they shared no personal bonds. On the basis of work by Herbert Gutman, we know that many black slaves tried to

---

develop a separate slave economy to supply the plantation. As a result, American blacks differed from their Caribbean counterparts in that they were more likely to be cut off from their African roots and resocialized into the mores of their white plantation owners. With no need for informal financial associations and their ties with Africa severed forever, the American black experience with rotating credit associations slowly faded from memory. An unanticipated legacy of America's distinctive pattern of slavery was that native-born blacks lacked one of the key social institutions that enabled Asians and West Indians to develop successful businesses.

However, many observers have asked why West Indians, who are successful entrepreneurs in America, have not shown a comparable tendency in their own homeland. The answer appears to be that West Indians who migrated to the United States probably (1) possessed a sojourner mentality which stimulated them to get involved in business, (2) adopted the values of American capitalism, and (3) developed a set of social institutions that enabled them to finance their business aspirations. By themselves, the adoption of a sojourner outlook, American values, or rotating credit associations may be necessary but not sufficient conditions for minority entrepreneurship to flourish. But when these elements are combined, the chances that minority groups will succeed in business are greatly enhanced.

overcome this communal vacuum by creating kinship-ties among slaves on the plantations.[26] But black families, unlike other ethnic groups, had to rely more on ad hoc and informal means of self-help. The communitywide organizations that Asians could rely on were not found in the more atomized plantation society. The resulting paucity of community ties prompted blacks to invest a lot of energy in building alternative institutions to provide cohesion to the black community. Some, like Booker T. Washington, tried to build business-development organizations, others social welfare and fraternal associations, and yet others strong church groups.

Unfortunately, many observers, including the well-known black sociologist E. Franklin Frazier, believe that the resulting business and social welfare organizations badly served the black population. In his book *The Black Bourgeoisie*, Frazier attacked most of these voluntary organizations as being selfish, bourgeois, individualistic, and unable to relate to the needs of the larger black community.[27] Only black churches and fraternal orders retained an appeal for the vast majority of blacks. The great popularity of the black church, which exists to this day, reflected the absence of other ties to bind the black community together. American blacks created and strongly supported their churches to serve as substitutes for the Old World linkages that had been destroyed by slavery. However, the proliferation of churches soon promoted competition for members, which hampered their ability to provide leadership for the black population. Unlike the Asian community, blacks were never able to develop the internal solidarity and cooperation that would help sustain an indigenous business class. Repeatedly, efforts by Booker T. Washington at the turn of the century, and later Father Devine during the Great Depression, to develop black-owned businesses and end welfare dependency achieved transitory success at best.

Cultural/Educational Explanations. Finally, the fourth and final factor that may determine the entrepreneurial success of ethnic groups is their cultural commitment to improving their educational skills. This is especially true in the 1990s, when the changing nature of our economy has created innumerable opportunities that did not exist a decade ago. But only those ethnic groups who possess technical skills will be able to identify—let alone exploit—these new niches in the economy. As we have seen, Japanese and Chinese Americans have placed a lot of emphasis on higher education, and when Asian Americans attend college, they are likely to major in difficult fields such as science, engineering, and business. By combining these new skills with their heritage of entrepreneurial activity, many young Asian Americans have been able to develop profitable computer, data management, and consulting companies. Unlike Asians who are more likely to concentrate on the sciences, blacks tend to major in fields such as education and the social sciences, which have less relevance for the business world. Even when blacks acquire advanced degrees, their human capital skills are often not conducive to establishing successful businesses in our increasingly technical economy.

Can the Future Be Different? If the above assessment of the cultural and educational problems of the black community is essentially correct, it raises a whole series of important policy questions. As we have seen, Thomas Sowell believes that the black population ought to follow in the footsteps of Asian Americans and adopt the same privatistic, entrepreneurial strategy they have pursued. He thus implies that the occupational strategy a group adopts is purely a matter of public choice. To stress that point, he is critical of much of the leadership of the black community for being preoccupied more with the pursuit of politics and governmental programs than with the creation of a black capitalist class.

However, many of Sowell's critics claim that his call for more "black capitalism" is not a feasible option for the black community. If the ability of an ethnic group to succeed as entrepreneurs primarily depends on its unique traditions or cultural values, then Sowell's policy recommendations are much more problematic than he likes to admit. It is thus interesting to note that Sowell spends very little time discussing historical figures like Booker T. Washington, who espoused a similar policy of self-help and economic development at the turn of the century. The failure of Washington's policies and of black business ventures eventually prompted Frazier to argue that it was a "social myth" to believe that the black population could ever develop an independent business class.

But such a pessimistic attitude is surely unwarranted and based on a faulty sense of historical determinism. There is no compelling reason why ethnic groups should be trapped by their past. While a group's cultural background and historical traditions may be difficult barriers to overcome, they are not insurmountable. Sowell is thus correct to argue that the black population, instead of constantly asking the larger white community for political concessions, can build a culture of self-help and economic independence. Ironically, certain government programs may even prove useful in furthering the development of a successful black entrepreneurial class. A variety of government agencies may act as surrogates for some of the institutions Asians relied on to develop their tradition of small businesses. The proliferation of business schools, for instance, may provide young blacks with the economic training their relatives never obtained. Similarly, the Small Business Administration's policy of guaranteeing minority loans may duplicate the role of the Asian rotating credit associations.

Black conservatives might also point out that instead of asking why Asians or Jews have a culture that stresses entrepreneurship, it might be more appropriate to turn the question upside down and ask why blacks have a culture that minimizes or even denigrates private enterprise. The biggest obstacle facing the black community is not that blacks lack the entrepreneurial tradition of Asians but that they have embraced an economic and political culture that is hostile to business activity and self-help programs. As pointed out earlier, all three elite black groups in this country have downplayed the "trades" and viewed education, individual deportment, and political power as alternative sources of status. In light of the cultural indifference and even downright opposition to private enterprise exhibited by many blacks leaders, it is not surprising that the black community has never emphasized entrepreneurship.

Since the 1980s, some civil rights leaders appear to have become even more hostile to Sowell's ideas. Their fear is that the inordinate fascination that American conservatives like Sowell have with Asian, Jewish, and West Indian entrepreneurial success is really a subterfuge to "blame the victims" of poverty for their own condition. When civil rights leaders claim that Sowell is blaming the victim, they overlook the possibility that they are doing a disservice to the people they are ostensibly trying to help. Sowell's main point is that minorities have the resources to be other than victims of society. He wants to convince the black leadership that the poor can take responsibility for their own lives and become financially independent. When his critics assume that the poor are trapped by circumstances and unable to help themselves, they abandon any hope of ever solving the causes of poverty. Sowell, in contrast, insists that with innovative leadership and willpower, the black community can turn the situation around and finally create an environment in which entrepreneurship is encouraged. Data from the most recent census of minority businesses lend mixed hope that blacks are finally becoming more effective as entrepreneurs. While their revenue growth lagged behind that of whites, the number of black firms grew by 37 percent, as opposed to a 14 percent increase for all businesses between the years 1982 and 1987.[28] If black entrepreneurs can sustain their ability to start new companies and improve their profitability, a significant black business class may yet emerge.

The Desirability of Black Entrepreneurship

Even if it feasible for the African American community to pursue "black capitalism," we need to know if it is a desirable goal to achieve. The second main criticism leveled against Sowell's belief in entrepreneurial activity is that the advantages of small businesses are illusionary as well as increasingly irrelevant in an age of large corporations.

Not surprisingly, American Marxists have been the prime advocates of the argument that entrepreneurial activity offers minorities limited opportunities for upward mobility. They insist that small companies are a retrograde form of capitalism, more suitable to an earlier rather than an advanced stage of capitalist development. In the Marxist scheme of things, small businessmen are nothing more than petite bourgeoisie who will eventually be superseded by large capitalists, who in turn will be replaced by monopoly capitalists. To argue that the black population should adopt an entrepreneurial strategy is to render them superfluous in a complex economy. The future of blacks as well as all Americans depends on the performance of large international corporations. While small businesses may have offered opportunities for ethnic groups in the past to achieve financial independence, they will be of no economic consequence in an age of giant corporations. In the 1950s, C. W. Mills seemed to offer conclusive evidence in support of this view by pointing out that the number of proprietors in the labor force had decreased in every census between 1880 and 1940.[29] Mills eventually projected that large corporations would absorb most small businesses and that the self-employed worker would disappear from the economic scene.

However, in the 1970s and 1980s a variety of studies began to challenge and eventually overturn the prevailing wisdom about the development of American capitalism.[30] Large companies often acted like dinosaurs and were unable to respond to shifting changes in consumer demand. Scott Fain found that in the 1970s the self-employed not only ceased declining as a percentage of the labor force but grew 28 percent faster than the wage and salary labor force.[31] Other studies found that a surprising number of jobs were generated by small businesses.[32] In the 1970s they created 3 million positions, while the one thousand largest corporations registered virtually no net gain in employment. More recently, the Small Business Administration reported that small firms (under five hundred employees) accounted for about 60 percent of all jobs created during the 1980s. However, there is evidence that the recession of the early 1990s has significantly slowed the job-creating ability of many small firms. But while it is important not to overstate the role

Table 5.4
Black Employment in Government

Percentage of Jobs Classified as Professional or Management, 1989			
Blacks		Whites	
Public Sector	Private Sector	Public Sector	Private Sector
53.5	46.5	28.5	71.5
Percentage of Total Black Employment in Government Service			
1960	1970	1980	
12.0	21.4	27.1	

Sources: Data from Selim Jones, employment analyst for the U.S. Bureau of the Census, as quoted in Thomas Edsall and Mary Edsall, *Chain Reaction* (New York: W. W. Norton, 1991); and U.S. Bureau of the Census, *Census of the Population*, 1980, Vol. 1, Part 1, Chapter C, United States Summary, "General Social and Economic Characteristics," PC 80-1-C1 (Washington, D.C.: U.S. Government Printing Office, 1983).

of small companies, it is still fair to argue that "small business" remains a large, visible, and important sector of the American economy.

The Government Option

Finally, just because entrepreneurial activity has many beneficial conse-quences, it does not necessarily mean that it is the only route ethnic groups can pursue to achieve upward mobility. The third and final complaint lodged against Sowell is that he has simply failed to realize that government assistance and political activity may be equally attractive ways for a minority group to achieve financial success. The fact that the black community is following in the footsteps of the Irish to escape the ghetto does not mean that this decision is inferior to the entrepreneurial path of Asian Americans. After all, as census data on ethnic income indicate (table 5.1), the Irish earn a family income that is above the median family income in the United States. The black community seems to agree with this assessment, for in the last thirty years its reliance on government employment and political activity has increased substantially. Currently, the number of black employees in government approaches the level of Irish government workers during the 1930s, their peak period of public employment.[33] When Sowell minimizes the role of government, he overlooks the fact that a large percentage of the black middle class in professional or managerial positions owes its financial success to government employment (see table 5.4).

Black interest in government no doubt reflects the undeniable benefits of civil service jobs. Like entrepreneurial activity, public employment has provided blacks with an occupation niche that takes them out of direct competition with working-class whites. If the split labor market explains why whites often resist the advancement of blacks, we can appreciate why the black community has pursued opportunities in government. Public employment has afforded black managers an opportunity to excel in occupations for which many whites are either educationally unqualified or unwilling to pursue. Government opportunities now seem to offer even more chances for upward mobility than in the early twentieth century when the Irish dominated public employment. With the growth of government in the last several decades and the expansion of the welfare state since the 1960s, the need for professional managers has increased substantially.

In spite of the advantages of working for the government, public employment also has its limitations. Steve Erie, who has perceptively written about the Irish in America, has suggested that their success was not necessarily due to their management of urban political machines.[34] As he points out, the Irish lagged behind other ethnic groups in developing a substantial middle-class population. Many of the jobs in the public sector were menial, and even those that required some professional training, such as fire fighting, offered limited opportunities for financial gain. Because they channeled so much of their economic energy into the public sector, the Irish "forsook opportunities in the private sector save for industries such as construction that depended on political connections."[35] Instead of seeing government employment as a ladder to upward mobility, Erie describes it as a noose. While government work provided security and marginal advancement, it hampered the ability of the Irish to achieve substantial financial gains. The decline of the machine, which forced the Irish out of the public sector, largely accounts for the economic success of the Irish today. As Erie notes, the development of the Irish middle class is really a phenomenon of the post-World War II period. When the Irish were forced to seek work in the private sector and pursued money and status rather than political power and security, their economic fortunes changed significantly for the better.

The interesting question is whether government employment will be a comparable dead end for blacks. Some recent trends in public employment may make the black experience in government very different from that of the Irish. As the size of the public sector has grown, many of the menial tasks of the urban machine have been replaced by complex managerial tasks requiring trained public administrators. The superficial similarity between black and Irish employment may thus be misleading. But as more and more blacks have gravitated toward government work, they have become increasingly vulnerable to shifts in public opinion. In the 1960s and 1970s, when the black middle class sought work in the government realm, the public seemed willing to support an ever-growing public sector. The black middle class thus sought work in a sector of the economy that could be best described as a growth industry. As the public sector expanded, so did the cost to the average citizen, which generated in turn a political backlash against further increases in the size of government. In the 1990s, the prospects for further growth in the public sector are uncertain at best. If well-educated blacks continue to seek employment with government agencies, they may find themselves looking for work in a static or even declining sector of the economy. Once again, the parallels with the Irish are not encouraging. While many factors contributed to the decline of the large urban machines, one factor was the growing disenchantment of middle-class voters with the costly employment practices of local government. Because President Clinton seems to be inclined to continue the Reagan policies of scaling back the size of the public sector, government employment may not be as attractive as it was in previous decades.

As Sowell has clearly demonstrated, individuals can achieve upward mobility by developing their entrepreneurial as well as their traditional educational skills. While many of Sowell's detractors say that it is neither empirically feasible nor normatively desirable for the black community to develop an entrepreneurial tradition of its own, the evidence suggests otherwise. More than anything else, the cultural hostility of the civil rights movement to entrepreneurial activity is undoubtedly the main reason why blacks have such a poor record of starting their own businesses. If the public is more restive than ever about expanding government and rising taxes, blacks may find that job opportunities in the federal sector will eventually dry up. To win the war against poverty, we may find as many answers by studying those groups that have escaped poverty as we do by studying those stuck in poverty. Instead of minimizing the accomplishments of Asian Americans, the civil rights movement might do well to emulate their entrepreneurial activities.

SIX
The Growing Instability
of the Family

If the lack of entrepreneurial skills poses a threat to the aspirations of poor blacks, the breakup of the family also has adversely affected their fortunes. Isabel Sawhill has argued that one reason why the pretransfer poverty rate has risen is because the number of vulnerable groups in society—especially single-parent families and their children—has also increased. As evidence of this connection, it should be noted that while the percentage of indigents who are elderly or in intact families has recently declined, the number who are in female-headed households has risen significantly over the last thirty years.

Despite Sawhill's insistence that there is an apparent link between the structure of the American family and the presence of poverty, the problem of single-parent families remains a highly controversial topic. While demographic changes in the family have certainly altered the face of poverty, numerous scholars, such as Mary Jo Bane, have minimized the relationship between female-headed households and the overall poverty rate. They claim that it is more the lack of economic opportunities than the changes in family structure that explains why the government has not won its war against poverty. In this context, the current debate over the status of the family recalls the controversy surrounding Daniel Patrick Moynihan's important study of family stability in the early 1960s. While many of his conclusions are still in dispute, Moynihan's central assertion—that the breakup of the family, especially the black family, represented a serious obstacle to the elimination of poverty—has held up remarkably well.

Before we substantiate this point, it is important to understand how family relations have changed over the last several decades. In aggregate terms, the American family is considerably less stable than in the past. But in addition

Table 6.1
Percentage of Female-Headed Families

Year	White	Black	Total
1940	10.2	17.9	n/a
1950	8.5	17.6	9.4
1960	8.1	21.7	10.0
1970	9.1	28.3	10.8
1980	11.6	40.2	14.6
1986	13.0	41.8	16.1
1990	12.9	43.8	16.5
1991	13.2	45.9	17.0

Sources: U.S. Bureau of the Census, *Current Population Reports,*
Series P-60, no. 161, "Money, Income and Poverty Status in
the United States: 1987"; U.S. Bureau of the Census, *Current
Population Reports,* Series P-20, no. 450, "Marital Status and
Living Arrangements, March 1990"; and U.S. Bureau of the
Census, *Current Population Reports,* Series P-20, no. 458,
"Household and Family Characteristics: March 1991."

there are significant differences in the evolution of white and black families.
Whether we examine the incidence of single-parent families, the reasons for
the emergence of female-headed households, or the alternative family structures that people join when the nuclear family breaks down, there appear to
be pronounced differences in the structure of white and black families.

For instance, the percentage of families that are headed by women varies
dramatically from one race to the next (table 6.1). When Moynihan published his study in the 1960s and announced that the black family was in a
crisis situation, slightly less than 22 percent of black and 8 percent of white
households were headed by females. Thirty years later the percentage of
single-parent families has dramatically increased. In 1991 a little over 45
percent of all black and 13 percent of whites were in female-headed households. If Moynihan was alarmed by the situation several decades ago, today
the status of the nuclear family appears more fragile than ever.

The reason for the emergence of single-parent families also appears to
differ from one race to the next. Black women are less likely to get married,
more likely to get divorced, and of those who do get divorced, fewer are
inclined to remarry than their white counterparts. However, never-married
women rather than formerly married women are increasingly responsible for
the growth of black single-parent families. The proportion of blacks aged 24–
44 who have never married has roughly tripled since the end of World War
II. The dramatic increase in single-parent families among whites, on the
other hand, is primarily caused by men and women's getting divorced and

Table 6.2
Percentage of Out-of-Wedlock Births,
Ages 15–44

Year	White	Black	Total
1940	3	14	3.5
1950	3	17	4
1960	3	22	5
1970	5	35	1
1980	11	55	18
1990	17	57	23
1992	17	67	24

Sources: National Center for Health Statistics, *Vital and Health Statistics*, Series 21, no. 36 (1980) and Series 24, no. 41 (1990). National Center for Health Statistics, *Monthly Vital Statistics Reports*, Vol. 32, no. 9 (December 1983); and U.S. Bureau of the Census, *Current Population Reports*, Series P-20, no. 454, "Fertility of American Women, 1990," and *Current Population Reports*, Series P-20, no. 470, "Fertility of American Women, 1992."

establishing independent households. Whereas whites marry but increasingly become divorced, blacks are more likely never to have married in the first place.

Third, among both black and whites there has been a substantial increase in the number of children born out of wedlock (table 6.2). While currently around 23 percent of all children are born out of wedlock, the figure has climbed to over 60 percent among black women. In spite of the troubling nature of these figures, many commentators insist that the problem of illegitimate births is not quite as serious as it may first appear. While the ratio of black children born out of wedlock has increased dramatically, the rate at which unmarried black women have children has declined since the early 1960s. From 1940 to 1960, the birth rate for unmarried black women rose from around 36 per 1,000 to a little over 98 per 1,000 and has since dropped to around 70 per 1,000. The big upsurge in the ratio of black children born out of wedlock occurred primarily because married black women are choosing to have fewer babies. Despite this caveat, black women are still roughly three times more likely to have children out of wedlock than their white counterparts.

More importantly, the tendency of middle-class blacks to refrain from having children also raises questions about upward mobility among blacks in the future. As ethnic groups move into the ranks of the middle class, they often invest heavily in their children to give them a head start. As intact two-parent black families, who are the most likely to become middle class, elect not to have children, their success in life cannot benefit any offspring. As a result, it is increasingly low-income individuals, rather than the more prosperous black middle class, who are bearing the primary responsibility to help their children establish themselves in society. The tendency of married black couples not to have children thus raises the danger that the black community, in contrast to other ethnic groups, will have a considerably harder time passing on to the next generation the significant economic gains of its emerging middle class.

Fourth, when confronted with the challenge of raising children in a single-parent family, different racial groups appear to cope with the problem in different ways. While Moynihan had suggested that the breakup of the black nuclear family eventually led to a highly disorganized family life in which people were caught up in a tangle of pathology, Carol Stack, as well as other sociologists have insisted that Moynihan's view of the black family was a distortion of reality.[1] On the basis of field research in a northern black ghetto, Stack found that female households often relied on kin-structured local networks of friends and relatives to help raise their offspring and achieve financial independence. It was thus wrong to think that the only family options available to poor blacks were either the stability of the nuclear family or the isolation of single parenthood. When poor black women became responsible for raising children on their own, they had the third choice of calling on an extensive network of relatives and friends for assistance. Rather than being isolated, female-headed households were often involved in highly complex and structured relationships with many people.

However, Stack's view of the single-parent household has itself been called into question. In drawing her conclusions about poor women, Stack relied on data gathered from a two-year case study of a northern urban ghetto. But Sheppard Kellam and his colleagues have reached very different conclusions in their longitudinal study of a poor black section of Chicago called Woodland.[2] In contrast to the disorganized picture of Moynihan and the kinship model of Carol Stack, Kellam has discovered a diverse array of living arrangements among poor black families. Out of a total population of almost 1,400 people, he identified some eighty-six different family structures, which he grouped into larger clusters that consisted of mother and father (41%), mother alone (37%), mother and grandmother (5%), mother and other (6%), and mother-absent relationships (7%). Kellam also found that mother-alone families tended to remain that way, as nearly three-fourths of such families had not altered their status over a ten-year period. But what was most disconcerting about Kellam's findings was the high incidence of social isolation among the 37 percent of the Woodlawn population that consisted of single mothers raising their children alone. He found that 60 percent of these mothers, as opposed to 6 percent of other family types, reported that there was no one besides themselves in whom their child could confide. In criticizing Moynihan for arguing that all poor black families were disorganized, Stack failed to see that a sizable number of black female-headed households were indeed isolated, with limited ties to friends and relatives.

The recent increase in our knowledge of poor black households has unfortunately not been matched by new insights into the family patterns of white female-headed families. But the little data that are available suggest that white single-parent households may be less inclined to rely on the type of kinship ties that Stack identified in the black community. However, counterbalancing this loss is the fact that whites are more likely to get remarried than blacks. While poor white females may have less external support in raising their children than indigent black women, they are more likely to find a new husband and reestablish a two-parent household.

THE LINK BETWEEN FAMILY STRUCTURE AND POVERTY

As we shall see, these recent changes in the family patterns of the poor have seriously affected their chances for escaping poverty.[3] While this point may seem obvious, it has generated considerable controversy. Today, as was true of the 1960s, many poverty analysts minimize the importance of the breakdown of the family as a cause of poverty. In the 1960s, some black activists even claimed that the rise of the single-parent black family was a healthy and adaptive response by low-income blacks to their bleak economic situation. For example, Andrew Billingsley typified this attitude in his well-known book *Black Families in White America* (1968), in which he criticized studies of black families that focused "on standardized objective measures which have been demonstrated to have meaning only in the white, European subculture."[4] He thus suggested that raising children in a two-parent family is not a desirable middle-class value but rather a white value which blacks should not necessarily feel compelled to follow. Yet other social commentators have also insisted that external factors alone, such as racial discrimination or the state of the economy, rather than family problems are the primary reasons for the economic plight of the black community.

But in light of the growing correlation between female-headed households and poverty, the claims of Moynihan's detractors are hard to substantiate empirically. Census data indicate that, increasingly, one's sex and marital

Table 6.3
Poor in Female-Headed Families

	1960	1970	1980	1991
Percentage of All Poor	18.3	29.5	37.1	38.7
Poverty Rate for F.H.F.	49.5	38.1	36.7	39.7
Percentage of Black Poor	25	55.8	67.7	64
Poverty Rate for Black F.H.F.	70.6	58.7	53.4	54.8

Sources: U.S. Bureau of the Census, *Current Population Reports*, Series P-60, no. 168, "Money, Income and Poverty Status in the United States"; and *Current Population Reports*, Series P-60, no. 181, "Poverty in the United States."

status appear to be the primary determinants of poverty. For instance, single-parent families constitute a growing proportion of the overall poverty population. As table 6.3 indicates, female-headed families have jumped from just over 18 percent of the poor in 1960 to over 38 percent by the start of the 1990s. Female-headed households now account for over 60 percent of all the black poor.

Finally, female-headed families are more likely than male-headed families to be persistently poor. In an analysis of the Michigan Panel Study of Income Dynamics, Greg Duncan found that female-headed households made up 61 percent of all those who had been poor for more than ten years.[5]

But while the overall percentage of the poor in female-headed households has increased, the news about single-parent families is not all bad. In fact, the incidence of poverty among these families has also declined since the 1960s.[6] Although it is common these days to talk about the growing feminization of poverty, we have to be careful in using that phrase. Even though more indigents are in female-headed households than ever before, an increasing percentage of women in such families are less likely to be poor today than thirty years ago.

WHY FAMILY CHANGES MAY LEAD TO POVERTY

The close connection between the incidence of poverty and the structure of family life raises the obvious question of why female-headed households are so much more vulnerable to spells of poverty than intact families. The answer appears to be threefold.

First, and perhaps most important, the breakup of two-parent families has affected the size of the poor population through its impact on the work record and earnings of women. Divorce often forces women who have had very little formal job training or work experience into the labor market. Among young women who are pregnant and elect never to get married, the situation is even more serious. The younger a woman is when she has her first child, the greater the likelihood that she is poorly educated and ill-prepared for any kind of job except the most menial.

Similarly, the breakup of the family may adversely affect poverty rates by isolating women from openings in the labor market. When women get divorced or are abandoned by the father of their children, they are likely to find themselves culturally cut off from people who are working outside the home. Martha Van Haitsma found that isolated single mothers are less likely to find out about possible job opportunities than are married mothers who associate with men who hold full-time jobs.[7] Carol Stack has also noted that single black mothers who are abandoned by their spouse and join extended kin groups often find that their new peers do not necessarily place a high value on becoming financially independent or securing an outside job. The "domestic networks" that indigent black women often join are in reality exchange relationships in which poor women share limited resources with those temporarily down on their luck. Stack has observed that while such kin ties help low-income women meet immediate and short-term needs, they may hamper the ability of poor blacks to escape from poverty over the long run. Young black girls may feel it is unnecessary either to complete their education or to acquire a skill because they know they can always fall back on their "domestic networks" if they get in trouble. Once young women start relying on relatives, the kin group acquires a vested interest in discouraging them from returning to school, saving money, or leaving the confines of the ghetto for outside work. When individuals move off welfare, they become more concerned with advancing their own careers than serving the interests of their relatives and friends.

Second, there is also growing evidence that the growth of female-headed households has a decisively negative effect on the economic prospects of their children. "Children in families disrupted by divorce and out of wedlock birth do worse than children in intact families on several measures of well-being."[8] For example, children who grow up in single-parent families are six times more likely to become poor than children in two-parent families. They are also likely to remain in poverty longer. While 22 percent of children in one-parent families will experience poverty during childhood for seven years or more, the figures drop to 2 percent for children in two-parent families.[9] The National Center for Health Statistics also found in a 1988 survey of families that children in single-parent families are two to three times more likely than children in two-parent families to have emotional and behavioral problems. Barbara Dafoe Whitehead reports that children from single-parent homes are also more likely to quit high school, to get pregnant as teenagers, to abuse drugs, and to be in trouble with the law. Sarah McLanahan and other researchers have echoed that point by finding that black children from single-parent families have slightly lower I.Q. scores and a 70 percent greater tendency to drop out of school than children raised in two-parent families.[10] They also discovered that daughters from female-headed households are more inclined to have children as teenagers, and are more likely to end up in single-parent families themselves. Even more disturbing, "having lived in a mother-only family approximately triples the probability of an individual becoming a welfare recipient."[11] "Contrary to popular belief, many children do not 'bounce back' after divorce or remarriage. Difficulties that are associated with family breakup often persist into adulthood. Children who grow up in single-parent or step-parent families are less successful as adults, particularly in the two domains of life—love and work—that are most essential to happiness."[12] The danger thus exists that the children born into poor single-parent families may literally inherit the poverty of their mothers.[13] The economic deprivation of one generation appears to be be passed on to future generations. As more and more individuals elect to pursue their own happiness at the expense of their families, the results are often a disaster for the well-being of children. As families ties break down, more and more children are at risk of becoming poor. While the percentage of children in this country who were poor had dropped to around 15 percent in the late 1960s, by 1992 it had increased to a little over 20 percent.

A third reason why broken families often end up in poverty is due to the erosion and growing polarization of aggregate family income. When poor couples with little education get divorced or when young poorly trained women establish independent households, their ability to earn a decent family income is likely to be limited. The fragmentation of the two-parent family has thus made divorced members of low-income families especially vulnerable when they are only qualified for low-skilled, low paying positions. As a case in point, assume that the parents of two teenaged children can find only menial jobs in the fast-food industry paying the minimum wage. If both adults work at least fifty weeks a year, they will earn $17,000, which is several thousand dollars above the poverty line for a family of four. If the couple subsequently gets divorced and the husband refuses to pay any child support, as is often the case in this country, the former wife and her two children will find themselves below the official poverty line. As an intact family, the couple had enjoyed earnings that were 34 percent above the poverty line. With the breakdown of the nuclear family, the odds are that both individuals will be classified as members of the official poor. In recent years, it has become fashionable to argue that low-paying jobs are the primary reason for the persistence of poverty in this country. But as the above example demonstrates, a cohesive family in which both spouses work may escape poverty even when the economy generates only minimum-wage jobs.

THE DEGREE TO WHICH FAMILY CHANGES INFLUENCE THE POVERTY RATE

To explain why the breakdown of the family causes spells of poverty still leaves unresolved the actual magnitude of the problem. Because roughly two-fifths of all the poor are currently members of female-headed households, it is tempting to argue that changes in family patterns are responsible for 40 percent of the current poverty problem in this country.[14] However, in a widely cited article on family breakup and poverty, Mary Jo Bane has argued that these figures greatly exaggerate the nature of the problem.[15] Like many of Moynihan's critics in the 1960s, Bane insists that there are methodological problems in assuming that the proliferation of female-headed households is the actual cause of a poverty. The most prominent of these mistakes is assuming that the women who end up in single-parent families are representative of the population as a whole, when, in reality, they may be more prone than the average person to become poor in the first place. If this is the case, then the apparent relationship between broken families and poverty may be spurious. Some other factor such as a decline in the economy or a lack of motivation may be the cause of both poverty and the breakup of families.

As a means of illustrating this point, Bane calls poverty resulting from an actual change in the pattern of family life "event driven poverty," and poverty caused by other factors "reshuffled poverty." The reshuffled poor are merely those women who are currently in a single-parent family but who would have become poor regardless of their marital status. To determine the size of either population, Bane has tried to identify whether indigent women began their poverty spells before, after, or simultaneously with the establishment of a single-parent household. She maintains that if an individual's financial status and her ties to her husband change simultaneously, then it is most likely that the breakup of the family is the cause of poverty. However, if a woman is already poor before she establishes her own family, another factor such as loss of a job probably explains her economic status. Similarly, if the woman became poor after the creation of her single-parent family, then others factors, such as her vulnerability to unemployment or illness, are probably responsible for her low income.

Based on the data from the Panel Study of Income Dynamics, Bane estimates that roughly half of the poverty among female-headed and single-person households in the country as a whole, and therefore about 20 to 25 percent of the official poverty rate, has been caused by the breakdown of the traditional two-parent family. Her data also indicate that the impact of family changes varies along racial lines: the breakdown of traditional family ties has forced fewer single-parent black families into poverty than comparable white households. Many poor black female-headed families have evidently been formed from households that were already poor to begin with. In spite of these findings, Bane has tended to minimize the importance of family ties in explaining the persistence of low income, arguing that "the problem of poverty should be addressed by devoting attention to employment rather than hand-wringing about the decline of the family."[16]

As impressive as Bane's research may be, her figures may understate the importance of the family as a cause of poverty for two very important reasons. First, because her definition of whether changing family ties are responsible for poverty deals only with actual events rather than counterfactual situations, she may have significantly underestimated the influence of family relations on poverty levels. To illustrate, imagine that a young girl dropped out of school and thus became poor before she got pregnant and established her own household. Under Bane's counting procedure, the breakdown of the family appears unrelated to the girl's economic plight. But if we imagine a counterfactual situation in which the girl got married after dropping out of school, and started working with her husband at a menial job paying the minimum wage, then it is easy to see how the woman's marital situation would have enabled her to escape the ranks of the poor. To find that many young women are poor before they establish their own households overlooks the fact that if these same women became part of a two-parent working household, they might have easily worked their way out of poverty. A recent Census Bureau study of low-wage earners makes the significance of marriage readily apparent. As table 6.4 indicates, among women who had low wages, 5.5 percent of those who were married fell below the poverty line, while the poverty figure jumped to around 28 percent for low-paid women in single-parent households. By pooling their wages, husbands and wives can collectively guarantee that their families earn their way out of poverty. While the point is simple enough, we must remember that if workers stay married, they can escape poverty even if as individuals they earn only poverty wages.

Second, in grouping women according to when they first became poor, Bane overlooks the intergenerational transfer of poverty from mothers to

Table 6.4
Poverty Rates for Women with Low Wages

	1984	1990
Wife in married-couple family	7.0%	5.5%
Female household, no spouse	30.2	27.8

Source: U.S. Bureau of the Census, *Current Population Reports*, Series P-60, no. 178, "Workers with Low Earnings: 1964–1990."

daughters. Because daughters from single-parent homes are less likely to graduate from school and tend to have greater job instability than children raised in two-parent families, they may very easily become poor before they set up their own households. Especially noteworthy in this regard is Sarah McLanahan's finding that black children from single-parent families have a 70 percent greater tendency to drop out of school than children raised in two-parent families.[17] When the daughters of these single-parent families subsequently established their own female-headed homes, Bane would merely count them as part of the reshuffled poor, as women who are prone to become indigent under any circumstances. But in reality, their poverty has been caused, rather than reshuffled, by the breakdown of the traditional family. Unfortunately, Bane has failed to measure, let alone account for, the devastating impact of single-parent homes on the psychological and economic well-being of children. Because this impact cannot be dismissed as a minor problem, the above development certainly warrants considerable hand-wringing. For the next decade or two, the signals are mixed as to whether this percentage will increase or decrease. While the breakup of the family appears to be stabilizing, albeit at a rather dangerously high level, it will continue to be a major cause of poverty. This will be the case especially if the intergenerational transfer of poverty from mothers in broken families to their children continues to perpetuate itself.

WHAT IS CAUSING THE RISE OF THE SINGLE-PARENT FAMILY?

Given the importance of family breakups as a major cause of poverty, it is important to ask what we can do to reverse the present pattern of family decay. To achieve that goal, it is essential to know why poor families have become so unstable over the last thirty years. As will be argued in more detail in later chapters, the breakup of indigent families may reflect changing cultural patterns in society. But this conclusion is controversial to say the least. Presently, there is no consensus among poverty analysts as to what factors are responsible for the decline of the two-parent family. Most explanations of the breakup of poor families tend to divide along two different dimensions. First, there is disagreement as to whether the breakup of the family among the poor reflects a larger pattern of change in society as a whole, or whether it is a dilemma specific to the poor. Second, there are intense disagreements as to whether spouses are leaving the family nest primarily for economic or for cultural reasons.

The Impact of General Trends

The argument that the breakdown of indigent families is simply a reflection of larger societal trends is based on the simple fact that all families, poor and non-poor alike, are in disrepair. As will be explained shortly, the weakening of traditional controls and values may explain the increasingly fragile nature of family ties in American society. To support this view, Barbara Ehrenreich has pointed out that in the 1950s and 1960s there was a general revolt by males against traditional family values.[18] She argues that as part of the sexual revolution and a more general concern for self-fulfillment and consumerism in the post-Vietnam period, many men elected to pursue a life-style that rejected family ties. As part of the counterculture movement, many men chose to adopt a self-centered and promiscuous life-style that spared them traditional family responsibilities. As male commitment to the family waned, it was inevitable that both the divorce rate and the number of single-parent families would increase dramatically.

Christopher Jencks has partially modified this view by arguing that changing attitudes among political elites toward sex, divorce, and parenthood have also led to the decline of two-parent families. As opinion makers began to view "moral constraints on premarital sex, premarital childbearing and divorce as inappropriate and unnecessary limitations on individual freedom, the state ceased to stigmatize such behavior."[19] As a result, public institutions such as the schools began to accept unwed mothers, and state legislatures passed no-fault divorce laws. As society indicated its indifference to traditional family obligations, it was perhaps inevitable that family ties would weaken. Since the poor have not been immune to the changes that occurred in the post-Vietnam period, it should not surprise us that so many low income families also have chosen to dissolve their family bonds.

Many neoclassical economists, however, sharply disagree with such cultural arguments. Operating from an exchange perspective, economists like

Gary Becker maintain that purely economic factors—such as the increasing tendency of women to enter the labor market—are the primary reason for the decline of the traditional family.[20] As women acquire an independent source of income, divorce becomes more economically feasible.

However, demographers like Richard Easterlin, who also uses an exchange framework, downplay the above trends and claim that the changing economic fortunes of men, rather than women, explain the breakup of the family.[21] Easterlin, who believes that family fortunes mirror changes in the economy, argues that in periods of economic depression males are less likely to establish two-parent families or to have children. When the offspring of these marriages reach maturity, as was the case in the 1950s, the demand for workers often exceeds the available labor supply because of the previously low birth rate. Under these favorable conditions, adult males marry early, have many children, and maintain strong family ties. However, when their children are ready to marry, as occurred in the early 1970s, population and economic conditions are reversed. Because of the previously high birth rate, it is harder for men to find work that will enable them to support their families in the same manner that their parents did. In light of these conditions, many men choose to postpone marriage, abstain from having children, or divorce their wives if they do get married.

While both Becker and Easterlin's arguments are clearly and elegantly executed, their explanations for the breakup of low-income families are certainly debatable. Because many low-income women are poorly educated and do not actively look for work, their opportunity costs for divorcing their husbands have probably not changed much over the past few decades. Similarly, since the breakup of the poor black family began in the early 1960s when economic conditions were still relatively robust, Easterlin's demographic explanation may be only part of the reason for the fragmentation of the low-income family.

Problems Unique to the Poor

Because there are problems with the above arguments, many poverty researchers believe that the high incidence of broken families among indigents is somehow rooted in the experience of poverty. But underlying this consensus are sharp disagreements about the social forces that have made indigent families so vulnerable. Most analysts tend to advocate one of four explanations, two based on control and two on exchange theories, to account for the fragmentation of the family among indigents.

The Legacy of the Past. For instance, in the 1960s, Moynihan used a control perspective to argue that the legacy of slavery, emancipation, and the mass migrations of blacks from the South to the North were the primary reasons behind the decline of the black family. In his view, the cumulative effect of these historical trends undermined the social and cultural discipline of the black community, thus weakening the stability of the two-parent family. Moynihan's insisted that the fragile nature of the black family had its origins in the antebellum period.[22] On plantations, most slave unions were not accorded the legal status of marriage as the slave owner, rather than the father, had primary responsibility for the care and maintenance of the slave woman and her children. Since males had limited power over the fate of their families, and families could easily be broken up by their master, black women developed a tradition of self-reliance that minimized the importance of marriage. Under these trying conditions, the black community developed a tolerance for out-of-wedlock births that has been carried on to the present. The trauma of emancipation and the black migration from south to north further weakened family ties and led to the proliferation of single-parent homes in the black community.

This latter theme has been developed in detail by scholars like Charles Johnson, who maintains that it was more the postemancipation period than slavery that fostered a tradition of illegitimacy among blacks.[23] Johnson argued that when blacks were freed from the constraints of slavery, they had to make a living as either tenant farmers or sharecroppers on white-owned land. In this protocapitalist environment, blacks saw children as a real asset because they could help the family harvest its crops. If children became pregnant out of wedlock, they were not ostracized by their parents. On the contrary, the parents viewed the additional children as potential laborers who would augment the family income. Illegitimate children, unlike the situation today, often worked to the economic benefit of the larger family unit during the postemancipation period. When blacks subsequently migrated north, they often carried these attitudes to the very different environment of the urban ghetto. Unfortunately, practices that had served some functional purpose in the rural South were often a detriment in the cities of the industrial North.

As plausible as these explanations may seem, they have not gone unchallenged. On the basis of new research, a variety of scholars have found that the breakdown of the black family has its origins in the present rather than the past. For instance, in his massive study of the black family from 1750 to 1925, Herbert Gutman noted that over 70 percent of all slave women were part of conventional two-parent households.[24] Anticipating Carol Stack's findings about more recent times, Gutman discovered that the remaining unmarried slave women tended to rely on extensive kinship ties to help them through rough times. Gutman also rejected the argument that emancipation and the northward migration of blacks caused the breakdown of black families. He noted that between 1855 and 1880, 70 to 90 percent of black households were headed by males, and that at least 70 percent of these households were conventional two-parent families. Thirty years later, a similar pattern of family life emerged in the urban ghettos of the north. In 1925, for instance, 85 percent of black families in Harlem were intact families, less than 15 percent were headed by single parents, and black teenagers raising their children alone were almost nonexistent.

By the 1960s, however, the above pattern began to change as the number of black single-parent families rose to roughly 22 percent in 1960, jumped to just under 29 percent in 1970 and leveled off in the 1990s at around 40 to 42 percent of all black families. Judging from these figures, the breakdown of the black family appears to be a post-World War II phenomenon. Contrary to Moynihan and the wisdom of thirty years ago, most scholars today argue that events since the late 1960s and early 1970s rather than the legacy of the past are responsible for the fragile nature of the black family.

The Role of Government. In light of the above findings, Charles Murray stirred up considerable controversy by arguing that the growth of the welfare state was the primary reason why families in low-income areas were breaking apart.[25] Working from an exchange framework, Murray maintained that welfare payments have altered the financial incentives for men and women to enter into marriage. If the earnings of men are minimal, the lure of welfare benefits may encourage women to establish their own households. Whenever women acquire an independent source of income, whether wages or welfare, the opportunity cost of divorcing their husbands declines dramatically. Murray likewise suggested that a generous welfare system may also provide incentives for young teenagers to have children out of wedlock.

In support of his argument, Murray points out that the substantial increase in welfare payments in the early 1970s parallels the accelerated dissolution of family ties in the same period. He also cites data from the much publicized Seattle-Denver Income Maintenance Experiment, which showed that the negative income tax transfer program increased divorce rates by more than 50 percent among targeted families. Furthermore, reports from self-help projects suggest that welfare payments may disrupt the creation of two-parent families. In Project Redirection, a program that tries to prevent additional births among unmarried teenagers in four cities, there is evidence that the availability of welfare is a crucial part of the teen pregnancy problem. This study observed that "Many teenagers were beginning to view getting their own welfare grants as the next stage in their careers. It became apparent that some participants' requests for separate grants and independent households were too often a sign of manipulation by boyfriends, in whose interests it was to have a girlfriend on welfare with an apartment of her own."[26]

However, a variety of other studies have raised serious questions as to whether the impact of welfare programs on family structure is all that significant. For instance, the relationship between variations in state welfare levels and the makeup of the family is mixed. As is well known, the benefit levels for programs like AFDC differ significantly for states in the North compared to the South. If welfare played a major role in breaking up families, there should be more out-of-wedlock births and single-parent families in high-benefit states. The evidence from a variety of studies on marital disruption is inconclusive. In some cases, states with the lowest benefits have the highest proportion of children in female-headed families. But the available data also indicate that welfare benefits have more impact on living arrangements and rates of remarriage than on divorce and illegitimacy, partly confirming Murray's contentions about the impact of welfare. For instance, Bane and Ellwood estimated that in 1975 a $100 increase in AFDC benefits would have led to a 10 percent increase in the number of divorced or separated mothers, as well as a further 25 to 30 percent increase in the formation of independent households.[27]

However, Murray's claim that the rapid increase in welfare payments in the early 1970s was responsible for the deterioration in the structure of the family appears to be only partly true. While benefit levels did substantially rise at that time, welfare benefits did not keep pace with inflation in the latter part of the decade. Between 1975 to 1985 the real value of the maximum welfare payments in the median state actually dropped 33 percent. As the benefit levels of transfer payments alternately expanded and then contracted, the breakup of families continued to increase.

While the relationship between the expansion of welfare programs and the breakup of the family is uneven, it would be wrong to conclude that the impact of government programs has been completely benign. In what is perhaps the most careful analysis of the available data, Sara McLanahan and Irwin Garfinkel estimate that as much as 30 percent of the growth of single-parent families between 1955 and 1975 was due to the expansion of the government's entitlement programs.[28] Since the children of these families in turn are more likely than most to live in female-headed households, the impact of transfer programs may be larger over the long run. While Murray has perhaps overstated the consequences of transfer programs on the structure of the family, the above figures nonetheless indicate that government programs have had an impact on the structure of family relationships in the 1960s and early 1970s. Today, with AFDC payments lagging behind inflation, and the recent decision of Congress to mandate that all states provide assistance to families with an unemployed parent (the AFDC-UP program), the impact of welfare programs on the family is probably minimal at best.

The Mixed Impact of the Economy. Because of the problems with Charles Murray's analysis, many liberals have developed a variety of economic or exchange arguments to explain the instability of family life in the ghetto. They insist that the dire state of the economy is the main reason for the breakup of the poor black family. For example, in the 1960s Elliot Liebow argued in his widely read book, *Tally's Corner*, that when men could not find jobs to adequately support their spouses, they became promiscuous and manipulated women to achieve a sense of self-esteem.[29] Liebow insisted that when men were economic failures, they would try to compensate for their deficiencies by becoming "macho" and sexually active. Dismissing all notions that the subjects of his study were acting out the values of a destructive culture of poverty, Liebow insisted that ghetto men were basically insecure individuals trying to obtain social status in a period of economic hardship. Unfortunately, the consequence of their behavior led to the breakup of traditional family ties.

An alternative version of the economic argument that has recently gained wide popularity has been developed by William Julius Wilson, who argues that it is women rather than men who elect not to get married when unemployment rates in the ghetto are high.[30] He insists that the black family is breaking up because the number of black men with well-paying jobs, or what Wilson labels the "marriageable pool," has declined sharply for every age group of black men over the last thirty years. As women find fewer desirable men for partners, they either become divorced or elect to stay single without necessarily cutting back on their sexual activity, resulting in the rise of single-parent families.

In spite of the current popularity of Wilson's thesis, the evidence in support of it is mixed. Using PSID data from Michigan, Saul Hoffman and John Holmes found that when husbands experience unemployment, there is a greater chance of marital disruption.[31] However, Alan Cohen as well as Heather Ross and Isabel Sawhill have found that unemployment and single-parent families are related, but only among whites.[32]

Similarly, if Wilson is correct that women are not getting married because of the dire economic prospects of men, he needs to explain why the historical shift in the marital behavior of low-income blacks occurred in the relatively affluent decade of the 1960s. The work patterns of black males between the ages of twenty-two and forty-four do not fully support his contention that the lack of "marriageable men" caused the breakup of so many poor black families. In the 1950s as well as the 1960s, while the ratio of marriageable men to women did not change to any significant degree, the black family began to break apart. Since there were roughly 70 employed black men for every 100 black women during both these decades, Wilson's thesis seems incapable of explaining why the problem of the black family became so much more acute during the 1960s. After the 1970s, the ratio of employed men to women did begin to decline but in a moderate rather than precipitous fashion.

Wilson's exchange argument likewise provides little guidance to account for the strengths of minority families in previous periods of financial hardship. Most scholars today agree that the breakup of the black family is a recent phenomenon that paralleled the rise of the civil rights movement in the 1960s. But if that is the case, we need to know why the black family was relatively stable during the antebellum days of slavery, why it endured the hardships of the Great Depression, and why it did not fall apart during the days of segregation. Wilson spends very little time talking about the period from the end of the Civil War to the beginning of the civil rights movement in the 1960s, a period when black males were excluded from most well-paying jobs and could not have been considered attractive mates based solely on their earning power. At the height of the Great Depression, the income of the average black was considerably lower than that earned by blacks today. Contrary to the predictions of Wilson, the black family was relatively stable during this period of time. The crucial point is that the acceleration in the breakup of the black family has occurred since the Great Depression and the dismantling of Jim Crow laws rather than before it.

In addition, Wilson's portrayal of black men is open to debate. In arguing that economic conditions have undercut the attractiveness of black males as marriage partners, Wilson has implicitly assumed that all unemployment among black men is involuntary. But as discussed in chapter 9, alternative studies indicate that some of the joblessness among black men could better be described as nonemployment rather than forced unemployment. Instead of being passive victims of society, many economically deprived black men may have voluntarily dropped out of the job market. The causal relationship between employment and broken families may be just the opposite of what Wilson has suggested. Mark Testa has recently found that when young black men want to marry the mother of their children, they are more likely to look for and find a job, rather than the reverse situation being the case.[33]

A final exchange argument that relies on both rational self-interest and peer pressure is found in Carol Stack's study of kin groups. Stack argues that with high rates of unemployment and a welfare system that rewards fatherless households, single mothers may rationally conclude that the kin group offers her family a much needed safety net. But, ironically, once a single mother becomes involved with a kin group, the kin group may hamper the ability of the single mother to remarry and work her way out of poverty. As soon as the kin group provides assistance to single mothers, it expects the mother in turn to share her resources, such as welfare payments, with her relatives. If the mother seeks to get married, the kin group knows it would lose an important source of emotional and financial support for its network. The kin group consequently applies subtle pressure to encourage women to limit their activities to the domestic network of friends and relatives, arguing that uneducated black men are likely to be unsuccessful breadwinners and thus poor prospects for marriage. In the short run, women can rationally calculate that they will be financially more secure if they stay in their networks of friends and relatives and shun the institution of marriage.

Stack is thus suggesting that the dynamics of modern-day ghetto life have created a conflict between the two sides of the black family which Gutman suggested coexisted and complemented each other in the past—marital ties and loyalty to an extended kin group. While the kin network complemented the nuclear two-parent family by helping out single slave mothers in the ante-bellum period, the two presently appear as conflicting alternatives for low-income blacks. As long as limited economic opportunities and the present welfare system continue, many of the poor may continue to opt for kinship ties over the bonds of marriage. If Stack's observations are correct, she has partially overturned Moynihan's view of the black female family as being disorganized, but substantiated his larger argument that single-parent families are caught in a "tangle of pathology" that adversely affects their financial well-being.

The Breakdown of Cultural and Social Controls. Finally, a fourth way analysts have accounted for the fragile nature of indigent families is by focusing on the breakdown of social controls in the ghetto. Increasingly, neither the social structure nor the cultural values of the inner city seem able to regulate the self-destructive behavior of the poor. This is especially true of the 37 percent of black mothers who live alone in single-parent families. Dennis Hogan found that in this type of family, teenage daughters were likely to become pregnant because they received limited parental supervision.[34] In contrast, Hogan discovered that when a single parent shared her parental duties with a grandmother or other relatives, teen pregnancy was comparable to the lower rates found in two-parent homes. Evidently, a grandmother or other relative can often take the place of an absent father and help a single mother control the behavior of her teenage daughters. Without assistance, single mothers seem to have trouble preventing their sons and daughters from having children out of wedlock.

The problem is further compounded when the breakdown of cultural values in the neighborhood also reinforces the lack of parental supervision. Both Dennis Hogan and Leon Dash have recently noted that in poor areas, unlike in middle-class neighborhoods, no real stigma is attached to having an illegitimate child.[35] Dash also maintains that very few children born out of wedlock are born because of inadequate sex education or lack of contraceptives. In the cultural milieu of many poor black teenagers, having a child is a sign of status. While many parents of poor teenage girls may prefer that their children not become pregnant, they may also live in a community where illegitimacy is tolerated. Or as Kenneth Clark has stated: "In the ghetto, the meaning of the illegitimate child is not ultimate disgrace. There is not the demand for abortion or for surrender of the child that one finds in more privileged communities. In the middle class the disgrace of illegitimacy is tied to personal and family aspirations. In lower class families the girl loses only some of her already limited options by having an illegitimate child."[36]

As the above discussion indicates, a variety of explanations can account for the fragile nature of the family among the poor, especially among black women. While the loosening of traditional values may be the primary cause for the breakup of the indigent family, factors unique to the inner city may have exacerbated the problem. For example, the shift in cultural values that Jencks and Ehrenreich have chronicled in the larger society has undoubtedly trickled down to the ghetto. When civic elites at the top of the social pyramid questioned traditional family values, those at the bottom of the social ladder, who were less committed to those values to begin with, were even more likely to reject conventional family arrangements. But as the moral constraints that stigmatized people who lived outside the two-parent family eased, the financial incentives for women to form single-parent families also increased. The growth of AFDC payments in the 1960s as well as the support system of kin groups made it economically possible for women to strike out on their own. It was thus inevitable that more people would choose to establish single-parent homes as their moral obligations declined and their financial ability to survive as a single parent grew. Once the number of broken families reaches a certain critical mass, the very real danger exists that single-parent families will become self-perpetuating.

DEALING WITH THE PROBLEM

While many scholars have minimized the problems associated with the breakdown of the family, it is very clear that the weakening of family ties is a major cause of poverty. However, suggesting ways to reverse the breakup of the family always elicits tremendous controversy. As Barbara Dafoe Whitehead has perceptively noted, such discussions are often seen as attacks on struggling single mothers and their children.[37] Many people ask, "Why blame single mothers when they are doing the very best they can? After all, the decision to end a marriage or a relationship is wrenching, and few parents are indifferent to the painful burden this decision imposes on their children."[38] Even if we recognize and appreciate the problems facing individuals in families that are devoid of love, we cannot ignore the adverse consequences of marital breakups. As more and more parents are forced to raise their children alone, they become increasingly vulnerable to economic fluctuations in the economy. But even more importantly, they increasingly put their children at risk of becoming future victims of poverty. The social science data overwhelmingly indicate that broken families adversely affect the future well-being of children. Society needs to balance the desire of parents to pursue their individual happiness with the needs of their children for "stability, security and permanence in their family lives."[39] If we cannot achieve this balance, then the prospects of improving the educational performance of our students, reducing teenage crime, or adequately preparing the work force for the future—all problems that are intimately connected with the viability of the two-parent family—may be jeopardized.

In light of the magnitude of the problem, the question is what, if anything, can be done to rectify the situation. In most discussions of single-parent families, advocates tend to offer one of three different policy options. First, analysts who believe that the problems of the family are essentially economic often imply that there is no need for the government to develop a family policy. If the deterioration of the family is an epiphenomenon of adverse economic consequences, then the government should be concerned primarily with improving the performance of the economy. But as noted earlier, it is still an open question whether poor economic conditions are the primary reason for the fragmentation of the family.

A second option is for the government to make a serious attempt to reverse the growing fragmentation of the American family. Despite the best of intentions, many well-meaning government programs have had the unanticipated consequence of undermining rather than strengthening the role of the family in American life. In the last half century, we have witnessed a dramatic increase in both the role of the state and the rights of the individual. But both of these changes have occurred at the expense of the family, which today occupies a diminished role in society. On most occasions, the state had the laudable goal of assisting the family, but in the process it often ended up replacing it. For instance, government officials have increasingly taken over many of the functions once performed by parents. In establishing schools, the state rather than the family now has primary responsibility for educating children and, increasingly, socializing them into the mores of society. A variety of other public institutions, such as Social Security and Medicare, have also relieved children of the responsibility for caring for their parents and other relatives when they retire from the workplace. Still other government institutions, such as mental institutions, social welfare agencies, and the juvenile court system, have supplanted the family in controlling family members who are hard to handle.

Besides displacing the role of the family, the state has also increasingly intervened in the family to promote the rights of individuals. These actions include a wide range of policies such as AFDC payments for pregnant teenagers, sex education in the schools, family planning and abortion counseling for children, and an active government policy to remove abused children from their parents. While most of these programs are designed to solve one social problem or another, they have nonetheless curtailed the power of the family to regulate its own members. In more cases than not, the biggest problem facing children is child neglect rather than child abuse. Too many parents are either unconcerned or indifferent about whether their children learn anything in school or engage in worthwhile activities. Even when parents do try to be conscientious and advise their children or punish them if they misbehave, they now have to worry about government officials second-guessing their actions. The understandable desire of many state agencies to protect the rights of children has often had the unanticipated consequence of superimposing legal relationships on the affective ties of parents and children. But in solving one problem, that of abuse, the state may have exacerbated another, that is, the growing inability of many parents to monitor and discipline their own children. It may not be too far-fetched to imagine that one day government officials will start writing and enforcing legal contracts between children and their parents. The affective ties between parents and children may thus give way to legal relationships that sharply delimit the powers of parents. The unfortunate result is that as individual rights and state power have expanded over time, the family has contracted in importance as a major institution. Besides the cultural and economic forces cited earlier, the altruistic efforts of government officials to help the family may also be contributing indirectly to its demise.

As a first step in developing an effective family policy, the government must try to modify the above trends so that the family's role is enhanced rather than totally eclipsed. Instead of completely taking over the educational and socialization role that parents once performed, the government should try to spend more time sharing this responsibility with parents. Coleman and others have found that when parents are highly concerned about the education of their children, student performance usually improves.

As a second step, public officials also need to reexamine the values they have tried to promote by intervening in traditional family matters. Besides advising young girls on their rights to contraceptives or abortions, public institutions need to encourage people to act more responsibly about sexual and family matters. If the breakdown of social controls is the primary reason for the fragmentation of the family, the state as well as families need to spend more time resocializing people into accepting responsibility for their children and spouses. When young men conceive children out of wedlock and then disavow any responsibility for them, they put their children and former girl friends at great financial risk. Unfortunately there are still too many institutions, such as public schools, that have not taken their socialization responsibilities seriously enough to minimize such disruptive behavior. Given the magnitude of the problem, such a laissez-faire attitude among government officials is a luxury we can no longer afford. In light of the fact that only around 14 percent of black mothers and 43 percent of white mothers receive any kind of financial help from the men who fathered their children, the state additionally needs to become much more aggressive in demanding that fathers recognize their obligations to financially support their offsprings.[40] With the 1988 Family Support Act, Congress finally began to address this problem by authorizing government officials to withhold payment from the wages of absent parents.

Finally, a third policy many liberals seem resigned to advocating involves treating the consequences rather than the causes of single-parent families. In light of the difficulties involved in the Humpty-Dumpty process of trying to put the family back together, perhaps the best that society can do is to make sure that single-parent families are adequately cared for. On the one hand, some commentators insist that the state should try to maximize the earning power of single women through programs like subsidized day care and higher minimum wages. Yet other analysts, who are pessimistic that poorly educated single women will ever be able to earn their way out of poverty, insist that more generous transfer programs are the solution to the financial needs of single-parent families. But there may be distinct limits to the effectiveness of such programs. As soon as the government makes entitlement programs more generous, it simultaneously makes it that much harder for officials to keep two-parent families intact. Garfinkel and McLanahan have called this trade-off the new American dilemma. In trying to assist families financially, the government may inadvertently help break them up. Despite the best of intentions to minimize the hardships of poverty, the government must be careful that its solutions do not become part of the problem.

PART THREE

Explaining Poverty: Motivational Explanations Accounting for the Growth of the Underclass

As the preceding chapters have shown, family ties, entrepreneurial talents as well as educational skills all play a significant role in determining whether people become trapped in poverty or achieve financial success. However, many analysts maintain that people's attitudes are equally important factors in determining the size of the poverty population in this country. In many cases the poor may be not so much unprepared as unmotivated to work their way out of poverty.

The third part of this book looks at the role motivation plays in enabling people to escape poverty. Of course, the distinction between skills, attitudes, and opportunities is essentially an artificial one. The attitudes of people will often determine what skills they elect to acquire in the first place. Also, cultural beliefs appear to influence how people respond to the presence of opportunities and how resourceful they are in overcoming obstacles to upward mobility. The stark contrast between the creativity of some ethnic groups that have successfully escaped poverty and the self-destructive behavior of the underclass may thus reflect very different belief systems. When people are properly motivated, they tend to be both highly trained as well as highly successful in identifying and exploiting opportunities for economic advancement.

If motivation is important in explaining why some people escape poverty while others do not, analysts are sharply divided as to whether it is economic incentives or cultural values that are the prime motivators of the poor. It is still an unresolved question as to whether indigents are pulled from the front by the possibility of economic gain or pushed from behind by their values.

We need to know if it is the presence of economic disincentives or the breakdown of traditional social values that has led to the rise of an underclass with its broken families and weak attachment to the labor force. Chapters 7 and 8 will examine these phenomena from a rational economic or exchange perspective, while chapter 9 will explore the importance of values—or more properly, the breakdown of values—in fostering the self-destructive behavior that characterizes the underclass.

SEVEN

Rational Economic Explanations: The Liberal Version

As the social behavior of the underclass deteriorated in the late 1960s, many analysts began to argue that attitude also influences whether people became poor or not. The self-serving behavior of many poor people, such as the neglect of their families or their indifferent work record, seems to indicate that a lack of motivation—rather than inadequate training or skills—is partly responsible for the country's inordinately high poverty rate. But liberals, who tend to view poverty from an exchange perspective, maintain that the behavior of the underclass is really nothing more than a rational response to limited economic opportunities. In contrast to conservatives who talk about the breakdown of values among the poor, they try to analyze the actions of the underclass in more traditional economic terms. The emergence of the underclass over the last several decades thus reflects the sluggish growth of the economy during the 1970s and 1980s. The reason why so many people have dropped out of the labor market is because they have become discouraged by the high unemployment rates in the country. If the economy revived and there were enough high-paying jobs, the underclass would quickly reenter the labor market and adopt more conventional forms of behavior.

Liberal exchange theorists also assume that tastes (which include what we would call values and beliefs) are basically the same for all individuals. They thus minimize the importance of focusing on the behavior of different ethnic groups, since they believe that all people behave like rational economic actors. The main question for policy analysts is to figure out how individuals will respond to changes in the costs and benefits of alternative courses of action. In an ideal world we could hope that the incentives of the marketplace would induce people to behave in a socially optimal fashion. But given the imperfections of our labor markets, those hopes are often frustrated. As a consequence, the spotty work record of the poor and their tendency to avoid their family responsibilities are the unfortunate but understandable responses of people to bleak economic circumstances. Rather than attacking the poor as pathological, exchange theorists believe that the behavior of the poor in general and the underclass in particular makes economic sense.

Poverty researchers as diverse as Richard Freeman, Sar Levitan, David Ellwood, and William Julius Wilson, among others, insist that indigents have a strong work ethic but are frustrated by the lack of high-paying job opportunities.[1] When the economy is healthy and there are plenty of jobs, the poor will naturally be enticed back into the labor market. Second, scholars like David Ellwood argue that many single mothers choose not to work because they feel a moral commitment to nurture their children in a family environment. Thus the conflict between the rational desire of the poor to work and their desire to be good parents explains why so many women are not active in the labor market.[2] Rather than suffering from a lack of values, many single mothers show an exemplary desire to maintain a decent home environment for their children.

While all of the above arguments are undoubtedly true under certain circumstances, they only partially explain the behavior of the underclass. To understand people's actions fully we need to distinguish between a major shift in their behavior as opposed to a short-term adjustment to harsh economic conditions. While fluctuations in the economy will affect people's employment practices, those cyclical shifts often obscure what is in fact a major secular change in the work habits of the poor. Even more importantly, we have to realize that changes in the work patterns of low-income individuals are part of a larger cultural shift in society as a whole.

THE POOR AND DECLINING PARTICIPATION RATES

The 1960s and 1970s were a period of growing ambivalence among the American public about the importance of work and traditional values. Given the social upheavals of the 1960s, the work patterns of the American people began to diverge and exhibit cross-cutting tendencies. With the rise of the women's movement and the stagnation of family income, an increasing number of women began to look for work outside the home. While the growth of feminism and new employment opportunities pulled more women into the work force, low family income simultaneously pushed them into the job market (see table 13.1). But as more women began to look for work, more men began to withdraw from the labor market. The 1960s witnessed the beginning of a long-term shift in the work patterns of American men as a whole. Moreover,

Figure 7.1
Nonparticipation Rates and Unemployment Rates for Males, Ages 25–54

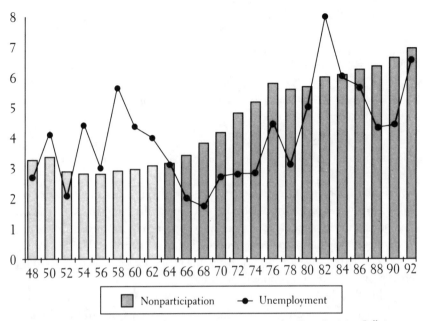

| ■ Nonparticipation | ●— Unemployment |

Sources: U.S. Department of Labor, Bureau of Labor Statistics, *Labor Force Statistics*, Bulletin 2340 (Washington, D.C.: U.S. Government Printing Office, 1989); and U.S. Department of Labor, *Employment and Earnings* (Washington, D.C.: U.S. Government Printing Office, 1991–1993).

this trend had no relationship to unemployment rates despite the conventional wisdom that high employment rates discourage people from looking for work in the first place. This point is illustrated in figure 7.1, which tracks the non-participation and employment rates of all men aged twenty-five to fifty-four. The nonparticipation rate is a key economic indicator that measures how many people in the economy have stopped looking for work, while the unemployment rate measures what percentages of those participating in the labor market have been able to actually find a job. As the following graph clearly indicates, in the middle of the 1960s there was a steady increase in the percentage of men who had decided not to seek work.

While a little over 2 percent of males aged 25–54 were not in the labor force in 1952, that figure had tripled to around 7 percent by 1992. In contrast to exchange arguments, the decision of these young and middle-aged men to drop out of the labor market appears to have no relationship to economic events. More and more men were electing not to seek work during the 1960s when, as the graph in figure 7.1 indicates, the unemployment rate for men

Table 7.1

Percentage of All Poor Families in the Labor Market

1959	1966	1970	1975	1980	1987	1990
61	54	48.4	48.5	50	47	41

Sources: U.S. Bureau of the Census, *Current Population Reports*, Series P-60, no. 54, "The Extent of Poverty in the United States, 1959–1966"; *Current Population Reports*, Series P-60, no. 106, "Characteristics of the Population below the Poverty Level: 1975"; *Current Population Reports*, Series P-60, no. 133, "Characteristics of the Population below the Poverty Level: 1980"; *Current Population Reports*, Series P-60, no. 163, "Poverty in the United States: 1987"; and March 1990 Current Population Survey tapes.

dropped to under 2 percent. Even when the economy became more robust and the number of jobs multiplied, more individuals chose to walk away from the labor market.

The same pattern also characterizes the poor, but unfortunately an even larger percentage of indigents has dropped out of the labor market. As table 7.1 indicates, the percentage of poor who appear to be interested in working has dropped roughly 30 percent over the last three decades. The biggest decline occurred in the early 1960s, when the economy was expanding and the unemployment rate was dropping rapidly.

Rather than being an isolated event, the growing propensity of the poor to abstain from participating in the labor market seems to reflect a general ambivalence about the work ethic in American society. While women were determined to be treated as equals with men and thus entered the labor market, the larger society became more equivocal about the virtues of work. As civic and political elites became more indifferent about work or family ties, subgroups like the underclass who had not been intensely committed to those values in the first place were likely to let go of those beliefs at a faster rate than the rest of society. The decline in the work record was thus more precipitous and more costly for poor families than for men in general. Similarly, when middle-class Americans dropped out of the labor market, the consequences were much more benign than when the poor adopted similar behavior. The accumulated wealth of middle America acted as a cushion, protecting those who no longer wished to work from dire consequences. But when such attitudes trickled down to the lower strata of society, the result was more acute, leading to serious impoverishment.

THE POOR AND DECLINING EMPLOYMENT RATES

The decline in the commitment of the poor to work their way out of poverty becomes even more obvious when we look at actual employment figures of

Table 7.2
The Changing Work Record of Poor Families

	1959	1967	1974	1978	1987	1988	1992
Worked full time, full year	31.4%	26.9%	22.1%	16.1%	14.6%	16.4%	18.4%
Unemployment rate	5.5	3.8	5.6	6.1	6.2	5.5	7.4

Sources: U.S. Bureau of the Census, *Current Population Reports*, Series P-60, no. 68, "Poverty in the United States, 1959 to 1968"; *Current Population Reports*, Series P-60, no. 102, "Characteristics of the Population below the Poverty Level: 1974"; *Current Population Reports*, Series P-60, no. 166, "Money, Income and Poverty Status in the United States, 1988"; *Current Population Reports*, Series P-60, no. 175, "Poverty in the United States, 1990"; *Current Population Reports*, Series P-60, no. 185, "Poverty in the United States, 1992"; and *Economic Report of the President* (Washington, D.C.: U.S. Government Printing Office, 1992, 1993).

indigents (the percentage of those who work) as opposed to their participation rates (the percentage of those looking for work). It is apparent from the employment record of poor families, who make up two-thirds of the indigent population, that there has been a dramatic 40 percent reduction in the number of poor who work full time (see table 7.2). In 1959 over 31 percent of poor families had a full-time worker, whereas the comparable figure for 1992 was a disappointing 18 percent, which is close to a 40 percent drop in the number of full-time workers. Most of the decline in the number working full time and full year occurred between 1959 and 1978. But once again, the tendency of the poor to work does not appear to be systematically related to fluctuations in the economy. The preceding data indicate that the poor had become less motivated to work even before the economy turned downward. In 1959, when the national unemployment rate was a relatively low 5.5 percent, over 31 percent of poor families had a member who worked full time. Contrary to the predictions of many economists, when the economy picked up in the 1960s and the unemployment rate dropped to a historical low rate of 3.8 percent, the number of poor working full time dropped to under 27 percent.

But perhaps the best test of the argument that a sluggish economy caused the poor to drop out of the labor market occurred during the 1980s. The surging economy and tight labor markets which were hoped to stimulate the poor to participate more actively in the labor market failed to result in higher employment rates among indigent families. After seven years of sustained economic growth, the unemployment rate in 1989 was roughly the same as that in 1959. But in spite of this dramatic improvement, the number of poor working full time was over 40 percent lower than during the Eisenhower years. The prosperity of the mid-1980s was a sweeping natural experiment that tested the hypothesis that employment rates and the work rates of the poor were connected, and it came up negative.

Richard Freeman has recently pointed out that at least on the local level, a rising economy did increase the employment rates of young black males.[3] Paul Osterman has echoed that finding, noting that the tighter labor market of the Boston area during the Reagan years enabled many indigents to work their way out of poverty.[4] In spite of these optimistic findings, the national data paint a very different picture. Cyclical shifts in the behavior of indigents in a few cities obscure what appears to be a major secular change in the work habits of the poor. When the U.S. economy enjoyed a prolonged period of prosperity in the late 1980s, the percentage of poor families with full-time workers remained at roughly half the level observed during the Johnson years. Any improvements in specific cities were not reflected in national statistics.

The above evidence suggests that cyclical changes in the economy are not the sole reason for the declining work effort of the poor. Census surveys which ask indigents why they are not working full time confirm this point. If exchange arguments were correct, we would expect that the vast majority of the poor would cite harsh economic conditions to account for their lack of work. When the poor have been asked this very question over the last thirty years, only 3 to 9 percent have cited the "inability to find a job" as a reason for their unemployment.[5] Even among people working part time, only 30 to 40 percent have mentioned the inability to find a job as the main reason for their part-time work.[6]

THE BAD-JOBS HYPOTHESIS: A BAD HYPOTHESIS

Despite the data cited above, many commentators insist that it is the lack of high-paying jobs rather than the availability of jobs per se that has caused the poor to drop out of the labor market. Despite the upturn in the 1980s, the economy has undergone a major restructuring in which the number of manufacturing jobs in most of our major urban centers has dramatically declined. As service jobs replace industrial positions, low-income individuals are increasingly finding that most available employment opportunities pay minimal wages at best. When times are hard and wages low, we should not be surprised that people's commitment to the work ethic will wane. If being employed is not lucrative enough to be worth their time, the poor as rational economic actors may choose to cut back on their work effort.

While there may be some merit to this argument, low wages do not appear to be the principal reason why the poor increasingly elect not to work at all. Over the last thirty years, the tendency of the poor to cease working has not necessarily paralleled the slowdown of wage growth in the American economy. The pattern of indigents dropping out of the labor market began years before the so-called problem of bad jobs, and bad wages. The slowdown in wage growth in this country primarily occurred at the end of the 1970s or early 1980s (see table 12.2). But as table 7.2 illustrates, the percentage of poor families with full-time workers had declined by close to 30 percent from 1959 to 1974. Similarly, by 1990 an unskilled worker's real wages were higher than they were in 1959, but the level of employment among poor families was significantly lower.[7]

Also, as Frank Levy has pointed out, "the 'good jobs–bad jobs' debate is more a story about men (in particular, young, less educated men) than women."[8] While the wages of most men stagnated, the wages of women, including those with only a high school degree, showed modest growth in the late 1970s and 1980s. Between 1973 and 1986 women aged 25–34 with only a high school degree saw their earnings increase by 4 percent while those aged 35–44 experienced a 13 percent increase.[9] In spite of these income gains, the number of poor women in single-parent families who chose to work full time declined by roughly 50 percent over the last thirty years (see table 7.3).

In fact, if the phenomenon of bad jobs is analyzed from a purely economic viewpoint, it is possible to argue that a slowdown in wage growth might produce more rather than less work effort by the poor. As students who have taken an elementary course in economics quickly learn, declining wages have two opposing effects, one which increases work effort and the other which decreases it. As wages drop, workers need to work more to maintain their income, but at the same time they realize that their labor has become less profitable. Falling income thus provides incentives for individuals to work additional hours to maintain their income, while low hourly wages reduce the payoff from work. Economists call the first the "income effect" and the second the "substitution effect." Conversely, if wages rise, the two effects work in the opposite direction. Because employees now earn more income, they have less incentive to work even though their payoff from their work has become more lucrative. From a purely exchange point of view, it is hard to predict beforehand how people will respond to a decline in income.

What is remarkable about employment practices in this country is that the income effect seems to have dominated the behavior of middle- and working-class women while the substitution effect appears to have influenced the work patterns of the poor.[10] As family income began to stagnate in the United States, many women who had previously elected to stay home began actively to look for work in order to supplement their husbands' earnings. The middle and working classes and the poor had thus reacted very differently to the slowdown of wage growth in the 1970s. As former housewives entered the labor market and put in long hours to compensate for sluggish growth in their husbands' earnings, many of the poor elected to do less. While it is possible to argue that the reaction of indigents was a rational if undesirable response to events, the behavior of middle- and working-class wives suggests the opposite. Even among the poor, the tendency to cease working altogether was not shared by all ethnic groups. As we will see shortly, in Chicago, Mexican immigrants who have been the most willing to take the lowest-paying jobs also have the highest rate of employment. When ethnic groups like Mexicans are determined to get ahead, they often use low-paying jobs as a stepping-stone to acquiring better jobs later on.

The above data thus indicate that individuals are not tabula rasa who automatically respond in the same way to economic incentives. If people have internalized norms that stress hard work or brought comparable values from their homeland, they may elect to work harder when their income stagnates or declines. But if those values decline over time, then the substitution effect may overwhelm the income effect. How people react to adversity appears to be shaped as much by their cultural values as by the presence or absence of economic costs. While some economists maintain that the slowdown in wage growth is a major deterrent to work, many of the non-poor have viewed it as a stimulus to work even harder.

SINGLE-PARENT FAMILIES AND DECLINING WORK

Regardless of the state of the economy, some economists insist that some sectors of the poor, such as single parents, should not be expected to work. For instance, David Ellwood has argued that many low-income women are not in the labor market for the simple reason that they want to care for their children. Ellwood insists that single mothers face a difficult trade-off of being either the provider or the nurturer in the family.[11] As women increasingly make up a larger percentage of the poor, the number of indigents who work may decline because there are more single women staying home to raise their children. Instead of being indifferent to the work ethic, low-income mothers may choose to drop out of the labor market because of their commitment to family values.

Although Ellwood makes a persuasive case, he provides no clues as to why fewer single parents are less likely to work today compared to twenty years ago. While the problem of deciding whether to nurture or to provide

Table 7.3
Poor Single-Parent Families
(Excludes Those over Age Sixty-Five, Disabled, or
in School)

	1968	1990
Worked full time, full year	19.0%	10.0%
Worked part time, full year	8.6	5.7
Did not work	32.5	48.6

Source: U.S. Bureau of the Census, March 1990 Current Population Survey tape.

for their children has always been a painful dilemma confronting women, their response to this conundrum has changed over time. As table 7.3 indicates, the work patterns of single-parent families, excluding those who are over age sixty-five, disabled, or in school, reveal that the number of poor single parents working full time, full year, has declined from 19 percent to 10 percent over the last thirty years, which is close to a 50 percent reduction in their work effort.

Even more disturbing is the number of single-parent women who did not work at all increased by roughly 50 percent over the same period, from roughly 33 percent to close to 49 percent. While it is conceivable that more low-income women are staying home to care for their children, it is equally plausible that more and more single-parent families, like the poor in general, are simply less motivated to work than ever before.

DECLINING WORK EFFORT AND THE LACK OF AFFORDABLE CHILD CARE

Finally, many commentators argue that low-income women are not entering the labor market because of the lack of affordable child care. However eager women may be to become productive working members of society, their ability to hold down full-time jobs will be affected by their prospects of obtaining affordable child care. Since most single-parent women have limited education and earn at best minimal wages, they are often priced out of the work force by the high cost of hiring someone to take care of their children. It is irrational for people to work full time if the cost of child care consumes most of their wages. Until the government provides more affordable day-care facilities, the prospects for a dramatic improvement in the work record of indigent women are likely to be slim indeed.

To support this argument, some surveys have found that over 25 percent of nonworking mothers say they stopped working because they could not find adequate, affordable child care. Other researchers have found that up to 60 percent of nonworking mothers state that they would choose to go to work if their employer or the government would guarantee them affordable as well as acceptable child care.[12] We also find that many low-income mothers who do work rely heavily on organized forms of child care. Presently 16 percent of poor children, 28 percent of black children, and 30 percent of all children in single-parent homes are enrolled in day care centers or nursery schools.[13] Most other working mothers in the labor force rely on either friends or relatives to take care of their children.

In spite of these numbers, it is debatable whether the lack of affordable child care is that serious an obstacle. Recent efforts by state governments to require single parents on welfare to work bear out this prediction. When states started requiring women to enter work programs, they were often surprised to find that child care was not a major obstacle preventing women from taking a job. In WIN, a nationwide work-incentive program for single mothers, poor parents placed only 8 percent of their children under 12 in organized child-care centers. Two-thirds of their children were taken care of by informal arrangements with either friends, relatives, or paid sitters.[14] While many women in workfare programs have trouble participating because of child-care problems, only about one in seven welfare mothers has cited the lack of child care as a principal reason for not taking a job. In Massachusetts, which has an elaborate employment and training program, large sums of money were set aside for child-care programs so that single mothers could work. However, to the amazement of the state, only 14 percent of the participants sought child care from the program.[15] Similarly in California, only 10 percent of those who were considered employable took advantage of state-funded day care.[16] While some welfare mothers mention child care as a problem in surveys, they do not seem to find it an insurmountable obstacle when they actually do have to work. But it is possible that as state programs for child care become better established, indigent women might be more inclined to take advantage of such subsidized facilities.

But perhaps the most serious drawback with the argument that the lack of affordable child care keeps women out of the labor market is its failure to explain why fewer indigent women are working today than in the past. If child care is that crucial an issue, we would expect work rates for poor women to be roughly the same from one decade to the next. But as we saw in table 7.3, the percentage of poor women working full time has declined by roughly 50 percent from 1968 to 1990. That decline has occurred despite the fact that poor women, who have fewer children than they did twenty years ago, also have more opportunities to enroll their children in government-subsidized day care. In a major reversal of their past practices, many states, such as Massachusetts and California, currently earmark funds for child care programs for low-income women. But as public officials have dramatically increased the resources available to indigent single women to care for their children, their hopes that their work record would improve has not materialized. On the contrary, as government entities have begun to set aside more resources to fund child care for indigent women, indigent participation in the labor market has dropped contrary to the predictions of the advocates for more child care. Too many advocates of child care have failed to see that the spotty work record of many poor women may reflect more a lack of motivation than a lack of affordable child-care facilities.

Given the large difference in the work habits of the poor and non-poor, it is hard to believe that the differing availability of child care for the two populations accounts for any significant part of the difference in their work records. Lawrence Mead has recently estimated that if the government dramatically increased its spending on child care, there might be a 10 percent increase at most in the share of poor women either working or seeking work, which would still leave them far short of the rates for the population as a whole.[17] While finding someone to take care of their children at an affordable price is undoubtedly a problem for indigent women, it does not appear to be an insurmountable one. Because providing more child care is not quite the panacea its supporters make it out to be, it does not necessarily mean that the state should cut back on its child-care facilities for the poor. On the contrary, if we want indigent women to one day work their way out of poverty, the government should actively encourage as well as subsidize single parents to participate in the labor market. We just need to be careful not to exaggerate the payoff from investing more funds in additional day-care facilities.

THE POOR AND THE DECLINING INCIDENCE OF WORK VIS-À-VIS THE NON-POOR

In light of the above discussion, it is instructive to compare the work record of the poor with the non-poor. To make sure that we are analyzing comparable individuals, we looked at the work records of only those respondents whom we would expect to work: that is, individuals who are neither disabled, over sixty-five, nor in school. As table 7.4 makes clear, both poor single-parent families as well as all other poor families work considerably less than their non-poor counterparts. Although only 20 percent of poor families (excluding

Table 7.4
The Work Record: Percentage Comparisons between the
Poor and Non-Poor Whom We Expect to Work
(Excludes Those Who Are Disabled, over Age Sixty-Five, or in School)

	Single-Parent Families		All Other Families	
	Poor	*Non-Poor*	*Poor*	*Non-Poor*
Worked full time, full year	10.0	65.2	20.1	74.4
Worked full time, part year	21.1	17.2	26.1	14.5
Worked part time, full year	5.7	5.0	8.1	3.4
Worked part time, part year	14.5	6.1	16.8	3.3
Total	51.3	93.5	71.1	95.6
Did not work	48.6	6.5	28.8	4.5

Source: U.S. Bureau of the Census, March 1991 Current Population Survey tape. All other families include married couples with or without children and all single people without children.

single parents) who are capable of working work full time, full year, the figure rises to almost 75 percent for non-poor families. We find a similar pattern of work activities among single parents. While slightly over 10 percent of poor single parents who are capable of working work full time, over 65 percent of non-poor single-parent families have a full-time job. Household heads and their spouses in non-poor families are more than three times as likely as their poor counterparts to hold full-time jobs, while among single-parent families the non-poor are six times more likely to work full time than their indigent counterparts.

The above data certainly indicate that one reason why the poor are so much worse off than the rest of society is that they are less inclined to be employed. As mentioned in chapter 2, ever since the 1960s the percentage of people working their way out of poverty (or escaping what is known as pre-transfer poverty) has declined. The dramatic drop in the percentage of poor people who work is undoubtedly one of the reasons why the war on poverty has failed. Unless this trend is reversed and the poor elect to become more involved in the labor market, the prospects of ever winning the war against poverty are slim indeed.

However, several ethnographic studies have recently suggested that there is a good deal of work effort among the poor, but that it occurs in the untaxed rather than in the taxed economy. Because such behavior is not socially sanctioned, it is not picked up in the traditional surveys of human behavior. While there may be an element of truth to this argument, it is hard to tell how extensive such underground work activity may be. Since the 1960s the government has progressively reduced the tax burden of the working poor.

During the Nixon administration Congress passed the Earned Income Tax credit, and in 1986 the legislature altered the personal exemptions and standard deductions of the IRS code so that the poor were excused from all federal income tax liabilities and part of their payroll tax responsibilities. In light of the above changes in the tax forms, it is possible that the poor are probably less likely to work in the underground economy today than they were thirty years ago. Likewise, if the tax code provides incentives for indigents to conceal their true work effort, it may also provide incentives for the working and middle class to underreport their true participation in the labor market. To maximize their take-home pay, carpenters, plumbers, or even accountants may at time moonlight on the side without officially mentioning it in any Current Population Surveys. If we thus consider the involvement in the underground economy by all segments of society, the stark difference in the work effort of the poor and non-poor may not change all that much.

Finally, the remarkable disparities in employment among various subgroups of the poor, as well as between the poor and non-poor, raise additional doubts about economic accounts of the work behavior of the poor. If employment patterns of the poor are a rational response to the harsh economic conditions found in many of our urban centers, then we need to know why the work record of inner-city residents should vary so much from one group to the next. Employment data collected by the Urban Poverty and Family Structure Survey from 1985 to 1987 in Chicago indicate that there are dramatic differences in the employment practices among ethnic groups. This project, which ironically was carried out by Wilson and his associates at the University of Chicago, surveyed 2,500 residents of Chicago's inner city, including interviews with roughly 1,200 blacks, 360 poor whites, 500 Puerto Ricans, and 450 Mexicans.[18] The data from Chicago are important because William Julius Wilson and John Kasarda have argued that cities like New York and Chicago were especially hard hit by the industrial restructuring that occurred in the late 1970s and early 1980s.[19]

Although Mexicans, poor whites, Puerto Ricans, and blacks in Chicago faced the same industrial mix and general labor conditions, their ability to find and hold jobs has varied sharply (table 7.5). If a dearth of jobs were the only factor responsible for the poor work record of indigents, it is hard to understand why poor Mexicans have been more successful than whites, blacks, or Puerto Ricans in finding alternative employment.[20] Despite a large number of plant closings in Chicago, Mexicans have enjoyed phenomenal success in holding onto jobs in the manufacturing sector of the economy. In the Urban Poverty and Family Structure Survey, 94 percent of Mexicans from the inner city of Chicago were employed, while the figures dropped

Table 7.5
Characteristics of Chicago Poverty-Area Fathers, Ages 18–44

	Percentage Employed	*Average No. of Years of Education*	*Percentage Who Read English*
Mexican	94	7.1	31.9
White	82	13.1	100
Puerto Rican	76	9.8	74.1
Black	67	12.1	100

Sources: The data are from the Chicago Urban Poverty and Family Structure Study, 1988, available from the Consortium for Political and Social Research, Ann Arbor, Michigan. See also Robert Aponte, "Ethnicity and Male Employment in the Inner City: A Test of Two Theories," paper delivered at the Urban Poverty and Family Life Conference, Chicago, 1991. Article is available from the Center for the Study of Urban Inequality at the University of Chicago. The above table is reprinted with permission of Robert Aponte.

to 82 percent for whites 76 percent for Puerto Ricans and 67 percent for blacks.

The case of Mexicans is especially impressive since most have had very little formal education and the vast majority are unable to speak or read English. While most low-income blacks and whites have the equivalent of a high school education, most Mexicans have little more than an elementary school education. In a tough labor market, native-born Americans should be much more qualified than their Mexican counterparts for any available openings. From a purely human capital point of view, one would predict that Mexicans would have the lowest rather than the highest rate of employment. The unusual employment rates of Mexican Americans demonstrate that if some groups are highly motivated, they may be able to find work even when they lack the ability to communicate in English and their educational skills are minimal. Even more noteworthy is the fact that the Mexican population in Chicago grew from slightly over 100,000 in the 1980s to 250,000 by 1990. In spite of the burden of being part of an expanding rather than a declining population that has had few long-term ties with the city, poor Mexicans have had a work record that few other indigents can match.

Ethnographic data also clearly indicate that there is a wide array of attitudes toward work. Unfortunately, exchange or rational economic explanations fail to account for the diversity of the views on work found by the Urban Poverty and Family Structure Survey. As Richard Taub noted, the Mexicans, like many immigrant groups before them, were demons for work.[21] Most Mexicans considered a supervisor to be a good boss if he provided them with opportunities for working overtime. Many of the men, who agreed that life was much more difficult in Mexico than America, also believed that they received worse jobs than white Americans of similar status.

But in spite of these obstacles, they repeated the same refrain: "I would like to be someone in a job. I am willing to work in order to have a decent life."[22] Many Mexican women also echoed the same sentiments as they spoke admiringly of their fathers, who taught their families to engage in hard work and "made speeches against being idle."[23] The case of Mexican immigrants is instructive in that it clearly demonstrates that if a group is determined to get ahead, regardless of its limited educational and human capital skills, it may prosper by sheer drive, initiative, and willpower. In contrast, Taub found that other inner-city ethnic groups had a very different attitude toward work. None seem to be as driven as the Mexicans in their desire to secure some form of gainful employment. Taub observed that many poor black men in the study indicated that they did not like the jobs that Mexican-Americans took, and that they would "not work as hard for those same low wages."[24] While most of the men believed in the American dream and recognized the importance of hard work, they were only marginally committed to actually achieving that goal.

Finally, the importance of values in shaping the work record of the poor is also clearly illustrated by examining the attitudes of the poor themselves. Many inner-city residents believe that the spotty employment practices of their peers reflects more of a lack of character than a lack of opportunities for advancement. But ever since Moynihan was harshly attacked for his study of poverty, most researchers have avoided criticizing the values of the poor for fear of being ostracized by their colleagues. It is of interest that the poor do not seem to share that reservation. To the surprise of researchers at the University of Chicago, some of the harshest critics of the work ethic of the poor are the poor themselves. "Repeatedly, low income respondents told ethnographers that their unemployed friends were 'lazy' and questioned the diligence of those who quit jobs or had been fired."[25] One argued: "The reasons why a lot of guys don't have jobs is because they don't put their minds to it. They are too busy up on the street. Once you get hooked on the street, you might not want to do nothing."[26] Another insisted that his friends don't want jobs "where they have to go leave their homeys or leave their friends."[27] He also mentioned that many of his unemployed friends did not even apply for temporary slots at a local food festival when he had arranged to have them hired. Clive lamented that too many people "don't want to work, and when I say don't want to work, I say don't want to work hard. They want real easy jobs, making big bucks."[28] Clive, like many of the poor, often strongly argued that his peers lack jobs not because of economic obstacles, but because of their own lackadaisical attitudes toward work.

While many analysts as well as politicians insist that the apparent lack of motivation of the poor and their increasing tendency to drop out of the work force are a perfectly rational and understandable response to bleak economic prospects, the situation may in reality be a cultural rather than an economic problem. The shifting work habits of the poor suggest that it may not be just changes in the economy that account for the rise of the underclass, but changes in the way many people respond to external events. Contrary to the views of exchange theorists who believe that people will always respond to adversity in the same way, people's values appear to determine how they react to financial difficulties. Perceptions of economic disincentives are always mediated by cultural beliefs. If individuals have an intact and stable set of values, they may respond to adversity by redoubling their efforts to secure work rather than engaging in aberrant behavior. But if the cultural gyroscope inside people breaks down, those same people may undertake self-destructive actions such as dropping out of the work force even when the external situation in which they find themselves is no different from that facing others. As we will see in chapter 9, it may be more the growth of normlessness, or what Durkheim calls anomie, than changes in the economy that accounts for the growing tendency of the poor to neglect their responsibilities to be productive members of the labor force.

EIGHT

Rational Economic Explanations: The Conservative Version

Like their liberal counterparts, many conservatives believe that the poor are rational economic actors who respond to the presence or absence of financial incentives. But instead of focusing on changes in the economy, conservatives like Charles Murray believe that the growth of the welfare state is responsible for the persistence of poverty. Although he often uses cultural arguments, Murray is best known for his argument that the growth of transfer payments has undermined the desire of many poor people to become financially self-sufficient. Unlike previous critics of the Great Society, who merely questioned the effectiveness of government programs to combat poverty, Murray has gone one step further and suggested that transfer programs often harm the very people they are designed to help, inadvertently creating a dependency mentality among the poor that is likely to perpetuate rather than eliminate poverty.

Since Murray believes that government activities provide obvious financial disincentives for the poor to remain married work or to work, government intervention more often turns out to be part of the problem rather than the solution. Murray tends to downplay the argument that the poor suffer from anomie or a pathological culture of poverty. On the contrary, he maintains that much of the indifference of the poor toward working is nothing more than a rational response to the perverse disincentives built into many government programs.

In evaluating Murray's argument, it is important to keep in mind the distinction we made earlier between government efforts to treat the origins as opposed to the effects of poverty. Many of Murray's critics have pointed out that the country's welfare program has often lifted millions of people above the official poverty line by substantially improving the living conditions of the elderly and the disabled as well as the poor in general. They thus reject his proposition that government welfare programs harm their recipients.[1] But this argument overlooks Murray's contention that public entitlement programs often make it more difficult to eliminate the causes of poverty than the consequences of poverty. It is hard to deny that public officials can always treat the effects of poverty by giving the poor more money. But such policies are a far cry from Lyndon Johnson's belief that the government should give the poor only a hand rather than a handout.

In this chapter I will argue that the welfare state has had a small yet significantly negative impact on the behavior of the poor. As will soon be clear, most studies which have dismissed the harmful affects of transfer programs have failed to look at the diverse and often subtle ways that welfare can adversely influence the behavior of the poor. But even then, it is important to realize that the disincentives built into many transfer programs are always mediated by people's cultural values. The real danger is that welfare programs are most likely to reinforce the actions of people who are already culturally predisposed to drop out of the labor market. More often than not, entitlement programs facilitate and subsidize, rather than actually cause, the poor to engage in actions that help to perpetuate poverty.

THE GROWTH OF THE WELFARE STATE

The welfare activities that Murray feels hurt the poor the most include both cash assistance as well as relief-in-kind programs. By and large the transfer program that has received the most publicity is Aid to Families with Dependent Children (AFDC), a cash-assistance program that was primarily designed to help female heads of household with children under age eighteen. The program has two parts: a "guaranteed" amount for families of different sizes, and a so-called reduction rate that reduces benefits at a specific rate if recipients enter the work force. The states determine the value of the guaranteed amount, while the federal government decides what the reduction rate will be. For example, in 1990 the maximum AFDC payment for a family of three ranged from $694 per month in California to $120 per month in Mississippi.[2] At the same time, the reduction rate was 100 percent, which meant that the government reduces dollar for dollar the value of AFDC transfer payments when a recipient earns income in the labor market.

Over the last twenty-five years the growth of AFDC has been erratic. From 1965 to 1975, the program exploded as the number of families on welfare rolls more than tripled. Following this period of rapid growth, AFDC

Table 8.1
Length of Time on AFDC

Expected Years on AFDC	Percentage of People on AFDC at a Point in Time
1 to 2	7
3 to 4	11
5 to 7	17
8 or more	65

Source: House Committee on Ways and Means, *Green Book: The Overview of Entitlement Programs*, 640.

grew only slightly from 1975 to 1980; after 1980, enrollment leveled off until 1988, when it slowly started to rise again. A major reason for the slight decrease in the number of AFDC recipients is that when Congress agreed to the 1981 Budget Reconciliation Act (OBRA), it limited AFDC eligibility. Presently around one-third of all people the government classifies as poor (or roughly 11 million individuals) are enrolled in the AFDC program.

In the 1988 Family Support Act, Congress also mandated that all states had to make intact families eligible for benefits by October 1990 in what is known as the AFDC-UP program (UP stands for unemployed parent). Before the passage of this act, less than half of the states provided assistance to two-parent families. However, because of stringent eligibility requirements, less than 10 percent of the total AFDC caseload consists of families with an unemployed parent.

Most defenders of the present welfare system generally downplay the fear that transfer programs create dependency among the poor by arguing that most people spend relatively short periods of time on AFDC. But a recent study (see table 8.1) found that the vast majority of people (65 percent) enrolled at any one time on AFDC are in the midst of a spell that will last at least eight years.

In addition to the AFDC program, the government provides indigents with a whole array of in-kind transfers such as food stamps, medical care, public housing, and rent subsidies. One of the largest transfers is the food stamp program, which provides food vouchers for families regardless of the marital status of the head of household. Along with Medicaid, it is the closest program in this country to a universal welfare program. While it was insignificant in 1965, serving only 400,000 individuals, it has grown substantially and today is twice as big as AFDC, serving around twenty million people. Similarly, Medicaid, which provides health care for the poor, has grown tremendously since the 1970s. While Medicaid is a federal program, it is administered by the states. Aside from the special problems of the disabled and aged, the program generally limits eligibility to those enrolled in AFDC. Given its rapid growth in the last two decades, Medicaid is presently the largest welfare program in the country, with over twenty-two million individuals receiving some kind of benefits. Finally, the third and smallest of the government relief-in-kind programs are public housing and rent subsidies. At most recent count, about 20 percent of AFDC recipients in particular and five million Americans in general received some kind of housing assistance.

The interesting question is, why did the AFDC caseload grow so rapidly in the 1960s? Murray argues that as welfare payments became more lucrative, more low-income individuals elected to become wards of the state. If individuals are rational economic actors, it is easy to understand why they would take advantage of government subsidies. To some extent, increases and subsequent decreases in welfare benefits did have a major impact on the number of welfare recipients. The value of AFDC benefits increased fairly dramatically from the late 1950s until it peaked in 1967. Over the next two decades, the economic worth of AFDC payments declined roughly 40 percent, until by the late 1980s the level of benefits equaled those in 1965. As benefit levels increased and then decreased, the percentage of women receiving AFDC also rose and fell. From 1967 to 1973, the number of female heads participating in the program increased from 36 percent to 63 percent, and then declined below 50 percent.[3] But as many commentators have noted, besides an increase in benefit levels, changes in the rules governing eligibility, as well as a decline in the cultural stigma attached to welfare, may also have played a role in increasing the AFDC caseload. Robert Moffitt, for instance, has noted that as transfer payments came to be viewed as a right rather than a dole, more female-headed households may have felt it was culturally acceptable to sign up for government subsidies.[4]

THE IMPACT OF WELFARE ON POVERTY: THE TENUOUS LINK BETWEEN WELFARE SPENDING AND LEVELS OF PRETRANSFER POVERTY

Do the transfer payments described above actually hamper upward mobility? As we mentioned earlier, the number of people climbing out of poverty on their own, or escaping what is more commonly known as pretransfer poverty, stopped declining in 1969. In 1965, for instance, the pretransfer poverty rate was a little over 21 percent, but in 1969 it dropped to under 18 percent and since the early 1970s it has remained stuck at around 22 percent of the population. Based on these data, Murray maintains that the disincentives associated with transfer payments are responsible for this unfortunate rise in pretransfer poverty.

But when we compare the changes in welfare spending with actual poverty, the alleged connection between expanding entitlement programs and the pretransfer poverty rate is not quite as clear cut as Murray implies. Sheldon Danziger and Peter Gottschalk have noted that "cash and in-kind transfers grew by about 35 percent in real terms between 1965 and 1969 when pre-transfer poverty was declining, and by about the same percent between 1969 and 1974 when it was increasing."[5] If there is a causal connection between these two events, it is not easy to identify. Similarly, more recently pretransfer poverty rates have remained stubbornly high even though welfare benefits have continued to decline in value. Between 1970 and 1991, the maximum AFDC benefits a median state provided for a family of three declined by 42 percent in constant dollars. The rising value of food stamps since the 1970s, however, has partially offset the fall in AFDC payments. Even after adjusting for the fact that food stamps have been indexed for inflation, the total value of the two programs has still declined by over 26 percent. Despite this rather significant drop in benefits, we have seen no real improvement in the percentage of people who have climbed out of poverty on their own initiative. If Murray were right, we would have expected the decline in benefits to have encouraged more of the poor to escape pretransfer poverty.

WELFARE, WORK, AND POVERTY

While the aggregate data on poverty and welfare expenditures raise serious doubts about Murray's welfare thesis, they are only suggestive rather than conclusive. To evaluate Murray's argument properly we also need to examine whether the welfare system actually discouraged indigents from actively participating in the labor market. To test this proposition, analysts have looked both at time series and at cross-sectional data. While the available studies are not in complete agreement, there is still ample evidence that entitlement programs have adversely affected people's desire to seek employment. But because welfare mothers have never worked much to begin with, the disincentives built into entitlement programs have had a limited impact on their work record.

Table 8.2

Work Record and Family Characteristics of AFDC Recipients

	1968	1969	1973	1975	1979	1981	1982	1984	1991
AFDC Work Record									
(in percentages)									
Mothers working full time	n/a	8.2	9.8	10.4	8.7	n/a	n/a	1.2	2.2
Working full and part time	16	15	18	18	16	14	7	5	6
Average family size	n/a	4.0	3.6	3.2	3.0	3.0	3.0	2.9	2.9
Education of Mothers									
(in percentages)									
8th grade or less	n/a	29	17	17	10	n/a	n/a	n/a	6
High school diploma	n/a	16	n/a	24	19	n/a	n/a	n/a	20
Some college	n/a	2	n/a	4	3	n/a	n/a	n/a	6

Source: House Committee on Ways and Means, *Green Book: The Overview of Entitlement Programs* (1991), 623; (1992) 669; (1993), 696.

Time Series Data

As table 8.2 shows, very few recipients of AFDC actually work. Over the last twenty-five years, the percentage of females on AFDC in the labor market has never exceeded 18 percent and more recently has hovered around 6 percent. In contrast to most single-parent women who are not poor, AFDC mothers are notable for their lack of participation in the labor market. This spotty work record is even more unusual when we consider that the average welfare recipient has fewer children than twenty-five years ago and is better educated. In 1968, the average AFDC family had four members, while today it is over 25 percent smaller with just three members. Also, the percentage of females on AFDC with an eighth grade education or less has declined from over 33 percent of the total population to just 6 percent today. But in spite of having smaller families and improved human capital skills, AFDC recipients are even less inclined to be in the labor market today than in the past.

As table 8.2 indicates, the number of AFDC recipients who work increased slightly in the mid-1970s, then slowly declined in the late 1970s before dropping precipitously in the 1980s. But we must be careful in interpreting these data. The shifting pattern of work among welfare mothers that we find in table 8.2 reflects as much a shift in the makeup of AFDC recipients as it does a change in the behavior of individual mothers.[6] In 1967 Congress lowered the AFDC benefit reduction rate from 100 percent to 67 percent in order to encourage more women to enter the labor market. But this action also increased the percentage of highly trained and motivated women who were eligible for AFDC and thus led to an improvement in the work record of welfare recipients. In 1981 Congress reversed its position and raised the benefit reduction rate back to 100 percent, thereby eliminating many women from the AFDC rolls. As the caseload of AFDC recipients changed, the work record of single mothers on welfare also fluctuated. The shifts in the aggregate data over time may thus tell us as much about the composition of AFDC's caseload as they do about the motivation of the average welfare recipient.

While keeping this caveat in mind, we can still ask if changes in either (1) the basic welfare guarantee or (2) the benefit reduction rate had any impact on the labor activities of AFDC recipients. If we look only at benefit levels, the answer appears to be a partial yes. As already mentioned, the combined total of AFDC benefits and food stamps rose in the late 1960s and early 1970s, at a time when employment rates for female heads declined slightly, a fact consistent with Murray's overall hypothesis. However, by the late 1970s welfare benefits fell and the percentage of AFDC mothers choosing to work initially rose and then dropped sharply. While the increase in working AFDC mothers supports Murray's argument, the decrease does not.

To account for this latter fall-off in work we need to look for some alternative explanation. Some economists point to the disincentives contained in the 1981 legislation that increased the benefit reduction rate back to 100 percent to explain why so few AFDC mothers were in the labor market during the 1980s. But the trouble with this argument is that welfare recipients worked less in the late 1970s, well before the 1981 act was enacted.[7] Moreover, the reduction in the benefit rate in 1969 apparently had no discernible impact on the willingness of AFDC recipients to work. Indeed, the employment rate of single mothers actually fell after Congress reduced benefits in 1969. The attempt by Congress to stimulate more work among welfare mothers appears to have been a failure. In light of the above data, it is remarkable how stable the employment rates of AFDC recipients have been "despite major changes in benefit levels, benefit reductions rates, and unemployment rates."[8] As some commentators have noted, this extreme "inelasticity does not augur well for the prospect of increasing work effort by any change in benefits or in benefit reduction rates."[9] This is a point we need to keep in mind when we consider Murray's proposals for scaling back the size of the welfare state.

Cross-Sectional Data

While studies of AFDC recipients over time suggest that welfare programs have had at best a minimal impact on the work behavior of the poor, cross-sectional data indicate otherwise. For instance, there is a significant difference in the employment rate between welfare mothers and nonwelfare married women or single parents. Since the late 1960s and early 1970s, the employment rates of married women slowly but steadily increased while those of women on AFDC declined slightly. As more and more women decided to join the labor market and struggled with the problems of simultaneously raising a family and earning an income, most welfare mothers elected not to work.

The same pattern becomes even more pronounced when we focus on the labor record of only those women who are eligible for AFDC (single parents with children under eighteen). As we have just seen, roughly 50 percent of all such families are on AFDC and the other 50 percent are in the labor market. Since table 8.2 indicates that only 6 to 15 percent of AFDC recipients have either a full- or part-time job, that means that roughly 80 percent of female heads who decided not to enroll in AFDC are actually working. The employment record of the two groups could not be more dissimilar. The above data suggest that the financial disincentives built into the AFDC program have reduced the work effort of most welfare recipients by close to 70 percent.[10] However, because people's decision to enter the labor force may be caused by a variety of factors—such as their level of education or cultural beliefs—we can still not be absolutely certain that welfare per se is the primary reason why so few AFDC mothers actually work.

To sort out these matters, a variety of scholars have tried to analyze how changes in AFDC benefits in various states have affected the employment record of female households. The best-known surveys of this copious literature, which have been conducted by Sheldon Danziger, director of the Poverty Institute at the University of Wisconsin, Robert Haveman, Robert Plotnick, and more recently by Robert Moffitt, equivocally find that AFDC benefits do discourage welfare recipients from seeking work.[11] This finding becomes obvious when we realize that in 1986 AFDC benefits exceeded the monthly earnings that full-time workers could make from the minimum wage in eight different states. The recent increase in that wage to $4.25 an hour has significantly improved the financial payoff from working. But as table 8.3 indicates, a woman who stays home and receives welfare from a moderately generous state like Pennsylvania is still fairly well off compared to someone who works full time at a minimum wage job. In a state like

Table 8.3
A Comparison of Welfare and Work
(Single Parent with Two Children, Pennsylvania, 1991)

Wage Level	Earnings	Day Care	Taxes	Welfare and Food Stamps	Disposable Income
No work	$0	$0	$0	$7218	$7218
Half-time, min. wage	4250	− 1500	425	5031	8206
Full-time, min. wage	8500	− 3000	588	2151	8239
Full-time, $5.00/hr.	10,000	− 3000	260	1881	9141

Source: Adapted from House Committee on Ways and Means, Green Book: The Overview of Entitlement Programs (1991), 590, table 4.

California, which offers a more generous guarantee, the value of AFDC and food stamp benefits is extremely competitive with part-time work.

Similarly, standard economic theory would also predict that both the income guarantee of AFDC as well as the benefit reduction rate would adversely affect the employment effort of welfare recipients. When the government provides benefits, the need to work naturally declines (the income effect) while the imposition of a 100 percent reduction rate on any earnings reduces the payoff from work (the substitution effect). The two components of AFDC thus financially reinforce each other: first, by enabling people to consume without working; and second, by imposing an extremely high tax rate on their wages if they do find employment.

While there is widespread agreement that the welfare system provides disincentives for people to remain in the labor market, the magnitude of the problem remains unclear. In Danziger's survey of the econometric literature he found that the AFDC program appeared to reduce the labor supply of welfare recipients anywhere from 10 percent to 50 percent.[12] Given this large discrepancy, Moffitt, in another, more updated survey of the same literature has split the difference and suggested that the present welfare system probably reduces the work effort of AFDC mothers by about 30 percent, a considerable reduction by any standard.[13] To use a metaphor developed by Arthur Okun, providing welfare to indigents is a lot like carrying a "leaky bucket."[14] Every time the government tries to improve the financial position of the poor, part of the benefits leak away because the recipients choose to work less.

At first glance, the above data appear to vindicate Murray's contention that government welfare programs are partly responsible for the persistent nature of poverty in this country. It is very clear that government payments have a significant negative impact on the employment of AFDC recipients. But there is an important catch to this conclusion. Since welfare mothers are not inclined to work very much in the first place, the disincentives of the AFDC program have had very little impact on their overall work record. This is the reason why the time series data also failed to measure the adverse impact of the AFDC program on work. Because women on welfare worked so little to begin with, it was hard to detect the adverse impact of AFDC on their work record over an extended period of time.

These studies suggest that transfer programs are not the main reason why so many single parents are poor. Because welfare recipients only work an average of 9 hours a week, AFDC has reduced their participation in the labor market by roughly 200 to 300 hours a year. At the present minimum wage of $4.25 an hour, most single mothers have lost at best around $1,200 in wages because of the disincentive effects of AFDC. By itself, that sum of money would not have lifted very many AFDC recipients above the poverty line. Despite the undeniable negative impact welfare has on the work habits of the poor, their spotty employment record appears to be more of a cultural than an economic problem.

THE QUESTION OF MOTIVATION RECONSIDERED

However, there are several considerations we need to keep in mind when assessing the influence of welfare programs on the behavior of the poor. Because the studies conducted by Danziger and Moffitt were concerned primarily with measuring the direct impact of transfer payments on the labor activity of female heads of household, they largely ignored the indirect influence that AFDC may have on the labor activities of men. As a result, the econometric studies of AFDC may have overlooked some of the worst consequences of transfer programs. First, as Murray argues, when women are enrolled in AFDC, their boyfriends will often lose interest in work and periodically sponge off their girlfriends.[15] This behavior is so destructive because most of these young uneducated males have limited opportunities for advancement. If these individuals are to have any hope of escaping poverty, it is imperative that they take advantage of available low-income jobs when they can find them. If they work steadily at a variety of low-income positions, it is hoped they will acquire skills and a good work record that will eventually enable them to find positions paying decent wages.[16] But the growth of transfer programs has often discouraged young males from pursuing this route. As welfare benefits became more generous in the 1960s, many young men realized that they could take advantage of their girlfriends by treating them as meal tickets. The easy money of welfare was often an attractive, albeit temporary, alternative to the tedious jobs available to them.

By intermittently moving in and out of the labor market in this fashion, many inner-city men squandered both their opportunities to gain valuable work experience as well as their reputations as reliable workers.

Second, the growth of the welfare system may also have indirectly helped to perpetuate poverty by discouraging people from migrating to areas where jobs are plentiful. William Julius Wilson has recently argued that many poor blacks have become isolated in the inner city, cut off from the growth of well-paying jobs in the outlying suburbs. But the key question is, why have so many poor become immobilized, unable or unwilling to follow the expansion of jobs outside the inner city? In the 1950s, many Southern blacks moved north in search of work and a better life. The key question is: "What allowed these hard working people, who'd uprooted themselves and moved hundreds of miles in search of better paychecks, to stop moving and stop working, in defiance of the pattern of every other migrant peasant group?"[17] Welfare is undoubtedly part of the answer. Without any other legitimate source of income, the poor probably would have continued to move to where the jobs were, as historically they had always done. John Kasarda has underscored that point by noting that in the 1980s some 40 percent of unemployed black males received either public or subsidized housing, food stamps, or AFDC and thus had little reason to migrate.[18] The very real possibility thus exists that without welfare, many lower-class residents of the inner city might have evolved into the working and middle classes of suburban America. To the detriment of the poor themselves, "the creation of 'urban welfare economies' allowed a large minority underclass to become 'anchored' in the isolated urban ghettos where there were no jobs."[19]

Third, and even more important, most econometric studies can also be faulted for overlooking the possibility that government welfare programs may have fostered a general sense of dependency among the poor which in turn has hampered their prospects for finding work and becoming financially self-sufficient. In his excellent case study of social dropouts, *The Underclass*, Ken Auletta noted that many of the inner-city men and women he studied often expressed conventional beliefs about the desirability of finding and keeping a job.[20] But because so many had grown up in an atmosphere in which the government provided for a significant portion of their needs, they came to believe that it was primarily the responsibility of the public sector to find them jobs. As a result, many of the poor had no sense that they needed to take charge of their own lives or that they had to show some initiative in finding work in order to become self-sufficient. To the contrary, most felt that the government had an obligation to provide for their children, to arrange their transportation, to guarantee that they were appropriately trained, and even to secure them a position before they could actually be expected to show up for work. This atmosphere of "organized altruism," as Christopher Lash has called it, often results in the poor adopting the self-destructive attitude that they are not responsible—and perhaps even incapable—of caring for themselves or their families.[21]

All too often, when the poor encounter problems, the government has intervened to alleviate their difficulties. But what proponents of the welfare state often fail to see is that by constantly stressing the theme of victimization and the need for more public intervention, they may undercut the ability of the poor to help themselves. The constant refrain that the government needs to do more for others can often be used as a crutch by the poor to do less for themselves.

The above examples clearly demonstrate that the economic incentives built into most government transfer programs may operate in complex and subtle ways. But we must be careful not to exaggerate the role of the welfare state in discouraging the poor from acquiring jobs. It is readily apparent that if AFDC were abolished, most of the recipients would simply not look for employment. The lack of work effort by female-headed households and their boyfriends is as much a cultural as an economic problem.

It is noteworthy that the cultural problems of the poor are not shared by all ethnic groups. Murray is often silent as to why indigents often vary in their labor records. If the disincentives contained in most welfare programs actually discouraged work among all poor, there should be little variation in the degree to which different ethnic groups either participated in AFDC or joined the labor market. But data collected from the Urban Poverty and Family Structure Survey found that the opposite is true. Low-income Mexican immigrants, for instance, who have minimal education and live in the inner city of Chicago, have generally avoided participating in AFDC. The participation rate of Mexican immigrants in AFDC is only 37 percent that of their black or Puerto Ricans counterparts.[22] Part of this difference is due to the fact that many Mexican immigrants have illegally entered the country and thus are not likely to apply for welfare. But different groups also have different perceptions about what constitutes acceptable behavior. For instance, Mexicans are also four times more likely than other ethnic groups to argue that work should be a precondition for receiving welfare. It should thus come as no surprise that Mexican Americans, whom Richard Taub has described as demons for work, have fared much better than other ethnic groups in finding and holding on to well-paying industrial jobs. The presence of a relatively lucrative welfare system in the state of Illinois thus appears to have had little or no impact on their work behavior. While Murray believes that the poor will be seduced by the generosity of AFDC, Mexicans immigrants in Chicago, who have had a cultural aversion to becoming beneficiaries of the welfare state, have proven otherwise. When ethnic groups have a value system that stresses the work ethic, their behavior is not likely to be influenced by the economic disincentives embedded in our current welfare system.

Marta Tienda has likewise found that the problem of welfare dependency is primarily a problem that troubles poor blacks and Puerto Ricans. She notes that the "the hazard rates for black mothers imply a 70 percent probability that a spell of AFDC would last 5 years and a 60 percent probability of a 10 year duration."[23] But it is important to realize that the differences between blacks and other ethnic groups reflect as much class as racial differences. In fact, as the black population has fragmented into a highly successful black middle class, a working class, and a black underclass, the class differences within the black population may have become more important than the racial characteristics that appear to unite them. Since a significantly higher percentage of low-income blacks are more likely to be members of the underclass than are Mexican immigrants, it is not surprising that Tienda and the Chicago Urban Poverty Survey found significant differences in the attitudes and reliance on welfare among various ethnic groups.

IS WORKFARE THE ANSWER?

Whether or not one agrees with Murray's assumptions, his book has sparked an important debate over the future role of AFDC. Many of his critics have insisted that it would be unwise to tamper with a welfare system that provides much-needed assistance to indigents. For instance, Richard Coe and Greg Duncan insist that the welfare system is "an indispensable safety net in a dynamic society, serving largely as insurance against temporary misfortune."[24] However, we know from our previous analysis that this argument minimizes the problems of AFDC. Work by David Ellwood and Mary Jo Bane as well as Marta Tienda indicates that many indigents are often highly dependent on AFDC payments, sometimes having "spells" that last over ten years.[25]

Because of these dependency problems, Murray has essentially advocated the scrapping of all major welfare programs.[26] He believes that completely cutting the Gordian knot of welfare will force AFDC recipients back into the labor market and eventually solve the problem of poverty. But like his opponents who defend the present AFDC system, Murray may be too optimistic about what his reforms would accomplish. As noted earlier, it is certainly an open question if eliminating most welfare programs would actually do much to provide incentives for indigents to find jobs or to shore up the family in the inner city. But whether AFDC is a major cause of poverty or not, asking people who often work long and tedious hours at modest wages to pay taxes to subsidize people who often choose not to work at all becomes an ethical problem. There is also a moral dilemma involved in expecting the poor to act in a responsible fashion when we often reward those who adopt socially and economically undesirable behavior. In his interesting study, *Poor Support*, a book that has not received the publicity it deserves, David Ellwood suggests that providing assistance to the poor is a conundrum, a problem for which there appears to be no satisfactory solution.[27] If we adopt Murray's recommendation and scale back the present welfare system, we may find ourselves in the position of inadvertently hurting many individuals suffering from real misfortune. Conversely, if we refuse to tamper with the present makeup of AFDC, we find ourselves in the equally unsatisfactory position of discouraging people from taking some initiative for improving their own lives by entering the labor market.

The only way out of this conundrum is to devise a welfare system that helps those in need without simultaneously encouraging them to be indolent. But unfortunately, previous governmental efforts to encourage welfare recipients to work have met with very little success. When Congress or state legislators have tried to offer the poor financial incentives by altering either the benefits or the benefit reduction rate, they have seen at most a modest increase in the work record of AFDC recipients. These reform efforts have failed because most welfare recipients have refused to act like the classical rational economic actors found in beginning economics textbooks. If we hope to avoid the present problems with AFDC, we must think more about instilling in welfare recipients some notion that they have obligations to become productive members of society. When individuals lack a cultural commitment to work or family, economic incentives are unlikely to be effective in dramatically changing their behavior. To achieve this goal, the government needs to establish some form of mandatory workfare in which people realize that they have a duty to be gainfully employed. Until more welfare recipients recognize that they have responsibilities as well as rights, obligations as well as entitlements, they are not likely to become productive members of society. As a temporary stop-gap, it would not be unreasonable for public officials to offer cash assistance to individuals or families suffering temporary misfortune. But over the long run, the government should insist that welfare recipients have an obligation to work. How to structure such a system of workfare needs more experimentation and research. President

Clinton is currently proposing that we scrap the existing welfare system and provide assistance for a minimum of two years. In place of long-term relief, the government would offer intensive work training and, as a last resort, government-financed minimum wage jobs for those unable to find employment on their own after their two years on welfare had expired. When defenders of our current system correctly point out that government transfer programs can serve a useful purpose in alleviating the hardships of the poor, they often fail to see that welfare programs can also help to perpetuate poverty. The important task is to design a welfare program that helps the poor help themselves regain responsibility for controlling their own lives. In this sense, Clinton's proposals for reforming the current entitlement system system represent a dramatic but overdue change in our existing welfare state.

NINE

Cultural Explanations

In light of the difficulties one encounters with rational economic explanations of the poor, it is important to realize that the rise of the underclass is a cultural rather than an economic phenomenon. While many liberals and conservatives often maintain that the apparent destructive behavior of the underclass is an unfortunate but rational response to bleak economic conditions or the disincentives of the welfare state, the data seem to indicate otherwise. The propensity of many poor to drop out of the labor force, to neglect their families, or to engage in criminal behavior seems to reflect less a rational response to limited economic opportunities than a breakdown of traditional norms in society. As the problems of the underclass have become more acute over the past several decades, even liberals like William Julius Wilson have begun to express alarm about the breakdown of civility among the poor. These trends are discouraging because they suggest that the pathological unraveling of the social fabric in our urban communities will eventually jeopardize the ability of many indigents to ever escape poverty.

THE RISE OF ANOMIE

If there is a growing consensus among poverty analysts that the problems of the poor are cultural rather than economic in nature, there is intense disagreement over exactly how cultural norms have influenced the destructive actions of the underclass. As we shall see shortly, many observers insist that the poor suffer from a unique and pathological culture of poverty that affects only the indigent population. This chapter will argue instead that the growth of the underclass is a result of what Emile Durkheim once called the development of "anomie," which literally means the absence of social norms in society as a whole.[1] The aberrant behavior of the underclass may simply reflect the fact that traditional social values have broken down over the last thirty years, leaving many indigents without a moral compass. Whenever the normative sanctions holding society together became fragile or brittle, the behavior of some will inevitably become impulsive and self-destructive, undermining the civility of the community as a whole.

The present concern with the underclass is not the first time that industrialized nations like the United States have had to deal with potentially disruptive actions by its citizens. Just like today, political and economic elites in the early and latter part of the nineteenth century worried about the rise of antisocial behavior among large sectors of the lower class. In fact, it was the prevalence of these disturbances in newly industrialized nations that stimulated scholars like Durkheim to develop the discipline of sociology in the first place. As societies became more complex and impersonal, Durkheim worried that they might become torn apart by the conflicting demands of their citizens. To minimize conflict in the public realm, he adopted the structuralist belief that the growth of impersonal structures such as the division of labor would somehow integrate society and minimize deviant behavior. But in his later work Durkheim came to realize that without some common values or beliefs to tie people together, individuals are more likely to engage in self-destructive actions that would threaten the cohesion of society as a whole.[2]

While Durkheim articulated the need for social control and developed the notion of anomie to describe its absence, a diverse array of institutions in the United States, such as the Progressive party and the temperance movement, tried to develop concrete programs for teaching self-control and discipline to the lower and working-classes in society.[3] These organizations realized that as an industrial country became more mobile and impersonal, it would be difficult to regulate people's behavior solely through the use of external controls or supervision. To provide some degree of stability in a rapidly changing society, the only feasible option available to public officials was to control people internally by inculcating in them a set of cultural values that stressed self-discipline and hard work. Most reform movements of the nineteenth century believed that the threat of disorder in society stemmed largely from the fact that individuals were often self-serving and impulsive. Unless public institutions could socialize people into accepting social norms that stressed restraint and hard work, there was a very real danger that the poor and working class would engage in antisocial behavior. In retrospect, many historians have called this period in American history the "age of Victorian morality." To prevent society from degenerating into a Hobbesian world in which the poor would harm themselves as well as the rest of society, civil, religious, and political leaders invested tremendous resources in promoting individual self-control.

In the 1840s, for instance, reformers created public schools, built YMCA buildings, fostered Sunday school instruction, and promoted religious revivals to inculcate the values of self-discipline and self-control. The YMCA believed that its facilities would serve as a waystation for young men who had left behind the more homogeneous life of the countryside. The public schools were also designed as much to develop the character of its students as to give them occupational skills. The hope was that society could turn out young men and women who would scrupulously observe traditional social norms.[4] Unless people recognized their duties to the rest of society, it would be hard to maintain civility and order.

Half a century later, another set of reformers loosely associated with the Progressive movement also tried to promote the moral character of the poor. By placing new immigrants in tenement houses, enrolling young men in highly structured organizations like the Boy Scouts, investing additional money in education, and developing a grass-roots temperance movement, these reformers stressed the importance of sobriety, social obligation, and hard work to a generation of laborers. The Boy Scouts also hoped to teach the virtues of discipline, self-reliance, and service to working- and middle-class youths by enrolling young men in highly disciplined, quasi-military type organizations. Even in the domain of architecture and land-use planning, reformers tried to advance some variation of the Victorian morality of the day. The "city-beautiful" movement, which sprung up at the turn of the century, believed that by designing attractive government centers, such as the one found in San Francisco, they would inspire the public, in general, and the poor, in particular, to take their civic duties seriously.[5] Likewise, the park movement at the turn of the century hoped to discipline the lower classes by draining off their excess energy in organized sporting activities that stressed the importance of teamwork and discipline. While Marxists insisted that such cultural beliefs were designed to keep the poor in their place, it is probably fairer to say that the reformers believed that their message of self-discipline was the key to getting ahead and achieving upward mobility in America. Only if workers remained sober, recognized their civic duties, and applied themselves could they hope to improve their financial standing.

THE REFORMERS COME UNDER ATTACK

Today the very notion of a "Victorian morality" has lost favor with many civic and political leaders, but it was remarkable how successful it was in eliminating the antisocial behavior we often associate with the underclass today. At the turn of the century, crime rates were extremely low, two-parent families were the norm, and the overwhelming majority of potential workers actively participated in the labor market. These achievements are even more impressive when we consider that the nineteenth century was a period of rapid industrial and social change that left many people financially insecure. Close to 40 to 45 percent of the population at the end of the nineteenth century would have probably been considered poor by today's definition of poverty. Despite these hardships, very few individuals who were economically poor engaged in the kind of self-destructive behavior that characterizes the underclass today. It is only when political and civic elites began to question the wisdom of the Victorian morality in the post-World War II period that the underclass emerged as a major social problem.

Even then, the challengers to the Victorian norms that dominated this country in the nineteenth and early twentieth centuries did not completely overturn all traditional values. While many individuals still found Victorian values appealing, they increasingly found themselves in competition with people advocating a more laissez-faire set of norms. The reasons for the breakdown in cultural beliefs are complex, but several factors stand out. First, after the sacrifice and discipline of World War II, some segments of society were receptive to embracing a less demanding civic philosophy. A growing number of academic, entertainment, and civic leaders began to see calls for self-control and discipline as nothing more than a priggish and parochial public philosophy that inhibited people's full self-development. In place of stressing character, self-discipline, and public duties, the new post-World War II morality emphasized self-expression and individual rights. The growing affluence of the 1950s likewise led many social critics to believe that we had entered a postindustrial age in which dedication and sacrifice were no longer required. The very success of a Victorian morality that stressed hard work and discipline may thus have contained within itself the seeds of its own self-destruction. Daniel Bell has pointed out that the discipline required of a capitalist economy might be destroyed by its own "cultural contradictions." "The consumerism and permissiveness that a capitalist economy promoted often undermined the very virtues—hard work, discipline, postponement of gratification—that capitalism depended on for its survival."[6] As people grew up in a society of affluence that instantly satisfied most of their needs, they no longer saw the need for self-discipline. Creativity and self-expression rather than restraint were now perceived to be the keys to economic prosperity.

The development of this alternative morality was further enhanced by the turmoil that grew out of the Vietnam War as well as the coming of age of the baby boomers. In protest of what they believed to be an unjust war, many youths began to reject the Victorian morality which they believed symbolized the arrogance of the political system as a whole. Since the sacrifices and duties of this war seemed unjust, many college students stressed their rights and entitlements rather than their duties and obligations. Instead of focusing on long-term goals and a sense of moderation, a generation of bright and articulate college students advocated the enjoyment of the present and "doing your own thing," an attitude that eventually worked itself into the vernacular of American life. As the post–World War II generation reached adulthood, people schooled in the old Victorian morality increasingly found themselves swamped by the legions of young people raised on the new morality. The dream of a new beginning espoused by so many students soon turned into what Myron Magnet has provocatively labeled "the nightmare."[7]

As American values began to change, they had a negative ripple effect on all segments of society, including work habits, education, and family life. In business, the nineteenth-century stress on hard work, investment, and productivity now had to compete with the doctrine of consumerism and instant gratification. As the ethic of self-expression and individual rights found its way into the school curriculum, even the quality of American education began to decline. The collapse of traditional values likewise affected the stability of the two-parent family. If Barbara Ehrenreich and Christopher Jencks were correct in saying that the fragmentation of the family reflected a shift in cultural attitudes among civic elites toward marriage and parenting, they failed to see that the problem was part of a larger transformation in American values. The old Victorian morality, which stressed duties and self-restraint, was now in competition with a more laissez-faire morality that did not take marital obligations or sexual fidelity seriously.

Once community leaders became ambivalent about the core values that had dominated the nineteenth century, they ceased administering rewards and sanctions in the clear and unambiguous fashion they once had. As a consequence, many low-income individuals, whose commitment and ability to live up to those norms were weak to begin with, abandoned the values of self-restraint even more quickly than the rest of society.[8] As the commitment of indigents to Victorian norms quickly became unwound, their financial standing was harmed in a way that the more affluent sectors of society could not even imagine. The wealth of the middle class helped to cushion them from the damaging effects of marital breakups and a lack of interest in work. But when the same beliefs trickled down to the lower strata of society, the erosion of traditional values destroyed the stability of life in the inner city. While the decline of the Victorian principles was at best an irritant for society as a whole, the weakening of social norms in the ghetto led to the unfortunate rise of the underclass.

THE GROWTH OF A WELFARE STATE THAT PROMISES MUCH AND ASKS LITTLE IN RETURN

If the breakdown of traditional values created the necessary conditions for the growth of the underclass, the problem was compounded by the growth of the laissez-faire nature of most government welfare programs. Besides growing up in a society whose core values were undergoing dramatic changes, the poor were exposed to a welfare state that was extremely ambivalent and even hesitant about endorsing the Victorian virtues of hard work and accountability. To appreciate this point, we must remember that some American political thinkers have always felt that government should refrain from altering the values of its citizens. The most clear-cut examples of this attitude were articulated by the founders of the republic, who had certainly entertained reservations about the character of the American people. But instead of attacking the root causes of people's behavior by altering their beliefs, the founders thought the republic could survive by balancing one segment of society with another.

While the government's neutral role in pitting ambition against ambition may have made sense in the early years of the republic when the only issue at stake was the development of a viable commercial economy, a similar attitude may be less effective in combatting poverty or encouraging people to enter the work force.[9] When the government began to address social problems in the 1960s, it unfortunately resurrected and modified the attitudes of the founders rather than the beliefs of their nineteenth-century predecessors. When Lyndon Johnson launched his Great Society, he conceived of government as a neutral broker that would assist interest groups to achieve their goals. In contrast to the social reformers of the nineteenth century who believed that government had a right to ask that individuals meet certain minimal obligations to society, the Great Society saw its job in more limited terms as distributing benefits to the various interests in society. Theodore Lowi eventually coined the term "interest group liberalism" to describe this conception of government as a broker among contending parties.[10]

When the behavior of the poor began to deteriorate in the 1960s, the war on poverty found itself at a loss for correcting the destructive actions of the underclass. Because it viewed itself as a neutral agent, the state was hesitant about playing an active role in altering the attitudes of the large number of poor who seemed increasingly indifferent about their social responsibilities. When advocates of the Great Society thought about the issue at all, they simply assumed as a matter of course that the poor possessed the motivation necessary to become productive members of society. They thus tended to reject the idea that society should either blame or hold the poor accountable for their actions if they chose to misbehave. The welfare state, in providing for the needs of indigents, promised the poor much but demanded very little of them in return.

The best way to illustrate this shift in attitudes is to look at how government agencies have labeled welfare programs. As Charles Murray has perceptively noted, when welfare programs were first established, public officials always referred to them as "the dole."[11] The clear implication was that assistance programs were a handout to be avoided at all costs. If receiving the dole was a stigma, then the flip side of the coin was that when the poor achieved financial independence by sticking with a job, they could enjoy a sense of pride in their accomplishments. Before the culture of the welfare state became widespread, many of the poor derived satisfaction from being employed and financially self-sufficient.

But as government programs grew, the welfare establishment insisted that aid programs were not "the dole" but "transfer payments" or "entitlements." While the change in vocabulary may seem technical in nature, it signified a major shift in how the government and the poor themselves perceived their role in society. If the poor could claim assistance as an "entitlement," it was unclear whether they had any obligation to become productive working members of society. As soon as social workers sought out the poor who had previously shunned welfare, and passed the word that welfare was a basic right, they inadvertently undermined the status of those working poor who previously had taken pride in their financial independence. Rather than enhancing the prestige of the working poor who had made it on their own, public welfare officials often suggested that such people were foolish not to take advantage of benefits to which they were entitled. Society no longer thought it was an embarrassment or a stigma to become a ward of the state. On the contrary, welfare was merely a right that all eligible people should properly exercise. The reformers and social workers who pushed this new welfare philosophy were undoubtedly sincere in their efforts to help indigents, but they failed to see that their actions had the unanticipated result of undermining the motivation of the poor to become self-reliant. The consequences of this new attitude were immediately evident in the declining rates of participation in the labor market. As political and welfare officials unintentionally undercut the work ethic, a growing number of indigents became increasingly indifferent about either looking for a job or holding on to a steady one. The more people dropped out of the labor market or became cavalier about developing a steady employment record, the harder it became for people to escape poverty on their own.

While the government's entitlements programs helped to erode people's willingness to work, its reluctance to ask much of the poor in return also adversely affected the quality of urban life. Lawrence Mead, among others, has passionately described how the laissez-faire attitude of government toward the public behavior of the poor resulted in a breakdown of decorum in our inner cities. Undoubtedly one reason why reformers did not believe in holding people responsible for their actions was their growing belief that structural factors were solely responsible for the actions of the poor.[12] But ironically, by constantly blaming only the economy or racial discrimination for the plight of the poor, many reformers may inadvertently have aggravated the undesirable and antisocial behavior that they were supposedly explaining away. Once analysts focused on the victimization of the poor—rather than on their responsibility to work and be productive members of society—they often tacitly excused and thus legitimized behavior that they should have tried to correct. In the process, they sent the wrong signal to inner-city residents.

Perhaps the most vivid example of how the new welfare morality had overturned Victorian principles is reflected in the government's attitude toward panhandling and the homeless. In the 1950s and 1960s most cities routinely enforced vagrancy laws and expected people to behave themselves in public. By the 1970s, these standards had broken down and urban areas had become more difficult places to live in. With more and more individuals aggressively begging on the streets, street crime rising, and the courts giving indigents more freedoms in public places, a growing number of individuals retreated to what Joe Garreau has called "edge cities," where they could isolate themselves from the harshness of public life.[13] If public officials had lost interest in maintaining a sense of order, developers were more than willing to fill the gap by enticing individuals to privately owned malls and gated residential areas where a sense of decorum was still maintained. But in inner cities vagrancy laws became more of a historical oddity than a useful tool for regulating the behavior of the poor.

The same pattern of change has also affected a wide range of other public institutions, often to the detriment of the poor themselves. Unlike the decision to overturn vagrancy or public drunkenness laws which primarily annoyed and frightened middle-class shoppers, alterations in government programs like housing have seriously eroded the quality of life in the urban ghetto. When the government initially built low-income housing for the poor, its policy was to screen applicants for apartments that became available. The public officials who ran the projects also notified residents that they would be expelled from the projects for acts of violence or disruptive behavior. However, as the courts and organizations like the American Civil Liberties Union attacked these practices, public housing authorities started to drop their screening procedures. When housing authorities were notified that residents were violating project rules or disturbing their neighbors, they often became more concerned about upholding the rights of the accused than of preserving order. Instead of holding indigents accountable for their actions, welfare officials insisted that the poor not be stigmatized in any fashion. But as Nicholas Lemann points out in his compelling story of black migration from the South, the results became a disaster for those living in low-income housing, who increasingly wished to escape the chaos of government housing projects.[14] When residents realized that government did not expect them to act with civility, their temptation to engage in self-destructive actions increased dramatically. By thus neglecting its responsibilities to hold people accountable for their actions, the government inadvertently played a major role in the growth of the underclass.

Nowhere is this fact more evident than in the dramatic rise of crime in this country. The breakdown in the behavior of people living in public housing projects was part of a larger collapse of law and order in society as a whole. As the 1960s began and the values of the welfare state reinforced changing mores in society, the crime rate in the country literally exploded. It affected all segments of society but was especially hard on the urban ghetto. For the first time criminologists started to talk about the problems of black-on-black crime, as minorities and the poor often victimized their own neighborhoods. Despite the rise in the crime rate, elected officials did not make the protection of their communities a priority. As figure 9.1 illustrates, when the number of part I crimes per one hundred people in the population shot upward, the judicial and political system elected to imprison fewer people. In 1960 there was over a 6 percent chance that an offender would receive a prison sentence, but by 1974 the odds had dropped to a little over 2 percent. Instead of isolating dangerous criminals, civic and political elites adopted a laissez-faire attitude toward crime which often had the unfortunate consequence of destroying the social fabric of many inner-city neighborhoods. At the same time that William Ryan was insisting that many conservatives were heartlessly blaming the victims of oppression for their actions, the government increasingly chose to turn the other cheek. The problem was that many of the poor were not innocent victims at all. The flip side of the argument that society should not blame

Figure 9.1
Crimes Rates and Prison Risk

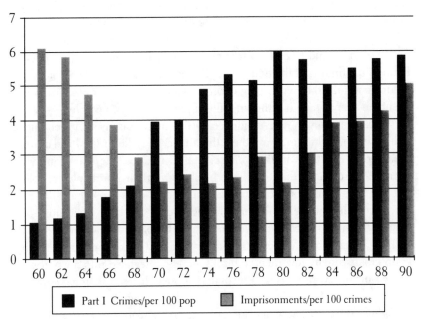

Part I Crimes/per 100 pop   Imprisonments/per 100 crimes

Sources: U.S. Department of Justice, *Sourcebook of Criminal Justice Statistics*, 1990 (Washington, D.C.: U.S. Government Printing Office); and U.S. Federal Bureau of Investigation, *Crime in the United States*, annual editions (Washington, D.C.: U.S. Government Printing Office). Crime data only reflect offenses known to the police. Part 1 crimes include homicide, forcible rape, robbery, aggravated assault, burglary, larceny-theft, and motor vehicle theft.

the victim was the dark and unfortunate fact that many low income people had lost all sense of self-control. In its desire to make sure that the "victims" of society were not blamed, the government inadvertently sent out the message that people would not be held responsible for their actions. In spite of their disparate nature, the thread tying together the explosion of crime in the sixties, the decline of the work ethic, the relaxation of academic standards in our schools, and the increasing fragility of the family among the poor was the weakening of traditional cultural values.

THE IMPORTANCE OF MEDIATING GROUPS

As political and civic elites ceased to administer symbolic rewards that upheld traditional values, it is not surprising that the poor, whose internalization of these values was weak to begin with, would abandon them faster than the rest of society. Because roughly two-thirds of all indigents in America are

Caucasians, and only 30 percent are black, a significant majority of the underclass is white, but percentagewise the underclass is much greater among blacks than whites. For instance, most of the long-term poor as well as those most dependent on welfare are black women, and even most troubling is the growing propensity of young black males to terrorize their own neighborhoods and to end up serving time in jail. One especially shocking figure is the finding of the Sentencing Project, a Washington-based nonprofit agency committed to sentencing reform, that one out of four black men aged twenty to twenty-nine is either in jail, on probation, or on parole.[15]

When we ask why the incidence of the underclass is so much higher among one minority than another, the answer may lie in the breakdown of mediating institutions in the inner city. For instance, the black family has become more fragile than ever, the black church has lost its pivotal role in holding together its poor constituents, and middle-class blacks have fled from the often inhospitable atmosphere of the ghetto. As these institutions have declined in importance, indigent blacks have become more vulnerable to the collapse of traditional values in the larger society. Unlike many of their white counterparts, many low-income blacks are less integrated into a whole array of well-organized primary and secondary groups that can help to slow down and even check the erosion of values in society as a whole.

As discussed earlier, when blacks were brought to this country by their slave owners, they often lacked a rich and diverse group life. To fill that void, the black community invested considerable resources trying to build up a sense of community that often revolved around the church. At religious services, which often were an all-day affair, young men and women were taught the importance of observing traditional values. While it is hard to quantify the benefits of this socialization process, Richard Freeman found that young black men were more likely to find work and succeed in their jobs if they attended church.[16] In *The Miracles of a Black Church*, a moving story of an inner-city neighborhood in New York, Samuel Freedman has shown how a dynamic black minister had infused some sense of meaning and purpose in the lives of his many low-income parishioners.[17] Rather than imitating the behavior of the underclass, the members of this congregation have shown promise of becoming worthwhile members of their community. Unfortunately, the positive influence of these church activities is in a state of decline. Lincoln and Mamiya have recently found that black churches are having trouble attracting young people, especially young black males, to their congregations. All too often, it is only elderly black women who consistently attend Sunday services.[18]

The problems of black churches have been compounded by the erosion of family ties. The precarious nature of the black family is both a consequence as well as a cause of the breakdown of traditional norms. As traditional principles of marital obligations have come under attack, fewer and fewer men have felt the need to support their families. As low-income black family ties have come unglued, the ability of parents to teach the virtues of self-discipline to their children has also become difficult.

A final development contributing to the rise of the black underclass has been the decision of middle-class blacks to flee to more affluent and heterogeneous neighborhoods. Given the restrictions of Jim Crow laws in both southern and northern cities, middle-income blacks were often physically unable to move outside the ghetto. This lack of mobility meant that the middle class provided the necessary leadership in the inner city that helped to restrain socially deviant behavior. As Elijah Anderson has pointed out in his book *Streetwise*, middle-class blacks in Philadelphia "served the black community well as visible, concrete symbols of success and moral value, living examples of the fruits of hard work, perseverance, decency, and propriety."[19] But as the discriminatory barriers against blacks in the larger society have weakened and conditions in the inner city have become more dangerous, black professionals have been both pushed as well as pulled by the lure of new opportunities. William Julius Wilson and more recently Elijah Anderson have argued that this exodus of successful blacks has served to isolate low-income blacks from the rest of society.[20]

But the exodus of the black middle class has not left a complete moral vacuum in the ghetto. As Mitchell Duneier has perceptively noted, many decent "working poor" blacks still remain in the ghetto and want to build a community in which people accept personal responsibility for building a livable, safe, and productive society.[21] But even the "working poor," the last bastion of stability and self-restraint in the inner city, find that they cannot compete with other influences shaping the mores of the ghetto. As traditional institutions like the family and church have declined, a whole series of new institutions has arisen to challenge and threaten conventional forms of authority. In all too many instances, drug dealers, gang leaders, and some rap musicians now seek to replace the churches, the schools, and the middle and working class as the dominant groups socializing people into what is appropriate behavior. As Duneier notes, this trend is epitomized by much of rap music, which works outside traditional institutions like the schools and churches, and frequently "legitimizes the most extreme forms of permissiveness, all of which function to distort the seemingly natural relations between ends and means and the working class conception of value."[22] The suggestion by the rapper Ice-T that ghetto youths should kill a cop is only the most destructive example of the attitudes espoused by the new cultural heroes of the inner city. In light of the challenge from these new institutions, it is not surprising that the remaining sources of traditional authority in the ghetto, such as the working poor and the clergy, have been fighting a losing battle trying to halt the growth of the black underclass.

In contrast, low-income whites are more likely to come from intact two-parent families who may have helped to check and override some of the permissive norms of the larger society. Although the data are sketchy, it also appears that low-income Caucasians are more likely to be attached to evangelical churches, which have often railed against the growing erosion of traditional values. While the growth of more permissive norms in society as a whole has led to the growth of an underclass that cuts across all racial barriers, the breakdown of the family and church and out-migration of the middle class have made low-income blacks especially vulnerable to these societal changes.

In spite of the problems plaguing the inner city, many scholars have resisted cultural explanations because they claim that the underclass appears to subscribe to the same Victorian values that have lost part of their legitimacy in this country. But the problem with the poor is not that they have adopted an alternative set of values but that their commitment to any set of beliefs is often shallow and of limited duration. We must not confuse control or anomic explanations, which believe that the underclass is suffering from a lack of well-ingrained and cohesive values, with the culture of poverty explanation, which insists that the underclass has adopted its own perverse and deviant cultural beliefs. As Lawrence Mead has argued in a slightly different context, "Lower class people profess attachment, just like other Americans, to the family, work and obeying the law. They are distinctive not in their beliefs but in their inability to conform to them as closely as other people."[23] In some cases the underclass will even violate norms whose moral legitimacy they accept and whose appropriateness they advocate. But like individuals who suffer from anomie, the underclass's commitment to such values is so weak that its members feel no sense of obligation to harmonize their beliefs with their actions.

THE UNDERCLASS AND ALTERNATIVE VIEWS OF CULTURE

Even if a reasonable case can be made that the breakdown of traditional values or anomie has caused the rise of the underclass, the argument has not gone unchallenged. Christopher Jencks, among others, has argued that the actions of the underclass are so disparate in nature that it is impossible to come up with a unified explanation for their destructive behavior.[24] But by now it should be clear that the breakdown in the family, the increase in crime, and the growing indifference of the poor to participation in the labor market are not isolated events at all. All the characteristics we associate with the underclass appeared at roughly the same point in time, which suggests that the emergence of the underclass reflects some larger changes in society.

While many analysts accept the fact that the behavior of the poor has become more pathological and that cultural values have played a significant role in this growth, they sharply disagree over how culture has influenced the actions of the poor. In rejecting the Durkheimian analysis subscribed to in this chapter, commentators suggest that the cultural difficulties of the poor stem either from false consciousness (the Marxist position), a separate and pathological "culture of poverty" (the Banfield and Harrington view), neighborhood effects and social isolation (Wilson's position), or a lack of congruence between the values of the poor and the opportunities available in society ("strain theory"). Despite their popularity, none of these theories offers a convincing explanation for the origins and growth of the underclass. In fact, as we shall soon see, they share a common flaw: they fail to explain why the cultural or attitudinal problems of the poor became so acute in the reform years of the 1960s. They are also unable to explain why those like Asian-Americans who have maintained their family ties and held onto traditional values have prospered, while those who have abandoned these values remain mired in poverty as part of the underclass.

The Marxist Position

These limitations are readily apparent in Marxist accounts of poverty. As explained earlier, Marxists believe that the poor are heavily influenced by the cultural traditions of society. But in contrast to the thesis of this chapter, they insist that the poor suffer not from the breakdown of cultural norms or anomie, but from a sense of false consciousness that leads to political quietism. Unlike Durkheimians who see culture as a mechanism for promoting social cohesion and individual productivity, Marxists maintain that culture is more often a source of dominance that elites use to maintain their status in society. Rejecting the argument that Victorian values enabled the poor to be productive citizens, Marxists believe that the norms espoused by associations like the Boy Scouts, the YMCA, the temperance movement, and the Progressives helped to pacify and exploit the poor. By convincing those at the bottom of the economic ladder to become sober, responsible, and hard-working individuals, Marxists alleged that the political system could guarantee that workers would not threaten the status quo. The objective of American culture has been to reinforce the position of elites while oppressing the poor. More recently, Samuel Bowles and Herbert Gintis, as discussed in chapter 4, have also leveled the same charge against education in this country by arguing that the stress in public schools on merit and achievement reflects an attempt by the ruling elites "to cool out" the poor and working classes so that they will accept their station in life.[25] They maintain that the whole ideology of discipline and hard work is really a facade that elites can use to legitimize as well as pacify the poor when they fail to achieve financial success. The schools help to guarantee that the lower rungs of society will meekly accept their financial standing in life as a legitimate reflection of merit principles and thus remain quiet about political affairs.

While many academics today embrace one version or another of the above Marxist views of culture, their assumptions about Victorian norms are open to debate. First, the assertions by Bowles, Gintis, and other Marxists about American values reflect a serious misreading of American history. The social movements that tried to shape the values of the working class in the nineteenth century clearly accepted the belief that sobriety and hard work would lead to financial success rather than political oppression. They would undoubtedly argue that controlling people's self-serving tendencies is a far cry from pacifying or politically controlling them to accept the status quo.

In response to this kind of criticism, a Marxist might reply that the Victorian norms that shaped American life have had the functional consequence of limiting the opportunities for those at the bottom of the social ladder to gain upward mobility. Regardless of the motives of those who preached self-restraint and self-control to the poor, the consequences of their actions so pacified the poor that no really significant social changed occurred. But if we look at the country's early successes in eliminating poverty, it is difficult to accept this argument. Since the poverty rate dropped substantially from the end of the nineteenth century to the early 1960s, it is unclear how traditional American values could have conditioned the poor to accept their lot in life. The rise of the underclass and the failure of the war on poverty coincide with the decline rather than the active transmittal of Victorian norms. When we look at ethnic groups who have financially succeeded in this country, the Marxist position seems even more vulnerable. As mentioned earlier, Harry Kitano has argued that Japanese Americans have done well in America because they willingly adopted the work ethic and entrepreneurial values of their newly adopted country. Unlike the underclass today, Japanese immigrants and their families eagerly embraced, and apparently still practice, the Victorian principles of self-discipline, hard work, and self-reliance. Today Vietnamese Americans appear to be repeating this pattern of success. In spite of Bowles's and Gintis's assertions that the public schools socialize the lower classes into accepting their status in life, Vietnamese children, who often go to poor inner-city schools, are enjoying impressive academic success. The educational achievements and financial accomplishments of Asian Americans, which most Marxists and liberals generally avoid discussing, suggest that self-control is still the key to upward mobility in this country.

Another difficulty with the Marxist view of culture is its assumption that the poor have internalized the values of society. As Dennis Wrong ably pointed out many years ago, many academics, and this is especially true of Marxists, tend to have an oversocialized view of mankind.[26] Marxists often naively assume that institutions like the schools and the family have successfully transmitted a unified and self-contained culture to those at the bottom of the economic ladder. They consequently fail to see that the dilemma facing the United States today is that too many of its low-income citizens feel no moral attachment to a publicly shared belief system.

As a result of these blinders, Marxists often cannot explain why the self-destructive behavior of the poor has arisen in the first place. Their conspiratorial theory of culture has forced them to exaggerate the pacified rather than the self-destructive actions of the poor. Indeed, as we shall see later, some Marxists even argue that the underclass exists only as a figment of the imagination of conservatives. When Bowles and Gintis talk about the "cooled out" lower class or other Marxists insist that the poor have been culturally coopted into accepting the status quo, they fail to see that many residents of the inner city are anything but submissive and docile. Whether we look at our schools or urban areas, the problem is not that society has pacified the poor but that it has lost its ability to discipline and teach the poor the virtues of self-restraint and hard work.

The Culture of Poverty

As an alternative to both Marxism and our anomic description of the poor, a rather disparate group of writers, sociologists, and political analysts have advanced another cultural explanation of poverty to account for the destructive actions of the underclass which is commonly known as the culture of poverty thesis. But the proponents of this school believe that the difficulties of the underclass reflect the fact that many of the poor have developed their own separate and "pathological" set of beliefs which is not conducive to upward mobility and financial prosperity. Once these low-income groups establish their own subcultures, they can constantly recruit new members and socialize them into the deviant values of their association. The danger thus exists that the pathological beliefs of the underclass can be passed on to the younger members of the ghetto, locking many people into a vicious cycle of poverty and despair. Until their isolation from the beliefs and values of the larger society is ended, there is little hope that the underclass will abstain from the self-destructive behavior that is keeping them mired in poverty.

Surprisingly, in the past decades a wide variety of writers from both sides of the political spectrum have promulgated one form or another of the culture of poverty thesis. For instance, in the 1930s the well-known author James Farrell tried to explain both the poverty of the Irish in general and that of the popular character of his novel *Studs Lonigan* in terms of their aberrant cultural beliefs.[27] Farrell argued that many young Irish Catholics who came from lower middle income families often hopelessly slipped into poverty when they adopted the false values of the street, the gang, and the poolroom. As the schools and the Catholic church failed to provide the appropriate values for young men to become respectable citizens, the streets took over and perverted their dreams by glorifying the impoverished notion of the "tough guy" as hero. In the 1960s the idea that the poor had their own separate and identifiable culture was further developed by social scientists like Michael Harrington on the left and Edward Banfield on the right. In contrast to Farrell's literary depiction of a "tough guy" ethos, Banfield, and to a lesser extent Harrington, talked about the poor embracing a subculture that stressed instant gratification and a concern with the present rather than the future. Banfield and Harrington consequently believed that many of the poor were unable to take advantage of the opportunities available in society because they had internalized a set of values that was at odds with mainstream American beliefs. More recently, in a surprising development, a variety of liberals have begun to revive the culture of poverty thesis by arguing that the residents of our inner cities are suffering from what has now become know as the problem of "neighborhood effects."[28] They see the cumulative effect of ghetto life as crowding out traditional beliefs and legitimizing in the minds of many ghetto residents the idea that petty crime, promiscuous sex, or other destructive actions are acceptable behavior.

In spite of the intuitive appeal of the culture of poverty argument, the theory is at best an incomplete description of both the poor in general and the underclass in particular. As a global explanation, recent historical developments have undermined its creditability as a viable theory of poverty. If the vast majority of poor people were suffering from a separate culture of poverty, we would not have seen the tremendous drop in the ranks of the pretransfer poor that occurred in the 1950s and early 1960s. As the Michigan survey also found, the vast majority of poor people seem to float in and out of poverty depending on fluctuations in their external circumstances. Similarly, the culture of poverty's troubles in explaining poverty as a whole is matched by its difficulties in accounting for the growth of the underclass in the late 1960s and 1970s. If the behavior of the underclass reflects their attachment to an alternative set of values, we are left in the dark as to why they increasingly came to follow a pathological set of values during the reform years of the 1960s. Both Banfield's and Harrington's accounts of the culture of poverty are historically unsatisfactory because they provide no adequate explanation as to why a deviant subculture would arise in the first place.

Nicholas Lemann has recently tried to solve part of this problem by tracing the difficulties of the ghetto back to the rural values of Southern blacks. In *The Promised Land* he argues that the actions of the black underclass may reflect the mores of the black sharecroppers who elected to migrate from the South to the urban cities of the North in the post-World War II period.[29] While recognizing that numerous factors may influence people's beliefs, Lemann argues that there is a link between the rural values of black Southerners and the destructive behavior of the underclass. Like the thesis of Charles Johnson, whose work we cited in chapter 6 on the black family, Lemann believes the legacy of the postemancipation period has hindered the ability of blacks to adjust to current urban conditions. Unfortunately, the evidence in support of the sharecropper thesis is not substantial. First, sharecroppers were not always representative of the vast majority of blacks who migrated north. Second, Lemann's account of the development of the culture of poverty is relatively silent as to why the problems of the ghetto became so much worse in the 1960s. Historically, the black migrations of the 1940s and 1950s had pretty much run their course years before the destructive behavior of the underclass became a real problem. Third, Southern-born blacks who have recently migrated to the North also tend to have higher earnings, lower unemployment rates, and a lower level of welfare dependence than their Northern-born counterparts.[30] If anything, the pathological behavior of the black underclass may represent more of a break than a continuation of historical Southern traditions.

In light of the above problems, there are two alternative ways to explain the origins of a culture of poverty. First, it is possible that many black Americans have retained a separate cultural tradition from their postslavery days, even if it is not the sharecropper culture described by Lemann. But because society vigorously enforced adherence to its larger cultural norms, the majority of inner-city residents might have wisely decided to hold their beliefs in check. Since the Victorian norms of nineteenth and early twentieth century America stressed the need for restraint and self-discipline, white society might have heavily censored behavior that was at odds with these mores. And it is only now with the relaxation of those societal values that the belief system of rural Southern blacks has begun to surface.

Another alternative is to combine the notion of anomie with the development of a street-oriented culture of poverty. The breakdown of society's values might have fostered the rise of a new and distinctive culture of poverty that had little or no relationship to the historical origins of either blacks or whites. As many young people became alienated from their families and church and were confused about what values to adopt, they may have embraced the values of the street in order to provide some structure to their lives. Like Studs Lonigan before them, many young males may have mimicked the values of the tough guy in order to fill a cultural void caused by the fragmentation of traditional controls. If this scenario is correct, then the rise of a separate culture of poverty is yet another consequence of the growth of normlessness in society. The general loosening of society's values may create incentives for people to create their own distinctive subcultures upon which they subsequently pattern their behavior. But if the problem of anomie pushes people to adopt deviant values, low-income neighborhoods and groups such as street gangs may help to socialize, as well as reinforce and solidify, that commitment. Many analysts insist that there are definite "neighborhood effects" or prevailing practices in the ghetto that reinforce and legitimize destructive behavior such as violent street crime or a cavalier attitude toward family responsibilities.

But the scope and significance of such neighborhood effects in particular, or the culture of poverty in general, should not be exaggerated. The main problem with the poor is that they are loosely committed to their values rather than being partisan advocates of a pathological or deviant set of cultural beliefs. In most cases drug dealers, gang leaders, and even rap musicians are merely expressing in exaggerated form the permissiveness and self-indulgence that is rampant in the larger society. While most poor people will at least verbally give lip service to values that are generally similar to those advocated by most Americans, their commitment to living up to those values is more shallow in nature. Their desire for self-expression and freedom merely stretches and weakens their belief that they also have an obligation to work and behave themselves. But the advocates of the culture of poverty, like Marxists before them, often insist on viewing the poor from an oversocialized perspective. They thus fail to realize that the underclass began to grow in the late 1960s, when traditional socializing agents broke down and the commitment of many of the poor to social norms began to weaken. The policy problem facing government officials is not that the underclass has embraced deviant values, but that it is increasingly unwilling to embrace any values at all that require self-discipline or commitment. The problems of the underclass have occurred—not because it has adopted its own distinctive and separate set of values—but because it has succumbed, in its own exaggerated fashion, to the breakdown of cultural norms in society as a whole.

The Social Isolation of the Poor

William Julius Wilson has developed a third alternative for explaining the rise of the underclass, often called the "social isolation thesis."[31] As mentioned in chapter 3, Wilson was one of the most prominent liberal commentators in the post-Moynihan era to note that the fabric of life in the ghetto was being torn apart. But instead of focusing on the deviant values of the poor or the rise of anomie and the decline of Victorian norms in society as a whole, he argued that the increasingly destructive behavior of inner city residents reflects the adverse economic changes occurring in the industrial heartland of America. In this sense Wilson, like most liberals, maintained that the apparent destructive behavior of the underclass is as much a consequence as it is a determinant of poverty.

Wilson maintains that the transformation of the U.S. economy and the migration of heavy industry out of the inner city to the suburbs have severely restricted the opportunities available to inner-city residents. This thesis, which is known as the "mismatch theory of urban development" (see chapter 11), argues that the out-migration of businesses to the city's suburbs has physically isolated poor blacks from any chance of upward advancement by limiting their opportunities for finding well-paying jobs. The deviant behavior of the poor is thus not an ahistorical event that is divorced from recent developments in the larger economy. On the contrary, Wilson maintains that as changes in the economy have led to the concentration of indigents in the inner city, the poor have been exposed to social norms (or what is now called neighborhood effects) that are not necessarily conducive to holding down a job or obeying the law. When people see their neighbors neglecting their family responsibilities, selling drugs, or engaging in other illegal activities, they will be inclined to mimic their behavior and engage in deviant actions themselves. The socio-psychological responses of the poor to their bleak economic conditions have thus acquired a life of their own, generating a pathological culture that is harmful to inner-city residents.

But according to Wilson, the deleterious impact of this physical isolation and its resulting neighborhood effects on the poor has been compounded by the fact that indigents have increasingly become socially isolated from the values and opportunities of mainline society.[32] By social isolation Wilson simply means "the lack of contact or of sustained interaction with the individuals or institutions that represent mainstream society."[33] When individuals are socially cut off from the larger society, they lack access to desirable role models and information about possible job opportunities. When middle-class blacks were forced to live in the ghetto because of Jim Crow laws, they helped check some of the adverse learning that went on in the ghetto by providing alternative role models for young men to follow, as well as information about possible jobs in the larger society. As middle-class blacks have fled the inner city, the residents left behind in the ghetto have lost the social connections that often kept them abreast of changes in the labor market. When people are part of larger social networks they are more likely to hear about employment possibilities and receive the social and cultural support they need to take advantage of any such openings.

While Wilson's argument has been widely cited and undoubtedly explains some facets of ghetto life, it remains to be seen if it is a complete explanation of the rise of the underclass in this country. First, there are problems with Wilson's chronology of events. As discussed earlier, the fragmentation of the family, the increase in crime, and the growing propensity of the poor to drop out of the labor market appear to have started in the late 1960s, at least a decade before the industrial dislocations stressed by Wilson.

Second, Wilson's assumption that businesses are moving to the suburbs solely for economic reasons is open to alternative explanations. Most obviously, he overlooks the possibility that the movement of businesses and people out of the ghetto is also due to the breakdown of cultural values in the inner city, rather than vice versa. When the social cohesion of a neighborhood is being torn apart, few merchants are likely to want to raise their children there, let alone invest their resources. In pointing out that businesses are leaving the inner city and that the remaining residents are acting in self-destructive ways, Wilson often overlooks the problems in determining which is the cause and which is the effect. While he is absolutely right to argue that the movement of jobs out of the inner city has been a disaster for poor blacks, the problem may be as much a cultural issue as an economic one.

Third, Wilson's argument that economic hardships inevitably lead to the problem of neighborhood effects, and eventually social isolation, appears to be an argument that does not apply across the board to all ethnic groups. Even if we assume for the sake of argument that the out-migration of businesses from the inner city is a result of economic forces, it is important to realize that people can respond in a variety of ways to such adversity. As already mentioned, when Japanese Americans encountered racial discrimination and were driven out of most jobs wanted by lower-income whites, they neither settled in neighborhoods where undesirable behavior was the norm nor did they allow themselves to become socially isolated from mainstream society. Given their desire to succeed financially, they located and exploited economic niches such as truck farming and fruit peddling where they faced little economic competition. The initiative of many Japanese Americans in identifying and then satisfying an unmet need in the local economy guaranteed their ability to survive and even prosper financially. The cultural values of Chinese Americans, who were even physically isolated in special enclaves, helped insure that in "Chinatowns" the destructive behavior we normally associate with an underclass was held to a minimum. Although Wilson suggests that social isolation is a process over which the poor have little control, the opposite situation may be closer to the truth. Those groups who are culturally committed to getting ahead have always seemed able to avoid the social isolation and pathologically destructive behavior that Wilson thinks inevitably follows from rough economic times.

Fourth, and most important, Wilson's thesis overlooks the extent to which the difficulties of the inner city reflect broader trends in the larger society. The problem with the black underclass is not that it is isolated from mainstream values but that it has adopted an exaggerated version of society's emancipated and often anomic culture. While the out-migration of the black middle class and the deterioration of other mediation groups have made indigent blacks more than other ethnic groups vulnerable to the erosion of traditional values in society as a whole, Wilson fails to realize the that the problems of the black underclass reflect the changing mores of society as a whole. Or as Michael Duneier has aptly summed it up, the "many pathological social trends in the ghetto are nothing more than . . . concentrated reflections of life in the wider society."[34] If that is the case, then it is the receptiveness rather than the isolation of the black ghetto to developments in the larger culture that explains the unfortunate rise of the underclass.

Strain Theory: A Strained Theory

Because of the limits inherent in Wilson's arguments about the social isolation of the underclass, many liberals have embraced yet another cultural explanation that often goes by the name of strain theory, to account for the apparent pathological behavior of the underclass. This explanation, which was initially developed by Robert Merton, argues that the self-destructive behavior of the underclass stems from the poor's commitment to traditional values and not, as Wilson contends, from their isolation from mainstream culture. Strain theory believes the poor have internalized the values of the larger society, which stress achievement and accumulation, but cannot realize their goals because of the highly stratified nature of our economy. In order to relieve the psychological strain resulting from this tension, the poor often engage in deviant actions by dropping out of the labor market, neglecting their family responsibilities, or committing crimes.[35] In contrast to scholars who take a Durkheimian view of the underclass, strain theorists, paradoxically, insist that the destructive behavior of many indigents is a result of their commitment rather than loose attachment to mainstream values. Or to paraphrase Merton, a cardinal American virtue such as ambition may promote a cardinal American vice, "deviant behavior."[36]

In its most general version, strain theory assumes that all people are equally socialized into a set of values that stresses achievement and worldly success. And it also holds that people engage in undesirable actions only when they are unable to realize their culturally induced goals. The actions of the underclass are merely a consequence, rather than a cause, of their difficulties in finding meaningful employment opportunities.

In making these two assumptions, strain theorists, like Marxists before them, seem guilty of operating with an overly socialized view of mankind. They naturally assume that the poor have internalized the larger values of society when in fact they may not have. To illustrate this point, we can critically look at how strain theorists explain deviant activities such as the high incidence of crime or the unusual number of failed marriages that we often associate with the underclass. While the criminal brutality of the underclass often shocks people, strain theorists explain away the phenomenon by blaming society for the criminal acts of the poor. Merton, for instance, suggests that because so many low-income people lack legitimate means of achieving financial security, they innovate by engaging in illegitimate means to achieve economic success. Crime, in other words, is nothing more than an alternative route for realizing upward mobility. Because the poor recognize that the structure of the economy makes a mockery of their belief in hard work and self-control, they engage in undesirable and criminal actions to express their frustration with the hypocrisy of American society.

Although the above description of events is intriguing, crime statistics are often inconsistent with the predictions of strain theory. If, as strain theorists suggest, indigents are likely to commit acts of crime whenever their values conflict with the harsh reality of economic conditions, we need to know why so many of the poor and non-poor have elected not to engage in this type of behavior at all. There are vast discrepancies in the amount of crime committed within poor communities. As numerous studies of criminal behavior have pointed out, as much as half of all violent crime is usually committed by a very small percentage of offenders. However, if strain theory were correct, then all poor people, and not just a segment of the underclass, should be hardened criminals.

The problem strain theorists have in describing current trends in crime is matched by their difficulty in explaining historical fluctuations in crime rates. Although nationwide data on most crimes did not become available until 1933, James Q. Wilson has been able to piece together a picture of historical trends in crime rates from a variety of sources, including detailed studies of American cities.[37] He notes that the level of crime and disorder in urban areas was extremely high in the early decades of the nineteenth century, but then it declined, albeit in an uneven and erratic pattern, through the end of the nineteenth until around the middle of the twentieth century. As a way of simplifying these data, we can think of crime during this period as being composed of a U-shaped curve. The initially high levels of crime in the 1830s fell dramatically until the 1960s when it began to rise again sharply, although it now appears to be leveling off. What is striking about these figures is that the overall level of crime in the U.S. appears to have no systematic or clear relationship to adverse economic conditions or bleak employment prospects. Only in the case of property crimes like burglary did crime rise and fall as the economy contracted and expanded.[38] But if we look at a more recent period of time, "the connection between economic conditions and criminality no longer seems to exist, or to exist to the same degree. In the United States crimes rates, insofar as we can tell, drifted more or less steadily downward between 1933 and 1960, although the first part of this period (1933–1940) included a severe economic depression and the second part part was one of reasonable prosperity (1941–1960). And the most recent increase in crime occurred during a period of unparalleled prosperity (1960–1980)."[39] If there is any period in American history when there was an acute strain between the values and the promise of American life and the opportunities actually available in society, it had to be during the Great Depression. But contrary to the predictions of Merton, the crimes rate did not go up in the harsh economic times of the 1930s (a period of great strain) but in the more affluent 1960s (a period of minimal strain). As Wilson has noted, even scholars who find evidence that economic factors have some effect on contemporary crime rates concede that "the major movement in crime rates during the last half century cannot be attributed to the business cycle."[40] Since the era of the Great Society, crime has become decoupled from shifts in the economy. This situation may have occurred because in the prosperous years of the 1960s there were both more targets and more opportunities for committing crime, as well as more young people in the labor market. However, most studies find that the shift in the age structure of the U.S. population probably accounted for less than half the increase in crime during the Kennedy years.[41] Even if we control for possible alternative explanations, the rise and decline of traditional cultural values still appears to be a major determinant of the nation's overall crime rate. As the public embraced the principle of self-control in the nineteenth century, crime rates declined. But with the overall loosening of values in the post-World War II period, crime rates have unfortunately soared, making life unbearable for many residents of inner cities.

This loss of values has led not only to crime but also to the breakup of the black family. In *Tally's Corner*, Liebow insists that the poor street-corner men he studied shared the traditional American values of wanting a strong two-parent family in which the father plays an important role in raising his children.[42] But Liebow argued that because the men who hung out on Tally's Corner were not able to provide for their spouses, they tried to hide their failures and relieved their resulting frustrations by sexually taking advantage of the women in the neighborhood. However, in talking to Tally's entourage, Liebow noted that the men claimed that their marriages failed because they had "too much dog in them" to remain sexually faithful to a single woman. But Liebow rejected such explanations, arguing instead that street-corner men sexually exploit women to compensate for their failures as successful breadwinners. By claiming they are "studs" with strong sexual drives, Tally's friends can effectively mask their failures as wage earners. In dismissing his subjects' own account of their sexual behavior, Liebow, like other strain theorists, runs the risk of attributing to their subjects a commitment to traditional values that may not exist. By assuming that the poor, including the men hanging out at Tally's Corner, are perfectly socialized, Liebow and other strain theorists look for external events to account for the breakdown of conventional behavior. But it is possible that Tally's friends were merely unmotivated and imperfectly socialized individuals exhibiting the signs of anomic behavior.

As an indirect way of testing these contrasting explanations, we can examine the historical pattern of single-parent families in this country. As table 9.1 indicates, the breakup of the family, especially black families, is a phenomenon that began in the 1960s, accelerated in the 1970s, and appears to be stabilizing, albeit at a very high rate, in the 1980s and 1990s. If strain theories and their overly socialized view of the poor were correct, we would

Table 9.1
Percentage of Female-Headed
Families

Year	White	Black
1940	10.2	17.9
1950	8.5	17.6
1960	8.1	21.7
1970	9.1	28.3
1980	11.6	40.2
1991	13.2	45.9

Sources: U.S. Bureau of the Census, *Current Population Reports*, Series P-60, no. 161, "Money, Income and Poverty Status in the United States: 1987"; and *Current Population Reports*, Series P-20, no. 458, "Household and Family Characteristics: March 1991."

expect to find more single-parent families during the Great Depression, when the national unemployment rate exceeded 25 percent, or during the 1940s and 1950s, when Jim Crow laws prevailed in the South. But in fact we find the opposite situation. It is only when the economy starts to take off in the 1960s and the laws discriminating against blacks are being swept off the books that the family situation begins to deteriorate. Ironically, in the early years of the Great Depression, when any alleged strain between American values and the economy should have been the strongest, the number of divorces actually declined in this country. While these data are only suggestive rather than conclusive they certainly imply that the problems of the underclass do not stem from a conflict between the values of highly socialized individuals and the often harsh realities of American life.

Second, the tendency of strain theorists like Liebow to overstate people's commitment to cultural values is compounded by their propensity to exaggerate the alleged difficulties that prevent people from realizing their cultural beliefs. An illustration of this point is found in Douglas Glasgow's sensitive and moving study, *The Black Underclass*, which looked at the troubled lives of young black men in the years between 1965 and 1975.[43] Glasgow readily admits that despite a decade of government programs involving compensatory education, antidiscrimination laws, and affirmative-action programs, the young men he studied seemed unmotivated to climb out of poverty on their own.

But like other strain theorists, Glasgow either minimizes this fact or tries to turn it on its head by claiming that many obstacles in society, such as racism, have actually gotten worse. As Glasgow repeatedly argues, the pervasiveness of racism in the job market modifies the aspirations and job-seeking strategies of inner-city youth.[44] But this analysis overlooks the fact that racial discrimination had become less severe in the years between 1965 and 1975. As a result, Glasgow, like other strain theorists, tries to argue that what on its face appears to be dramatic improvement in the conditions of the poor masks the more difficult and serious obstacles facing them. As one hurdle facing the poor is struck down, strain theorists often search for yet another obstacle to take its place. For example, in discussing racism Glasgow argues that "the almost total absence of human evaluators in the rejection process intensifies the helplessness of the ghetto youth. . . . When discrimination was much more overt and not so embedded in organizational procedures, Blacks were at least able to focus their resentment accurately on those who screened them out because they were Black."[45] Thus Glasgow maintains that as overt and personalized forms of racial discrimination fell by the wayside in the late 1960s, they were replaced by a more subtle and therefore more pernicious form of discrimination. Because of Glasgow's evident concern for the young men he studied, and his desire not to criticize them, he inadvertently suggests that minorities were somehow better off in this country when open bigotry was common and public ordinances officially discriminated against the poor. Because of their a priori assumption that structural obstacles are responsible for the plight of the poor, strain theorists are constantly searching for the alleged "obstacles" that are responsible for the rise of the underclass. As old obstacles are knocked down without any appreciable improvement in the lives of the underclass, they constantly have to identify other institutional factors to explain away the troublesome data. But in the process they are often blind to the possibility that a breakdown in values, rather than the emergence of some new hurdle, is the primary cause of the deviant behavior they are trying to explain.

Finally, in addition to overemphasizing the degree to which the poor are socialized as well as the obstacles confronting the poor, strain theorists fail to appreciate the central point of control theory: when people have internalized traditional norms of behavior that stress self-control, they are not likely to engage in self-destructive actions merely because the are unable to realize their aspirations. In the past, indigents who suffered from a lack of appropriate skills and opportunities apparently did not also lack the appropriate values for controlling their behavior. For instance, even when they were driven out of traditional white jobs, and their aspirations for economic success were frustrated by lower-class whites, Chinese and Japanese Americans did not divorce their spouses, disengage from the labor market, or engage in crime to any appreciable degree. If individuals have internalized a coherent set of values that stress discipline and self-control, they are not likely to misbehave or engage in deviant behavior. Although strain theorists insist that the growth of the underclass is due to the discrepancy between the values of the poor and the opportunities in society, the opposite situation may be closer to the truth. It may be the breakdown rather than the presence of values among so many poor people that explains why the underclass is unable to take advantage of the opportunities available in society.

While numerous analysts have tried to explain why the behavior of the poor became so much more self-destructive in the 1960s, the Durkheimian notion of anomie seems to provide the most insight into the origins and growth of the underclass. As we have seen, alternative cultural explanations suffer from two serious flaws. First, most of the theories have trouble explaining why the problems of the underclass began to develop in the relatively affluent decade of the 1960s. Second, they are at a loss to explain why some groups like Asian Americans who have held on to their values have overcome economic deprivation and prospered, while those who have let go of traditional values have often become mired in the ranks of the underclass.

Given the importance of the problem, the critical issue for policymakers is how society should deal with the actions of the underclass. The most obvious answer is that public as well as private organizations should imitate their nineteenth-century predecessors rather than the policy activists of the 1960s, and promote the values of self-discipline and individual control among the underclass. But this policy recommendation has touched off an ongoing debate among conservatives as to what should be the optimal size of the welfare state. Those on the right, who believe that the generosity of the welfare state is the primary reason why the poor have dropped out of the labor market, want to scale back the size of government programs and rely on economic incentives to encourage the underclass to be productive citizens. In contrast, analysts like Lawrence Mead who insist the problem of poverty is more cultural in nature want to keep the present welfare state essentially intact. They believe that if the government requires the poor to participate in so-called workfare programs, these programs can begin the difficult but necessary task of resocializing the poor into accepting responsibility for their own lives. But certainly government efforts to instill some sense of self-control in the poor must go beyond the idea of workfare. Programs like Head Start and the Job Corps, which often see their mission as teaching their participants academic or job skills, must also play a larger role in trying to inculcate the appropriate values in young people. Public officials need to make it clear to indigents who have dropped out of the labor market or who engage in violent actions that they have obligations as well as entitlements in a society as complex as ours.

To make further progress, all sectors of society and not just the government must recognize as well as deal with the pervasive normlessness that characterizes life in our inner cities. But the willingness of society to recognize the nature of the problem is still very much in doubt. The tendency of many analysts to focus solely on structural factors while dismissing criticism as blaming the victims of poverty for their own plight probably distorts more than enhances our understanding of the underclass. The truth of the matter is that anomic behavior of the poor is a reflection of larger trends in society. Political elites, opinion makers as well as the poor all must share responsibility for the growth of the underclass and the breakdown of civility in the inner city. Instead of blaming the victim, society and the government must begin the difficult process of articulating and upholding standards of conduct that hold people accountable for their actions. While many liberal Democrats have rejected laissez-faire policies on economic matters, surprisingly enough, they have often embraced laissez-faire principles involving matters of conduct or values.

However, there is evidence that some liberals may be rethinking their attitude toward workfare. One of the reasons for this change of heart may be found in the convoluted nature of present-day American politics. In spite of the attack on traditional cultural norms, the population's reaction to the situation has been less than uniform. The most enthusiastic advocates of the new, more relaxed postindustrial outlook have been the civic, academic, and political elites at the top of the economic ladder and the poor at the bottom. The erosion of traditional values among the working class has been less pervasive. Historically, when institutions like the YMCA or the temperance movement tried to instill in people the virtues of self-discipline and self-restraint, they concentrated most of their efforts on resocializing the working class. As recent polling data seem to indicate, they were more successful than they could have imagined. At the same time that many elites and indigents celebrated the demise of traditional norms, many working and lower middle class people reacted strongly against the weakening of traditional beliefs. But the fact that was most disconcerting to liberal Democrats was that the Republican party appeared to be making tremendous political gains by appealing to the traditional values of what at one time had been a solidly Democratic working class. To counter this tendency, President Clinton has started to talk about the need for the poor to be accountable for their actions. In his successful run for the presidency in 1992, Clinton even mimicked his Republican opponents by using biblical language to call for a "new covenant" between the government and the poor. To repeat his often-cited campaign slogan, Clinton suggested that welfare should be extended only to those who agreed to play by the "rules of the game." If Clinton actually follows through on his promise to build a new covenant he will have dramatically reversed the growing tendency of post-1960s liberals to treat only the consequences rather than the causes of poverty. While Clinton deserves considerable praise for trying to alter the laissez-faire outlook of modern liberalism, his call for a change in attitudes cannot come soon enough. Until both the left and the right recognize that poverty is a cultural as well as a purely economic problem, the government will never undertake the strenuous effort needed to resocialize the poor into playing by the "rules of the game."

PART FOUR

Explaining Poverty: Structural Explanations

While most conservatives emphasize government disincentives or the breakdown of traditional values, liberals generally insist that structural factors are responsible for the failure of the war on poverty. In their minds, it is a waste of scarce resources to upgrade the skills or to alter the attitudes of the poor. The problem with the poor is not that they are untrained or unmotivated, but that they are unable to find meaningful opportunities for achieving upward mobility. However, analysts who view poverty from a structural perspective differ on the reasons why opportunities in this country are limited. As we shall see in the following four chapters, some scholars believe that racial discrimination is the main barrier that keeps low-income blacks from escaping poverty, while others insist that the sluggish growth of salaries or the nature of American capitalism is the primary reason for the dire straits of the poor.

As convincing as these arguments may be, structural explanations of poverty are at best only a partial explanation. First, in pointing solely to the importance of external factors, structuralists are often at a loss to explain why there is such a wide disparity in the economic success of ostensibly similar groups in society. While structuralists seem to offer plausible explanations for changes in aggregate poverty levels, they are far less successful in accounting for the relative success and failure of different ethnic groups. If race is one of the primary determinants of mobility, then it is problematic as to why the average incomes of West Indian blacks and American-born blacks are so radically different. If racial discrimination is the primary detriment of economic success, the financial well-being of minority groups with the same racial characteristics should be more or less the same.

Similarly, if structuralists insist that the point in time in which various ethnic groups came to this country or the degree to which they exercise political power is the key to determining upward mobility, then we would expect groups like Caucasians to have the highest family income. But when we look at the census data we find that more recent immigrants like Japanese or Chinese Americans, who have been the victims of serious racial discrimination and exercise only minimal political power, earn considerably higher incomes. If, as many other structuralists insist, the makeup of the economy is the essential factor in explaining financial success, we would expect that the poverty rates would be the same for different ethnic groups. As seen earlier, the opposite situation is the case. The above examples suggest that both the training or values of various ethnic groups, as well as the country's economy, may be crucial in shaping people's economic fortunes. We must not assume, as most structuralists do, that people are merely passive victims of society who are unable or unwilling to overcome obstacles they find in their way. It may be the skill and resourcefulness with which individuals respond to obstacles, rather than the presence of obstacles per se, that determine whether people become stuck in poverty or not.

A second and even more serious drawback of structural explanations is that they fail to realize that, even if government removes the obstacles allegedly blocking ethnic mobility, there is no guarantee that the alleged victims of society will have the determination or willpower to take advantage of their newfound opportunities. Too many structuralists have confused what is at best a necessary explanation of why some people are poor with a sufficient explanation. When people are poorly motivated or suffer from anomie, the dismantling of barriers will not automatically lead to upward mobility. To paraphrase Jon Elster, even if we open the fence of the corral, there is no guarantee that the cows will leave their enclosure and search for new pastures. As we saw in the previous chapters, when unemployment rates tumbled in the late 1960s, the number of poor electing not to work, deserting their spouses, or engaging in crime dramatically increased. Although efforts by public officials to remove obstacles may facilitate upward mobility, people must still be appropriately motivated if they are going to successfully exploit their new opportunities. While public efforts to undermine structural factors like racism or low wages may facilitate the elimination of poverty, such policies may not be a complete answer to the problems of the poor today.

TEN

The Barrier of Racial Discrimination

Of all the institutional explanations advanced to explain the persistence of poverty, racism has been the most hotly debated one. In the early 1960s, civil rights leaders correctly argued that widespread discrimination made it difficult for blacks to either escape poverty or achieve upward mobility. Viewing American society from a structural perspective, they insisted that external constraints had so overwhelmed the ability of minorities to achieve financially success that it was not surprising that blacks were stuck at the bottom of the economic ladder. The Johnson administration tried to rectify the situation by vigorously lobbying Congress to pass Title VII of the 1964 Civil Rights Act, which forbids, among other things, racial discrimination in hiring practices. Shortly thereafter Johnson issued several executive orders which also required federal contractors to establish affirmative-action programs to comply with Title VII.

Besides trying to improve the educational skills of the poor, Great Society activists argued that eliminating racial prejudice was necessary to effectively eliminate poverty in this country. If discrimination was widespread, it stood to reason that minorities would have few incentives to upgrade their human capital skills and become productive employees. The ability of minority indigents to participate in the labor market effectively and thereby earn their way out of poverty would be compromised. The more employers looked at the racial traits rather than the work skills of potential employees, the greater the odds that the Great Society's programs to improve the human capital skills of the poor would prove to be another costly government failure. In order for the government to offer the poor a hand rather than a handout, there had to be some guarantee that minorities could find productive, well-paying employment.

However, two and a half decades after the passage of the Civil Rights Act, there is considerable controversy as to whether racial discrimination is still a

Table 10.1
Poverty Rates for Blacks, 1969–1991

1969	1972	1976	1980	1983	1991
32.2%	33.3%	31.1%	32.5%	35.7%	32.7%

Sources: House Committee on Ways and Means, Green Book: The Overview of Entitlement Programs (1991), 1138. Also U.S. Bureau of the Census, Current Population Reports, Series P-60, no. 181, "Poverty in the United States: 1991."

major cause of poverty. Currently, over two-thirds of all indigents are white and roughly 30 percent are black. As a simple matter of mathematics, the complete elimination of discrimination would still leave the country with a large poverty problem to solve. Nonetheless, a prima facie case can be made that racial prejudice still exists if we look at the incidence of poverty among different ethnic groups rather than the aggregate rate among the population as a whole. The most recent data indicate that over a third of the black population is stuck at the bottom of the economic ladder compared to only 11 percent of whites. While prejudice may be unimportant in determining the overall level of poverty, it conceivably explains why the burden of poverty weighs so much heavier on the shoulders of minority members than it does on whites.

Unfortunately, the changing nature of race relations raises questions as to whether the link between prejudice and the high incidence of poverty among blacks is actually that clear-cut. In the late 1960s, when the government was just beginning to dismantle segregation in the South and prejudice toward blacks was prevalent, the poverty rate among blacks stood at 32.2 percent. In the last twenty-five years, the federal government has struck down most overt forms of racial discrimination and encouraged the implementation of affirmative-action programs to increase employment opportunities for blacks. At the same time, public opinion polls show that the vast majority of Americans have become increasingly supportive of the civil rights of African Americans.

In spite of these dramatic changes, the incidence of poverty among the black population has stubbornly remained at roughly 30 percent. If discrimination caused poverty, a reduction in prejudice toward blacks should simultaneously lead to a decrease in the rate of poverty. While overt forms of racial discrimination have declined dramatically, there has been no substantial progress in lowering the level of poverty among blacks (see table 10.1). On the basis of these unexpected trends, we need to examine in more detail what role, if any, discrimination has played in generating substantially higher poverty rates among minority groups.

The thesis of this chapter is that while prejudice is still a lingering problem in the marketplace, it is neither an insurmountable barrier to upward mobility nor a primary cause of poverty. Even if whites at times treat minorities unfairly, their actions may not be the primary reason why so many individuals remain mired in poverty. As mentioned before, groups such as Asian Americans, who have also suffered from intense racial prejudice, have enjoyed unusual economic success as well as low rates of poverty. Instead of relying exclusively on governmental assistance to escape poverty, those minority groups enjoying the most success in escaping poverty have relied on self-help projects and entrepreneurial activity to achieve financial independence.

THE ROLE OF DISCRIMINATION

In light of the above observations, it is important to realize that Thomas Sowell has recently advanced the provocative argument that racial discrimination will eventually self-destruct and thus poses little or no danger to minorities.[1] Viewing race relations from an exchange perspective, Sowell tries to show that if employers rationally calculate the costs and benefits of discrimination in a competitive economy, they will inevitably abandon discriminatory behavior and embrace merit in employment practices for the simple reason that discrimination harms the perpetrator as well as the victim. He maintains that racial discrimination will disappear in a competitive economy because the marketplace will make it too expensive for businesses to ignore the talents of minorities. While Sowell's arguments shed new light on the problem of discrimination, we will see that his belief that the marketplace will tame discriminatory practices is unfounded. Before developing this argument in more detail, it is important to understand why more traditional views of race relations have also rejected Sowell's rather optimistic assumptions about discrimination.

Policy analysts who view discrimination as a cultural phenomenon maintain that discrimination reflects well-ingrained beliefs that are not easily changed. But advocates of cultural explanations disagree among themselves as to how sharply racial prejudice is woven into the fabric of American society. In the 1950s, Jan Myrdal argued that American cultural values worked to mitigate and soften the worst effects of racial discrimination.[2] In many cases, racial bias even reflected ignorance as much as deeply ingrained beliefs. Myrdal insisted that the American public was torn between a belief in American ideals, or what he labeled the American creed, and the practice of racism and discrimination. The gap between egalitarian and democratic ideals and racial practices was troublesome to most Americans because they wanted to treat all people in a just and equitable manner. This discrepancy, which Myrdal called the "American dilemma," applied psychological pressure on most Americans to alter their behavior in a positive fashion. As an optimist on race relations, Myrdal believed that gentle government prodding and increased instruction in the tenets of the American creed would eventually guarantee the civil rights of black Americans.

In the 1960s and 1970s, other scholars took exception with Myrdal's sunny assessment of American values, and advanced a cultural explanation in which racism was a central as opposed to a peripheral element in our belief system. Some analysts went so far as to argue that anti-black sentiment was "a cluster of deeply rooted or primordial sentiments brought from Europe" that reflected a central tenet of Western culture.[3] However, others insisted that racial prejudice was an indigenous development of American history that grew out of the country's exploitation of slaves. Once developed, prejudice acquired a life of its own and "created a powerful, irrational basis for white supremacist attitudes and actions."[4] Many commentators have pointed to the violence and hostility with which white Southerners greeted efforts to dismantle Jim Crow legislation in the 1960s as proof that Myrdal's faith that moral suasion would end racial prejudice was an incorrect reading of the American racial landscape. It was more the threat of legal sanctions, and even the use of army troops, rather than economic pressure or moral suasion that convinced the South as well as the North to recognize the basic rights of black Americans.

Marxists analysts, who have likewise written extensively on race relations, also agree that competitive market forces are not likely to check racial considerations. But Marxists as well as neo-Marxists maintain that racial oppression reflects class interests more than community values.[5] According to orthodox Marxist theory, racial conflict is merely a special case of class conflict. Racial prejudice, discrimination, and attitudes and ideologies of racism are simply part of a superstructure that reflects the class interests of capital. Since the owners of capital want to maximize profits, they will engage in race baiting and foster prejudice to divide the working class and weaken its demands for higher wages. Rather than expressing well-ingrained beliefs, managers are cynically playing on racial fears to divide the working class so that it cannot provide a unified threat to management. Whenever owners feel threatened by the demands of their employees, they will stir up more racial conflict to advance their economic interests.

Neo-Marxists, or what more commonly has become known as split labor theories of discrimination, also agree that racial oppression reflects class interests.[6] But they insist that it is the white working class rather than capitalists who want to limit opportunities for minorities and perpetuate segregation and discrimination. In an open and competitive labor market in which no discrimination exists, competition among workers will hold down wage gains and limit labor costs. To prevent such competition from occurring, the working class will try to exclude minorities from gaining employment in particular industries. By stratifying the labor market and limiting the hiring of black employees, white workers can reap higher wages than they would in a nondiscriminatory environment.

In contrast to these views, Sowell as well as other conservative economists view discrimination primarily as an economic problem facing companies trying to maximize profits. Whereas previous commentators focused on the harm inflicted on the target of discrimination, Sowell has perceptively pointed out that in a competitive marketplace discrimination will also hurt the perpetrators as well as the victims of racial bias. To understand why, we have to remember that if a business wants to prosper it will try to hire its employees as cheaply as possible while meeting the demands of its customers. When a firm consequently decides to discriminate against minorities, it will face some difficult choices. As soon as employers choose not to hire black employees because of racial prejudice, they will be stuck with higher labor costs. If all firms in an industry agreed to abide by such discriminatory practices, the higher costs of doing business would be easily passed along to the customer. When such agreements break down and competition is intense, nondiscriminating firms will quickly acquire a competitive advantage.[7]

However insightful the above comments may be, Sowell's analysis appears incomplete in comparison to cultural, Marxist, as well as other exchange theories of discrimination. The two main flaws with his analysis are that Sowell may have overstated the costs while downplaying if not ignoring altogether the benefits of discriminatory hiring. For example, Sowell maintains that in a competitive marketplace, firms will suffer financially if they refuse to hire capable minority members. But as Sowell himself admits, the costs will vary immensely with the degree of competition. The more monopolistic a particular industry is, the less damage the company's balance sheet will suffer.

Similarly, Sowell assumes that companies and their managers are concerned primarily with economic considerations. In so doing, he overlooks the fact that many companies may have a cultural taste for discrimination that will override their desire to maximize profits. Managers who have internalized values hostile to blacks may in fact minimize the economic costs that Sowell believes will force companies to change their practices. As we argued earlier, individuals more often are pushed from behind by cultural values than they are pulled from the front by the lure of economic gains. By assuming that individuals are primarily rational profit maximizers, Sowell fails to understand the cultural intensity with which companies will often cling to racially biased hiring practices.

Sowell's tendency to overstate the potential costs of discrimination is compounded by his inclination to minimize the many advantages of discriminatory behavior. In trying to show how the marketplace will limit the extent of prejudice, he overlooks three occasions on which firms or workers will benefit from refusing to hire minorities. For example, a company may gain from engaging in what has become known as statistical discrimination. In this practice employers discriminate against individuals because they belong to a group that often has labor problems. Imagine that a company discovered that a particular minority group was more likely to get into trouble with the law, miss work, or have trouble adjusting to the rigors of a 9-to-5 job. While the firm would realize that not all members of an ethnic group were likely to be unproductive workers, they might still be reluctant to recruit any in the group because the transaction costs involved in identifying capable employees would be so high. Companies often find it extremely difficult and expensive to predict who will be a competent worker. The marginal costs of acquiring more data on their prospective employees may exceed the benefits they would reap from gaining more accurate information on their employees. A company may thus have no taste for discrimination at all. But to minimize labor problems and to realize possible gains in the productivity of its labor force, it may decide to discriminate against all blacks. Recent data from the Chicago Urban Poverty and Family Life Study suggest that many employers often rely on the social status and color of job candidates to predict who will be a productive worker.[8] Although few employers express overt racist sentiments or categorically state that they dislike all blacks, they often avoid hiring young black men because they see them as poorly educated, unreliable, and likely to be uncooperative in the workplace.

Second, a corporation may also gain from racial discrimination if it recognizes that its customers are prejudiced against minorities.[9] While a company may have benign intentions and not be opposed itself to hiring blacks or Hispanics, it may institute discriminatory hiring practices because it senses that its customers prefer to deal with white employees. Obviously, companies that are most solicitous of their clients' wishes will expand their market share and earn higher profits. Because Sowell focuses primarily on a firm's desire to hold down labor costs, he minimizes the gains a company can reap from respecting and even catering to the prevailing values of its consumers.

Finally, Sowell overlooks the possibility that workers may benefit from higher wages if they force companies to discriminate against minorities. While conservatives like Sowell are correct in suggesting that firms may prefer an integrated labor market because it holds down the cost of labor, they ignore the fact that companies may lack the political power to counter the demands of white laborers for preferential treatment. As mentioned earlier, Asians on the West Coast and blacks in the South were often denied employment opportunities because workers had instituted a split labor market. By creating a two-tier market, white workers knew they could hold down the supply of available laborers and thus bargain for higher wages and more job security. Given their political influence as voters as well as their economic power as consumers, the working class had more than enough clout to limit the opportunities open to minority groups, especially in the South, where poor whites strongly supported Jim Crow policies.

In arguing that the marketplace will limit the effects of discrimination, Sowell has focused too much attention on the costs as opposed to the benefits of racial prejudice. He has also failed to see that cultural values or economic interests will often override the financial calculations of firms trying to maximize their profits. When it comes to issues of race, the beliefs of people or the politics of class may cancel out the tendencies of a capitalist economy to promote color-blind hiring practices.

THE DECLINING BUT RESIDUAL IMPACT OF DISCRIMINATION

On the basis of both theoretical and historical grounds, Sowell's optimistic assumption that discrimination would economically self-destruct on its own account overstates the case. In spite of this fact, there is clear evidence that discrimination has significantly declined over the last forty years. From 1939 to the mid-1970s, the disparity in wages between blacks and whites narrowed significantly but began to widen again in the 1980s. Presently, most black males earn roughly 60 percent of what their white counterparts make. And contrary to the arguments of conservatives, the government's efforts in the 1960s and 1970s to promote 'civil rights appear partly responsible for the improved position of black Americans. As table 10.2 indicates, blacks made their most significant wage gains between 1965 and 1975, a period in which the federal government passed both the 1964 Civil Rights Act and established the Equal Employment Opportunity Commission (EEOC). In aggregate

Table 10.2
Black-White Earning Ratios
(Ages 15 and Older)

	All Workers		Year-round Workers	
Year	Males	Females	Males	Female
1939	0.41	0.36	0.45	0.38
1955	0.59	0.43	0.64	0.57
1960	0.60	0.50	0.67	0.70
1965	0.58	0.58	0.64	0.68
1970	0.66	0.85	0.70	0.85
1975	0.60	0.88	0.74	0.96
1981	0.59	0.89	0.71	0.90
1985	0.63	0.85	0.70	0.88
1990	0.61	0.81	0.71	0.89
1991	0.61	0.82	0.73	0.89

Source: U.S. Bureau of the Census, *Historical Statistics of the U.S. Colonial Times to 1970*, Part 1, 304–5; *Economic Report of the President* (Washington, D.C.: U.S. Government Printing Office, 1993), 380.

terms, there is no denying that blacks have made significant financial and occupational gains since the days of the Great Society, especially young, well-educated blacks, who currently earn around 80 percent to 85 percent of the wages of comparable white employees.

While wage discrepancies have narrowed, they have not completely disappeared for the majority of blacks. In the late 1970s and 1980s, blacks even saw some of their earlier gains disappear. But most studies of earning ratios have concluded that anywhere from 40 to 60 percent of these wage differences is due to lingering racial bias.[10] If that is the case, then discrimination is a societal tax that effectively lowers the average wages of blacks from 10 to 20 percent below that of comparable white workers (multiply 40 percent times the difference between the black to white ratio of 63/100). But conservatives like Sowell have countered that many of these studies fail to take account of the size, geographic location, attitudes, family composition, or educational attainment of different populations. He insists that when proper controls are instituted for these variables, the impact of racial discrimination almost completely disappears. Although Sowell's reservations about the extent of discrimination are well taken, his argument that it has completely disappeared is unconvincing. There still seems to be a small yet significant residue of discrimination that adversely affects the economic fortunes of blacks.

Table 10.3
Relative Income of Various Groups
(Percentage of National Average)

Structuralist Prediction of the Most Affluent Ethnic Groups		Ethnic Groups with the Highest Relative Income	
All Whites	101	Japanese	138
English	101	Jews	138
French	99	Asian Indians	127
Germans	108	Chinese	115

Source: U.S. Bureau of the Census, *Census of the Population: 1980*, Vol. 1, Part 1, Chapter C, United States Summary, "General Social and Economic Characteristics," PC 80-1-C1 (Washington, D.C.: U.S. Government Printing Office, 1983).

WILL DISCRIMINATION PREVENT UPWARD MOBILITY?

But the important point from a policy perspective is that even if discrimination remains a troublesome yet diminished problem in American society, it does not necessarily mean that minority groups cannot escape from poverty. A variety of factors other than racial prejudice may account for the relatively high incidence of low income among black Americans. As discussed earlier, structuralists, who emphasize the importance of racism in determining who gets ahead, often maintain that the obstacles on the racetrack and the relative starting positions of the runners will determine the economic well-being of various ethnic groups. But the strategy individuals use to run the race may be just as important as where they initially line up. If racism were that important in explaining financial success, skin color or the point in time in which an ethnic group came to this country should determine how prosperous that ethnic group had become. As a result, Caucasians in general or subgroups like the English or French should have the highest median income in America. But as noted earlier, the ethnic groups with the highest relative income are all minorities who have experienced severe discrimination (see table 10.3).

If we also scrutinize the record of black Americans in this country, it becomes apparent that racial discrimination does not necessarily prevent upward mobility among minority groups. Despite the existence of discrimination, there has been a remarkable expansion of the black middle class in the last twenty years. The census data on wages cited in a previous section of this chapter often hide this fact because they report only the average wages of minority members. As many commentators have noted, the black community may be fragmenting into a sizable group of haves and a persistent group of have-nots. As Margaret Bush, the former president of the NAACP, described the situation in 1980: "Over the last fifteen years in many urban black communities there has been developing a widening income gap. For example, the number of middle-income blacks has doubled during this period so that some 25 to 45 percent of all black Americans have middle incomes. However, the size of the black low-income group has hardly changed."[11]

Structuralists' predictions about upward mobility and family income have often proven to be faulty because they fail to see that individuals can take steps to minimize racial discrimination. In this country, middle-class blacks as well as other ethnic groups that have overcome prejudice and achieved financial success have done it through two different routes. As was already discussed, minorities have often sidestepped the worst consequences of discrimination by establishing their own businesses and occupying previously untapped market niches. If groups like the Japanese, Jews, or West Indian blacks call on their cultural traditions and acquire educational skills that are in great demand or exploit business opportunities that few whites have tapped, they can take themselves out of direct competition with the working class. This was especially the case when Jews acquired postgraduate degrees in medicine or academia, or Japanese and Chinese Americans obtained advanced training in subjects like engineering, biology, and computer science. By pursuing careers that required specialized human capital skills, minorities could often overcome anti-Semitism or anti-Asian sentiments in the larger society and still earn lucrative salaries. The same advantage accrued to minority groups that had a flair for entrepreneurship. By occupying specialized business niches, many Jewish and Asian businesses quickly learned that they would encounter very little competition from working-class whites. In spite of a general climate of racial hostility, minority groups like the Jews and Japanese have prospered by recognizing and servicing unmet needs in the marketplace. The same pattern holds true for West Indian blacks, who have substantially higher family incomes than their American-born counterparts. Because they have been able to develop an entrepreneurial tradition, they have been able to circumvent the discrimination that has plagued native born blacks.

A simple exercise in mathematics will illustrate how a comparable entrepreneurial tradition among American-born blacks would help many inner-city residents avoid the worst consequences of discrimination. If the rate of black business ownership were to rise from its present 12.5 per thousand to the national average of 64, an additional 1.5 million new black businesses would be created.[12] If 40 percent of these new black businesses would hire one African-American employee, they could significantly reduce the number of unemployed black workers, who currently number around 1.5 million. Like Asian Americans or West Indians, blacks could insulate themselves from some of the worst effects of discrimination if they would only develop a viable entrepreneurial tradition.

Second, ethnic groups have also thrived when discrimination is practiced in a limited rather than universal manner. As Christopher Jencks has perceptively noted, only when discrimination has been universally applied across the board has it had a major impact on the financial standing of minorities in this country.[13] In contrast, when it is practiced by only a fraction of businesses, minority groups can usually work around biased restrictions and achieve financial independence. For example, if you were Jewish and graduated from a top law school in New York in the 1930s, prejudice would not have kept you from getting a lucrative law position.[14] While anti-Semitism was widespread at that time, and many firms recruited gentiles only, there were still plenty of law firms that hired Jews. Bright and competent Jewish lawyers thus had no trouble earning salaries comparable to their Angle-Saxon counterparts. While anti-Semitism no doubt stigmatized Jewish attorneys and was socially annoying, it probably had little or no impact on their financial success.

The economic impact of discrimination was undoubtedly very different on black attorneys during the same period. Prior to the 1960s, discrimination against blacks was much more universal in nature and affected most occupations. The wages of black lawyers consequently lagged significantly behind their white counterparts. However, as Jencks has correctly pointed out, in the last couple of decades the situation confronting blacks has changed dramatically. While racial discrimination has not completely disappeared, the situation is more like that confronting Jews fifty years ago than that confronting blacks in the pre-civil rights age. Hypothetically, if only one business out of ten were willing to hire and promote blacks, there should still be ample employment opportunities for blacks who, after all, make up only one-tenth of the labor force. As blacks increasingly discover those firms that hire on the basis of merit rather than skin color, the pay differences between equally competent white and black employees should begin to disappear. By selectively choosing where they try to find work, blacks can narrow if not achieve outright wage parity with the majority of white workers. Undoubtedly, one reason why so many blacks have moved into the ranks of the middle class is that they have been able to identify employers who do not discriminate on the basis of color. The undeniable fact that racial discrimination still exists and is morally indefensible does not necessarily mean that it will seriously hamper the economic success of minority groups in this country.

IS DISCRIMINATION RESPONSIBLE FOR DOWNWARD MOBILITY AND THE EXISTENCE OF POVERTY?

While discrimination does not necessarily make it impossible to achieve upward mobility, it may likewise be a minor factor in explaining downward mobility and the persistence of poverty in this country. Over the last thirty years, discrimination has declined dramatically but the incidence of poverty among blacks has remained roughly the same. In addition, just as the civil rights movement began to win its battle to dismantle Jim Crow laws and end segregation, poverty became more intractable and even brutal in nature, jeopardizing the civility of life in many urban cities. Beginning in the 1960s black-on-black crime, the breakup of the family, and growing disinterest in the labor market all started to increase. The fact that these forms of self-destructive behavior became more prevalent in the 1960s suggests that recent events, rather than the legacy of slavery and racial discrimination, explain why poverty has become so persistent among many black Americans. As William Julius Wilson notes: "It is not readily apparent how the deepening economic class division between the haves and the have-nots in the black community can be accounted for when (the racism/discrimination) thesis is involved, especially when it is argued that this same racism is directed with equal force across class boundaries in the black community. Nor is it apparent how racism can result in a more rapid social and economic deterioration in the inner city in the post-civil rights period than in the period that preceded the notable civil rights victories."[15] To explain this perplexing trend, analysts have pointed in two different directions. Liberals like Wilson have argued that the main causes of poverty are primarily economic rather than racial in nature.[16] Wilson claims that blacks currently have an unacceptable level of poverty because of the deterioration of the economy. To appreciate the present dilemma of the black population, it is important to realize that many of the economic opportunities once open to white ethnics are no longer available to blacks. When Eastern Europeans came to this country in large numbers at the turn of the century, they quickly found employment in the industrial sector of the economy. Because manufacturing has traditionally paid generous wages, large numbers of workers easily climbed into the middle class. As these families became more affluent, they could afford to invest in the human capital skills of their children by sending them to college. Once white ethnics became better educated and escaped

Table 10.4
Labor Market Participation

Non-White/White Ratio				Black/White Ratio				
1954	1959	1964	1969	1969	1974	1979	1984	1991
1.051	1.029	1.027	1.001	.995	.918	.888	.864	.876

Source: *Economic Report of the President* (Washington, D.C.: U.S. Government Printing Office, 1990), table C-38, 337, as quoted in Christopher Jencks, *Rethinking Social Policy* (Cambridge: Harvard University Press, 1992). Data updated by *Economic Report of the President* (Washington, D.C.: U.S. Government Printing Office, 1992), table B-36, 339.

into the service sector, opportunities opened up for blacks in the relatively high-paying industrial sector of the economy.

Unfortunately, the recent emergence of Japan as an industrial superpower has effectively eliminated this avenue of upward mobility. As American firms saw their products replaced by Japanese consumer goods, they closed plants and trimmed their labor forces. The resulting decline of the manufacturing heartland of America has been particularly hard on poorly educated blacks. When industrial firms employed a substantial share of the work force, even unskilled blacks were able to earn wages that could make them financially independent. The closing of American factories has had the unanticipated effect of simultaneously closing off a well-traveled route out of the ghetto. Regardless of whether discrimination has disappeared or not, it is of little importance to those poor who are unable to find any work at all.

Many conservatives, like liberals, have also concluded that race is presently a relatively minor factor in explaining the high incidence of poverty among blacks. But conservatives feel that the persistence of poverty among blacks is as much a supply as a demand problem. Instead of blaming the economy for the plight of blacks, as Wilson does, conservatives also point to cultural and demographic shifts in the inner city to account for the high incidence of poverty among blacks. The breakdown of social values has had an especially devastating impact on the black ghetto, canceling out many of the gains achieved by the civil rights movement. As mentioned earlier, many institutions that once helped socialize young people in the inner city to become productive members of the work force are in decline or leaving the inner city. As table 10.4 indicates, during the period of Jim Crow, non-whites participated more actively than their white counterparts in the labor market, but today the opposite situation is true. The pattern of black unemployment has also undergone a fundamental change. In the Eisenhower years, black men experienced considerably more short-term unemployment than did their white counterparts, but they were only marginally more likely to drop out of the labor market. But beginning in the middle 1960s through the 1980s, the proportion of black men aged twenty-five to fifty-four who had no paid work for an entire calendar year rose from 5 percent to 14 percent. Among a comparable group of whites, the proportion increased from 3 percent to 5 percent.

Regardless of whether it is the primary cause or merely a contributing factor, the breakdown of traditional values has also affected the stability of the black family. Although the current incidence of poverty among blacks is three times that of whites, Mary Jo Bane has predicted that the rate would be only twice that figure if the black family structure mimicked that of whites. Presently, 42 percent of blacks live in single-family homes and a little over 50 percent of those families are classified as poor. In recognition of these problems, Bane has estimated that about 44 percent of the discrepancy in white and black poverty rates is due to differences in the makeup of households. Had black parents been as likely to stay together as white couples, the percentage of blacks stuck in poverty would have declined to around 20 percent instead of its present 30 percent.

The tendency of many black males not to support their former wives and children has hurt female-headed families in the ghetto. Presently only 14 percent of black mothers and 43 percent of white mothers receive any kind of help from their ex-spouses.[17] The significantly lower figures for black mothers may reflect an attitude among many inner-city residents that they have no financial responsibility for their own children. Too many men are likely to father children out-of-wedlock, desert their wives after marriage, and provide little or no emotional or financial aid for their offspring. Until family relations in the ghetto are stabilized, many female-headed households will be unable to earn enough money to work their way out of poverty.

Finally, the growth of the violent underclass has also impeded the ability of the black poor to move into the mainstream of American society. As minority neighborhoods become more violent, it is harder for black-owned businesses in particular and the inner city in general to generate meaningful job opportunities for its residents. While Jesse Jackson is certainly no conservative, he captured the urgency of the problem when he wrote: "It is time for a new civil rights struggle to take back our neighborhoods. Yes it is true that this horrible plague has external sources. As gang members in Los Angeles' Nicherson Gardens have told me, drugs are not grown in the city. But the agents of death are homegrown. They are young, black and proud. But they are killing our children and must be stopped. The killers will burn the race up unless those in the neighborhood tell it and stop it."[18]

While the huge disparity in poverty rates among whites and blacks suggests that racism may be the culprit, the actual situation may be far more complicated. The Johnson administration may have been right in the 1960s in asserting that discrimination made it difficult for non-whites to escape poverty on their own, but that assessment no longer appears to be true. In the 1990s, the combination of a changing economy, the breakdown of traditional values, a fragile family structure, and the emergence of a violent underclass rather than racism may be the real cause of poverty among African Americans. Even when employers practice statistical discrimination, the problem stems not only from the unfair hiring practices of business but also from their reaction to the behavior of the underclass. If the record of the last thirty years tells us anything, it is that ending discrimination is not the same thing as winning the war against poverty.

WHAT SHOULD GOVERNMENT'S ROLE BE?

Because the causes of poverty are complex, we need to consider how government programs to combat racial discrimination may affect the incidence of poverty among blacks. Many analysts insist that public support of affirmative action programs will solve the problem of black poverty. Surprising as it may seem, the track record of quota hiring programs suggests that the opposite situation is closer to the truth. Instead of assisting indigent blacks, affirmative action programs may actually end up harming those who are most in need.

To understand why this situation has occurred, it is important to realize that the creation of the Equal Employment Opportunity Commission (EEOC) and the agency's subsequent affirmative action guidelines have made it very difficult for employers to fire unproductive workers. If a firm decides to let an employee go because of inadequate work performance, the fired worker has the right to appeal to the EEOC, a process that may be very expensive and time-consuming for the firm. Unfortunately, these procedures may discourage employers from hiring workers whose chances for promotion are slim at best. Thus, affirmative-action programs have had the unanticipated result of dramatically raising the cost to a firm that elects to employ high-risk applicants. As a consequence, the EEOC's personnel practices have inadvertently harmed those who are most in need of a helping hand.

As the price of hiring young and unexperienced blacks has dramatically increased, government agencies have created numerous incentives for the private sector to employ only middle class or "desirable" black applicants. The more hiring practices become rigid and cumbersome, the more employers prefer to deal with minorities who can quickly adjust to the workplace. As a result, the main beneficiaries of affirmative action programs turn out to be well-educated and mature blacks, many of whom would have been financially successful in any case. The losers, in turn, come from the ranks of low-income blacks whose serious behavioral problems identify them as high-risk job candidates.

However, it is conceivable that the cultural values of companies may lead them to ignore the economic costs of hiring and training untested job applicants. As discussed earlier, Sowell's analysis of discrimination is questionable because he assumes that firms are only concerned with maximizing their profit margins. In the same way that employers with a cultural taste for discrimination may ignore the economic costs of selective recruitment, firms with a cultural commitment to advancing race relations may heavily discount the financial costs of hiring poor blacks. Unfortunately, this scenario appears to be only a theoretical possibility.

As Christopher Jencks has found, wage and employment data indicate that affirmative-action programs have a negative impact on young blacks. In the 1970s, employers significantly raised the wages of black college graduates but not of black high school graduates. For whites the situation was reversed. As pointed out in chapter 4, the rates of return for Caucasians with college degrees fell to a postwar low in the 1970s, while the earnings of high school graduates rose at a faster clip than those of college graduates.[19] In similar fashion, employers raised the wages for non-white high school graduates over age 35 but not for young black high school graduates. Jencks also notes that a similar pattern has occurred in unemployment statistics. In the year that Title VII was enacted, the unemployment rate among young black men between the ages of twenty to twenty-four was twice the figure of black males aged thirty-five to forty-four.[20] Fifteen years later the younger group was experiencing three times the unemployment rate of the older group. But no such trend was apparent among whites. These data thus suggest that while Title VII may have benefited many minorities, especially well-trained middle-class blacks, it may have harmed young, poorly educated blacks. The latter group clearly lost ground after the passage of the Civil Rights Act of 1964. As if cultural and family problems were not troublesome enough, government affirmative action programs now made it harder for high-risk blacks to work their way out of poverty.

The problems caused by affirmative action programs raise troublesome questions about what role the government should play in helping minorities. Many liberals would undoubtedly argue that the deleterious effects of affirmative action programs on the poor are a small price to pay for the overall gains the black community has made in the last thirty years. After all, the civil rights legislation of the Johnson administration clearly improved the economic standing of most black employees. Also, as pointed out earlier in this chapter, Sowell's belief that racial discrimination will self-destruct because of economic pressure from the marketplace seems unwarranted in the light of recent economic events.

As convincing as these arguments are, there are still grounds for skepticism about the role of government. On the basis of past events, minority groups need to realize that the decisions of the government are reversible and that elected officials can just as easily curtail as advance the interests of minority groups. Unfortunately, the nonhistorical outlook of many civil rights advocates has fanned rather than tempered their almost uniform commitment to more government intervention in the civil rights arena. The civil rights movement should not exaggerate the government's role in overturning Jim Crow laws. In fact, it was not until the 1950s, when the historian C. Van Woodward published *The Strange Career of Jim Crow*, that commentators became fully aware of the government's somewhat checkered role in enhancing the individual rights of minorities.[21] Initially, most analysts assumed that the segregation laws of the late nineteenth and early twentieth centuries were merely an outgrowth and codification of earlier racial practices.

But Woodward showed that Jim Crow laws represented a conscious effort by many government officials to wipe out the civil rights that blacks enjoyed during Reconstruction. In the early twentieth century, Woodrow Wilson, among others, tried to resegregate the federal bureaucracy, which previously had enjoyed a fair amount of color-blind hiring. After advancing the civil rights of minorities during the first reconstruction from 1863 to 1877, the government dramatically altered its position and turned its back on the aspirations of black Americans. From the end of the nineteenth century until the advent of the Johnson administration, the government's civil rights record left much to be desired. One reason why the civil rights movement of the 1960s found discriminatory practices so difficult to overturn was because many government officials had implicitly if not explicitly helped to enforce them. If the government could alter its position at the turn of the century and embrace segregation, it might choose at some point in the future to again ignore the rights of minority groups.

Government decisions, after all, usually reflect the changing moods and sentiments of either special interests in society or the public at large. If the constellation of forces bringing pressure on elected officials changes, all government policies, including civil rights acts, may be revised. Since race relations reflect cultural values or economic interests, there is always the possibility that the beliefs of the majority may come into conflict with the goals of blacks. In recent years, the public has become much more tolerant and supportive of ending discrimination against non-whites than ever before. But at the same time, survey data indicate that public support for the total civil rights agenda, such as school bussing, has leveled off since the early 1970s. While it is difficult to predict the future, there are three reasons, in addition to those given at the beginning of the chapter, why we might expect public support for civil rights to fluctuate over the next two decades.

First, if Marxists are correct that racial attitudes reflect primarily class interests rather than cultural values, racial tolerance will reflect the ebb and flow of the country's finances. As long as the economy remains healthy, and American industry is generating enough jobs to absorb the white working class, discrimination will be a minor problem. But when the performance of the private sector falters, causing family income to decline further or unemployment rates to increase, the situation could change and pressures could build to restrict the opportunities of minorities.

Second, public opinion polls suggest that many whites, who increasingly reject discrimination as a national policy, still have serious reservations about programs that require hiring quotas.[22] While the majority of whites still support laws restricting discriminatory practices, they have problems with government programs that seem to confer preferential treatment on minority groups. Ironically, as the majority of whites have come to accept the original goal of Martin Luther King to develop a color-blind society, many members of the civil rights coalition have insisted that the government should create a color-conscious society in which race permeates all hiring, education, and housing decisions. As the civil rights movement has abandoned its agenda of the 1960s that advocated equal opportunity and color-blind hiring standards, it has often stirred up considerable controversy. While Myrdal's thesis was that the American creed worked to the advantage of the civil rights movement in the 1960s, today the opposite situation may be true.

Third, Senator Patrick Moynihan has recently argued that the growth of the black underclass may also jeopardize popular support for civil rights programs. While survey data indicate that the vast majority of citizens increasingly believe that all Americans should be treated fairly, a growing number of Americans, including working-class blacks trapped in the ghetto, are troubled by the violence and pathology of the inner city. Many civil rights leaders and liberals understandably do not want to talk about the problems of the black underclass for fear that it will revive racism, but their neglect of what Moynihan previously called the "tangle of pathology" in our cities may indeed create more racial hostility. As the chaos and gratuitous violence of the inner city grows, many whites have moved their homes and companies to the suburbs to insulate themselves from the problems of the inner city. The tendency of many liberals to minimize the legitimate concerns of many neighborhoods about urban decay only exacerbates the problem. This fear may eventually cause many whites to bring pressure to bear on government officials to ease up on the enforcement of antidiscrimination laws, thus unraveling many of the gains of the civil rights movement. To maintain as well as improve race relations in this country, it is essential that public officials and civil rights leaders try to correct the problems of the underclass.

If Sowell is overly optimistic in believing that the corrective pressure of the marketplace will restrain discriminatory practices, liberals are also naive in assuming that public officials and their constituents will always be enthusiastic about advancing the civil rights of blacks. The indifference if not downright hostility of the Reagan administration toward many of the civil rights laws of the 1960s may very well indicate that the country's second reconstruction period has come to an end. Regardless of who occupies the presidency, the executive branch may find that public support for further integration is so problematic or controversial that it will lack the energy to push the agenda of the civil rights movement with vigor.

CONCLUSION

As we have seen, there are many reasons why discrimination may periodically reappear in American politics. But as we have also noted, racial prejudice will not necessarily prevent an ethnic group from escaping poverty and enjoying considerable upward mobility. As a hedge against changes in public opinion or group interests, all minority groups, including blacks, need to balance their political activities with self-help projects. A potentially fickle government may not always be there to address their grievances.

The civil rights movement must realize that by constantly stressing the problems of racial discrimination and the need for corrective government intervention, the danger exists that their warning may turn on its head and become a self-fulfilling prophecy. If civil rights groups continue to claim that blacks are victims of society, black Americans may come to believe that there is little they can do by themselves to improve their status. But over the long run, the upward mobility of the black population is likely to depend as much on their ability to become self-reliant as it is on their ability to extract concessions from Washington. As we have seen, those ethnic groups who have relied more on their own initiative have enjoyed the most financial success. When they likewise have stable families, well-behaved and well-educated children, and a tradition of pursuing business opportunities, minority groups of all colors have compiled an impressive record of overcoming the hardships accompanying discrimination. Despite the progress we have made in dismantling the worst aspects of racial bias, there is no reason to believe that it may not flare up in the future. And the more self-reliant and financially independent an ethnic group can become, the more successful it will be in weathering the dangers of discrimination.

ELEVEN

The Economy I: The Lack of Jobs

As analysts increasingly came to perceive racial discrimination as a relatively minor factor in explaining the persistence of poverty in America, they began to argue that changes in the economy play a more significant role in shaping the financial prospects of the poor. Liberal economists and sociologists have correctly pointed out that if the economy turned sour, it would be harder for individuals to work their way out of poverty. If we hope to reduce the ranks of the poor in this country, we need a healthy economy that can successfully generate an ample supply of jobs. Given the severity of the downturn that occurred in the American economy after the oil embargo of 1973, it is not surprising that the poverty rate ceased declining in the 1970s.

Many liberals have insisted that the failure of conservatives like Charles Murray to recognize this point led them erroneously to blame public welfare programs for the failure of the war on poverty. Sheldon Danziger and Peter Gottschalk argued that the country's efforts to eliminate poverty had been derailed for simple macroeconomic reasons.[1] During the 1970s and early 1980s, the slowdown in job growth due to cyclical fluctuations in the economy made it difficult for many indigents to work their way out of poverty. The biggest obstacle to eliminating poverty was the simple fact that the economy seemed unable to generate enough jobs to employ the working poor. In response to the Arab oil shock of the early 1970s, the government proved to be inept in fine-tuning the economy. With fiscal policy in disarray and unemployment rates rising, the poor found themselves squeezed out of the labor market and unable to find decent-paying jobs.

This problem was compounded by the large influx of baby boomers who were beginning to enter the labor market. At the same time that the economy experienced a downturn, the number of workers joining the work force reached an all-time high, exacerbating in turn the problems of the poor. As John E. Schwartz, the author of *America's Hidden Success*, has pointed out,

"The number of Americans aged 16 to 34 looking for employment between 1963 and 1980 expanded by an extraordinary 26 million, a 14-fold increase over the 1947 to 1963 period when the same age groups increased in the labor force by fewer than two million."[2] This dramatic increase in the supply of workers naturally made it easier for employers to be "particularly choosy about whom they wanted to hire."[3] If the economy had been growing at a substantial rate, the large influx of new employees would probably have had only a marginal impact on those with low incomes. But when fluctuations in the economy combined with the changing demographics of the American population, the prospects of the poor inevitably took a turn for the worse.

The observations of Danziger, Gottschalk, and Schwartz clearly demonstrated that structural factors like the economy play a key role in the fight to eliminate poverty. But even more importantly, they also highlighted the fact that there was a significant segment of the poor, the working poor, whose outlook on life and prospects for advancement were radically different from those of the underclass. In contrast to indigents whose attachment to the labor force was questionable and whose observance of the rules of the game had become problematic, a substantial number of the poor were trying to remain productive and hard-working members of the community. But their ability to prosper was directly tied to the economic health of the country. When the economy was booming and labor markets were tight, the opportunities of the working poor for upward mobility improved dramatically. This phenomenon, which has often been called "trickle down economics," often saw the poor as the chief beneficiaries of successful government fiscal policy. But just as the "trickle down" thesis began to gain widespread popularity among academics and poverty analysts, the relationship between poverty and economic expansion was called into question.[4] While cyclical fluctuations appeared to have played a major role in shaping the fortunes of the poor in the 1960s and to a lesser extent in the 1970s, they appeared to have less impact during the 1980s. Between the start of the fourth quarter of 1982 and the comparable quarter of 1990, the American economy experienced its second-longest period of economic expansion, yet very few of the poor appeared to work their way out of poverty. Any connection between macroeconomic shifts and the plight of the working poor had evidently been severed by the end of the 1980s. This chapter and the next will explore possible reasons why cyclical fluctuations in the economy had apparently ceased to influence poverty rates. Before examining the impact of this change on the poor, we need to examine in more detail how large the population of the working poor is and how their behavior and attitudes differ from those of the underclass.

THE PLIGHT OF THE WORKING POOR

Unfortunately, this task is easier said then done. While the destructive behavior of the underclass has received considerable attention from scholars and the press, the working poor are the forgotten subjects of poverty research. In the large body of literature on poverty, few studies try to probe the attitudes and values of indigents who work full time. In most cases, ethnographic studies either fail clearly to differentiate the working poor from other inner-city residents, or they focus exclusively on "street-corner" men and women. While studies by Elijah Anderson and by the Urban Poverty and Family Structure Survey, to name two, have significantly enriched our understanding of the poor, they fail to give us a clear picture of how the behavior of the traditional working poor may differ from that of other residents in our urban communities.[5]

The major exception to this trend is Mitchell Duneier's excellent book, *Slim's Table*, which is a study of the outlook and values of working and retired black men living on the south side of Chicago.[6] In a series of moving chapters, Duneier demonstrates how the working poor have often come to feel isolated and alone in the neighborhoods they have always called home. As the breakdown of traditional values has spread through the ghetto, working-class blacks in particular have not been able to flee to the relative safety of suburban America. Lacking the resources of middle-class blacks, they find themselves trapped in the ghetto, victimized by the destructive actions of the underclass. But despite the harshness of their surroundings, the subjects of Duneier's study have held on to their values and manage to exhibit a quiet sense of dignity and strength.

The individuals who make up "Slim's table" are a group of elderly black men who regularly eat at Valois, a well-known restaurant a few blocks from the University of Chicago. While many male members of the underclass often drift in and out of the labor market, exploit their women friends, and think nothing of engaging in criminal activities, the working men who share a lunch table with Slim have embraced very different values. As Duneier notes: "Slim and his buddies want to live in accordance with notions of appropriate or correct behavior. The idea of 'respectability'—defined as a mode of life conforming to and embodying notions of moral worth—has a great significance for them."[7] Although most of the men are lifetime Democrats, Duneier notes that they often sound like Republicans when they talk about the need for greater personal responsibility, hard work, and self-discipline.[8] Their concern with trying to be decent citizens leads them to be critical of the young lower-class blacks who have often taken over their neighborhoods. They are easily upset by the aggressiveness, laziness, and lack of personal responsibility exhibited by so many in the inner city. Patterns of impulsive and self-destructive behavior "are taken by Slim and his sitting buddies to be features of a social disorganization that has ruined the ghettos of their youth."[9] The working poor who regularly patronize the Valois restaurant see too many inner-city residents engaged in behavior that "is beneath the level of moral worth they associate with their own existence."[10] As middle-class blacks have fled to the suburbs in search of a better life, the working poor who remain behind in the crumbling inner cities have often valiantly tried to maintain some sense of order and dignity within their neighborhoods. But with the growth of street gangs and drug dealers, their ability to set the moral tone for the neighborhood has been overcome by competing elements in the ghetto.

The central question Duneier addresses in his provocative book is how Slim and his friends are able to remain faithful to their values as well as retain some sense of dignity in light of the turmoil that surrounds them. After all, he notes, the "black regulars at Valois sense that they are isolated from institutions which serve to propagate and maintain symbols of decency that were once embodied in ghetto life but now also seem to have declined in mainstream culture."[11] The answer, interestingly enough, lies in the restaurant that they patronize daily.

As political officials have lost either the willpower or interest in maintaining a sense of public order, Valois has helped fill the remaining void left behind by the permissiveness of the larger political system. The two tough Greek immigrants who own and operate the restaurant are "committed to maintaining a state of absolute order at Valois."[12] It is this sense of discipline that attracts Slim and his associates and helps stabilize their daily routine. Their ability to find and visit a well-run and orderly institution around which they can structure their lives "helps black regulars overcome the aloneness created by their sense of living in a moral vacuum."[13]

In many respects, the restaurant has become the black working class counterpart to Ed Garreau's "edge city."[14] Just as whites have fled to their own enclosed malls and neighborhoods protected by private security guards, so the working poor have sought out the protection and order imposed by two crusty Greek immigrants. When Duneier asked, "What is it about the cafeteria that makes it a haven for men who seek an orderly environment?," he found that "part of the answer lies in the existence of a set of expectations that guides behavior there."[15] Men know that there are certain things they cannot do at Valois that they might do elsewhere. As Slim's friend Murphy remarked, "This restaurant is a place where a woman with a baby can come and not be accosted."[16] Even some of the unemployed street-corner men at Valois—people who act differently at other places—behave themselves in the restaurant. Boom boxes, foul language, fighting, or harassing women are simply not tolerated. Duneier's insight suggests that Valois is not only a poor man's edge city, but also a graphic metaphor of what happens when society— as well as the officials presiding over the modern welfare state—no longer publicly expect people to behave themselves. If, as Bill Clinton repeatedly stressed in his 1992 presidential campaign, government programs fail to establish the expectation that only those who abide by the rules of the game will be rewarded, then people will try to seek out private alternatives where they can reaffirm their own values and sense of moral worth. Or as Duneier has put it: "The paucity of visible leadership and public symbols embodying and crystalizing the moral components of a separate, authentic black image symbolized by a belief in personal responsibility, integration and the impor- tance of social order with which they can identify helps explain the tremen- dous desire on the part of such people for informal private primary groups of the kind they form at Valois."[17] Perhaps we should not be surprised that in this particular neighborhood in Chicago, two Greek immigrants who still cling to their old-world heritage are the ones who have created a safe haven for the black working poor. The owners of Valois have realized, as many proponents of the liberal welfare state have not, that if we hold out high expectations for people, the quality of life is often improved.

HOW MANY INDIGENTS ARE MEMBERS OF THE WORKING POOR?

The plight of Slim and his associates raises the question: How typical are they of most poor people? If the working poor have very different attitudes than the underclass and are highly dependent on cyclical changes in the economy, it is imperative that we have some reasonable idea about how large a population they represent. If we count people as members of the working poor only if they work full time for at least twenty-six weeks or part time for twelve months of the year, we find that roughly 20 percent of all the poor aged sixteen and up can be considered members of the working poor. If we include their spouses and children, roughly 40 to 50 percent of the poor are parts of working families. Slim and his associates are thus a small and not necessarily representative sample of all the poor. To put this employment information in some kind of larger context, we can also compare the work record of the poor with the non-poor (table 11.1).

Although 60 percent of those above the poverty line appear to be actively working, only about a fifth of the poor have a comparable record. However,

Table 11.1
The Work Record of the Poor and Non-Poor, 1990
(Ages 16 and Up)

	Poor	Non-Poor
Full time, full year (50 weeks, 35 hours)	10.1%	45.6%
Full time, part year (27–49 weeks)	5.3	8.0
Part time, full year (50 weeks, 35 hours or less time)	4.7	6.2
Total	20.1%	59.8%

Source: U.S. Bureau of the Census, March 1991 Current Population Survey tapes.

as mentioned earlier, some ethnographic studies maintain that survey data often understate the true participation of the poor in the labor market. Because the poor often want to minimize their income taxes or remain eligible for welfare, they often work in the underground economy and thus fail to report the full extent of their participation in the work force. At present there are very little hard data on how widespread participation in this underground economy is among either indigents or their non-poor counterparts. While we can always speculate that these hidden forms of employment might slightly improve the work record of the poor, there is little evidence to suggest that they would dramatically alter the very different work record of the poor and non-poor.

HAS TRICKLE DOWN TRICKLED OUT?

The phenomenon of trickle-down economics and the fate of the working poor are naturally intertwined. The financial well-being of the working poor, however small their numbers may be, has always been highly dependent on the fortunes of the economy. When the economy is growing and labor markets are tight, employers are likely to be less selective about whom they hire. Likewise, as jobs become more plentiful, Slim and other members of the working poor will find it easier to locate better-paying positions that will enable them to earn their way out of poverty. In the 1960s and 1970s, many economists repeatedly stressed the strong association that existed between economic growth and the overall poverty rate. In fact, between the 1950s and 1980s the simple correlation between changes in real GNP per household and changes in the percentage of people below the poverty line was a significant -0.69.[18] In reviewing data spanning the years from the Kennedy administration through the Carter presidency, Rebecca Blank and Alan Blinder estimated that if a recession lasted for two years and led to a two-point rise in prime-age male unemployment, it would add roughly about one percentage point to the overall poverty rate.[19] While the elderly were relatively immune to changes in the economy, the impact of cyclical economic changes was especially strong among male-headed households.[20]

As encouraging as this news was, it did not mean that if the unemployment rate dropped to zero, the poverty population would also disappear. After all, in the 1960s and 1970s the poverty rate was usually two to three times the size of the unemployment rate. Even in the best of years, trickle-down economics would still have left behind a large residue of poor people. Regardless of this situation, it was still apparent that economic upturns had a significant impact on the financial well-being of the poor. As John F. Kennedy had once remarked, a rising tide lifts all boats, and that certainly seemed the case with the majority of the poor. Slim and other members of the working poor appeared to gain the most relative to the rich in periods of cyclical upturns.[21] Conversely, when the economic tide ebbed and expansion gave way to recession, the poor also suffered the most.

But no sooner had it become clear that an expanding economy benefited the poor than new data raised doubts about its continued importance. Despite the sustained expansion of the U.S. economy under Reagan and Bush in the 1980s, the nation's overall poverty rate ceased to drop as expected.[22] Cyclical fluctuations in the economy, which many liberals had stressed in their disputes with Charles Murray, appeared to have lost their effectiveness in fighting poverty.

What was so remarkable is that the expansion of the 1980s appeared very similar to the expansion of the 1960s.[23] To put these two periods in context, we must understand that in the last thirty years the country has enjoyed two decades of considerable prosperity, and one decade of sluggish growth and constant recessions. From 1970 to 1982, the economy suffered through rising rates of inflation and unemployment as well as five years of negative growth in the GNP. In contrast, from 1963 to 1969 and from 1983 to 1989, the United States enjoyed sustained periods of economic growth. As Rebecca Blank has pointed out, both decades had similar records on employment and GNP. In the 1960s, real GNP grew by a substantial 34.7 percent, while in the 1980s it expanded by an almost identical 30.1 percent. Similarly, unemployment fell by 37 percent during the Kennedy and Johnson years and by a slightly higher 45.3 percent in the Reagan/Bush era.[24] Even more remarkable, the number of workers entering the labor market in the 1980s declined dramatically from the 1960s when baby boomers flooded the market. Regardless of these favorable comparisons, Rebecca Blank discovered that the cyclical upturn of the 1980s had not trickled down to the poor as it had in the 1960s.[25] While the economic prosperity of the 1960s saw a significant drop in poverty rates, those same poverty rates were relatively stagnant during the 1980s. When the economic expansion of the 1980s came to an end in 1989, the actual aggregate poverty rate of 12.8 percent was 2 to 3 percentage points higher than what we would have predicted based on trends in the 1960s.[26] As the rising tides of the recent decade lifted all boats, the poverty boat appeared to have sprung a leak. And Slim and his associates were the passengers most at risk.

As the link between improvements in the economy and the poverty rate became severed, the inevitable question people began to ask was, why? What had changed since the 1960s to undermine the effectiveness of economic expansions in helping people to climb out of poverty? Although the issue remains controversial, there are a variety of reasons why cyclical changes in the economy have declined in importance. First, when the economy expands rapidly, it will have only a major impact on the overall poverty rate if a sizable group of indigents is in the work force. But as was pointed out earlier, the population of the working poor has dramatically declined over the last thirty years. Fewer and fewer indigents share the work ethic of Slim and his friends. If we look at the employment record of indigent families, we find more than a 40 percent reduction in the number of people who are employed full time. If a rising tide is going to lift people out of poverty, the poor must be in the labor market (or metaphorically speaking, at least their boats must be floating in the water) before an economic expansion can improve their financial situation.

However, William Julius Wilson and John Kasarda have recently suggested that cyclical changes have lost their punch because the nationwide economic expansion was not spread evenly around the country.[27] This argument, called the "geographical mismatch theory," maintains that many inner-city blacks have been economically bypassed by the expansion of the last decade. What may be important is not whether the overall economy prospers, but whether that prosperity has found its way to the residents of the inner city. Even if economic tides are rising, it is possible that they may not wash all shores equally.

THE PROBLEM OF REGIONAL MISMATCH

In support of this argument it should be noted that in the 1980s variations in unemployment from state to state reached a twenty-year peak. The differences in unemployment rates between depressed regions like the Midwest and the booming Sunbelt were extreme to say the least.[28] This contrast occurred because of a dramatic restructuring that has taken place in the

American economy. Over the last forty years, there has been a major shift of American firms first to the West and then to the South. Part of this shift was due to the rise of the Cold War and the decision of the government to enlarge U.S. military power. As America elected to invest more in defense and in the aerospace industry, cities like Seattle and Los Angeles on the West Coast began to boom. Likewise, the expansion of the semiconductor industry and the growth of a high-technology, information-based economy also led to the growing affluence of California's Silicon Valley and the San Francisco Bay Area.

With the expansion of the interstate highway system, the growth of jobs and affluence also began to trickle down to the South, transforming in the process a region that had once been plagued by limited employment opportunities. As the cost of shipping goods began to decline, many firms were attracted to the Southern states because of their climate, probusiness attitudes, and low tax rates.[29] This prosperity was reflected in the creation of new jobs. Between 1960 and 1985, seventeen million jobs were created in the South, eleven million in the West, a little over seven million in the Midwest, and only five million in the Northeast.[30] But even more telling, while manufacturing positions, normally filled by low-skilled workers, declined by over a million between 1960 and 1985 in the old industrial heartland of America (the Midwest and Northeast), they grew by over two million in the once rural South.[31] In the economic recovery of the 1980s, the Northeast showed surprising strength, and the dramatic growth of jobs in the South slowed. But the old industrial backbone of the country, the Midwest, continued to experience hard times and eventually acquired the nickname the "Rustbelt of America."

If indigents like Slim were located in regions hardest hit by the restructuring of American industry, it is easy to see why the economic expansion of the 1980s might not have trickled down to the poor. Although the overall economy enjoyed relative prosperity, the working poor may have been stranded in slow-growing areas of the country that were bypassed by the economic "go-go" years of the 1980s. If this scenario had actually happened, we would expect to find that the distribution of the poor and non-poor among the various census tracts of the country would have significantly changed during the Reagan/Bush years. The number of people below the poverty line in stagnant regions of the country should have dramatically risen while the opposite situation should have occurred in rapidly expanding states. However, attempts to verify the regional mismatch argument have produced mixed results. Paul Jargowsky has discovered that the proportion of low-income blacks living in ghettos shrank along the eastern seaboard, but ex-

Table 11.2

Regional Distribution of Poor and Non-Poor Family Units

	1979		1989	
	Percentage of Poor	*Percentage of Non-Poor*	*Percentage of Poor*	*Percentage of Non-Poor*
New England	4.7	5.7	3.1	5.7
Mid-Atlantic	16.1	17.2	13.3	15.9
East North Central	14.9	19.5	15.5	17.7
West North Central	6.4	7.9	6.4	7.5
South Atlantic	18.7	15.2	17.5	17.0
East South Central	9.9	6.0	10.0	5.8
West South Central	13.0	9.7	15.5	10.0
Mountain	4.5	4.8	5.5	5.4
Pacific	11.7	13.9	13.1	14.9

Source: Rebecca Blank, "Why Were Poverty Rates So High in the 1980s?" in *Poverty and Prosperity in the U.S. in the Late Twentieth Century*, ed. Dimitri Papdimitrious and Edward Wolfe (New York: St. Martin's Press, 1993). Reprinted with permission of St. Martin's Press and the Macmillan Press, Ltd.

panded in the industrial Midwest.[32] In contrast, Rebecca Blank has found that the distribution of poor and non-poor family units in the country was relatively the same in 1989 as it was in 1979.[33] While more poor live in the South Atlantic, East North Central, and West South Central regions than anywhere else, the overall distribution of poor family units in this country has been relatively stable from one decade to the next (see table 11.2).

THE PROBLEM OF URBAN MISMATCH

There is, however, the possibility that the urban location of the poor rather than their regional distribution is the cause of their limited upward mobility. This variation, known as "urban mismatch theory," was first developed by John Kain in the 1960s and has been refined and popularized more recently by John Kasarda and William Julius Wilson.[34] The proponents of this theory argue that the regional transformation of American industry has been accompanied by a concurrent and parallel urban restructuring of American companies that has served to isolate the poor in urban ghettos, making it difficult for them to find any kind of work at all. While the theory has many variations, the argument essentially revolves around two themes.

First, proponents of the theory, such as Kasarda and Wilson, argue that the fragmentation and dispersal of economic activity in major cities is oc-curring primarily for structural and economic reasons. Historically our urban centers were primarily responsible for the growth of the blue-collar jobs that eventually employed this country's immigrant population. With rapid changes in technology and transportation costs, most of these same industrial firms have now moved to the suburbs and taken their jobs with them. As companies have adopted production systems involving continuous material flow systems, they have bought cheaper land on the outskirts of municipalities to develop sprawling manufacturing plants. In built-up urban areas it is often too costly to acquire and assemble the large blocks of land needed by modern factories. Even more importantly, companies have decided to leave inner cities for transportation reasons. Before the 1960s most firms had to remain downtown because they needed quick access to rail terminals in order to ship their goods. When the interstate highway system was essentially completed by the end of the 1960s, it was economically feasible for companies to ship their goods from outlying suburban areas.

The resulting loss of manufacturing jobs in the inner cities was accompanied by a major restructuring of urban centers. As soon as cities started to decline as industrial centers, they began to emerge first as service centers (in the 1950s and 1960s) and later as informational and technological centers (during the 1970s and 1980s).[35] In the 1980s we also saw a renaissance in downtown areas as investors poured money into new and expensive high-rise office buildings. Many companies, including law and accounting firms, found urban space attractive and began to expand their activities downtown. Unlike factories, which require an extensive amount of room to manufacture material goods, workers involved in processing, storing, and transmitting information require limited space. By stacking workers on top of one another in downtown skyscrapers, law firms and other technologically oriented companies could see their productivity increase.[36] As the young and often well-paid workers employed by these firms also sought diversion after work, cities also began to prosper as cultural and entertainment centers.

The second part of Wilson and Kasarda's thesis is that as urban economies have changed, the poor increasingly find that their skills are either irrelevant or mismatched with the job opportunities present in the ghetto. "The transformation of major northern metropolises from centers of goods-processing to centers of information-processing has been accompanied by a major shift in the educational requirements for employment. Whereas job losses in . . . large urban centers . . . have been greatest in industries with lower educational requirements, job growth has been concentrated in industries that require higher levels of education."[37] The unfortunate result is that the replacement of low-skilled manufacturing jobs by high-tech positions has made it difficult if not impossible for inner-city workers to find jobs in their neighborhoods. The only openings readily available required educational credentials that few ghetto residents possess.

If that is the case, then the obvious question is, why don't the working poor either migrate or commute to the suburbs where their former employers have relocated? After all, thousands of suburbanites commute ever day from outlying areas to work in the skyscrapers that anchor our downtowns. But Kasarda and Wilson argue that it is unfair to compare indigents and suburban commuters because they confront very different obstacles in finding work. Because many homeowners in all-white areas are reluctant to sell their houses to inner-city residents, minority members often lack the mobility of white suburbanites.

Likewise, commuting to outlying areas is difficult for the poor given their limited means of transportation as well as lack of information about job opportunities in the suburbs. When companies shut down their downtown operations and move to the suburbs, the poor often become isolated and cut off from information about job prospects in outlying areas. Unlike white suburbanites, inner-city residents confront high search costs that make it difficult for them to become informed about suburban jobs, and many of them lack transportation to travel to suburban worksites. Because of the dispersed nature of many large urban communities, bus transportation to outlying areas is often sporadic or nonexistent. Given their lack of funds, many inner-city residents often do not own a car, or if they do, the cost of maintaining it is prohibitively expensive. In light of these difficulties, it is easy to see why Wilson and Kasarda believe the prosperity of the 1980s passed by so many of the poor. Despite the cyclical upturn in the economy, too many indigents were stranded in inner cities and unable to take advantage of the growth of jobs in society as a whole.

While at first glance the urban mismatch theory seems convincing and even compelling as an explanation of the plight of the poor, the theory's explanation of poverty is not always consistent with the available data. The evidence in support of its two main tenets is mixed at best. First, the assumption that companies are moving out of the inner city for purely structural reasons is certainly open to debate. While many firms have been pulled to the suburbs by the attraction of cheap land and excellent highways, they have also been pushed by the erosion of civility and the collapse of working conditions in the inner city. As the breakdown of values has trickled down to the poor, both the security of the ghetto as well as the motivation of the inner city work force has seriously deteriorated. In 1992, for instance, Chrysler Corporation announced that it was moving its automobile headquarters to the suburbs of Detroit because it could no longer guarantee the safety of its workers. Although Wilson and Kasarda often suggest that the poor have been victimized by structural forces beyond their control, they overlook the fact that the isolation of the poor and the mismatch of their work experience has also been self-imposed. Rather than being merely help- less victims of economic changes, the underclass must bear some responsibil- ity for the demise of job opportunities in the inner city.

The same judgment applies to the laissez-faire policies of our present urban welfare state. Because the courts have made it difficult for cities to enforce vagrancy laws or to maintain some sense of law and order in down- town areas, companies and workers alike have fled to outlying suburban areas. With public authorities either unwilling or unable to enforce the observance of societal norms, there has been an unfortunate breakdown of any sense of community life in America. As public disorder grows, people have fled downtown areas for privately owned industrial parks, shopping malls and fenced-in residential areas where the courts cannot overturn their "codes of behavior." The begging and violence of the public street now exist alongside the decorum and predictability of the mall and the privately maintained and supervised industrial park. Unlike the old classical notion of cities as public spaces in which individuals from all walks of life would meet and interact with one another, America's urban areas have become transformed into highly stratified societies. While the black working poor congregates at Valois, white suburbanites and private companies have often fled to the safety of suburban communities. Contrary to the suggestions of Kain, Wilson, and Kasarda, the geographical dispersion of jobs in this country may reflect as much the rise of anomie and the inability of govern- ment to maintain order in our large cities as it does changes in transporta- tion costs.

Wilson and Kasarda's second assumption that the poor are unable to find any meaningful work is also open to question. The fact that the costs of locating and applying for jobs have increased does not necessarily mean that the poor will automatically drop out of the labor market for lack of work. Unlike analysts who rely on structuralist assumptions, we must not assume that the poor are merely victims who are incapable of showing some degree of initiative and self-help. This point becomes readily apparent when we look at aggregate data. From a national perspective, the urban mismatch theory basically applies to the larger and older industrial cities of the Midwest and Northeast. It is thus hard to see how the dramatic break that occurred in the late 1970s and 1980s between cyclical fluctuations in the economy and changes in the aggregate poverty rate can be primarily due to the dispersion

Table 11.3
The Urban Location of Poor Family Units

	Percentage of the Poor Living in	
Year	*Central City*	*Remainder of SMSA*
1964	32.8	17.9
1970	33.9	20.8
1980	36.9	23.0
1990	35.2	22.9

Source: Rebecca Blank, "Why Were Poverty Rates So High in the 1980s?" in *Poverty and Prosperity in the U.S. in the Late Twentieth Century,* ed. Dimitri Papdimitrious and Edward Wolfe (New York: St. Martin's Press, 1993). Reprinted with permission of St. Martin's Press and the Macmillan Press, Ltd.

of industry in the industrial heartland of America. There is no evidence from the location of the poor and non-poor in this country over the last thirty years that the number of indigents living in urban areas has dramatically increased as industry has moved to the suburbs. As table 11.3 indicates, in the 1960s roughly 33 percent of the poor lived in central city locations, compared with a little over 35 percent in 1990. If the poor are being abandoned and isolated in urban ghettos, we would have expected a more dramatic upsurge in the percentage of poor trapped in large urban locations.

Aside from its inability to explain national trends, the ability of the urban mismatch theory to explain joblessness in particular cities has had only limited success. Analysts who undertake comparative urban studies insist that there is a relationship between the location of industry within a city and the job record of minorities. In support of the mismatch theory, Joseph Mooney and later John Farley, who used census data on the employment rates of blacks and whites in large metropolitan areas, found that the gap between the two races became larger when a city's manufacturing, service, and trade jobs were highly suburbanized.[38]

However, when other scholars tried to evaluate the mismatch theory by conducting neighborhood studies, they came to the opposite conclusion. The analysis of neighborhoods, in contrast to comparative urban studies, tries to determine if blacks who live adjacent to highly industrialized areas with plenty of blue-collar jobs have higher or lower rates of employment than blacks residing in more isolated communities. In one of the best-known neighborhood studies, David Ellwood examined employment patters in two large ghettos in Chicago: the west side, which is a major center of warehouses and manufacturing plants, and the south side, which is more residential and relatively nonindustrialized.[39] If the urban mismatch theory is correct, we would expect that blacks on the west side, who have lower search and transportation costs, would have much higher employment rates than their peers on the south side. But aside from the case of teenagers, Ellwood found that physical closeness to work had a minimal impact on employment records in the two neighborhoods. Separate studies of Los Angeles and Pittsburgh also found that proximity to places of employment had a negative (though statistically uncertain) effect on the probability that black males would be gainfully employed.[40]

Finally, ethnographic studies and survey data which look at the economic fate of different ethnic groups within large cities also raise serious doubts about the accuracy of the mismatch theory.[41] The main problem with both the comparative urban and neighborhood studies is that they try to make predictions about individual behavior based on aggregate data. But even if we find that there is a high correlation between the dispersal of manufacturing jobs and the persistence of poverty in an area, we cannot be sure that the two factors are related.[42] To assume otherwise is to commit what is known as the "ecological fallacy." While manufacturing plants are moving out of inner cities that have high concentrations of poor people, their actions may not be responsible for the economic plight of the poor. To determine if this is the case, researchers must gather direct information on the fortunes of individuals within the inner city. Studies such as these have found that only 20 percent of the population has lost jobs due to plant closings or automation.[43] While structural factors like the out-migration of companies may throw many people out of work, it apparently is not the predominant cause of unemployment.

In addition, when researchers questioned inner-city residents who were successful in finding jobs, they discovered that the alleged high costs of commuting to the suburbs, or the growing demand for more well-educated employees, was not a major obstacle for all of them. As table 11.4 indicates, in the city of Chicago, even when low-income Mexicans lack a car and have no high school degree, close to 90 percent are still able to find work.[44] In sharp contrast, only 36 percent of comparable black workers were able to do so. Because the Chicago survey found that the wages of the various ethnic groups in the study were roughly comparable, they concluded that the impressive work record of Mexican immigrants was not a result of the Mexicans' accepting lower-paying, menial jobs.[45]

While the proponents of the mismatch theory are correct when they insist that the lack of transportation makes it harder for indigents to find jobs in the suburbs, it does not necessarily follow that these additional costs will deter

Table 11.4

The Work Record of Chicago's Inner-City Residents

	Black	*White*	*Mexican*
Percentage employed	66.0	82.0	93.0
Percentage employed with no car in household	45.9	77.4	90.1
Percentage employed with no car and no high school degree	36.0	n/a	89.0

Sources: Robert Aponte, "Ethnicity and Male Employment in the Inner City: A Test of Two Theories," paper delivered at the Urban Poverty and Family Life Conference, Chicago, 1991. Article is available from the Center for the Study of Urban Inequality at the University of Chicago. The above table is reprinted with permission of Robert Aponte.

the poor from looking for work. In focusing on the costs of commuting to the suburbs, Kain as well as Kasarda and Wilson have overlooked the gains one derives from securing work. In economic terms, the relocation of industrial jobs has confronted the poor with the conflict between the substitution and income effect. While the high cost of commuting between the inner city and the suburbs may reduce the payoff from work and thus discourage the poor from participating in the labor market, the prospect of being unable to purchase life's necessities makes finding a job all the more attractive. As a simple economic problem, it is certainly possible that the out-migration of jobs might stimulate more rather than less work effort by the poor. While Mexican immigrants have been successful in finding jobs even when they lack basic transportation, other minorities have been overwhelmed by the substitution effect and dropped out of the labor market. If by sheer force of willpower Mexicans can secure gainful employment, what is to stop other ethnic groups from achieving comparable success?

The answer may lie in the fact that the out-migration of industry from the inner city has aggravated and enlarged all the problems associated with the breakdown of traditional values.[46] While Wilson and Kasarda are correct that the transformation in our urban economies has compounded the problems of the poor, they have failed to distinguish between the primary and the secondary cause of low employment in the inner city. Although the changing nature of urban economies has exacerbated the difficulties facing the poor, it is the secondary reason for the economic plight of inner-city blacks. The primary reason for the plight of indigent blacks in cities like Chicago is the growth of the black underclass, which lacks the motivation and drive to cope with its quickly changing environment. To the distress of Slim and his friends, many inner-city residents often do not share the same values of their working-poor counterparts. As Mexican immigrants have clearly demonstrated, as long as individuals are highly motivated, they will find a way to adjust and even prosper in a demanding and sluggish economy.

The growth of the welfare state has further compounded the difficulties of the black underclass by enabling many of them to take a more lackadaisical approach to finding work. While historically poor people have always been willing to pull up stakes and overcome immense obstacles in the search for work, their incentive to obtain employment diminishes once they become hooked on welfare. As more and more low-income blacks receive governmental assistance, the financial gain from commuting to the suburbs has naturally declined. Although many commentators have approvingly quoted John Kasarda's mismatch theory to disprove Murray's contention that transfer payments caused people to drop out of the labor market, they overlook his argument that the growth of the welfare state may have enabled many indigents to search less intensely for work. The well-meaning efforts of many public officials to help indigents may have "inadvertently increased the plight of the poor by bonding distressed people to distressed places."[47]

If the above problems were not worrisome enough, there is the distinct possibility that as the size of the black underclass has grown, more and more companies have relied on statistical discrimination to hire their employees. While overt forms of racism have dramatically declined over the past several decades, many companies in the Chicago area have expressed concern to researchers over the "costs and quality of the available labor supply, especially the lack of basic skills and a good work ethic among inner city residents."[48] Employers who sing the praises of immigrant workers often express reservations about hiring blacks. Their ability to distinguish accurately between the very different attitudes of the separate classes that make up the black ghetto has been colored by the work record of the black underclass. As Kirschenman and Neckerman point out, in light of these perceived problems, "employers coped though various strategies. Some . . . used . . . recruiting and screening techniques to help select 'good workers' . . . [such as] . . . referrals from employees [and] . . . targeted newspaper ads to particular neighborhoods or ethnic groups."[49]

Obviously, the injustice of this procedure falls most heavily on individuals like Slim and other members of the black working class. Too many employers in Chicago overlook the fact that many black working men and women who are eager to find full-time work would undoubtedly prove to be productive employees. In the same way that the black underclass has isolated and made life more trying for the black working poor inside the ghetto, the underclass has also helped isolate and make life more difficult for the black working poor outside the ghetto. The conduct of the underclass often makes employers hesitant to hire anyone from the inner city. While Slim and his associates were able to shield themselves from the chaos of the ghetto inside Valois, they have been less lucky in finding comparable shields to distance themselves from the underclass in the labor market. As pointed out earlier, if discrimination is practiced in a limited rather than universal manner, minorities can still find work and achieve upward mobility. But the actions of the underclass have certainly made it harder for other blacks to identify and apply for jobs with those employers who wish to treat them fairly. Surprisingly, the stigma of the underclass also affects poor blacks who are trying to improve their educational skills. In the Chicago survey, researchers found that if low-income blacks enrolled in government training programs, they might actually hurt their prospects of securing a job.[50] Many companies often "mistakenly assumed that blacks who resorted to training programs were not able to cut it on their own and represented the welfare poor."[51]

GOVERNMENT POLICIES FOR URBAN MISMATCH

As the above discussion clearly demonstrates, even if American industry decided to relocate outlying factories to the inner city, there is little evidence that this action would significantly reduce the number of people stuck in poverty. Until the larger problems of the ghetto are resolved, the presence or absence of industry in downtown areas may be relatively unimportant in lowering the overall poverty rate in this country. The dispersal of local industry is not per se the main reason why cyclical upturns in the economy have lost their effectiveness in helping the poor become self-supporting.

But the fact that the out-migration of companies from the inner city may be relatively insignificant from a national perspective should not blind us to its importance for the black working poor. To assist Slim and his friends, we need to ask what we can do to assist the black working class in finding well-paying jobs. Aside from the obvious point of improving the skills of the working poor, poverty researchers have proposed two very different policies for dealing with the out-migration of companies from the inner city: either attract industry back into the city, or facilitate the ability of local residents to move out of the city. Some, especially conservatives, have adopted the first proposal, advocating either enterprise zones, a national development bank, a Reconstruction Finance Corporation, or a new government-business-labor partnership to reindustrialize or otherwise rebuild the blue-collar employment bases of our urban centers.[52] But these jobs-to-people strategies are as economically unrealistic as they are nostalgic. At present, the evidence seems to indicate that the only kinds of firms that will thrive in our urban areas are information-rich companies that store, transmit, and interpret knowledge.

Unless public officials become more serious as well as more successful in eliminating the pathologies that characterize the inner city, there is little hope that efforts to stimulate more job creation for blue-collar workers by the reindustrialization of our cities will be effective. In spite of the regulatory concessions and tax breaks embodied in most enterprise zones or urban reconstruction proposals, it remains unclear how inner-city companies can make a financial go of it. The financial incentives that have pulled companies to the suburbs and the deteriorating social conditions that have pushed them out of the inner city are not likely to change any time soon. At the very least, public efforts to reindustrialize the inner city would have to be part of a much larger program to alter the attitudes of the poor and enhance the safety of the urban core if they are to have any chance of success. The employment problem of the inner city has as much to do with culture as it does with the lack of capital.[53] Even with the best of intentions, it is highly likely that public efforts to create a significant number of jobs in the inner city will simply become yet another costly government failure.

A second and perhaps economically more feasible proposal is to facilitate the efforts of the working poor to commute or migrate to outlying areas. While liberals often argue that such programs might significantly reduce the overall poverty rate, their expectations are probably unrealistic. However, the payoffs from adopting such a policy for individuals like Slim may be considerable. Just as the millions of blacks who moved from the South at the turn of the century eventually prospered, so the black middle class that migrated out of the inner city during the 1960s saw an improvement in their financial standing. But unlike the black middle class, which possessed adequate resources to relocate to the suburbs, the working poor may need financial assistance to be equally mobile.

To achieve that goal, the government might consider a wide array of policies to help the working poor commute from urban centers to outlying areas, such as improved bus service, subsidized job searches in outlying suburban areas, an enhanced information system listing up-to-the-minute data on job openings, and vigorous enforcement of employment-discrimination laws.[54] To go one step further, the government might also experiment with transfer programs like housing vouchers that would enable the working poor to migrate to suburban areas. A variation of this kind of policy has recently been tried by Chicago's Gautreaux program, which helps tenants in public housing projects find private dwellings in the suburbs. While all of these programs may achieve some success, their overall impact on the nation's poverty rate will probably be minimal at best. But at the margin, they may enable the black working poor to have a better chance of achieving upward mobility. For that more modest but still significant reason alone, these are policies worth pursuing.

CONCLUSION

As we have seen, many liberal analysts have argued that to eliminate poverty in this country it is essential that we have a healthy economy that generates an ample supply of jobs. It is hard to deny the simple fact that every time the economy has slipped into a recession, there has been a major increase in the overall poverty rate. In the 1970s and early 1980s, many economists stressed this point as the government's efforts to eliminate poverty ran out of steam and appeared ineffectual and poorly conceived. When Charles Murray audaciously argued that the welfare programs of the Great Society had hampered the ability of the country to eliminate the causes of poverty, his opponents countered by pointing to cyclical fluctuations in the economy. They maintained that the culprit causing the war on poverty to fail was the sluggish growth and recurring recessions that marked the Nixon and Carter administrations. But as the 1970s gave way to the prosperity of the Reagan years, it appeared that the connection between cyclical fluctuations in the economy and the overall poverty rate has been severed. While the recession of 1990 and 1991 proved that economic downturns would still increase the overall poverty rate, the prosperity of the mid-1980s indicated that cyclical upturns were increasingly less effective in decreasing the poverty rate. In spite of past historical trends, trickle-down economics had apparently trickled out.

The reasons for this dramatic decline in the efficacy of trickle-down economics remain highly controversial. While many scholars claim that the changing nature of urban economies explains why national economic trends are no longer lifting the poor out of poverty, the evidence in support of their arguments is mixed at best. The alleged mismatch of jobs in our inner cities appears to be merely a surrogate measure of the behavior problems plaguing the slums of large urban centers. But an alternative thesis is that the major economic problem facing the poor is not the lack of jobs but the lack of decent high-paying jobs. Even if they find work, the poor may be stuck in such "lousy jobs" that they will never be able to earn their way out of poverty. But as we shall see in chapter 12, the alleged problem of low-paying jobs may be as much a behavioral as it is a structural problem.

TWELVE

The Economy II: The Lack of High-Paying Jobs

As the economic upturn of the 1980s did little to significantly lower the overall poverty rate analysts searched for new reasons to explain why poverty had become such an intractable problem. A wide array of liberal commentators began to suggest that structural changes occurring in the American economy were partially overshadowing the benefits of cyclical upturns in the economy. While the economy had enjoyed substantial growth during the Reagan years, that expansion masked the fact that the country had lost many high-paying jobs in the auto, steel, textile, and consumer electronics industries. The meteoric rise of Japan and the subsequent demise of our traditional manufacturing base had thus canceled out many of the gains generated by the cyclical recovery that would normally have trickled down to the poor. The resulting problem facing the poor was not a lack of jobs, but a lack of high paying jobs. But many commentators insisted that the significance of these structural changes went beyond their obvious negative impact on the take-home pay of the working poor. The growth of "lousy jobs" had allegedly thwarted one of the two traditional routes of achieving upward mobility.

In the first route, individuals secured better jobs because they either acquired additional training or showed such zeal for work that they became extremely attractive to prospective employers. In the second route, people achieved upward mobility through the constant differentiation and upgrading of the occupational structure in this country. As Peter Blau and Otis Duncan have shown in their insightful book, *The American Occupation Structure*, even when the marketplace failed to equalize the starting line for all Americans, it still enjoyed reasonable success in multiplying the economic prizes available to people through the growing sophistication and improvement of employment opportunities.[1] The marketplace has thus enabled millions to climb out of poverty—not by equalizing the opportunities for individuals to compete fairly with one another, but by constantly upgrading existing jobs.

By the 1980s it was feared that this process of occupational differentiation had essentially ended, thwarting the second route of escape from poverty. As many U.S. firms began to deindustrialize or ship their manufacturing jobs to Mexico or the Far East, numerous commentators believed that the American economy was generating so many low-paying jobs that it was impossible for the working poor to support themselves or their families. On the one hand, the pay difference between good and bad jobs appeared to grow, while on the other hand wage increases in many jobs leveled off or even declined. With the industrial heartland facing intense pressure from Pacific Rim countries, American society appeared to be in danger of turning into a dual economy of low-paid hamburger flippers and high-paid financial executives.

However, we will argue that the so-called good jobs–bad jobs argument badly distorts what is happening to the American economy. While many analysts are correct to argue that structural changes are partly responsible for the persistent nature of poverty, they may have misread the events currently transforming American corporate life. In contrast to the above doomsday scenario, it is possible to argue that the differentiation and upgrading of jobs may be accelerating rather than decelerating, thus increasing the need for highly trained employees. To understand why this is the case, it is necessary to explore more thoroughly how the American economy has evolved over the last several decades.

THE WIDENING GAP BETWEEN GOOD AND BAD JOBS

The supposed expansion of bad jobs in this country stems from the constant growth and transformation of the American economic system. Since the turn of the century, the economy appears to have gone through three distinct phases, which we shall call the age of (1) mass production, (2) hyper-mass production, and (3) mass customization. While many analysts have focused on the shift from a manufacturing to a service and information-based economy, the more important difference from our perspective is the way in which companies actually operate. In each of the above stages, the evolving nature of the economy has presented the poor with very different kinds of employment problems. Even though, at first glance, the problem of low-paying jobs may seem simple enough, there are three competing explanations as to why the wages of the poor are falling behind the rest of society, each based on a different phase of economic development in this country.

MASS PRODUCTION AND THE DUAL LABOR MARKET: A RIGID BARRIER BETWEEN GOOD AND BAD JOBS

Those who focus on the mass production phase of the economy insist that the poor are stuck in "lousy jobs" because there is a rigid barrier between good and bad job opportunities in society. In the 1960s, a group of labor economists, including Peter Doeringer and Michael Piore, argued that the rise of large industrialized companies had fragmented the economy into a dual labor market of high-paying and low-paying positions.[2] While workers in the primary labor market enjoyed high wages and stable employment, the poor were supposedly limited to the secondary labor market, where wages were erratic and prospects for promotion limited. Because the dual labor theorists of the 1960s believed that the growth and evolution of the dual market separating "good jobs" from "bad jobs" was rooted in the very nature of a mass production economy, they were not optimistic that the poor would ever be able to work their way out of poverty.

The mass production phase of industrialization, which was epitomized by the management principles of Taylorism, developed at the turn of the century and prospered well into the late 1960s or 1970s, spreading from manufacturing firms to companies in the service and information fields. The main goal of mass production companies is to turn out a standardized product or service for the mass public at the cheapest price possible. To achieve that goal, companies stressed the development of a smooth-running and highly specialized production process capable of generating economies of scale in the provision of uniform products or services. This production philosophy eliminated the craft industries of the nineteenth century, which had relied on highly skilled artisans to turn out unique and relatively costly commodities responsive to the individualized and often fickle tastes of their customers. Instead of tailoring their products to the specialized needs of their customers, mass production companies tried to attract mass consumers by offering relatively inexpensive and standardized products.

In delivering goods to the marketplace, mass production firms broke the work of the craftsman down into a series of menial and repetitive tasks that required little training or imagination on the part of the worker. Henry Ford and the advocates of scientific management urged companies to simplify and deskill work whenever possible so that any worker, regardless of his training or skills, would be able to fill the available job slots on the assembly line. They believed that employees were merely cogs in highly capitalized, machine-driven workplaces who needed to exercise very little imagination or initiative. The corollary of the deskilled worker was the notion that managers, and not workers, were responsible for eliminating inefficiencies and promoting quality control. To insure that the highly specialized production process worked smoothly, mass production companies developed hierarchical organizations staffed by professional managers to supervise the work force.

In addition, mass production firms constantly tried to expand their operations in order to benefit from economies of scale in the production process, thus lowering the cost of their goods and services. The result of these tendencies was the emergence of large centrally managed companies that came to rule over various segments of the marketplace. As the age of mass production solidified its hold on the American economy, large and pervasive oligopolies came to dominate industries as diverse as automobiles, television, and consumer electronics. The internal logic driving this system was as obvious as it was simple. The more companies lowered their costs, the easier it was for them to reduce their prices, thus making their products more attractive to the average consumer. As the number of consumers who could afford their products grew, the easier it became for businesses to expand their production and lower their prices once more, thus completing the cycle.

Given the large investment they were required to make in production facilities and inventory, mass production companies sought to stabilize their labor force and minimize friction in the workplace. Their fear was that if workers became unhappy or refused to show up for work, it would be difficult to realize the economies of scale necessary to turn out inexpensive products for the marketplace. Accordingly, many companies developed what became know as internal labor markets to limit the turnover of their labor force and to facilitate the smooth operation of the production process. The rise of the dual labor market thus reflected the desire of large mass production firms to buy labor peace. The interchangeable, menial employment opportunities in what became known as the primary sector of the economy were generally much better paying and steady than those found in the secondary sector. Employees who were lucky enough to find work in the primary sector generally had some degree of job security, established rules governing work conditions, the opportunity to join a union, and, most importantly, prospects for advancement through a union-blessed seniority system. Because most mass production companies were relatively profitable, they were more than willing to share part of their profits with their work force in order to guarantee harmonious labor relations and thereby preserve the stability of the production process. Although workers in the primary sector usually performed relatively routine or in some cases even "deskilled" work, they received ample financial rewards for their labor. Until the 1980s, most commentators viewed employment opportunities in the primary sector as "good jobs" that were highly desirable.

But workers who were usually confined to the secondary market of small, thinly capitalized firms—including teenagers, women, minorities, and the poor—were more likely to find themselves in financially unattractive, "lousy jobs." All too often, they worked in low-paying, unstable jobs with minimal prospects for upward mobility, such as those found in fast-food restaurants. In the secondary market, jobs were often self-terminating, with little prospect for promotion and marked by frequent layoffs and limited prestige. Because unions tended to concentrate their efforts on organizing large oligopolistic companies, very few workers in the secondary sector enjoyed the benefits of union membership. Given the "bad or lousy" nature of these job opportunities, workers often had few incentives to develop a stable history of work experience. They tended to shuttle from one badly paid job to the next with very little prospect for financial improvement.

In the view of the dual labor market theorists of the 1960s, the working poor were stuck in "lousy jobs" because too many indigents had become trapped in the low-paying secondary market of the economy.[3] They also maintained that the rigid barrier between the two sectors made it difficult for the poor to enjoy any degree of upward mobility. Since the fragmentation of the labor market grew out of the needs of large corporations for labor stability, government policies to alter the training or attitudes of the work force would do little to enhance upward mobility. In a sharp break with the war on poverty, dual market theorists attacked the views of the Johnson administration, which had insisted that additional schooling and work experience were the keys to obtaining meaningful, well-paying jobs.

As noted earlier, the proponents of the human capital movement had argued that once workers acquired additional human capital skills and experience, their wages would rise because their marginal productivity would increase. Dual market advocates, however, sharply rejected these arguments, insisting that the problem of low wages was a structural one endemic in the labor market, rather than a supply problem reflecting the limitations of the poor. It made no sense to acquire additional experience if the experience always led to just another dead-end job in the secondary labor market. The human capital movement had failed to realize that wage rates only imperfectly reflected the skills or marginal productivity of workers. Primary-sector firms often paid wages above the marginal productivity of workers, while companies in the secondary market often paid below marginal productivity rates. Given the profitability of large oligopolistic firms, mass production companies were more than willing to offer premium salaries in order to buy labor peace and stabilize the work force. Conversely, the erratic and marginal nature of many secondary firms often led them to compensate their employees in ways that only loosely reflected worker productivity. When indigents who acquired additional years of schooling were confined to jobs in the low-paying secondary market, their rate of return on their educational investment was likely to be minimal indeed. The ability of the government to increase the wages of workers by improving their education was often limited by the norms and procedures of internal labor markets.

In spite of the intensity with which they argued their point, the dual market advocates never enjoyed widespread popularity among poverty analysts in the 1960s or thereafter. Their limited faith in the prospects of upward mobility for minorities and the poor seemed unduly pessimistic and out of step with the optimism of the war on poverty. Given their sharp attacks on the human capital assumptions of the Great Society in the 1960s, their views were not always welcomed by policy analysts in the Johnson administration. But even more importantly, the dual labor theorists played a peripheral role in the poverty debate of the 1960s because they seemed guilty of exaggerating the degree of occupational rigidity in the economy. Until forces at work in the U.S. and the international marketplace began to produce fissures in the American mass production economy in the 1970s, it appeared that there was considerable mobility from the secondary to the primary labor market.

Michigan's longitudinal study of over five thousand people discovered that few people were stuck in low-paying secondary jobs for most of their lives, thus belying the views of the dual labor theorists.[4] The boundary that separated secondary from primary jobs appeared more elastic than rigid in nature. In a very encouraging sign, it seemed that large numbers of people constantly moved back and forth between primary and secondary jobs.

Furthermore, the dual labor advocates seemed unfairly to minimize the importance of education in helping people achieve upward mobility. They tended to dismiss too quickly the possibility that if the poor acquired additional education and were temporarily forced to work in the secondary sector, they later could acquire better-paying jobs in the primary sector. To point out that a variety of factors besides marginal productivity may affect wages does not necessarily mean that education has only a minor impact on salaries. After surveying wages among different companies, William T. Dickens and Lawrence F. Katz discovered that "average years of education in industry is positively related to wages in every study in which it is included."[5]

But even more importantly, the proponents of the dual labor theory were guilty of working with a static view of the economy. They often downplayed the fact that the number of jobs in the primary and secondary sectors of the economy has repeatedly expanded and contracted over time. Historically, we now know that the growth of mass production companies over the last thirty to forty years was associated with rising wages and increasing family income. The reason why so many low-income workers benefited from the growth of mass production companies is relatively simple: whenever there was a cyclical upturn in the economy, the primary-sector companies started to grow, and mass production companies recruited employees from previously excluded sources of labor. "The logic of this form of 'queuing' would indicate that a policy of full employment, if pursued long enough and far enough, would either eliminate the secondary sector, through competition for scarce labor, or cause secondary sector jobs to conform more closely to those of the primary sector."[6]

Aside from minimizing cyclical changes in the economy, dual labor advocates also overlooked the possibility that structural economic changes might also lead to the expansion of so-called good jobs. As mentioned previously, Blau and Duncan have found that most American workers experienced mobility because the occupational structure has been constantly upgraded over the years.[7] With the growth of mass production companies, the number of lucrative jobs has expanded over time and in the process eventually crowded out low paying "lousy" occupations. As soon as large industrial companies lowered their prices and thereby expanded their market share, they hired additional workers in the well-paying primary sector. When these periods of upgrading in the occupational structure coincided with cyclical improvements in the economy, very few poor people, as the Michigan study indicated, were likely to be confined to low-paying jobs for any length of time.

The advocates of the dual labor theory were thus vulnerable to the charge that they had exaggerated both the unimportance of supply traits as well as the rigidity of the barrier separating the secondary and the primary labor markets. By insisting that most supply side theories of poverty have rather parochial views of labor markets, they failed to realize that their view that the poor were permanently locked into low-paying "lousy jobs" was equally naive and empirically unfounded.

THE RISE OF HYPER-MASS PRODUCTION AND THE DECLINE OF THE PRIMARY SECTOR

By the 1970s, a number of liberal commentators, including Bennett Harrison and Barry Bluestone, began to argue that the process of occupation differentiation, which had been ignored by the dual labor market theorists, had come to an end.[8] Like their predecessors of the 1960s, they focused on structural economic factors to provide a second explanation as to why many people had become trapped in low-paying jobs. Regardless of whether or not there was a rigid barrier between so-called good and bad jobs, Harrison and Bluestone insisted that the problem of "lousy jobs" was due to the contraction of the primary sector of the economy. Instead of the primary sector continuing to grow at the expense of the secondary sector, secondary jobs were now cannibalizing and crowding out previously well-paying primary jobs.

As dire as the misgivings of the dual labor theorists may have been, they paled in comparison to the dramatic events that were reshaping the American economy in the late 1970s. Harrison and Bluestone worried that the American economy had entered a new phase, which, although they did not use this terminology, can be appropriately dubbed the period of "hyper-mass production." To some extent, these structural changes transforming America were a result of both the success of the post-World War II economy as well as the rise of Japan. As mass production companies stepped up their production of consumer goods in the postwar period, they eventually saturated the markets for cars, refrigerators, TVs, textiles, and a host of other goods. The ability of firms to find profitable outlets for their products appeared to be drying up. At the same time that their prospects for expanded sales in the American marketplace began to decline, American businesses found themselves in tough competition with countries from Asia. In a variety of markets, Japan and other Pacific Rim nations started to sell high-quality but relatively inexpensive goods to customers who had normally purchased only American-made products. If these two changes were not daunting enough, the accelerating pace of technological change also began to alter the way business was conducted. The growth of sophisticated new products like fiber optics, microprocessors, color copying machines, and fax machines was rendering many manufacturing companies obsolete while simultaneously creating new business opportunities.

As Harrison and Bluestone readily admitted, the process of structural change was nothing new in the American economy. The famous Austrian economist Joseph Schumpeter had previously argued that all economies periodically go through what he labeled periods of creative destruction.[9] Companies constantly had to adjust to changing circumstances as old technologies died and new competitors emerged in the marketplace. Those firms which were the most successful in disengaging from shrinking markets and investing in new technologies were the most likely to prosper. What had changed, according to Harrison and Bluestone, was that American companies had failed to respond to the new challenges in a creative and productive fashion. As soon as foreign competition took aim at American companies and began to cut into their profit margins, American corporations responded by falling back on the organizational practices that had previously served them well. By the 1970s, they tried to take those management tactics to such an extreme that they ended up adopting a form of hyper-mass production. To hold off their foreign competitors, too many companies sought to restore their profitability by becoming the lowest-cost producers in the marketplace. Instead of developing new products, improving their productivity, or exploring new market niches, they tried to lower overall costs while continuing to turn out standardized products. Like an old dog unable to learn new tricks, American companies kept trying to refine practices that had once served them well.

Although their actions were relatively profitable in the short run, their policies were both detrimental to the well being of the economy and harmful to the interests of their employees. With the passage of the American economy from a mass production phase to a hyper-mass production phase, many managers began to abandon the internal labor markets they have previously worked so hard to develop. Since the practices of internal labor markets were expensive to maintain, as corporate profits began to drop, firms started to chip away at the benefits they once had willingly granted to their employees. Indeed, Harrison and Bluestone have argued that many corporations decided to go one step further and "sweat" their labor force by adopting a wide range of personnel policies that literally destroyed millions of "good jobs."

To achieve this goal, firms tried to lower their costs, in ascending order of severity, by either cutting the wages of new workers only, lowering the salaries of all employees, new and old, or abolishing employment opportunities in America altogether by moving jobs overseas. For example, companies often used a variety of tactics—from the development of a dual wage structure within the company to the replacement of permanent employees with temporary workers—to lower the salaries of new employees. General Motors, for instance, asked the United Auto Workers in its recent contract negotiations to agree to a new wage schedule in which newly hired workers receive only 85 percent of the previous base wage. Besides reducing the wages offered to new workers, American corporations also attempted to reduce the wages and benefits of their existing labor force. While policies varied from one corporation to the next, many firms either froze salaries, extracted wage concessions from their employees, employed temporary workers, or in extreme cases even busted their unions. In the 1960s and 1970s, wage freezes or pay cuts almost never occurred in the unionized sections of the American economy.[10] Generally, workers could expect to see their wages rise more or less in lockstep with increases in their productivity and the cost of living. But with the 1981 recession, management was able to impose freezes or extract other wage concessions from slightly under 50 percent of all union workers. The previous stability of wages in the primary sector was increasingly a thing of the past. When organized labor objected, companies were prepared to wait out strikes, lock out their employees or even try to bust their unions in order to lower their overall labor costs.

Finally, the most draconian measure that companies used to lower their labor costs was to move their operations offshore in the hopes of finding cheaper labor. By exporting jobs and production facilities to other countries, American corporations hoped to compete with their Japanese rivals by holding down their costs. In the 1970s, as America's share of world exports declined, the export share of foreign affiliates of U.S. companies actually increased.[11] Akio Morita, the co-founder of the immensely successful Sony Corporation, even coined the phrase, "the hollowing out of American industry," to describe this process.

In light of these developments, Harrison and Bluestone looked back wistfully on the 1950s and 1960s as an era in which the economy produced high-paying jobs. As more and more companies began to abandon their U.S. manufacturing activities and restructure their organizations, Harrison and Bluestone concluded that the number of "good jobs" in the economy was declining. Disregarding altogether the previous complaints of the dual labor market advocates, they suggested that the growth of mass production companies with their internal labor markets had been a boon to the American working class. The earlier complaints that most minorities, women, and the poor had been confined to dead-end jobs in the secondary sector with little hopes for advancement were somehow forgotten. Harrison and Bluestone even seemed to agree indirectly with William Julius Wilson's argument that the growth of the industrial sector had especially benefited African Americans. Historically, the rise of mass production companies had given black immigrants from the South the opportunity to find industrialized jobs in northern cities like Detroit, Cleveland, and Pittsburgh, and thus eventually move into the ranks of the middle class. Whatever problems the black working class had to overcome to secure work in the primary labor sector appeared insignificant compared to the structural changes they now had to confront.

To protect as well as to guarantee the continued growth of well-paid industrial jobs, Harrison and Bluestone advocated a variety of neo-protectionist policies to shield American corporations from the onslaught of foreign

Table 12.1
Poverty Rates of Full-Time, Full-Year Workers, Aged 16–64

	1964	1969	1974	1979	1984	1992
All workers	7.5%	3.0%	2.2%	2.1%	2.9%	2.6%
Female-headed household	15.4	8.6	5.5	5.4	6.8	7.9

Sources: U.S. Bureau of the Census, *Current Population Reports*, Series P-60, no. 178, "Workers with Low Earnings: 1964 to 1990"; *Current Population Reports*, Series P-60, no. 181, "Poverty in the U.S., 1991"; *Current Population Reports*, Series P-60, no. 185, "Poverty in the U.S., 1992."

competitors. While they did not explicitly deal with the problems of the poor, they implied that public officials might have to rely on higher minimum wages or even government-sponsored work programs like the CETA programs of the 1970s to protect the poor. Without some form of direct government protection or stringent regulation of existing labor markets, the tendency of companies to ship good jobs overseas or to cut back the wages of their employees would only continue, jeopardizing the number of high-paying primary jobs in the economy.

Whether these protectionist policies will alleviate the problems of "lousy wages" naturally depends on the extent to which Harrison and Bluestone's pessimistic views are actually true. If we look at the employment record of the working poor, it is clear that the situation is not as bleak as they portray it. The phenomenon of bad jobs has become more acute only since the start of the 1980s. As table 12.1 shows, the phenomenon of low wages and bad jobs actually declined from the early 1960s until the end of the 1970s, when it slowly turned upward. Among full-time employees, the percentage below the poverty line dropped from a little over 7 percent in 1964 to 2.2 percent ten years later, and then rose to 2.6 percent at the start of this decade. By 1992 the overall percentage of people working full time who were trapped in poverty was roughly one-third of what it had been in 1964. While the phenomenon of low wages has become more troubling for indigents over the past decade, the situation is still much better than in the 1960s, when American manufacturers faced little or no foreign competition.

But not all Americans have emerged equally unscathed from the economic changes outlined by Harrison and Bluestone. As indicated in table 12.2, it is more the working and lower middle class, rather than the poor, who are being squeezed by the problem of low wages. While the percentage of full-time workers who have slipped below the poverty line has barely changed over the last decade, the working class has fared less well. The percentage of males receiving low wages dropped from a little over 15 percent of the total male population in 1964 to just under 7 percent ten years later,

Table 12.2

Percentage of Full-Time, Full-Year Workers with Low Annual Earnings, Ages 18–64

	1964	1969	1974	1979	1984	1990
Total	23.1	13.5	11.4	11.6	14.2	17.8
Males	15.4	7.8	6.6	7.3	10.1	13.6
Females	44.5	26.9	21.8	20.0	21.0	24.1
Black Males	38.0	21.6	13.8	14.0	17.5	22.4

Sources: U.S. Bureau of the Census, *Current Population Reports*, Series P-60, no. 178, "Workers with Low Earnings: 1964 to 1990."

and then it eventually rose to roughly 14 percent by 1990. Although many commentators are often nostalgic for the days when America's mass production companies reigned supreme in the international marketplace, their fond memories of the past may not be warranted. In spite of the woes troubling the American economy today, fewer people are earning lower wages today than in the supposedly prosperous decades of the 1960s.

McKinley Blackburn and Richard Freeman of Harvard have also estimated that only a small fraction (25 percent) of the increase in low-wage jobs filled by poorly educated workers was due to the decline of traditional well-paying jobs in primary-sector jobs like the auto or steel industry.[12] Harrison and Bluestone's overall assessment of the labor market may thus represent an incomplete and even outdated picture of the structural changes remaking the American economy. In the 1980s a variety of studies discovered that the number of high-paying or primary-sector jobs was increasing rather than decreasing. As mentioned before, most Americans have enjoyed upward mobility because the economy has constantly been differentiating and upgrading the quality of available work. In an important study, William Dickens and Kevin Lang have recently found that this process has continued throughout the 1980s. Or as they have expressed it: "We fail to find any evidence to support the view that the US has undergone a severe loss of good skilled high-wage jobs. If anything, there seem to be significantly more good jobs now than before. This does not mean that the effects of trade are not present in some industries and that there are no negative welfare consequences. However, to the extent that they are present, they are either swamped by other forces in the economy, or obscured by the process of adjustment."[13] The only issue in doubt is whether the rate of occupational upgrading has been constant over time. Although many commentators have wrongly suggested that the process of occupational upgrading has ended, some studies indicate that the rate of increase in highly skilled jobs has slowed over the past several decades.[14] While predicting the future is risky, there is a good possibility that this process may soon be reversed.

While the hardships so graphically described by Harrison and Bluestone should not be minimized, their analysis overlooks the surprising strengths of many American firms in fields as diverse as automobiles and semiconductors. The Commerce Department reports that the U.S. trade surplus in what it calls "leading edge products" more than doubled from $16 billion in 1986 to over $36 billion in 1991. The willingness of many corporations in the 1970s to embrace one form or another of hyper-mass production was overshadowed by the fact that the American economy appeared to be entering a new phase by the early 1980s that we shall call "mass customization."

The reason for this evolution is rooted in the flawed practices of hyper-mass production. However appealing the lure of cutting labor costs may initially have been to American corporations, the policy is basically self-defeating. If U.S. companies lower their costs by shipping work to Third World nations, they will no longer have any local customers to purchase their goods. In holding down wages and dismantling their internal labor markets, firms face the risk of killing the demand for their products. Wages play a dual and even contradictory role in a market economy: while they are an unwelcome labor cost, they are also a much sought-after source of consumer demand. At the same time that companies want to hold down their production costs, they have an equal desire to create affluent workers and consumers with the resources to buy their goods.

Even more importantly, the failure of hyper-mass production reflects its flawed reading of the challenges facing American companies. As mentioned earlier, by the 1960s the market for many standardized products was saturated. Regardless of their income, most Americans appeared to own a car, refrigerator, color TV, and even a VCR. Even though American firms cut wages and slashed other costs, they soon found that their ability to sell their traditional goods had not necessarily improved. Moreover, American companies soon discovered that the main threat from the Japanese did not come from the production of cheap, standardized products but from sophisticated, high-value goods. Japanese firms quickly recognized that the way to improve their profitability was to upgrade their products and to differentiate them from those of their competitors. If customers came to view Japanese products as unique or somehow superior to their American counterparts, they might be willing to pay premium prices for them.

Sony's successful marketing of the Trinitron® television set in the United States is the classic example of this strategy. When Asian electronic firms like Sony first started selling TVs to American customers, U.S. companies responded by adopting hyper-mass production strategies. They quickly moved their production offshore and eliminated thousands of high-paying jobs in order to reduce their labor costs. American firms believed that they could beat out their rivals by turning out a standardized product at extremely low prices. Sony, in contrast, decided to customize and differentiate its TV sets from American-made counterparts by stressing the exceptional quality of its color monitors. By adding all kinds of other electronic bells and whistles to its television sets, such as color adjustments and remote control devices, Sony appealed to affluent and discriminating buyers. While Sony and other Japanese consumer electronic firms increasingly acquired market share in the TV market and a reputation as producers of high-quality goods, American companies were forced out of business.

Japanese firms realized that the economy had entered a new phase in which companies who tailored their products for specialized niches were likely to grow and prosper. Stan Davis, who originally coined the term "mass customization" to describe this new stage, argued that the companies which are prospering are those that combine seemingly contradictory practices.[15] Rather than producing either standardized goods or customized products, today's companies must learn how to combine mass production techniques with the development of customized goods to service a heterogeneous and fickle public. This new stage in the evolution of the economy appears to be overlapping and slowly displacing the business practices described by Harrison and Bluestone.[16]

MASS CUSTOMIZATION AND THE PROBLEM OF SKILL MISMATCH

Unfortunately, however, as American companies become more innovative in differentiating their products, the poor may find that they increasingly lack the skills or motivation to qualify for well-paying jobs. The third explanation for the disparities in wages in this country is that the United States may be experiencing a growing "skills mismatch" between the qualifications of the poor and the demands of the economy. As the economy enters this new phase of mass customization, companies need highly trained, skilled workers to meet the specialized demands of the marketplace. But the decline in the motivational and educational levels of many low-income people means that they are often unqualified for many job openings.

To understand why, we need to examine in more detail how business has evolved over the last decade. As noted above, with the saturation of domestic markets for mass-produced goods, those firms producing customized goods and services on a mass basis have proven to be the most profitable. By altering their products and appealing to distinct segments of the market, many companies have learned to thrive in what once were considered mature industries. Unfortunately, the Japanese were quicker to adapt to this new phase than their American counterparts, possibly because they had a more established craft tradition predating their mass production economy. Because of their late start, many American companies have had to scramble to catch up with their foreign competitors.

Whereas classic mass production industries such as auto makers turned out relatively inexpensive and undifferentiated products with only cosmetic differences from one year to the next, today's mass customization companies must compete primarily on the basis of their ability to provide high quality and differentiated products that appeal to specialized niches in the market-place. While General Motors has languished with its standardized Chevys, Chrysler has enjoyed unusual success with its specialized jeeps and minivans. Similarly, as Sears has had to close its catalog business because of waning demand for its standardized products, firms like Lands End and L. L. Bean have seen their businesses grow by catering to a specialized set of customers. The most prosperous companies are increasingly those who appeal to customers on the basis of quality, response time, unique features, and service rather than price.

But the rise of mass customization has forced many companies to reinvent the American corporation. Unlike the centralized operations of mass production firms in which management constantly monitored the activities of rank and file workers, companies today are in the process of slimming down and decentralizing. James Womack and his associates have coined the phrase "lean production" to describe the organizational makeup of mass customized firms.[17] To foster innovation, firms are developing cross-functional teams to encourage the diffusion of new ideas. Companies realize that if they can develop products with unusual features, they can charge premium prices for their goods or services. In place of midlevel managers issuing orders to subordinates, firms are trying to encourage more interaction among workers in order to speed up the process of developing new ideas. When product engineers, production employees, and sales personnel work closely together to develop new products that integrate consumer demands with the dictates of the production process, they eliminate much of the wasted time required by the compartmentalized structure of mass production companies in bringing new products to market.

Once firms have refined and targeted the products they wish to produce, their next step is to rely on flexible manufacturing to keep up with the changing demands of the marketplace. Rather than seeking to lower unit costs for undifferentiated products through economies of scale, mass customization firms have tried to achieve what Joseph Pine calls "economies of scope," that is, the application of a single production process to the output of a variety of goods and services.[18] In place of seeking long production runs, mass customization companies want the flexibility to be able to respond quickly to shifts in the marketplace. Whereas mass production companies flourished by lowering their costs and thus stimulating more demand for their products, mass customization firms thrive by lowering their response time in developing and manufacturing novel products that cater to select niches in the marketplace. As consumer demand shifts and technology changes, products and services may become obsolete in relatively short order. Unlike their mass production predecessors, firms today have been forced to evolve into decentralized, cross-cutting organizations that stress flexible production processes, shorter product cycles, and the rapid development of innovative and specialized goods and services.

In making these painful organizational changes, corporations have had to hire a very different type of worker from those employed by mass production firms. In place of scientific management's stress on deskilling work and simplifying tasks so that even poorly trained employees can accomplish their assigned tasks, companies today need better-trained workers who are able to exercise initiative and creativity on the job. Rather than treating workers as cogs in a machine, firms are recognizing that they need to expand the responsibilities of their employees by promoting job enlargement. Whereas mass production companies relied on high-paying managers to monitor the behavior of their employees, mass customization firms must depend on the ability of skilled workers to supervise their own work and to suggest improvements in the production process.

While the adoption of these new management tendencies may reduce the number of high-paying managerial positions, these practices often obscure the overall improvement in the skill level of most jobs. As companies have shoved more responsibility further down the production line, they often find that they no longer need as many of their well-educated and generously paid corps of midlevel managers. As more and more jobs become upskilled rather than deskilled, companies have less need for managers to cajole, discipline, or monitor the work of their previously untrained labor force. As the process of occupational upgrading spreads to more and more industries, some high-paying jobs will accompany the disappearance of low-paying menial work. Likewise, some companies will reduce their hiring of well-educated college graduates who would traditionally have occupied midlevel management positions. But in recognizing this point, we must not lose sight of the aggregate improvement in available occupational opportunities as well as the need for a better-trained work force.

Although many liberals insist that the primary sector of the economy is contracting and that society is producing too many dead-end, "lousy jobs," the evolving nature of the economy will eventually accelerate the growth of high-paying "good jobs." This conclusion remains true even after we subtract out the loss of midlevel management jobs that were necessary to operate mass production companies. Mass customization firms are often able to pay relatively high wages to their workers since they can charge premium prices for the value-added customized goods or services they provide. The more successful that corporations become in producing unique and customized products, the more likely they are to employ a highly skilled and well-paid labor force. The lament of Harrison and Bluestone about the disappearance of "good jobs" in America is really a complaint about the decline of menial and tedious jobs that happened to pay high salaries. The only good thing about the boring production jobs that started to disappear at the end of the 1970s was their hourly wage. As mass customization firms recruit the kind of skilled workers they need to remain competitive in today's marketplace, they will generously compensate well-educated workers for performing sophisticated and demanding tasks. As the Department of Labor has stressed in its widely disseminated Workforce 2000 report, the sooner the economy upgrades the goods and services it offers the customer, the quicker we will see high-paying and high-value positions crowding out low-value, poorly paying jobs.[19]

Ironically, the growth of high-paying, high-value jobs may worsen rather than alleviate the lot of the working poor. An unanticipated consequence of the expansion of so-called good jobs is that many indigent workers are unqualified for the more sophisticated and demanding work of a mass-customized economy. As explained earlier, there has been a slowdown in the growth of the supply of well trained and highly motivated workers. While the number of unproductive and untrained workers has increased, the evolution of mass customization has caused the supply of unskilled jobs to decrease. In fact, it is the combination of these two factors that has exerted downward pressures on the wages of the working poor. If, as argued by Harrison and Bluestone, the economy were generating too many "lousy jobs" because of a shift away from high-skill to low-skill jobs, the wages of unskilled workers should be rising relative to the salaries of college-educated workers. But the opposite situation is occurring. Chinhui Juhn and his associates recently found that by 1990 the inflation-adjusted wages of the bottom 20 percent of

American workers, who presumably are not very well educated and skilled, had fallen some 25 to 30 percent below their level in 1973.[20] Increasingly, the economy faces a shortage of skilled workers rather than a shortage of skilled jobs.[21]

Meanwhile, as mass customization increases the demand for highly skilled workers, the wages of the well-trained continue to grow, exacerbating the phenomenon of polarization of income. According to data compiled by Katz, the wages of college graduates are rising generally (an 11 percent increase from 1979 to 1987), as are wages for workers with specialized knowledge, such as computer science.[22] The recession of 1990 and the adoption of lean production have temporarily slowed this polarization of wages, but it is bound to accelerate again as the economy regains steam and businesses complete the process of mass customization. Even within the same educational levels, pay differentials are likely to increase because of the premium placed by mass customization on innovation and skill, traits which were less important in an era when companies turned out standardized products. This latter phenomenon, which has been called the "Hollywood effect," reflects the growing demand for people with unusual abilities. As long as workers were engaged in menial tasks producing standardized products like widgets for industrial firms, there was probably very little difference in the quality of work between the most and least capable worker on the widget assembly line. Unless the product of the company actually disintegrated, a firm had little or no reason to pay one worker more than another. But if these same workers have responsibility for completing more demanding tasks, such as writing software or securing financial backing to fund new companies, the situation looks very different. Not every computer hacker is a Bill Gates, nor is every investment banker a Michael Milken. A system dependent on innovation and skills is likely to reward its "stars" generously. Although mass customization companies will reward well-trained people, they will compensate even more generously those with the same formal level of training whose job performance is unusually meritorious.[23] As Mickey Kaus has noted, there is a big difference between being merely competent and being really good, just as there is a big difference between earning a decent salary and an enormous salary in a company that rewards excellence.[24]

Ironically, therefore, the growth of the mass customization sector, or primary labor market of high-paying jobs, may worsen rather than alleviate the growing polarization of income in society. While many commentators argue that the economic well-being of the U.S. depends on reversing the growth of the secondary sector at the expense of the primary sector, the continued growth of a mass customization economy will further polarize the differential between the haves and the have-nots. It is because the policy objectives and aspirations—rather than the fears—of Harrison and Bluestone have been realized that the wages of lower-income workers are declining. As the number of good jobs continues to increase at the expense of bad jobs, the wages of the working poor are likely to continue falling while those of the highly skilled are likely to continue rising so long as the education and skills of the poor do not improve.

To date, there are few policy options for breaking out of this conundrum. As mentioned before, many liberals have called for either higher minimum wages or more subsidies to the poor to compensate them for their low wages, as well as for significant tax increases to limit the economic gains of the well-to-do. By combining higher income taxes on the wealthy with stepped-up transfer payments to the poor, they hope to soften the consequences of the increasing polarization of income in society. Given their general pessimistic view of the economy, liberals increasingly seem resigned to treating the effects of poverty rather than alleviating its causes. But since the public shares a cultural commitment to rewarding individual achievement that is fundamentally at odds with an egalitarian society based on redistribution policies, their proposals have elicited mixed popular support at best.

The domestic agenda of most liberals might be politically more palatable if the country were willing to embrace a different set of values for compensating individual achievement. For instance, we know that the Hollywood effect is less pronounced in Japan, where the cultural emphasis on group cooperation and harmony has prevented the extraordinary salary differentials between the lowest-paid employees and CEOs that are common in large American companies. In contrast to the norms in this country, Japanese culture has tended to frown on wage disparities that disproportionately work against the interests of blue-collar workers.

Even in America public perceptions about what are appropriate "rules of the game" have been subject to historical change. As pointed out earlier, Lester Thurow has argued that if we want to find a period in this country in which wages became more equal rather than less, we have to go back to the period of World War II.[25] As the war raged on, there was widespread support for government policies that helped equalize market wages because the population believed that the burden of financing the war should be shared by all. Once people's perceptions of what constituted a "fair wage" changed, they adopted programs that limited the polarization of income in society. The economic laws of supply and demand always operate within, rather than outside, the confines of a society's culture. If America (or, for that matter, its corporations) ever became more egalitarian, companies would probably imitate the Japanese and limit the rewards paid to "Hollywood" stars.

Thurow's insightful observations illustrate the fact that culture plays a dual role in influencing people's economic fortunes. Cultural norms determine both the rules of the game by which people compete for economic gain as well as how successful they are at playing the game. On the one hand, society's values influence the rules governing the race for upward mobility, what obstacles on the racetrack will be tolerated, and what kind of prizes will be awarded to the winners and losers of the race. On the other hand, once having established the rules that govern the conduct of the race, a nation's culture also determines how well different people will run the race. In the competition to get to the top, individuals or groups that have internalized important cultural values such as hard work and self-discipline are likely to prevail over those who have abandoned these traditional norms. While chapter 7 pointed out that people's values will determine how successful they are in achieving upward mobility, we must not lose sight of the fact that culture also shapes the rules that determine what society considers to be a fair and equitable payment to the winner of the contest. There was more public support during World War II than there is today for policies that contain wage polarization. But the unusual nature of the World War II situation suggests that public willingness to support a comparable frontal attack on wage differences is not likely to repeat itself any time soon.

If that is the case, then the most feasible and long-term solution for containing the growing disparities in wages is to upgrade the quality of the American educational system. As previously mentioned, education has been one of the most important routes out of poverty in the past. Given the structural changes at work in the U.S. economy today that are placing increasing demands on the skills of workers, that route will become even more important in the future.

CONCLUSION

In light of the above analysis, governmental efforts to alleviate the causes of poverty will have to be twofold. To make sure that the American economy remains competitive with the Japanese, the government will need to encourage more and more companies to adopt the techniques of mass customization. But presently economists have few insights about how to accelerate the tendency of companies to upgrade and differentiate their products. Because the Great Depression had a major impact on the economics profession, most economists have spent their careers trying to figure out how the government can smooth out cyclical fluctuations in the economy. But the economics profession may want to spend as much time in the future figuring out how to create high-paying jobs as it presently does in trying to stimulate full employment. Even if public officials learn how to smooth out fluctuations in the business cycle, they will do little to promote upward mobility unless more companies succeed in generating high-value and high-paying employment possibilities.

But as soon as more firms produce better-paying jobs, the government will have to spend more time insuring that the poor are sufficiently trained and motivated to qualify for the new openings. The importance of the above observation illustrates that the distinction many liberals make between structural and individual explanations of poverty is highly misleading. As the economy structurally upgrades its practices to remain competitive in world markets, the demands on the labor force, including the working poor, will also intensify. To avoid the trap of "lousy wages" and work their way out of poverty, the working poor will need to acquire the skills and motivation required by the age of mass customization.

Perhaps there is no better metaphor of the challenge facing the United States than that embodied in the "Cathedral of Learning," a large Gothic building that dominates the University of Pittsburgh. From the turn of the century until the early 1980s, Pittsburgh represented the typical affluent, industrial, mass production city that thrived by turning out standardized products. The Monongahela Valley, which forms the southern border of the city, was world famous as the steel capital of the world. To staff their plants, Andrew Carnegie, Henry Frick, and James Laughlin, among others, hired thousands of workers at decent salaries to turn out raw slabs of steel. Given the good wages they made as blue-collar workers, the Polish, Italians, and African Americans who had migrated to Pittsburgh in search of the good life saw no use for higher learning in the city's foundries.

To alter that perception, John Bowman, chancellor of the University of Pittsburgh in the 1920s, wanted to construct a building that would both physically and psychologically dominate the industrial landscape of the city.[26] The future for the children of the industrial workers that made up the bulk of Pittsburgh's population lay in acquiring an education that would equip them for more skilled positions. Chancellor Bowman thus raised funds for the construction of the Cathedral of Learning, a fifty-five story towering landmark at the center of campus to advertise the importance of education. As a visionary, Bowman knew that the supremacy of the iron triangle of steel and aluminum would eventually come to an end. When it did, in the 1970s, as part of the process of hyper-mass customization, Pittsburgh experienced a renaissance, in the 1980s, in no small part due to the educational skills and resultant adaptability of its population. In a fitting tribute to Bowman's vision, upon the demise of the Monongahela steel plants the University of Pittsburgh became the largest employer in the city.[27]

While circumstances have certainly changed since Bowman raised his Gothic tower, his message, like that of Lyndon Johnson's in the 1960s, is as true today as it was then. As more American companies switch to mass customization, the only feasible way to contain the growing polarization of income is to improve the educational skills of the working poor. Until more workers and their children recognize the importance of attending the cathedral of learning, they will continue to end up as the unfortunate victims of "lousy wages."

THIRTEEN

The Economy III: Stagnating Productivity and the Lack of High-Paying Jobs

The alleged growth in so-called lousy jobs is really a dual problem: the wages of the working poor not only have fallen further and further behind their better educated peers, but also have ceased to grow in an absolute sense. As table 13.1 indicates, wages and fringe benefits have stagnated during the 1970s and 1980s compared with the prior two decades. Since the run-up of oil prices in 1973, most workers, including the working poor, have seen the annual growth in their wages slow to less than 1 percent, a sharp drop from the 3 percent increases of previous years. The failure of the economy to provide low-income workers with decent raises and increased purchasing power means that it cannot cushion the blow of the growing polarization of wages. When workers have more disposable income to spend on their families, they are likely to be less concerned with the fact that their economic standing vis-à-vis other workers has deteriorated.

The reasons for the slowdown in the growth of wages are twofold. As every beginning economics student quickly learns, wages are determined by both demand and supply factors. In the previous chapter, we saw that the demand for workers slowed considerably in the 1970s. Faced with intense pressure from competitors from Japan and Europe, many U.S. companies embraced the tenets of hyper-mass production and slashed their labor force. American firms either shipped manufacturing operations overseas or held down the wages of their low-skilled labor in the U.S. in order to control costs. Even though the efforts of companies to "sweat" their work forces did not always improve their profitability, their reduced demand for workers kept wages from rising. But as more and more businesses adopt the practices of mass

Table 13.1
Average Annual Growth Rate for Wages, Fringe Benefits,
and Family Income

	1955–1973	1973–1990
Wages and fringe benefits	3.2%	0.7%
Family income	3.1	0.5

Source: Charles Schultze, *Memos to the President* (Washington, D.C.: Brookings Institution, 1992), 225. Reprinted with permission of the Brookings Institution.

customization, there is reason to believe that the downward pressure on wages will eventually ease, and even disappear.

However, supply factors—in particular, labor's inability to add value through increased productivity—have also prevented wages from rising in an absolute sense. If workers increase their productivity, companies can pay their employees higher salaries without raising the prices of their goods and services. Conversely, if the growth in productivity slows down, firms will find it extremely costly to raise wages. For example, if a company's wages rise 5 percent per year but productivity rises only 2 percent per year, the differential must either be passed on to consumers in the form of higher prices or be absorbed by the company. But neither option is a realistic possibility in a highly competitive global economy.

The key to improving wages and curtailing the growth of "lousy jobs" is to increase productivity, a task that unfortunately will not be easy to accomplish. Over the last thirty years, improvements in productivity in the United States have slowed significantly. In the post-World War II era, annual productivity increases were around 4 percent per year, then dipped to 3 percent and finally fell below one percent in the 1980s.[1] As table 13.2 shows, the slowdown in real compensation per hour closely tracks the slowdown in the increase in output per person. In the 1960s, as output per hour increased by a little over 2 percent per year, compensation per hour also rose at close to 2 percent. But as output increases in the 1970s and 1980s slowed to a little over one percent, increases in real compensation literally came to a halt.

Over the past twenty-five years we find that significant gains in productivity have occurred only in the manufacturing sector of the economy. But the dismal record of the service sector, which employs over two thirds of the labor force, has dragged down the economy's overall productivity rate.

While many commentators concede that higher productivity will lead to better-paying jobs, they fear that solving the problem of low-paying jobs will create yet another problem, that of declining job growth and rising

Table 13.2
Average Yearly Increases in Output per Person and Compensation
per Hour (All Businesses)

	1960–1970	1970–1980	1980–1990	1990–1991
Increase in output per hour of all persons	2.14%	1.16%	1.11%	0.40%
Increase in real compensation per hour	2.25	0.83	0.37	0.70

Source: *Economic Report of the President* (Washington, D.C.: U.S. Government Printing Office, 1993), 398.

unemployment. The danger thus exists that increasing productivity may confront the country with a difficult trade-off between generating either low-paying jobs or fewer high-paying positions. But luckily the so-called trade-off between wages and work may never actually arise. Whenever the economy becomes more productive, business can produce more goods and services at cheaper prices. As the prices of goods and services drop, people have more money left over to buy additional products, which will generate new employment opportunities. There is no theoretical reason why increases in productivity should necessarily lead to a reduction of the aggregate number of jobs available in society. As William Baumol has demonstrated in his insightful study, *Productivity and American Leadership*, periods of increased productivity have usually been associated with periods of sustained job growth.[2] Since 1870 there has been a twelvefold increase in output per labor hour in the United States, but at the same time there has been only a slight increase in the country's unemployment rate.

If increasing productivity is essential to generating well-paying jobs for the working poor, the key question is, what can we do to improve the efficiency of American companies? At present, there are sharp disagreements as to why productivity growth has been so sluggish over the past couple of decades. It certainly seems clear that inadequate investment in both human and financial capital has contributed to the overall slowdown in productivity growth, although the relative importance of each is still unresolved. For instance, we know that the quality of educational achievement in this country is not what it used to be. While productivity, measured in terms of output per worker hour, has failed to rise at the rates experienced in the past, educational performance, measured in terms of standardized tests, has actually declined in an absolute sense. Between 1963 and 1980, Scholastic Aptitude Test (SAT) scores dropped 10 percent, with the average math and verbal scores declining from 980 to only 890.[3] While half of this decline is accounted for by the increasing proportion of high school students taking the SAT, the remaining half reflects weakening academic skills. By contrast, in the 1950s there was an absolute improvement in test scores, rising productivity, and an increase in the wages of workers. John Bishop has pointed out that the declining academic skills of U.S. students may have an even greater adverse effect on productivity in the future as the labor force increasingly comes to rely on students who attended high school in the 1980s, when SAT scores were at their lowest levels.[4]

While human capital skills appear to be related to productivity rates and will become even more important in the future, there also appears to be a direct relationship between financial capital and productivity. With the exception of Canada, all of the countries listed in table 13.3 experienced higher productivity growth when they increased their investment in nonresidential capital stock. The United States, which had the lowest rate of growth in nonresidential capital stock, also had the lowest rate of increase in productivity. In contrast, Japan, which increased its nonresidential capital stock by over 8 percent, had the highest growth in GDP per work-hour.

These statistics bear out the arguments of supply siders of the 1980s, who sought to create more incentives for savings and investment in order to fuel increases in productivity upon which economic growth depends. They argued that more capital per worker is required, both directly in the form of equipment such as computers, and indirectly in the form of infrastructures such as telecommunication networks. Unless companies in areas as diverse as the trade, service, and financial sectors of the economy better equip

Table 13.3

Productivity and Capital Investment: A Comparison of Seven Countries, 1950–1979

	Percentage of Growth in Capital-Labor Ratio	Percentage of Growth in Nonresidential Capital Stock	Percentage of Growth in GDP per Work-Hour
U.S.	2.44	3.61	2.30
Canada	2.95	5.03	2.58
U.K.	3.55	3.29	2.85
France	4.18	4.11	4.64
Italy	5.10	4.82	4.99
Germany	5.66	5.28	5.52
Japan	7.11	8.36	6.92

Source: Angus Madison, *Phases of Capitalist Development* (Oxford: Oxford University Press, 1982). Reprinted by permission of Oxford University Press.

their work forces, they will have trouble lowering the costs of their much-needed services.

However, liberal critics of supply siders have disputed the notion that incentives for more investment would lead to higher productivity. During the Reagan years, they made two very different and even contradictory arguments against the supply-side agenda. First, they pointed to studies by Robert Solow and Edward Denison indicating that increases in productivity primarily stemmed from technological change, or what Solow and Denison term "residual total factor productivity," rather than from labor or capital investment.[5] As table 13.4 shows, America's growth from 1929 to 1982 was much larger than what one would expect based on the increases in capital and labor during those years. Denison suggested that economic growth and rising productivity depended more on technological advances and increases in knowledge than on acquiring more physical and financial capital. However, many supply siders argued that Denison and Solow's argument seriously understated the impact of capital investment on productivity since many technological advances, for example, computer-based information systems, depend in large measure on capital investment.[6]

Certainly, a large part of what we consider technological advances is embodied in new capital investment. Stimulating additional investment would thus generate larger increases in productivity than indicated by Denison's "static" calculations. Furthermore, supply siders argue that if you look at international comparisons there is a clear relationship between investment

Table 13.4
Sources of American Productivity Growth, 1929–1982

	Average Annual Growth (in percentages)	
	1948–73	1973–82
Output per worker	2.3	0.2
Changes due to:		
Average weekly working hours	−0.4	−0.5
Quantity of education	0.4	0.4
Quantity of capital	0.5	0.3
Economies of large scale production	0.3	0.2
Other identifiable factors	0.4	−0.3
Residuals (advances in technology)	1.1	0.1

Source: Edward Denison, Trends in American Economic Growth, 1929–82 (Washington, D.C.: Brookings Institution, 1985), 114. Reprinted with permission of the Brookings Institution.

and productivity. J. Bradford De Long and Lawrence Summers have also found in a major study of industrialized nations that there appears to be a significant and robust association between additional capital investment and increases in productivity and long-term growth.[7]

Second, many liberal economists also attacked supply-siders for relying on tax breaks or private incentives to stimulate more capital investment. To the extent they are willing to concede that additional investment does promote productivity (thus downplaying the findings of Solow and Denison), liberals criticized supply siders for attempting to promote investment by focusing on supply as opposed to demand factors. As Evsey Domar pointed out in his famous theory of economic growth (the Harrod-Domar growth theory), tax breaks for encouraging private investment will fail to produce their intended effect if there is no additional consumer demand to purchase the increased production made possible by increased investment.[8] Business will only want to invest additional capital if it can reap a profit from that investment through additional sales. But because increases in business investment merely raise production capacity, they do not necessarily create demand for the goods and services made possible by that additional capacity. Or as Jack Walker has put it, "The more excess capacity we produce, the less likely we are to get the large increase in investment that we need to produce the demand to buy the output of the past investments and any new ones we undertake."[9]

Liberals thus insist that if we want to stimulate more investment in plant and equipment, we need to rely on demand and not supply-side proposals. Instead of cutting taxes or providing financial incentives for businesses to invest, government ought to adopt a policy of stimulating aggregate demand by increasing government spending. Increases in aggregate demand create its own supply—that is, higher government spending will provide the fiscal stimulus to activate consumer demand that is required in turn to stimulate private investment. In the view of liberals, the government can literally tax, spend, or borrow its way to higher investment, higher productivity, and, eventually, higher wages.

However appealing the above views may be, liberals often ignore the fact that if the government raises corporate tax rates to support more government spending, it will divert resources from the private sector and crowd out private investment by reducing individual savings rates and the retained earnings of business. Moreover, the use of deficit spending to stimulate consumer demand ultimately will lead to higher interest rates, which will hamper private investment by making it more expensive to raise capital for new plants and equipment. Even if liberals are correct in their diagnosis that demand conditions play a role in stimulating investment, they may be incorrect in believing that additional government spending will call forth additional capital investment.

But the need for increased capital investment is readily apparent if we hope to ease the plight of the working poor. If indigents are ever going to work their way out of poverty, the economy needs to generate more high-paying jobs. To accomplish this task, more companies will have to adopt the mass customization techniques outlined in the previous chapter. But at the same time, businesses will have to make the additional investments necessary to raise their overall level of productivity. Besides guaranteeing that the wages of the working poor do not fall more and more behind the salaries of highly trained workers, we need to see wage growth approach its pre-1973 rates. Unless the productivity of the labor force increases dramatically, too many of the poor will be stuck with "lousy wages," and the government, instead of eliminating the causes, will be forced to treat the effects of poverty.

FOURTEEN

The View from the Left: Economic Exploitation and the Lack of Political Power

A final institutional explanation that we need to look at is the argument of the left that poverty is rooted in the very nature of capitalism. In the opinion of many American Marxists, who view social relations in class terms, the problems of the poor are a direct outgrowth of the effort of capitalists to maximize their profits, rather than an accidental by-product of a market economy. They maintain that attempts by liberals and conservatives to explain poverty by either the educational skills or motivation of indigents or the structure of the economy overlook the functional role that the poor serve in a society dominated by class interests.

As we shall see in the remainder of this chapter, there are subtle yet significant differences among Marxists about the exact role played by the poor in a capitalist economy. The more common Marxist position, advocated by scholars as diverse as Francis Fox Piven, Richard Cloward, and Michael Katz, is that the poor serve a vital economic role by keeping labor costs low for industry.[1] If labor strikes for higher wages, employers can use the threat of hiring the poor to neutralize the bargaining power of their unions. Given their lack of power, indigents are often helpless to alter their precarious position in American society. The poor are often the unwitting pawns of management, which wants to extract as much surplus profit as possible from its workers.

However, many radicals, and liberals for that matter, have recently developed a second and softer version of the argument that poverty is rooted in the evolution of capitalist institutions. They argue that the poor are more the victims of political neglect and manipulation than economic exploitation.

Because of their lack of influence the poor are often ignored by the larger political community, which is often preoccupied with its own concerns.[2] Indeed, it is the very superfluous nature of the poor that renders them politically powerless, unable to find either the allies or resources necessary to alter their situation.

While both the Marxist and radical view of the poor enjoyed widespread support in the 1960s and early 1970s, especially among academics and college students protesting against the war in Vietnam, we shall see that both arguments are deeply flawed. In spite of the intensity with which they have argued their point, commentators from the left have provided little empirical evidence in support of their claim that poverty plays an important functional role in a capitalist society.

MARXISM AND MARXISM'S VIEW OF THE LUMPENPROLETARIAT

The tendency of many American social scientists of a Marxist bent to espouse the cause of the poor is itself surprising in light of Marx's well-known hostility toward indigents, whom he derisively labeled the "lumpenproletariat." In *The Communist Manifesto*, Marx argued that indigents were the dangerous class, a passively rotting mass of people thrown off by the lowest layers of the old society. Marx's decision not to embrace the poor reflected three concerns of his about the evolution of socialism. First, he argued that the ability of business interests to extract surplus profit from the working class was the key to understanding the dynamics of a capitalist economy. The poor, as opposed to the working class, were at best marginal players in the evolution of capitalism and had little or no impact on the profitability of the bourgeoisie. While Marx viewed the bourgeoisie as the enemy, he at least believed they played a historically necessary role in the process of class conflict. However, because the poor or the lumpenproletariat had no relationship to the means of production, they were essentially a non-class that had no significant part to play in the class struggle.[3]

Second, Marx was wary of embracing the poor because he believed too many of them lived chaotic lives. Like his bourgeois counterparts, he felt that the poor lacked the discipline as well as the work ethic that was necessary to built a new industrialized society. While many Marxist historians have criticized capitalism for imposing a rigid and dehumanizing life-style on the working class that was more attuned to the rhythms of the assembly line than to the needs of the worker, they overlook the fact that socialism itself was dependent on the creation of a highly disciplined and productive work force. As Gertrude Himmelfarb has noted, there was a "Sunday side of communism," which talked about the new socialist man who would be free to fish in the morning and hunt in the afternoon, and a more prosaic or "workday side" of communism, which saw man as only laboring man.[4] Hannah Arendt has echoed that point, arguing that Marx was unique among philosophers in giving absolute primacy to the idea of work and the proposition that people's identity is inextricably linked with their relationship to the means of production.[5] Since a successful socialist state would require a high degree of planning and coordination, Marx often saw the poor as incorrigibly antisocial as well as antisocialist. Unlike modern-day liberals who advocate a libertarian welfare state, Marx was hostile to what he perceived as the permissive and often self-indulgent behavior of the poor.

Finally, Marx was wary of the poor because he felt that they could very easily "be suborned by the bourgeoisie and made the 'bribed tool of reactionary intrigue' of counter revolution."[6] In Marx's scheme of things, the revolutionary force that would bring about a transformation of the capitalist economy was to be found among the proletariat. As more and more workers lost their jobs in a capitalist economy, they would become members of an industrial reserve army that would eventually overthrow the corrupt bourgeoisie society that had impoverished them. The lumpenproletariat, in contrast, were social deviants who were neither reformable nor amenable to the well-intentioned designs of socialist planners.[7] The danger thus existed that the lumpenproletariat would be coopted by their bourgeoisie oppressors and thus help to suppress any chance for radically restructuring the makeup of capitalist society. Marx's worst fears were realized during the 1848 revolution, when the lumpenproletariat fought with the bourgeoisie against the proletariat in Paris and helped to extinguish any hope for erecting a socialist society.

THE AMERICAN REVISION OF MARXISM: THE FUNCTIONAL ROLE OF POVERTY

In spite of Marx's doubts about indigents and his belief that they play a peripheral role in a bourgeois economy, many present-day radicals have tried to argue that poverty plays a functional role in American society. While somewhat ambivalent about Marx's fears that the poor might be coopted by the bourgeoisie, most American Marxists have generally rejected all three of Marx's reservations about the poor.

First, in their eyes, the captains of industry as well as their political supporters in government have been able to use the poor to discipline, tame, and moderate the economic demands of the working class for a larger share of the economic pie. Instead of being a non-class, indigents play a crucial role in helping employers extract the maximum amount of surplus value from their employees. American Marxists thus insist that the capitalist class no longer needs to rely on brute force to keep unruly employees in line. By pitting one segment of the labor force against another, employers can use the threat of hiring indigents to contain the demands of workers for higher wages, and thus drive up the profits of corporate America. The existence of a large reserve army of poor people gives corporations and the state ample leverage in regulating the wages of the working class. American Marxists like Frances Fox Piven, Richard Cloward, and Michael Katz have thus built on and slightly revised Marx's understanding of class conflict in capitalist societies by suggesting that the plight of the poor and the working class is inextricably linked. In their view, this dependence has become even more important in a period of growing international competition.[8] As American companies find it harder to hold their foreign rivals at bay, they increasingly have chosen to rely on indigents to hold down wages in order to shore up their position in world markets.

Second, most American Marxists also reject Marx's arguments that the poor lack the discipline and self-control necessary to participate in a highly industrialized society. Michael Katz, for instance, has recently argued that efforts by conservatives to revive the fears of Marx by talking about the problems of the underclass tell us more about the social outlook of poverty analysts than the attitudes of the poor themselves. He believes that the current preoccupation with the alleged misdeeds of the so-called underclass and the decline of civility in our inner cities is nothing more than a smoke screen to stigmatize and punish the poor.[9]

Finally, the left in American society is ambivalent about Marx's warning that the poor may be suborned into supporting reactionary policies. While rejecting Marx's argument that the poor lead disorganized and destructive lives, American Marxists recognize that the poor may at times succumb to a false consciousness and oppose desired social change. Piven and Cloward, for instance, claim that by manipulating the generosity of welfare payments, the government has learned how to regulate the poor, suppressing in the process their ardor for radical change. However, Piven and Cloward have always remained hopeful that the poor might one day refuse to be bought off. In their book *Regulating the Poor*, they insist that if indigents would recognize that the welfare state is part of the class struggle, they might learn to ignore its seductive nature and eventually bring about meaningful social reform in America.[10] Yet in a surprising turnabout, by the 1980s Piven and Cloward vigorously defended programs they previously criticized for coopting and pacifying the poor. While at times they justified their contradictory views by vague references to the dialectical and contradictory nature of social reform in general, or to the changing nature of American welfare programs, they were primarily concerned with defending entitlement programs against the growing tide of conservative thought in America that wanted to scale back the size of the welfare state. But in so doing, Piven and Cloward undermined both the credibility as well as the coherence of their Marxist interpretation of the welfare state.

American Marxism's Blindness to Poverty's Dysfunctional Role

The most obvious problem with the views of American Marxists, aside from their logical inconsistencies, is their inability to explain why the fortunes of the poor have improved so dramatically over the last century. If Marxists and neo-Marxists are correct when they claim that poverty plays a functional role in a capitalist economy, why has the poverty rate declined so dramatically during the last century? As mentioned earlier, by today's definition of poverty, roughly 40 percent of the population was poor at the turn of the century, while today anywhere from 13 to 15 percent of the population is in comparable economic straits. If businessmen were that dependent on the poor for low wages and high profits, they would not have tolerated let alone accepted a dramatic shrinkage in the poor. The answer may be that poverty undoubtedly results less from the functional demands of a capitalist economy than from the failures of capitalism to generate enough well-qualified workers as well as enough high-paying jobs. When a capitalist society has both a disciplined labor force and a smoothly functioning and productive economy, the ranks of the poor are likely to decline dramatically. In place of their penchant to see exploitation behind every social problem, Marxists need to understand that it is because of the flaws—rather than the functional needs of capitalism—that poverty exists at all.

Marxist also must recognize that poverty probably hampers more than it helps the profitability of American companies. While Piven and Cloward are right to insist that firms want to hold down their labor costs, they overlook the simple fact that companies also have the contradictory goal of increasing the purchasing power of their employees. As discussed earlier, the profitability of companies in a market economy must reflect both demand as well as supply conditions. While companies have periodically tried to lower the wages of their employees, their actions may prove to be self-defeating. In the 1920s even the tightfisted capitalist Henry Ford recognized that he needed to raise the salaries of his workers if he wanted them to have the income necessary to purchase his Model Ts. As Bennett Harrison and Barry Bluestone have noted, what is a labor cost to American companies is also the primary source of income for the vast majority of consumers in the population.[11] Finally, from a supply-side perspective, the existence of a large poor population may also prove to be a drain on the pocketbooks of most businesses. The taxes many companies have had to pay to support entitlement programs and other social services that help indigent families have undoubtedly driven up the cost of doing business in the United States.

Even the alleged reductions in labor costs are probably more illusory than real. Sixty years ago, John Maynard Keynes perceptively noted that wages and other prices in a market economy are often downwardly sticky, likely to decline relatively slowly, if at all.[12] Keynes's observations certainly seem as relevant today as they were in the 1930s. The vast majority of companies that hire low-wage workers are usually covered by minimum wage laws and thus have limited control over their labor costs. Regardless of how many poor people are in the labor market, companies like McDonald's and Burger King are prevented by law from lowering their wages. Similarly, in the manufacturing sector, industrial unions like the United Auto Workers and the Steel Workers help determine the salaries of their members through the process of collective bargaining. Thus, whether the poor actively look for work or not, their decision to enter the labor market is not likely to have a significant impact on the wages of blue-collar workers. The same pattern of behavior is even more true in high-tech sectors of the economy. Even if the poor seek work, they lack the educational credentials necessary to qualify for jobs with companies like Apple and Intel that require a high degree of skill and training. Instead of playing an important role in shaping labor policy in this country, the poor seem like peripheral actors in the dynamics of modern-day capitalism, with little influence over the wage decisions of most corporations.

More importantly, the tendency of Marxists to greatly exaggerate the impact of the poor on labor costs may reflect their outdated view of modern-day capitalism. Most Marxists tend to underestimate the degree to which American capitalism is presently undergoing a major process of change and renewal. While many companies still rely on cheap labor to mass-produce goods, it is apparent that most of those menial positions will eventually be shipped overseas to Asia or Mexico. Because Piven and Cloward wrote *Regulating the Poor* in the 1970s, they overlooked the possibility that the future of American capitalism may depend more on the creation of high-tech, high-value jobs than menial low-value work. If this scenario is correct, Marxists have totally misinterpreted the role of the poor in modern-day capitalist economies. The intractable nature of poverty in this country reflects the fact that indigents are increasingly superfluous rather than functional to the operations of modern-day capitalism.

Marxism and the "Mythical" Underclass

If attempts by Marxists to show that poverty plays a central role in a capitalist economy miss the mark, their dismissal of the problem of the underclass likewise is controversial. Michael Katz has recently argued that conservatives who echo Marx's complaints about the problems of the underclass harbor a hidden agenda for exploiting the poor. In contrast to William Julius Wilson, who believes that the underclass is a reaction to declining economic conditions, or conservatives who believe that the underclass is a result of the breakdown of traditional social values, Katz offers a third view that the underclass is nothing more than a political myth which conservative analysts have used to stigmatize and penalize the poor in order to help control the labor costs of corporate America. He thus insists that the anomic behavior of the underclass only exists in the eyes of the beholders. But in making this charge, he is silent as to why Marx himself was so displeased with the antisocial actions of the poor. Is it possible that Marx likewise had a secret agenda to penalize the poor? Without answering this question, Katz stoutly insists that the present concern with the destructive actions of the poor tells us more about the political agenda of the right in America than about the activities of the poor. However, he is never quite sure whether the present focus on the underclass reflects a sincere yet authoritarian streak among conservatives or whether it is merely a devious and cynical attempt by the right to ostracize the poor in order to drive them into the labor market, thus lowering the wages of corporate America. Surprisingly, Katz generally ignores the efforts of Wilson and other liberals to talk about the underclass and the breakdown of civility in the inner city. But his selective attacks on those who talk about the problems of the underclass illustrate how controversial and even polemical the debate about the poor has become.

When we ask why American Marxists are so hostile to discussions of the behavior problems of the poor, the answer may be found in their attempt to revise and update traditional Marxism along more libertarian lines. While scholars like Katz and Piven and Cloward are willing to adopt Marx's principles of class exploitation and power to explain the existence of poverty, they have never really accepted his principles of building a socialist community in which all people are expected to be productive citizens. In this sense American leftists are best described as analytic rather than normative Marxists. In agreeing with Marx that class conflict and the exploitation of labor are the keys to understanding society, Katz appears indifferent and even hostile to the Marxian vision of creating an egalitarian community in which all people are hardworking, disciplined, and productive members of society. Rather than trying to achieve a sense of social justice within the confines of a larger community, American Marxists, like Katz, have preferred to pursue the more limited agenda of expanding the rights and entitlements of individuals.

Given this libertarian bent, Katz is naturally suspicious of all commentators, whether conservatives or Marxists, who talk about instilling in people a sense of concern for themselves and their communities. He thus tends to label those who disagree with him as either moral authoritarians or advocates of big business who merely want to increase the availability of cheap labor. While he clearly is deeply concerned about eliminating the hardships of poverty in America, Katz refuses to concede that his conservative opponents might be equally sincere individuals who likewise want to help the poor become financially independent. He thus dismisses the belief of the right that the underclass needs to act in a more responsibly fashion as nothing more than a punitive and mean-spirited attack on the poor. In the process, Katz refuses to acknowledge that indigents might act in ways that might be considered irresponsible, hedonistic, or even self-destructive. The neglect and indifference of many indigents toward their children, their disinclination to hold a job, and their often violent and destructive behavior toward their peers is either ignored or regarded as being unimportant. Similarly, the findings of ethnographic studies that many poor men treat their girlfriends on welfare as "meal tickets," have little attachment for a life of work, and drift in and out crime are nowhere to be found in Katz's version of poverty in America.

Even more importantly, Katz also fails to recognize that the working poor are often victimized by the behavior of the underclass. In his efforts to protect those at the bottom of the social pyramid from criticism, he often fails to realize that many indigents do not share his belief that the underclass is merely a myth concocted by the right to punish the poor. The most unfortunate victims of poverty are often the black working class who lack the resources to flee from the social decay that surrounds them. Despite Katz's Marxist tendencies to view social problems in class terms, he has committed the worst Marxian mistake of failing to appreciate the often sharp class differences that separate the working poor from the underclass.

Finally, Katz can be criticized for having a very narrow version of what duties, if any, people owe to society, to their families, and even to themselves. In an extended discussion of Lawrence Mead's book, *Beyond Entitle-*

ments, he attacks Mead's argument that "The capacities to learn, work, support one's family and respect the right of others amount to a set of social obligations alongside the political ones (such as voting, paying taxes and serving in the military)" that all people must respect.[13] He maintains that before the poor are obligated to live up to any such social obligations, the state is obligated to assist them. Or as he puts it, "If obligation is mutual, wage labor and civic competence should be considered payment for resources or services rendered by society . . . to its least fortunate members. Unless it provides the prerequisites of competence, society lacks a moral title to obligation."[14] And Katz quickly concludes (without citing a lot of evidence) that since society has failed to provide adequate schools, health care, or decent jobs for its citizenry, the poor have no obligations to society and presumably to themselves.[15] He thus overlooks that fact that throughout most of American history, people came to this country and worked hard, looked after their families and were law-abiding citizens whether or not they received anything from the government. Until the growth of the modern welfare state in the 1960s, the decision of most people to be productive and well-behaved citizens was not dependent on the belief that such actions should only be considered payment for services rendered by the state. At the very least, most people in the past probably felt that their obligations to their families or even to the law were unconditional obligations that had little to do with the generosity of society's entitlement programs.

While the left may feel that it must attack the motives of its conservative opponents and even the ideas of Karl Marx himself in order to contain the apparent threat of moral authoritarianism, their attacks are not likely to improve the prospects of the underclass or the quality of life in the inner city. By assuming that the very concept of the underclass is a myth that has been conjured up to punish the poor, the left fails to recognize the cultural nature of today's poverty as well as the seriousness of the problems plaguing our inner cities. When phrases like "stigmatizing the poor" or "blaming the victim" are repeated enough, they act as intellectual blinders that prevent analysts from understanding the true nature of poverty. Unfortunately, the breakdown of social authority and the spread of self-destructive, irresponsible behavior among the poor will not go away by merely pretending they do not exist.

Similarly, the attempt by Katz to stigmatize analysts who use the concept of the underclass raises disturbing parallels with the attacks on Patrick Moynihan in the 1960s. The critics who stridently attacked his work on the black family effectively censored how people studied poverty for over fifteen years. If we want to eliminate poverty, researchers must feel free to raise and investigate controversial topics without fear that their motives will be impugned. The last thing the country needs in its fight to eradicate poverty is another questionable debate about the ulterior motives of poverty researchers.

Marxism and the Machiavellian Welfare State

Nevertheless, in the same way that Katz suggested that conservatives have a secret agenda to punish the poor by talking about the underclass, Piven and Cloward have insisted that liberals have an equally punitive desire to control and regulate the poor by expanding the scope of the welfare state. Whether they are talking about conservatives or liberals, Marxists at least appear evenhanded in arguing that their opponents' claims are not to be taken at face value. Piven and Cloward maintain that the conventional liberal view of the welfare state as an altruistic and caring institution masks its true intentions of intimidating and pacifying the poor. They argue that the real and, unfortunately, punitive function of entitlement programs in a capitalist economy is to enforce work, especially very low-wage work.[16] In their view, during periods of stability, the government deliberately tries to keep welfare payments low in order to ostracize and humiliate the poor so that they will willingly accept menial jobs. Or as Piven and Cloward express it, the welfare state is always willing to let a few of the young and the old become wards of the state. "But once there, they are systematically punished and degraded, made into object lessons for other poor people to observe and shun, their own station raised by contrast."[17] Because Piven and Cloward realize that many indigents may not be responsive to economic incentives, they see the social humiliation of the poor as necessary to motivate them to participate in the labor market. But the ridicule of welfare recipients is also meant as a warning to others not to slack off or withdraw from the labor market. If the attachment of the poor to work should weaken, their only option is the scorn and humiliation of society.

While in most cases government entitlement programs work as planned, periodically the welfare state breaks down and the poor become rebellious, jeopardizing the stability of the political system. Under these circumstances, Piven and Cloward argue that government officials will try to buy off the poor by temporarily expanding the scope of the welfare state. But these efforts to placate them are merely temporary palliatives designed to undercut the need for more significant and lasting reforms. As soon as the rioting dies down, the government reveals its true intentions and begins to dismantle the welfare state.

In the early 1970s, many students and academics found the arguments of

Piven and Cloward extremely appealing. Because of their cynicism toward Lyndon Johnson and their alarm over the turmoil convulsing U.S. cities in the late 1960s and early 1970s, the academic community often wanted to believe that government transfer programs were designed to coopt the poor. But on closer examination, the data relied on by Piven and Cloward are subject to alternative explanations. For example, the growth of the AFDC program had little or nothing to do with encouraging indigents to seek low-wage occupations at all. When FDR originally proposed establishing a welfare program for families with dependent children, he was primarily concerned with helping widows whose husbands were casualties of war, illness, or accidents. Rather than serving some sinister objective, AFDC was designed to assist poor widows who had fallen on hard times. Roosevelt's proposals initially generated very little controversy because AFDC did not appear to be a very large or expensive program. What most policy analysts failed to see was that with the breakdown of the family among indigents, enrollment in AFDC would dramatically increase over time.

However, Piven and Cloward tend to ignore the history of AFDC because it does not support their Machiavellian view of the welfare state. To be fair to Piven and Cloward, it is possible to argue that the program may still have had the consequence, if not the actual intent, of lowering wages by driving the poor into the labor market. Regardless of whether or not the liberal architecture of the welfare state was designed to penalize the poor, the implementation of AFDC may have had the unanticipated consequence of ostracizing the poor so much that they actively looked for and accepted low-paying jobs. But, as even Piven and Cloward grudgingly admit, neither indigents nor the general public has ever held such a negative view of welfare. AFDC is more commonly perceived as a government welfare program that encourages and subsidizes people to abstain from participating more actively in the work force. Since Piven and Cloward did not look at the labor record of AFDC recipients, they fail to mention that very few of the beneficiaries of our largest cash transfer program have ever held a permanent, year-round job. Over the last thirty years, not more than one in ten AFDC beneficiaries has ever worked full time. It is thus clearly an exaggeration to argue that the welfare system "systematically punishes and degrades the poor" and thereby forces them to take low-paying jobs.

Similarly, Piven and Cloward's claim that the expansion of entitlement programs was intended by liberals to pacify the poor rests on a misreading of the recent past. A more likely explanation is that liberals merely wanted to enlarge the scope of the welfare state in order to protect people from the harshness of the marketplace. In debating the expansion of the AFDC program, the administration and the legislature cited the need for the country to act quickly in order to assist people who had come upon hard times. The major thesis of Piven and Cloward, that the welfare state was designed to "regulate the poor," may reflect more the creative and fertile imagination of the authors than the intentions of our elected officials. While insisting that the goals of the welfare state were more sinister and devious, Piven and Cloward never cite any internal government memos or public speeches by Lyndon Johnson or his advisors to support their contentions. Like most Marxists, they rely more on intuition and supposition than hard evidence to prove their point that Johnson cynically manipulated the poor.

But if we recall that the expansion of AFDC was accompanied by a government effort to portray transfer programs as public entitlements—and not as public dole—it is clear that the growth of relief programs was a sincere, if possibly flawed, effort to help the poor. The growth of transfer payments was neither a temporary nor a tactical measure to coopt the poor into working for cheap wages. On the contrary, it was part of a larger shift in the thinking of liberals that people had "entitlements" or rights that society was obligated to recognize. Most liberals insisted on expanding the scope of the welfare state because they altruistically believed that the state needed to do more to protect individuals from the fickle nature of the marketplace. When efforts were finally made to scale back the scope of the welfare state in the 1980s, it was not because riots in the inner cities had abated (in fact, they had stopped a decade earlier).

Finally, the growth of transfer payments such as AFDC may be as much a cause as a consequence of the 1960s riots. The very growth of entitlement payments, instead of being a response to the urban disturbances in cities like Watts, may be partly responsible for the breakdown of civil order in the first place. As mentioned earlier, in the 1960s Johnson promised the poor that the country would win the war against poverty. While at first there was some hope that his efforts would prove effective, the expectations of the poor outran the actual improvements in their lives. As the government expanded entitlement programs and launched a series of educational programs to improve the human capital skills of the poor, the poor may have felt that they would soon become integrated into the financial mainstream of American life. As their expectations for the future soared, they were bound to be frustrated by the limited increases in welfare expenditures and job opportunities. In spite of the government's best efforts to improve their lot, the poor may have felt a growing sense of relative deprivation. When they finally discharged their frustrations by rioting in the 1960s in our major cities, they may have stimulated the government to reexamine its policies. But to argue as Marxists do that the growth of the welfare state was merely an effort to placate the poor overlooks the role the expansion of the welfare state may have played in helping to create those riots in the first place. Instead of cynically manipulating the poor, the growth of the welfare state may be guilty of nothing more than unduly raising their expectations.

THE LACK OF POLITICAL POWER AND THE FALSE PANACEA OF POLITICAL ACTIVISM

In light of the difficulties surrounding Marxist explanations of poverty, many radicals like Saul Alinsky, civil rights leaders like Jesse Jackson, and even some liberals have developed a second and softer version of the argument that poverty is rooted in the very nature of capitalist societies. Instead of contending that poverty serves some functional purpose in society by lowering the wages of corporate America, this second approach argues that the poor are more the victims of political neglect than the casualties of economic exploitation.[18] According to this view, the biggest obstacle confronting the poor is that they are often politically invisible to most Americans and thus are ignored by decision makers. When it comes time for political officials to redress social problems, they often overlook the legitimate demands of the poor because of their lack of power. Until the poor become better organized, they are not likely to enjoy the opportunities that are afforded to other segments of society. The sad fact is that in our pluralistic society, which prides itself on giving everyone an equal opportunity, those groups that have political power tend to be more equal than others.

To rectify this situation, many political activists on the left have insisted that the poor need to become more vigorous in defending their economic interests. In the early 1960s, many civil rights leaders argued that until more poor African Americans registered to vote and elected more minorities to federal, state, and local government, they would never be able to improve the economic status of low-income blacks. Because the poor lacked the political muscle to challenge incumbents at election time, they often found that politicians were indifferent to their plight.

A second and even more dramatic attempt to enhance the political power of the poor involved the creation of the Community Action Program (CAP). While initially Lyndon Johnson may have thought this antipoverty program would merely try to coordinate the diverse efforts of his war on poverty, he could not have foreseen how CAP would become transformed instead into a major advocate for the interests of the poor. Admittedly, in some big cities like Chicago, mayors like Richard Daley quickly captured control of the agency and used it to disburse public funds to supporters of the administration. But in other cities the Community Action Program became an independent power base from which poverty activists launched major attacks on the policies of city hall. In cities like Newark and Detroit, community action agencies even help elect more blacks to public office. The hope of poverty activists was that by mobilizing the poor at the grass-roots level and electing sympathetic black officials, the poor would become a political force with which society would have to reckon. If the lack of political power had made the poor invisible, their mobilization would finally force the political system to deal with the nagging problem of poverty in America.

In the politically charged atmosphere of the 1960s, many liberals applauded the activities of the Office of Economic Opportunity and the Community Action Program. For all those who believed in the efficacy of an active government, it was essential that the poor acquire more political power. However, it quickly became apparent that political power had very little to do with either the existence or the abolition of poverty. Over the past one hundred years, the amount of power wielded by the poor seemed to have had a negligible impact on their overall level of poverty. As the advocates of community action and the civil rights movement clearly pointed out, the poor have never been a major political force in American society. While the short-lived populist movement in the South tried to organize poor whites and blacks in a broad-based coalition in the 1890s, it was eventually torn apart and destroyed by racial conflict. That being the case, radicals and liberals needed to explain why the poverty rate had dropped so dramatically during the twentieth century, falling from over 40 percent at the turn of the century to around 15 percent by 1992.

Similarly, the advocates of political power were often silent as to why groups like the Japanese or East Indians, who were relatively powerless in American politics, had enjoyed unusual upward mobility in America while the Irish, who had enjoyed unusual success in acquiring and wielding power, had been slow to move into the ranks of the middle class. Japanese Americans, in particular, not only had been politically ignored, but they also had been interned in relocation camps during World War II and were harassed by their own government. But the Japanese, Chinese, and Asian Indians had all prospered in America and currently enjoy extremely high median family income without exercising any appreciable degree of political power. It is very clear that their climb to the top reflected more their educational and entrepreneurial talents than their ability to win elected office. Furthermore, if the acquisition of political power was necessary to achieve upward mobility, the left was at a loss to explain why the war on poverty had been established in the first place. As many commentators have noted, the war on poverty sprung from the fertile mind of Lyndon Johnson and his advisors rather than from grass-roots activism.

Finally, if the lack of power had not hindered the ability of people to climb out of poverty in the past, the acquisition of power by the poor in the late 1960s did little to eliminate poverty in the country. When community organizers used government-funded programs to challenge city hall, they stirred up so much controversy that community action programs were eventually disbanded. Similarly, the successful efforts of many black officials to capture city hall and to implement policies sympathetic to indigents made little impact on either the overall poverty rate in the country or on the poverty rate of black Americans. By the 1970s the poor and their allies were probably politically more powerful than at any other point in American history. At the very point in time in which the poor had become politically more influential, the decline in the overall pre-transfer poverty rate eventually leveled out and slowly began to rise again.

Despite their newly won political power, neither civil rights nor poverty activists have been able to use their political clout to significantly lower the incidence of poverty among blacks over the past twenty-five years. While many liberals and civil rights advocates still insist that turning out the voters and capturing political power are the key to helping the poor achieve financial success in America, the evidence indicates otherwise. The impressive electoral achievements of blacks over the last two decades and the growth in the influence of welfare agencies that cater to the poor seem to have done very little to reduce either the high incidence of poverty among minorities or the aggregate poverty rate among all Americans. In this sense the experience of blacks parallels the problems that Irish Catholics encountered once they achieved political power in American cities. Despite their electoral success, Irish Catholics often lagged behind the economic accomplishments of other ethnic groups who were only marginally involved in politics.

The trouble with the radical agenda for eliminating poverty was that its proponents had no clear idea of what to do with political power once they acquired it. To argue that the poor needed to become better mobilized begged the question of what the poor hoped to achieve once they became organized. If people were financially poor because they were neglected, it is unclear how paying more attention to them would solve their problems. Despite their popularity during the 1960s, radicals, civil rights groups, and liberals often seemed vague as to how they would eradicate poverty in this country.

Admittedly, the state can always spend more money treating the effects of low income. If the poor have more political power, public officials may very well feel pressure to expand entitlement programs to treat the consequences of poverty. But if our objective is to eliminate the origins of poverty, it remains unclear how the political mobilization of the poor will actually achieve that end. In some cases the exercise of political power might even make things worse. If the state treats the consequences of poverty by increasing the subsidies available to the poor, it may foster an attitude of dependency rather than independence among the indigent population and thus slow down their movement into the middle class. However, should public officials successfully use monetary or fiscal policy to stimulate aggregate demand, as was true of the 1980s, low unemployment rates may have little impact on the aggregate poverty figures. Trickle-down economics appears to have trickled out. Even if the state responds to the political clout of the poor by investing resources in worthwhile programs like education and human capital, there is no guarantee that the money will be spent wisely or effectively. As discussed earlier, there appears to be no clear relationship between government expenditures on education and student performance in school.

The important issue may not be whether the poor and their advocates have any appreciable degree of power but how they choose to exercise that power. And even then, we must not exaggerate the ability of the government to solve a problem as complex and multidimensional as poverty. The structural changes occurring in the economy and the deterioration in the attitudes and educational skills of the poor will not automatically disappear merely because the poor have become mobilized. The fact that many radicals, members of the civil rights movement, and liberals are actively involved in politics has often led them to exaggerate the importance of political activity.

Contrary to the suggestions of Piven and Cloward and Katz, there is little evidence either that the poor play a functional role in society or that they have been manipulated and pacified by the welfare state. Nor are radicals and liberals more convincing when they argue that the financial plight of the poor reflects their their lack of political power. On the contrary, the economic problems of the poor reflect the fact that too many of them are unprepared and unmotivated to compete effectively in our rapidly changing and demanding global economy. While the government can play a role in helping them adjust to the demands of the new international marketplace, there are definitely limits to what public officials can accomplish.

PART FIVE

The Changing Views of Poverty in America

FIFTEEN

Changing Perceptions of the Causes of Poverty: A Summary

As the preceding chapters have demonstrated, there is no shortage of explanations as to why poverty is such a persistent social and economic problem. The paradoxical reversal of positions by conservatives and liberals over whether the state can actually eliminate the origins of poverty reflects their changing perceptions of the causes of poverty. This reassessment has been precipitated in turn by the apparent failure of President Lyndon Johnson's war on poverty to significantly reduce the pre-transfer rate of poverty in this country. Despite the best of intentions, the government's efforts to lift people over the poverty line essentially came to an end by the early 1970s. Even more disturbing has been the growth of a sizable underclass in our major cities that appears to be caught in a downward spiral of poverty and self-destruction. Recent longitudinal studies indicate that the problems of the poor may be getting worse rather than better. Researchers at the University of Michigan have found that children of poor parents had greater difficulty achieving upward mobility in the prosperous decade of the 1980s than in the sluggish 1970s.[1] The only bright light in this picture is the unusual financial success of Japanese, Chinese, Vietnamese, and, to a lesser extent, Mexican immigrants. While the country's overall record in helping the poor to become financially independent leaves a lot to be desired, the achievements of these ethnic groups are remarkable and warrant further attention. To understand the origins of poverty adequately, we may find as many answers by examining those who have achieved upward mobility as by looking solely at those who have remained mired in poverty.

The perennial search for the causes of poverty has elicited a variety of responses over the years. At the risk of overgeneralizing, explanations of poverty appear to have gone through four distinct phases since the early

1960s. During the Johnson era, commentators disagreed whether the lack of human capital, a specific culture of poverty, or "capitalist exploitation" accounted for the existence of poverty. Aside from Marxists, liberals and conservatives basically agreed with each other that poverty was primarily a supply problem. Too many indigents were either insufficiently trained or sufficiently motivated to become financially self-supporting. But as government spending on education appeared to have little or no impact on the overall poverty rate, the human capital movement came under criticism, and as various ethnic groups made substantial economic progress in the 1970s, the culture of poverty argument likewise fell out of favor. When the economy experienced rough times in the 1970s, the Marxist argument that the poor were being exploited as a source of cheap labor also appeared increasingly untenable. The problem facing the poor was that they were superfluous—rather than exploited—members of the labor force who had few skills to offer an economy already troubled by high unemployment rates.

In light of these developments, poverty analysts began to focus on either changes in the economy, or on the nature of government welfare programs as the sources of poverty. By the 1970s, liberals maintained that downturns in the business cycle as well as the movement of baby-boomers and immigrants into the labor force explained the failure of President Johnson's Great Society. The government's lack of success in eliminating poverty stemmed from the inability of the poor to find decent, well-paying jobs in the sluggish economy of the 1970s. Conservatives, however, insisted that the persistence of poverty was rooted in the growth of the welfare state. As transfer payments became competitive with entry-level jobs, the poor lacked financial incentives to seek work. Like their counterparts of the 1960s, conservatives believed that indigents were unmotivated to climb out of poverty, but they blamed government programs rather than a distinct culture of poverty for the behavior of the poor.

In the late 1980s, the debate over poverty entered a third and even more complex phase. As the leveling effect of inflation eroded the value of transfer programs like AFDC, it quickly became apparent that government entitlement payments were not the sole cause of poverty. Conservatives consequently began to argue that the persistence of poverty was due to the breakdown of traditional values, the pervasive decline of the two-parent family, and the erosion of work habits among the poor. They maintained that the decline of the traditional work ethic and the moral indifference of the state toward the behavior of its citizens also explained the rise of the underclass in our inner cities. Liberals, however, insisted that the structural changes occurring in the U.S. economy, rather than mere fluctuations in the business cycle, were the primary reason why poverty had become such an intractable problem. The creative destruction of manufacturing jobs in the American economy and their replacement by low-paying service jobs had made it increasingly difficult for low-income individual to work their way out of poverty. Unlike their counterparts of the 1960s, who attacked Moynihan's thesis that many indigents were caught up in a "tangle of pathology," liberals finally agreed that the growth of a large underclass was a cause for concern. But they claimed that the often destructive behavior of the underclass was more a consequence than a cause of poverty. While the arguments varied, liberals pointed either to the phenomenon of social isolation or to the unfortunate effects of strain theory to account for the actions of the underclass. Rather than becoming preoccupied with altering the values of the poor, they maintained that the creation of meaningful job opportunities was the key to helping people escape from the ranks of the poor. The destructive actions of the underclass were merely an unfortunate but inevitable epiphenomenon of the transformation occurring in the U.S. economy.

As we move into the 1990s, it is time for the poverty debate to enter a fourth phase in which we incorporate portions of the above views into a more comprehensive explanation of poverty. However divergent the earlier arguments have been, each may partly explain why poverty has become such a persistent problem in this country. While liberals insist that poverty is a demand problem reflecting the changing nature of the U.S. economy, and conservatives insist that it is primarily a supply problem, they overlook the possibility that the interaction of both factors is responsible for the present plight of the poor. It is hard to deny that the last thirty years have seen both a serious deterioration in the educational skills and attitudes of the poor and a dramatic change in the makeup of the U.S. economy.

But the process of creative destruction is nothing new in the American economy. In the last 150 years, the marketplace has constantly undergone structural change and renewal, altering the way millions of people work. In the early nineteenth century, the rise of the steam engine, the railroad, and basic industries like steel revamped the American economy, while the growth of utilities and the chemical industry at the end of the century further accelerated the mass movement of workers from the countryside to large urban centers. The geographical mismatch between the industrial centers and the available labor supply resulted in the mass migrations of workers to the growing urban areas of the country. This period of change was followed by the 1920s, when the growth of the automobile as well as the rise of modern manufacturing ushered in yet another period of creative destruction. At the end of World War II the pace of industrialization accelerated in the

United States, enticing large numbers of Southern blacks to Northern cities to become factory workers rather than farm hands. The subsequent decline in the late 1970s and early 1980s of the manufacturing heartland and its replacement by a technologically driven and information-based service sector is only the latest of many transformations of the American economy.

But in previous periods of creative destruction, American business did not have to worry as they do today about either the educational skills or the motivation of the work force. As the country began to industrialize, most manufacturing jobs required only a minimal level of education. In many cases companies relied on the management techniques of Taylorism to simplify or "deskill" work so that it could be performed by any uneducated blue-collar worker. If a company needed skilled workers, it could always satisfy its personnel needs by either establishing an in-house training program or relying on its apprenticeship practices.

And even more importantly, while farm workers and immigrants initially faced some motivational problems adjusting to the routines of the manufacturing sector, they quickly acquired the self-discipline needed to become industrial workers. In order to prepare workers for the demands of the new industrial age, America relied on the dual policy of socialization and selective immigration to meet its labor needs. For example, with the growth of large companies, the mass migration from the countryside to the city, and the influx of immigrants from Europe and Asia, nineteenth- and twentieth-century America invested considerable resources in teaching workers a sense of individual responsibility and social discipline. As society became more mobile and impersonal, a whole array of institutions such as the YMCA, the Boy Scouts, the temperance movement, the public schools, and even the Progressive party realized that it would be difficult to regulate behavior solely through the use of external controls or supervision. To prepare individuals for the demands of the changing American economy, these institutions socialized workers into adopting a set of cultural values that stressed duties to society and the need for self-discipline. Many reformers believed that the threat of disorder stemmed from the fact that workers were often self-serving and impulsive. To prevent the working class from engaging in antisocial and self-destructive actions, numerous institutions tried to inculcate in them the need for self-restraint and hard work. Although deprecated by Marxists, these institutions enjoyed remarkable success in preparing workers for the demands of a highly industrialized society.

In the case of Japanese and Chinese workers, the process of resocialization was simplified by the fact that most Asians already possessed a cultural outlook that was compatible with the Victorian work ethic. Because the values of Chinese and Japanese Americans stressed the virtues of hard work, education, merit, and discipline, Asians quickly acquired a reputation as valuable and productive employees. Unfortunately, their capacity for hard work also won them the enmity of fellow workers who often discriminated against them as well as lobbied the government to limit their entry into America.

Despite the hardships imposed on the country by the constant process of structural change, American industry generally had no trouble finding conscientious and motivated workers. When it could not inculcate the values of discipline and self-restraint in the labor force, it could always find immigrants from abroad, especially from Asia, who were more than happy to perform the jobs that native-born Americans refused to perform.

Today, as opposed to previous periods of structural change, American industry is entering a new phase of capitalism in which companies must constantly differentiate and update their products. In earlier periods of economic growth, companies were primarily in the business of making mass-produced consumer goods that differed only in price. By streamlining their production techniques, firms competed with one another by manufacturing standardized goods that required relatively little skill or imagination. Henry Ford's Model T epitomized this stage of production. But it is now apparent that early phases of capitalism are in the process of being eclipsed by a new form of capitalism that is based on mass customization and individualized service. In this new competitive and information-based economy, only those companies that are especially innovative and capable of constantly churning out new products are likely to survive and prosper.

As the nature of the business world has changed, there has been a dramatic change in the nature of existing labor markets. With the rise of a technologically driven, information-based economy, all segments of the business community increasingly need well-educated and highly trained workers, especially companies adopting complex statistical methods to guarantee the quality of their finished products. Even in old-line manufacturing companies, the pressure to modernize has forced industry to significantly upgrade the skills of their employees. But employers are having a harder time finding enough skilled workers to fill the available openings.

U.S. employees are also discovering that the sense of self-discipline and commitment to the Victorian work ethic that was instilled in workers by a whole series of public and private institutions has been replaced by a much less demanding and even self-indulgent attitude among indigents. Even when the working class in the past century did not earn high wages, they managed to avoid the pathological and destructive behavior that so characterizes the underclass today. High crime rates, violence, drugs, broken families, and an unwillingness to work are problems primarily of the post-1960s.

We are currently witnessing two fundamental changes in the American economy. At the very point in time in which the marketplace is more demanding of its work force, we are finding that the poor are less motivated and less well trained than ever to respond to the challenge. While the poor have become less attractive as workers, business has become more selective about whom it wants to hire. With the demise of mass production and the growth of a mass customization economy, employers need a highly skilled labor force to remain competitive. In light of these two divergent tendencies, it should not shock us that fewer indigents are earning their way out of poverty while well-educated Asians are prospering. While the marketplace is generously rewarding those individuals who have the talents and attitudes that businesses need, it is severely penalizing members of the underclass who lack the appropriate skills. The war on poverty is at present failing in this country because of the growing mismatch between the skills and attitudes that industry wants and the qualifications that many of the poor can offer.

TROUBLESOME FUTURE PROSPECTS

In light of the dual nature of poverty, it will require considerable patience, as well as novel government policies, to make significant progress in eliminating the actual causes of poverty. Because of the changing nature of our economy, the problems facing the work force are likely to grow rather than diminish in intensity. In spite of the new economic environment, there is little evidence that the schools have the knowledge to improve the training of the working poor or that society has the willpower to alter the values of the underclass. Likewise, it is clear that the pressure on American companies to upgrade their products and improve service will only accelerate with time, thus intensifying the demands placed on the labor force.

As mentioned earlier, the economy currently suffers from two distinct structural problems. First, the lack of growth in productivity has led to a slowdown in the absolute increase in wages; second, the demand for highly skilled employees has led to a growing polarization in the wages paid to poorly trained as opposed to well-trained workers. In the age of mass customization, either one of these two structural problems will make it extremely difficult for indigents to pull themselves above the poverty line.

Because American industry became complacent after World War II, it invested too little in new factories, technology, and management practices to constantly generate new products and raise overall productivity levels. But it is also clear that the shift to a technologically driven information economy has currently surpassed our ability to master the new technology. The slow-down in productivity growth appears to be a result of faulty knowledge as well as faulty investment practices. Even when companies have invested millions of dollars in computer and information technology, they seem to have trouble raising productivity. Until American companies learn to use their technology more effectively to become more productive, we are not likely to see the significant gains in personal income that Americans enjoyed in the early 1950s and 1960s.

However, solving the productivity problem will be a double-edged sword. As soon as the business sector raises productivity and salaries start to rise in absolute terms, wage disparities between poorly trained and highly trained workers are likely to become more pronounced. While the rising tide of higher salaries will lift more people above the poverty line, the income differences among different sectors of society are likely to grow. As companies strive to become more productive as well as more innovative in differentiating their products from their competitors, they will increasingly either spin off low-paying, low-value jobs to Third World countries like Mexico or elimi-nate them altogether through automation. The remaining high-value, high-paying jobs are thus likely to require an increasingly well-educated labor force. In an economy dominated by innovation and mass customization, the highly skilled (the beneficiaries of the so-called Hollywood effect) and the highly trained are likely to prosper.

At the same time that the economy has become much more technologi-cally sophisticated and thus more demanding of its employees, a second and more serious problem has been the decline in the educational levels of the poor. We know from a variety of international tests that American students are not as proficient as their Asian and many of their European counterparts in the fields of science and mathematics. Besides a decline in the quality of education, there is evidence that Americans are less likely to obtain a college education than in previous decades. The growth of college students in this country has slowed down considerably from its peak levels in the 1970s. Even more disturbing, fewer and fewer students from low-income families are obtaining college degrees, thus limiting their future opportunities for upward mobility. The big winners in this changing labor market are univer-sity graduates, whose wages have increased dramatically over the last decade. Although many analysts see poverty as primarily a structural issue, it is more accurate to portray it as a human capital problem. Lyndon Johnson's argu-ment in the 1960s that solving the problem of poverty depended on enhancing the education of the poor may, ironically, be even more true today than when he originally proposed it.

In addition to having a large population of working poor who lack the educational skills necessary to earn adequate wages, we also have an underclass that appears unable to work its way out of poverty. Their inability to hold down a job, as well as their inclination to drop out of the labor market, to engage in violent crime, and to neglect their families, often dwarfs the difficulties created by the transformation of the economy.

These phenomena cannot be explained, as liberals attempt to do, purely as a consequence of poverty or as a reaction to the structural economic changes that emerged in the 1970s. The growth of the various subgroups that make up the underclass is more a cultural than an economic issue. The expansion of the underclass began in the relatively prosperous decade of the 1960s, years before the dislocations engendered by a competitive global economy. In fact, the emergence of the underclass can best be explained by the loosening of traditional values, the growth of a welfare state that stressed entitlements instead of obligations, the breakdown of traditional agents of socialization in the inner city (including the family), and the flight of the black middle class to the suburbs. The combination of these factors led to a pervasive sense of anomie in the inner city that fed on itself in a downward spiral, eroding traditional forms of social control. But among the causes for the growth of the underclass the decisive element was undoubtedly the growing indifference of society's leaders in promoting the principles of individual responsibility. When civic and political leaders became hesitant about defending such traditional values, they ceased to administer the rewards and sanctions that require respect for the law and support of the work ethic. As a result, many low-income individuals whose commitment to these norms was weak to begin with abandoned the values of self-restraint and hard work even more quickly than the rest of society. The individuals who came to make up what Jencks has labeled the impoverished, the reproductive, or the violent underclass thus started to lose the ethical gyroscope that had previously shaped their behavior. Like the character in Camus' novel *The Stranger*, they increasingly became detached from society and indifferent to the rules of its games.

Because the old Victorian work ethic has eroded, many indigents have elected to engage in self-destructive actions that limit their ability to achieve upward mobility. For instance, the pervasive breakdown of the two-parent family in the inner city has made many of the poor more financially vulnerable. Without a second wage earner in the household, single-parent families have not been able to imitate their intact middle-class counterparts who compensated for the slowdown in earning power by sending more wage earners into the labor market. By choosing to abandon their family responsibilities, many fathers have cut away the safety net that previously protected their indigent children. While the economy has become more demanding, the amoral attitude of many inner-city parents has made it harder for their children to deal with the harsh realities of the marketplace.

But the most glaring problem of the underclass is their seeming lack of interest in finding gainful employment. While the shifting nature of the economy and the lack of appropriate educational skills have adversely affected the wages of many indigents, a growing number of the poor appear unmotivated and unwilling to work their way out of poverty. An increasing number of them are either dropping out of the labor market altogether, working only intermittently, or pursuing unlawful and often dangerous activities in lieu of finding a job. When inner-city youths do decide to look for work, their provocative attitudes often discourage employers from hiring them. Among the three million women enrolled in the AFDC program, only 6 percent have chosen to work either part time or full time.

This unfortunate shift in the attitudes of the underclass has also undercut the ability of the economy to lift people out of poverty. The benefits of trickle-down economics have apparently trickled out, leaving many people stranded in lifelong poverty. Even when the business cycle is generating large number of new jobs, too many of the underclass remain unable to take advantage of the opportunities available to others in society. Without the motivational drive or the educational and entrepreneurial skills demonstrated by successful minority groups, many of the people currently stuck in poverty may be left behind by this present period of creative destruction. While the government, society, and the economy have offered the poor a helping hand, too many seem unable to grasp it.

At the same time that the behavior of the underclass started to deteriorate in the 1960s, many Asian Americans began to prosper economically. Despite their superficial differences, these two groups are the reverse image of one another. While the breakdown of values is responsible for the rise of the underclass, the ability of the Japanese, Chinese, and others to hold on to their traditional values explains their remarkable success in overcoming economical and racial adversity. When people have internalized a well-developed set of values, they are not likely to act irresponsibly or drop out of the labor force merely because they encounter tough times or economic strain. As the American economy has begun a new cycle of change and renewal in the 1990s, the respective strengths and weaknesses of Asian Americans and the underclass are likely to become even more pronounced.

SIXTEEN

Maybe Something Will Work after All: The Fight against Poverty Revisited

The fact that poverty increasingly appears to be an intractable problem in the United States raises anew the question of how the government should deal with it. Over the last thirty years, there has been a dramatic shift in the policies that the left and the right have proposed for alleviating the hardships of the poor. As soon as liberals and conservatives altered their views about the causes of poverty, they simultaneously had to revise their opinions about what the modern welfare state could hope to accomplish. Although this paradoxical shift in the attitudes of liberals and conservatives toward the poor has received little attention, the story is one of the more remarkable developments in recent American politics. In the 1960s most liberals argued that the government ought to launch a war on poverty to eliminate the causes of poverty, but today, as their fears about the economy have grown and their optimism about the effectiveness of government has faded, liberals have increasingly become resigned to alleviating the consequences of poverty instead. In contrast, conservatives, who earlier argued that Lyndon Johnson's efforts to attack poverty would prove ineffectual and should be abandoned, today express guarded optimism that the causes of poverty can be treated.

While both the right and left have vehemently argued with one another over the makeup of the country's poverty programs, the government would be well advised to be cautious in adopting either of their proposals. The thesis of this book has been that both the pessimism of liberals as well as the optimism of conservatives is empirically unjustified. If poverty is the result of the interaction of a variety of factors, then a renewed war on poverty may eventually prove to be winnable. If literally "everything"—such as the breakdown of the schools, the fragmentation of the family, the erosion of the work ethic, and the evolution of the economy—is responsible for the intractable nature of poverty, policymakers might be able to intervene at a variety of points to break the cycle. The tendency of liberals since the 1970s to advocate government programs embracing protectionism, racial quotas, and equal results rather than equal opportunity is thus an unfortunate policy development that will hopefully soon be reversed. By renewed experimentation and the adoption of novel programs, the government may yet develop policies that effectively reintegrate the poor, and especially the underclass, into the mainstream of American life.

But to argue that we know how to eliminate the causes of poverty does not necessarily mean that this objective can actually be achieved. While there may be numerous points at which the government might successfully attack poverty, there is no guarantee that its intervention will prove to be effective in helping the poor to help themselves. That is especially the case when many on the right as well as the left fail to see that the problems of the underclass are cultural rather than economic in nature.

As a result, liberals with their proclivity to rely on government spending, as well as market conservatives with their tendency to talk about the benefits of the marketplace and work incentives, often fail to address the key reasons why poverty has become such a persistent problem. The central contention of this book has been that people's cultural beliefs, family ties, entrepreneurial traditions, and their willingness to follow socially acceptable rules of conduct even in the face of racial and economic hardship are the primary reasons why some individuals escape poverty and others remain mired in it. Thus it is primarily sociological factors like culture and family relationships rather than government programs or market incentives that will determine if the causes of poverty will ever be eliminated.

THE EVOLUTION OF LIBERALISM: FROM A HELPING HAND TO PROTECTIONISM

At present there are mixed signals as to whether the country will ever try to adopt policies that will effectively lower the pre-transfer poverty rate. To appreciate why those on the left in particular have become unduly pessimistic about the prospects of winning a war against poverty, and thus have adopted policies that are likely to exacerbate the problems of the poor, it is important to understand how liberalism has evolved since the era of Franklin Roosevelt and Lyndon Johnson. From the late 1930s to the end of the 1960s, liberals sought to champion the interests of the have-nots in this country by pursuing two different but complementary policies. First, they tried to make sure that workers were not exploited by guaranteeing them the right to join unions and engage in collective bargaining. Liberals naturally assumed that American workers were hard-working and productive, but doubted that workers always received adequate or fair compensation for the fruits of their labor. This was true especially for black employees, who were often financially short-changed because of their color. In passing the Civil Rights Act of 1964, the Johnson administration sought to extend the protection previously afforded to work-ing-class whites by outlawing racial discrimination in the workplace as well.

Second, traditional liberalism also tried to enhance the opportunities available to the working class and the poor by investing additional money in education. The hope of liberals like Johnson was that the sons and daughters of the poor would eventually acquire the educational skills necessary to move into the ranks of the middle class.

But as the 1960s faded into obscurity and the American economy started to fall behind its Japanese competitors, the belief that it was possible for the government to eliminate the causes of poverty was called into question. Despite its best efforts to extend a helping hand, the poor in our inner cities appeared increasingly unable to grasp it. Protecting the rights of workers and minorities in the workplace would do little to advance their economic situa-tion if a sluggish economy failed to produce new jobs. Similarly, governmen-tal efforts to enhance the educational skills of the poor would prove to be ineffective if the American economy lacked the capability to employ those at the bottom of the social ladder.

In light of these developments, liberals began to abandon their belief that the government could actually win a war against poverty and argued instead that the government should treat the effects of poverty. As Japanese firms began to challenge and even displace American companies, liberals grew increasingly concerned with protecting indigents from the competitive pres-sures of what Joseph Schumpeter has labeled the "process of creative destruc-tion." Liberals recognize that in the give and take of market-oriented econo-mies, this process often casts aside inefficient and unprepared companies while rewarding innovative and productive ones. The unforgiving nature of capitalist economies explains why Western market-oriented countries have proven to be so much more creative and efficient than their socialist counter-parts. But to remain competitive in this kind of environment, the United States must constantly upgrade the skills of its work force as well as revitalize its industries. To hold off newly industrialized Third World countries, Amer-ican companies must inevitably either automate or spin off low-value work to Third World countries while developing high-value occupations that employ well trained and disciplined workers in the U.S. As liberals came to recognize that the costs of preparing people to deal with these major structural changes were likely to be painful and even disruptive in nature, they grew wary about paying the price. In the process, the left decided to place less priority on preparing the work force and the poor for the challenges of the global economy than on policies that would protect people, especially indigents, from the costs of creative destruction.

The growing tendency of liberals to treat the consequences of poverty rather than eliminate its causes is merely part of a larger shift in the attitude of liberals toward the demands of a market economy and the process of change in general. On the issue of international trade, American liberals, who once championed free trade, increasingly defend protectionism. While liberals in the 1930s believed that American workers did not receive fair compensation for their labor, liberals today recognize that the growing inability of American workers to compete internationally jeopardizes their wages. Although many on the left currently espouse one form or another of an industrial policy, they often seem less interested in preparing the American economy for this new age than in protecting the work force from foreign competition. In his new book, *Head to Head*, the prominent liberal economist Lester Thurow argues that Eastern Europe should accelerate its adjustment to a market economy, but he insists that America should slow down and partly insulate itself from comparable changes in the world economy.[1]

Even in the area of education, which Lyndon Johnson believed was the key to eliminating poverty, liberals seem uncertain about whether they should stress achievement and performance or protectionism. As the quality of American schools has lagged behind that of their Asian counterparts, liberals have called for investing more money in education. But if any proposition has been repeatedly confirmed in the social sciences, it is James Coleman's discovery that allocating more resources for education does not necessarily lead to an improvement in the quality of our public schools. If our schools continue to rely on their existing instructors and curricula, it is hard to see how additional funds alone will make them more effective. Because the educational lobby has been one of the most loyal and vocal supporters of the Democratic party, liberals have generally not been enthusiastic about funding education through a voucher system that would hold teachers accountable for their actions. As a result, liberalism, which once prided itself on its willingness to experiment and to promote change, has become an extremely conservative force in society, determined to protect its constituents from the need for reform.

This shift from performance to protection is even reflected in proposals for educating minority students. As Ravitch and Kramer have noted, many liberals often claim that society's inordinate concern with excellence and competition is partly to blame for the present plight of minority students. Instead of emphasizing academic standards, they feel that the public schools should concentrate their energies on making students feel good about themselves and their heritage. In his new book, *Two Nations*, Andrew Hacker has articulated the views of many other liberals by calling on teachers of black children to "be tolerant of a more casual approach to syntax, time and measurement."[2] While Hacker undoubtedly means well and believes his suggestions will promote the best interests of minority children, it is unclear whether his proposals would actually achieve that goal. The left in American politics often overlooks the fact that the best way to make minority students proud of themselves is to train them adequately to compete in a highly demanding world. Whatever their skin color may be, students will feel good about themselves when they have the skills necessary to qualify for high-paying jobs. But given the cost of this adjustment, many liberals often balk because of altruistic concerns about forcing minorities to pay the harsh price of meeting these standards. The current inclination of liberals to treat the effects of poverty rather than eliminate its causes is thus part of a larger shift in their overall attitude toward social change.

An Attitude of Laissez-Faire

At the same time that liberals have expanded entitlement programs to protect the poor from the demands of the marketplace, they have tended to ask very little of them in return. The modern welfare state is remarkable for its permissiveness as well as its protectionism. The left has traditionally minimized or dismissed altogether the obligations and duties of the poor to society while emphasizing instead their rights and entitlements. From the late 1960s to the middle 1980s, many liberals turned a blind eye even to the misdeeds of the poor. Until William Julius Wilson acknowledged that some of the poor were engaged in self-destructive actions, they even refused to admit that an underclass existed. While Wilson should be commended for forcing those on the left to address the problems of the underclass, it is still apparent that liberals remain uncomfortable with the idea that the state should encourage its citizens to act in a responsible fashion. In creating a humane welfare state, they have been singularly quiet about what kind of individual behavior, if any, the state should try to encourage or promote. Or as the journalists E. J. Dionne has expressed it: "Liberals tout themselves as the defenders of the community. Yet when the talk moves from economic issues to culture or personal morality, liberals fall strangely mute. Liberals are uncomfortable with the idea that a virtuous community depends on virtuous individuals. Liberals defend the welfare state but are uneasy when asked what moral values the welfare state should promote—as if billions of federal dollars can be spent in a 'value free' way."[3]

The historian Fred Siegel has observed that the consequence is a welfare state "whose jurisdictional reach has been dramatically extended, but whose moral grasp recedes before the privatization of life."[4] As they push for more government programs to shield indigents from the demands of the marketplace, liberals often seem indifferent as to whether or not the poor will discharge their obligation to be productive members of society. In spite of their recognition that many low- and moderate-income families toil away at demanding jobs, liberals frequently reject the idea that welfare recipients have similar obligations to work. Although an increasing number of women are trying to nurture their families as well as participate in the labor market, liberals often maintain that conservatives are mean-spirited to expect poor women to incur comparable responsibilities. When the public justly complains about the violence and lawlessness of the inner city, liberals frequently dismiss these complaints as disguised racism, overlooking the fact that the people who suffer the most from the breakdown of law and order in the inner city are themselves minority members.[5] Even when liberals acknowledge that many inner-city residents often engage in violent and self-destructive behaviors, they tend to reject the idea that the public sector should promote, or, in the case of violent crime, even enforce community standards of behavior.

The key question is, why have liberals been so adamant about stressing the entitlements of the poor while minimizing their social duties and obligations? From a policy perspective, both society and the poor might be better off by rejecting what E. J. Dionne has called our "value-free" welfare state. Given the difficulties of our present society, which is suffering from a surfeit of rights, we must also emphasize people's social responsibilities. It certainly is reasonable for a welfare state that goes out of its way to protect people from the competitive pressures of the global economy to expect in return that people honor their social responsibilities.

While there are no easy answers to this question, many liberals may favor a laissez-faire view of the welfare state out of simple prudence. As all poverty analysts quickly learned in the 1960s, when Patrick Moynihan raised questions about the black family, they may be subject to intense and even unfair criticism if they discuss, let alone criticize, the behavior of the underclass. While the attacks on Moynihan are certainly not one of the proudest moments in social science research, they continue to have a chilling effect on the ability of liberals to openly discuss the problems of the poor.

Similarly, the growing popularity of structuralist and exchange arguments among liberal poverty researchers may also have blinded them to the behavior problems of the underclass. As more and more sociologists and economists argue that structural changes are the primary determinants of economic well-being, they have tended to deemphasize the importance of individual action.

Perhaps the main reason that liberals have been reluctant to stress the obligations of the poor is their libertarian belief that the government should refrain from altering the values of its citizens. There has always been a conflict in Western political thought over whether the state should be responsible for molding the character of its citizens. The Greek founders of our Western heritage felt that it would be impossible to develop a harmonious state unless the polity instilled a sense of duty and self-restraint among the people. If a citizenry lacked a sense of virtue, no amount of economic prosperity would ever generate the conditions required for the maintenance of a virtuous state. Aristotle, like many other Greeks, recognized that achieving this goal would not be an easy task. It would take considerable training and practice for people to acquire the sense of balance and discipline necessary to discharge their responsibilities effectively. In contrast to today, the Greeks believed that questions of character were rightly considered to be a matter of important public as well as private concern. In the nineteenth century, the French sociologist Emile Durkheim and other control theorists gave the Greek preoccupation with "virtue" a cultural twist by insisting that society might very well disintegrate unless there were some common beliefs binding people together. A variety of private and public reform movements in the nineteenth century, including elements of the Progressive party, also embraced the idea that the government had a responsibility to instill in people a sense of civic virtue.

In contrast to the legacy of the Greeks and their emphasis on civic behavior, a second tradition in Western political thought associated with the Enlightenment has always been hostile to the Greek concern with public virtue. As the sons and daughters of the Enlightenment recalled that Europe had torn itself apart in the religious wars of the seventeenth century, they became wary of governmental efforts to shape the character of its citizens. The founders of the Enlightenment feared that if authorities promoted a shared set of beliefs among their subjects, they might very well create a morally despotic and intolerable political climate. Thus they downplayed people's obligations and duties while stressing their right to dissent from majority beliefs. People's character, they believed, was essentially a private matter, of minimal concern to public officials.

When the American republic was founded, Madison and the other architects of the Constitution echoed the reservations of the Enlightenment about governments tinkering with the values of its citizens. But Madison's belief in limited government was tempered by his doubts about the wisdom and character of the American people. Rather than attacking the root cause of people's behavior by altering their beliefs, Madison felt that the American political system could survive by balancing one segment of society against another.[6] The founding fathers felt that instead of trying to instill a sense of virtue in the citizenry, they could control people's behavior through an elaborate system of checks and balances.

When present-day liberals began to expand the modern welfare state in the 1960s, they embraced the libertarian notions of the founding fathers. But their adoption of Madisonian principles was highly selective, overlooking Madison's warnings about the tendency of people to engage in self-serving behavior. Hesitant about taking a stand on moral issues, today's liberals have gravitated toward either structural or exchange explanations of poverty that have allowed them to avoid moral commentary on the behavior of the poor. As Lyndon Johnson launched the Great Society, he optimistically saw government as a neutral broker who would assist the bottom strata of society to become conscientious and productive members of the middle class. In contrast to the Greek notion that governments had a right to expect people to meet certain minimal obligations to society, the war on poverty saw its job in more limited terms as distributing resources to previously ignored groups.

When the behavior of the poor began to deteriorate in the late 1960s, liberalism was at an intellectual loss as to how to correct their destructive actions. Besides rejecting the classical idea of public virtue, modern liberalism also ignored Madison's warning that people's behavior had to be checked and balanced at least externally, if not internally. The liberal state, which knew how to dispense resources to the needy, naturally assumed that indigents would become productive citizens if the economy were expanding. The growth of the underclass thus presented liberals with a new social issue outside the range of their previous experiences. Given its reservations about public virtues and its indifference towards external checks, post-World War II liberalism had no tradition for dealing with social problems that required changing people's behavior. In stressing the rights and entitlements of the poor, liberalism became a victim of its own libertarian views of government.

The Political Dilemma of Liberal Democracy

The growing tendency of liberals to treat the consequences rather than the causes of poverty has been costly to the presidential aspirations of Democratic contenders. Because the political price of continuing the existing welfare state has been relatively high, there is hope that liberals may eventually alter their policies regarding the poor. With the slowdown in the economy, the public has become increasingly less sympathetic with government efforts to protect those who often violate traditional working- and middle-class values. As families have struggled to maintain their standard of living by sending additional workers into the labor market, many have resented the laissez-faire and protective nature of the current welfare state. From the late 1960s until 1992, Republican presidential candidates enjoyed unusual political success in exploiting this anger. In their excellent book, *Chain Reaction*, Thomas and Mary Edsell examine how Republican presidents from Richard Nixon to George Bush have fractured the traditional Democratic coalition by attacking the apparent moral indifference of liberal Democrats toward the breakdown of the social fabric in the inner cities. As they note, "The symptoms of social disorder, which the Democratic left . . . excluded from public debate for most of the past twenty-five years, and which black leaders have resisted talking about in morally unambiguous terms, have become so severe in the nation's cities—and . . . so closely associated . . . with liberalism—that continued Democratic avoidance of these issues risks the national party's already-eroded credibility with the voting majority."[7] By dismissing rather than trying to understand the legitimate concerns of many Americans about the condition of our cities, the Democratic party often alienated voters. But many liberals were hesitant to alter their policies because they were hostile to the idea that public officials should interfere in the private lives of its citizens. If the state tried to inculcate in the poor a set of values, the danger existed that the modern welfare state would take on an Orwellian cast. While the concern of liberals that the adoption of a common set of beliefs would lead to a modern version of the Inquisition is understandable, their fear that teaching people the virtues of self-restraint and hard work will lead to intolerance seems exaggerated. In spite of their libertarian leanings, liberals must recognize the distinction between the government enforcing a despotic moral code and merely endorsing a set of core values that "are beneficial to both society and the individuals who practice them."[8]

Even if liberals turn their back on the libertarian outlook of the Democratic party and begin to address the problem of permissiveness, their political problems may not completely disappear. The continued sluggish growth of family income in this country since the early 1970s confronts liberals with an unappealing dilemma. As they see more and more indigents failing to achieve financial independence, their natural inclination is to shield yet others from the competitive demands of the marketplace. But as the financial prospects of most Americans deteriorate, forcing them to struggle to make ends meet, they have become more hostile to paying the costs of welfare programs. A dilemma therefore confronts liberals: the financial conditions that make them eager to expand the generosity of the welfare state simultaneously erode their political support for enlarging entitlement programs.

It is perhaps not surprising that Republicans started to do well in presidential elections in the 1970s just as the post-World War II increases in family income came to a screeching halt. Because average Americans have seen no significant increase in their disposable family income since 1973, most Americans have correctly perceived that their disposable income will further decline if the size of the U.S. government is enlarged through increased taxes. While most Americans may be willing to support an expansive role for government when their take-home pay rises faster than taxes, they are hesitant to do so in periods of slow income growth, especially when additional taxes are used to support entitlements for others.

To overcome this dilemma and counter the growing public hostility to entitlement programs, liberals have entertained two different proposals for altering the welfare state. First, William Julius Wilson, Theda Skocpol, and others have recently suggested that the political left should redesign its entitlement programs so that they benefit the public at large rather than target solely the poor.[9] When government programs are specifically tailored to benefit indigents only, liberals cannot generate enough public support to retain their hold on public office. Wilson, Skocpal, and others hope to blunt the political opposition to redistributive programs by enlarging eligibility for welfare programs and thus coopting the working and middle classes. "Their aim is to ameliorate poverty though broader social programs that include whites alone with people of color, middle-class citizens along with economically disadvantaged Americans."[10] In place of programs like AFDC, which benefit only single parents, the welfare state would implement programs such as family allowances for children, universal medical protection, and child care that would benefit everyone. While liberals like Wilson recognize that most of the benefits in their "reformed" welfare state would accrue to the middle class, they nonetheless hope that enough resources would trickle down to the poor to substantially improve their lives.

However appealing the revamping of existing welfare programs may be, the call for universal entitlement programs is not without its difficulties. The efforts by Wilson and Skocpol to change the scope of the welfare state will be expensive and require a major increase in taxes. Even if members of the middle class are the major beneficiaries of this revamped welfare state, they may be hesitant about paying the increased taxes needed to fund the new programs. But aside from the economic price tag of universal welfare programs, the more fundamental question is whether the commendable desire of liberals to shield the poor as well as other constituents from the brutal demands of the global economy is a policy worth pursuing. Whatever guise welfare programs eventually assume, the problems of the poor are likely to become more acute with time. As discussed earlier, the marketplace increasingly demands workers who are better trained and motivated. Given the number of workers and businesses that have had to make painful adjustments to head off foreign competition, we are likely to find mounting pressure for the poor to make comparable sacrifices.

In light of the difficulties associated with expanding the scope of entitlement programs, President Clinton has developed a second option for minimizing public hostility toward liberal welfare policies. His reform proposals have essentially called for liberals to abandon their libertarian outlook of the 1970s and 1980s and to embrace the traditional values of equal opportunity and self-discipline which the Democratic party advocated in the 1960s. Instead of expanding its welfare policies so that they appeal to more people, Clinton hopes to shore up popular support for the Democratic party by extending one more a helping hand—rather than a handout—to the poor. In this sense Clinton's attempt to substitute a welfare state based on the principles of the "New Covenant" for the entitlement programs of the 1970s represents a return to as well as a major revision of the discarded policies of Lyndon Johnson. Like Johnson, Clinton and his secretary of labor, Robert Reich, have pointed to the importance of education and retraining as a means of achieving upward mobility. Despite Clinton's self-characterization as a "new Democrat," his policies involve embracing the principles his party once espoused in the 1960s and later chose to abandon. Instead of stressing quotas and equal results, the Clinton administration has tried to identify the Democratic party with the principles of investing in human capital and promoting equal opportunity. Unfortunately, the administration's ability to generate novel ideas for improving the quality of our schools and the educational skills of the poor have not kept pace with its rhetoric.

But to appreciate the significance of Clinton's proposals, we have to realize that he is also proposing a major revamping, rather than a mere duplication, of Lyndon Johnson's war on poverty. In a major departure with the libertarian heritage of his own party, Clinton appears willing to invoke cultural sanctions to criticize the behavior of the jobless underclass by insisting that the beneficiaries of the welfare state act in a virtuous fashion. While William Julius Wilson forced liberals to admit there is an underclass in this country, the president is willing to entertain proposals to change their behavior. Clinton, unlike his liberal predecessors, seems more than willing to use the state to prod and cajole the poor into becoming productive members of society. He has even used the biblical language of the religious right to talk about the need for a new covenant between the government and the poor. In order to flesh out the meaning of the new covenant, Clinton has become an enthusiastic supporter of programs such as national service for students and workfare for the poor. By limiting the length of time indigents can spend on welfare, his administration is sending a message that the poor have duties as well as rights. In return for granting entitlements to indigents, the state will insist that the poor abide by the "rules of the game" by eventually seeking work in the labor market.

THE EVOLUTION OF CONSERVATISM: FROM PESSIMISM TO A HELPING HAND

Although the decision of Clinton to turn his back on the laissez-faire outlook of the Democratic party and embrace traditional values like self-restraint is an extremely positive development and undoubtedly contributed to his election victory, it is still an open question whether he will succeed in transforming the cultural beliefs of his party. If we are ever going to win a war against poverty, we are more likely to find the answers from the political right than the left. While Clinton's proposals for reforming the welfare state are a step in the right direction, his views may be more of an aberration than a reflection of mainstream liberal thinking. The president may even find more supporters among Republicans than his own party on behalf of his efforts to redesign government entitlement programs and eliminate the actual causes of poverty.

This newfound faith among conservatives that a war against poverty can be won represents a radical departure from their previous attitudes. In the immediate post-World War II period, most conservatives were skeptical about the government's ability to solve any kind of social problem. A variety of analysts on the right like Edward Banfield, who believed that the poor were victims of their own indigenous "culture of poverty," held out little hope that the poor would ever achieve any significant degree of upward mobility. But beginning in the 1970s many intellectuals on the right, including Thomas Sowell, Charles Murray, Lawrence Mead, Diane Ravitch, and

James Q. Wilson, began to recast conservatism as a political ideology capable of dealing with some of society's most pressing social problems.[11] As the economy turned sluggish in the 1970s and family income ceased growing, the political right in American politics searched for an alternative to the prevailing liberal orthodoxy that then dominated American politics. Rather than defending the protectionism and permissiveness of the liberal welfare state, conservatives stressed the need to better motivate and prepare indigents for the demands of the new international economy. As liberals became more concerned with shielding the poor from the demands of society, this diverse group of conservatives literally hoped to create a new "opportunity society" that relied on market incentives and cultural values to promote upward mobility. But in place of the present welfare state, which offers the poor a handout and asks very little of them in return, these conservatives wanted to develop a poverty policy that would encourage indigents to become more self-reliant. Like Lyndon Johnson, their goal was to win the war against the causes of poverty by helping the poor to help themselves.

But even though they agreed that an alternative to liberalism was urgently needed, the political right was divided over what course to follow, offering two plans that embraced overlapping yet contrasting strategies for attacking the causes of poverty. The first alternative, which we shall call "market conservatism," hoped to rely on a diverse array of economic incentives to reduce the ranks of the poor and better prepare people for the demands of a highly technological society. Instead of merely opposing government initiatives, they wished to apply the market principles of financial gain, competition, and public choice to the delivery of government services such as welfare, housing, and public education. The second alternative, which we shall call "civic conservatism," argued that efforts to eliminate the true causes of poverty in this country would prove ineffectual until the community, businesses and the poor recaptured some common sense of shared values. They maintained that the breakdown of traditional beliefs, or what Durkheim called anomie, not only had eroded the willingness of the underclass to become financially independent but it had also hampered the ability of American industry to generate jobs and compete effectively in a global economy.

Market Conservatives

Of these two strategies, the call for market-oriented reforms has received the most attention in the press and undoubtedly dominates conservative thinking today. While many market conservatives have come up with a number of innovative recommendations for bringing about social change, their proposals may have little or no impact on the overall poverty rate. By claiming that the poor lack economic incentives to behave themselves, they have failed to see that the issue of poverty is more of a cultural than an economic problem.

Despite this drawback, the unique appeal of market conservatism lies in the fact that it embodies a simple yet powerful message. They insist that if the poor are to become better prepared for the new international economy, they must be financially rewarded for adopting the required behavior. Conversely, to discourage undesirable and unproductive behavior, it must be taxed or penalized. Unfortunately, most liberals have ignored this simple yet important lesson in designing the panoply of programs that cater to the needs of the poor. When market-oriented conservatives look at the legacy of the current welfare state, they insist that it has left too many indigents both unmotivated and untrained to pull themselves out of poverty. Given their supply-side concerns, they also maintain that the lack of adequate financial incentives has led to a slowdown in both capital investment and productivity increases, which in turn adversely affects the wages of the working poor.

These changes in the work force and capital investment have led to three disastrous consequences. First, an increasing number of the poor have either dropped out of the labor market or become indifferent about their obligation to work, thus undercutting their appeal to potential employers. Second, the pattern of income inequality in the United States has become more rather than less pronounced with the passage of time as the poor increasingly lack both the family ties that might help them ride out harsh economic times as well as the educational skills necessary to qualify for sophisticated, high-paying jobs. Third, earned income has ceased growing in an absolute sense because there has been no increase in productivity. The hope that the poor would one day become self-sufficient has been dashed because the worst of all possible scenarios has occurred. Not only are more and more indigents choosing not to work, but when they do their wages and family income have become more unequal and their salaries have stopped growing in an absolute sense.

Motivating the Poor with Financial Incentives. In light of these problems, market-oriented conservatives hope to attack poverty in a variety of ways. By altering either singularly or cumulatively the educational training, family ties, attitudes, or work opportunities available to the poor, they hope to significantly reduce the pre-transfer rate of poverty.

For instance, market conservatives maintain that the problems of the underclass reflect their lack of incentives to reenter the labor market, to obey the law, and to act generally as productive members of society. Like their liberal counterparts and America's founding fathers, market-oriented conservatives don't agree with the Greek assumption that government should actively try to mold the character of its citizens. But in rejecting the politics of virtue, market-oriented conservatives have enthusiastically embraced, as well as slightly revised, the tradition of James Madison and his principles of external checks and balances. They argue that if people engage in unproductive behavior, the state should rely on a combination of economic inducements and legal sanctions to control their self-destructive tendencies. In order to make it more lucrative for the poor to reenter the labor force, market-oriented conservatives have called for the following financial incentives:

- An expansion of the earned income tax credit coupled with a decrease in AFDC payments to make work more attractive
- The raising of the standard tax deduction to reward the working poor and their children
- Child-care tax credits instead of an expansion of government-run child-care programs to assist working mothers
- The sale of public housing to tenants to foster a sense of individual responsibility and home ownership among the poor.

To cut down on the criminal activities of the underclass, Presidents Reagan and Bush, and other market conservatives, have focused on reversing liberal efforts to pare down the number of arrested felons serving time in jail. In the heyday of liberal judicial activism in the 1960s, the number of people serving time in jail for acts of criminal behavior dropped to an all-time low. By intensifying punishments for violent crimes while increasing economic rewards for holding down a job, market-oriented conservatives hope to make the adoption of more conventional behavior by the underclass an attractive alternative. They believe that if public officials indirectly control the actions of the poor through the selective use of financial incentives and external checks it will be unnecessary to alter their character.

Reducing the Polarization of Income and Reviving the Growth of Wages. To stem the growing polarization of income in America, market conservatives also favor the use of financial incentives to shore up low-income families as well as improve their educational skills. But they recognize that the problem of income inequality confronts decision makers in Washington with a tough policy dilemma. To hold off our foreign competitors and generate high-paying positions for our labor force, we need to encourage American firms to upgrade and produce high-value products. But in solving the problem of American competitiveness, we may exacerbate the problem of income differences. The more innovative our companies become, the greater their demand for educated employees, which in turn will help polarize our wage structure.

To give the poor the educational skills they need in order to compete in the new economic world order, market conservatives want to guarantee indigents the same option that middle-class parents presently enjoy of choosing their children's schools. Like Lyndon Johnson, they realize that government needs to improve the training of the poor in order to check the growing inequality of wages as well as prepare people for the changing demands of an increasingly complex society. Instead of granting monopoly power to public schools, they would give educational vouchers to parents, who would then decide which schools their children would attend. In defense of their proposals, they would point out that 40 percent of urban public school teachers with school-age children now enroll their children in private schools. Many public school teachers seem to realize that the educational establishment—just like the underclass—needs the judicious use of financial checks and balances to improve its performance. In light of the bureaucratic makeup of our existing school systems, administrators and teachers have little or no financial incentives for achieving academic excellence. When parents have the right to vote with their feet, they will undoubtedly be more effective in holding the schools accountable for their performance.

In case their educational policies fail, market conservatives want to soften the growing polarization of income by using selective financial incentives and penalties to shore up and strengthen indigent families. By simply staying married, low income families can insulate themselves to some extent from the growing polarization of wages. When low-income families have only one wage earner, they are financially more vulnerable to economic trends in the larger society than their two-parent counterparts. Market conservatives believe that indigent families are more likely to stay together if society reduces the generosity of its welfare payments. The present system of transfer payments encourages too many women to walk away from their marriage responsibilities. By forcing fathers to pay child support when they abandon their marital responsibilities, conservatives also hope to encourage men to take their marital duties more seriously.

Finally, the government can also intervene to assist the poor by stimulating more business investment. Market-oriented conservatives believe that if public officials provide additional tax incentives for companies to invest more resources in their plants and equipment, they will boost productivity and raise the wages of the working poor. When plants become more productive, they can grant higher wages to their workers which will in turn help to compensate for the growing inequality of wages. With the challenge from Asia becoming more intense each year, it is imperative that American companies upgrade their capital stock and adopt the latest developments in technology. The sooner American firms become more competitive and increase their productivity, the easier it will be for them to hold their foreign rivals at bay and pay their employees higher real wages.

Civic Conservatives

Despite the intellectual coherence and apparent simplicity of the market-conservative agenda, these proposals have met with only limited success in dealing with the causes of poverty. While the efforts of market conservatives to entice the underclass back into the labor market and to contain the growing polarization of income deserve high praise, they have failed to realize that these problems are not solely economic in nature. If we are ever going to build a new "opportunity society" it is essential that the poor and the larger community share in the development of a shared set of values. This doctrine, which I wish to call "civic conservatism," contends that a war against poverty will work only if the country can agree on a new covenant in which the rights and duties of the poor as well as other citizens are equally respected. The financial rewards and penalties of the marketplace are most effective when workers and managers alike have internalized a coherent set of beliefs that value hard work, discipline, respect for individuals, and a healthy regard for the well-being of the larger community. If society cannot address Durkheim's fear about the rise of anomie, Adam Smith's invisible hand will be ineffectual in enticing the poor to reenter the labor market.

Motivating the Poor through Resocialization. The failure to recognize this point has led both liberal economists as well as market conservatives to exaggerate the degree to which the poor respond to either market incentives or adverse economic conditions. Repeated efforts by Congress over the last thirty years to make work economically more attractive and welfare less remunerative have had little impact on the employment of AFDC recipients. In 1969 and 1981 Congress significantly altered the amount of money AFDC recipients could keep if they accepted full-time work. But regardless of the benefit levels, benefit reduction rates, or even unemployment rates facing welfare recipients, they have consistently chosen not to seek work. Welfare recipients have never had a tradition of participating actively in the labor market even when job opportunities were plentiful and the welfare tax on work was minimal.

The efforts of Presidents Reagan and Bush to crack down on illegal activity have likewise had at best mixed results in helping to contain the growth of street crime in the inner city. When the Reagan and Bush administrations combined tougher sentences for crimes with a reduction in welfare benefits, the work record of the underclass still failed to improve. The Madisonian belief that society can externally control the behavior of the underclass through external checks and financial incentives has repeatedly come up emptyhanded because it is based on questionable assumptions about human motivation. Market incentives and external controls are always mediated by people's cultural beliefs. When individuals suffer from anomie and lack an internal sense of self-discipline, they are not likely to be swayed by incremental changes in their external environment.

If we want to make a serious effort to address the problems of the poor in general and the underclass in particular, it is essential that government concern itself with the character of its citizens. As the American economy has increasingly faced global competition, the problems of the underclass have begun to resemble the difficulties facing the working class during the nineteenth century. At that time, a whole array of institutions invested considerable resources in socializing people so that they would be properly prepared for the demands of an industrialized society. But in the post-World War II period, many civic and political elites began to reject and even make light of the values that originally helped make America so wealthy. In place of stressing character, the work ethic, self-discipline, and public duties, the new post-World War II morality has emphasized instant gratification, self-expression, and "doing your own thing." Once civic and business leaders ceased administering rewards and sanctions clearly and unambiguously, many of the poor abandon traditional values much faster than the rest of society. While some scholars insist that the collapse of the inner-city family, the high and often gratuitous level of crime in the ghetto, and the poor work record of many indigents are often unrelated problems, they in reality reflect the increasing anomic nature of life in the inner city.

To correct this problem and prepare indigents for the demands of the global economy, government officials, school administrators, philanthropic groups, and civil rights leaders must try to inculcate in the underclass a realization that self-discipline and hard work are the keys to achieving upward mobility in America. At present the most prominent civic conservative is undoubtedly Lawrence Mead, who has repeatedly stressed the need to institute a program of workfare to replace our current welfare system.[12] Mead's hope is that when public transfer programs emphasize responsibilities as well as entitlements, they can begin the difficult but necessary task of resocializing the underclass into behaving responsibly again. But Mead's proposals have stirred up considerable controversy among those who espouse libertarian views of government. His critics on the left, who are queasy about proposals combining individual rights with social duties, insist that mandatory work requirements impose too heavy a burden on the poor. But if Mead's recommendations warrant any criticism at all, it is not that they require too much of the poor but that they require too little. In light of the cultural difficulties afflicting the poor, it is apparent that governmental efforts to instill a sense of self-control among the underclass must go significantly beyond the idea of workfare. The country may have to spend as much time culturally preparing the underclass for the demands of the current economy as the social reformers of the nineteenth century spent on preparing the working class for the age of industrialization. To reduce the ranks of the underclass, all sectors of society and not just the government must recognize as well as deal with the pervasive normlessness that characterizes life in our inner cities.

Reducing the Polarization of Income through Revitalizing the Importance of Family and Education. The same principles apply to limiting the growing inequality of wages in this country. In order to shore up family income and overcome the growing skill mismatch between the demands of the labor market and the supply of trained workers, we need to improve the educational skills of the work force. For example, efforts to experiment with apprenticeship programs (as currently practiced in Germany) as well as vouchers should be encouraged. At present, it is still unclear whether increased competition among public schools will actually improve the educational skills of the poor and reduce the growing inequality of wages. Aside from the limited yet excellent studies by Coleman, Chubb, and Moe, no long-term research has been conducted that measures the effectiveness of vouchers.[13] However desirable it may be to hold teachers accountable for their actions, educational competition may be at best only a partial solution to the country's educational woes. If, as discussed earlier, many teachers are opposed to educating students with rigor, the danger exists that vouchers may lead schools to compete with one another by lowering rather than raising academic standards. The only way to prevent this unfortunate scenario is to hope that the majority of parents as well as students disagree with Hacker's flawed suggestion that teachers should take a more relaxed attitude toward training minority students in the intricacies of language and mathematics. It is only when poor minority parents place their children in academically demanding schools that vouchers may work. Regardless of how much money we pour into the schools or how much public choice parents enjoy, low-income students are not likely to show much academic improvement until they and their parents, as well as our culture generally, place a higher value on academic achievement. In an unfortunate cultural turn of events, many students have even come to look upon their well-educated counterparts as "nerds" or "propeller heads" who are to be avoided rather than emulated. Despite the economic advantages of excelling academically, many middle-class students as well as indigents appear to lack the discipline as well as the cultural commitment necessary to apply themselves in the classroom effectively.

Besides improving their educational skills, indigents can escape poverty by choosing their spouses more carefully. When indigent women who work at low-paying jobs stay married to working men, they can insulate themselves from the growing polarization of wages in this country. But the continuing high level of broken families among indigents has made many poorly educated women extremely vulnerable to the growing inequality of wages in the economy. As discussed earlier, neither the growth of welfare payments nor the lack of "marriageable men" may be the principal reason for the collapse of indigent families. As the generosity of welfare payments has declined over the last decade, the family life of indigents has remained as unstable as ever. The breakdown of family life among indigents reflects broader cultural changes occurring in American society and is not a problem unique to the poor. But these changes have hit the poor particularly hard given their lack of economic resources.

Overcoming the Slow Growth of Wages through Cultural As Well As Economic Reform. Finally, the extremely important goal of increasing investment in the private sector and raising the wages of the working poor cannot be achieved by financial incentives alone. The record of market conservatives in stimulating overall investment has often failed to achieve it objectives. While Reagan believed that cutting tax rates for individuals and businesses would increase savings and stimulate investment, the results have been mixed at best. In the 1980s personal savings rates actually dropped to a post-World War II low. While the ratio of nonresidential fixed investment to GNP did increase significantly after the 1982 Reagan tax cut, the level was merely comparable to rates achieved in the 1950s. And even then the investment rate of the Reagan years was significantly below the rate achieved during the middle years of Lyndon Johnson's presidency.[14] This reduction in savings and investment in America occurred at the same time that the

Japanese dramatically increased their investments in new plants and equipment. Besides earmarking fewer resources for manufacturing plants, American businesses also invested less than their foreign counterparts in R & D and employee training.[15]

Even more importantly, much of the investment that occurred in the 1980s went to finance leveraged buy-outs that often overburdened many American companies with onerous levels of debt. If the additions to the outstanding debt of American companies had led to the much-needed purchase of new plants and factories, the leveraging of American companies might have increased their productivity. Unfortunately, the deterioration in the balance sheets of American firms often benefited stockholders, investment bankers, and attorneys at the expense of the company. By offering financial incentives to the business community to invest and raise the productivity of American firms, market conservatives overlooked the fact that the financial community was often more interested in reaping short-term gains than in improving the financial health of their takeover targets. While the situation naturally differs from one company to the next, the leveraged buy-out spree of the 1980s may have saddled many companies with so much debt that they cannot find the resources necessary to increase their productivity. As with many of their suggestions to combat poverty, market conservatives often promised more than they could deliver.

More recently, Michael Porter has suggested that the capital decisions of American companies might be significantly improved by encouraging investors to take a longer-term interest in the companies in which they buy stock. Among other proposals, the government might consider allowing banks to own an equity interest in the companies to which they lend.[16] Although Porter's economic proposals for stimulating more investment undoubtedly have their advantages and warrant further attention, his suggestions are at best only partial solutions to America's investment problems.

While market conservatives, like all exchange theorists, insist that the key to increasing investment and hence productivity is to design financial incentives that appeal to people's self-interest, they are often silent on how companies or people interpret "self-interest." How CEOs and their companies define their "self" may vary considerably according to the values they have chosen to internalize. To some extent the excesses of the private sector in the 1980s reflected the same problems that plagued the underclass. As traditional norms of self-restraint and discipline have broken down, many investors have engaged in self-serving, impulsive, and even illegal activities analogous to the behavior in our inner cities.

In praising the obvious advantages of the private sector and its emphasis on competition, many conservatives have failed to see that the financial incentives of a capitalist economy may also contain the seeds of its own self-destruction. As Daniel Bell noted many years ago, the stress on financial gain and permissiveness that a capitalist economy often encourages may undermine the very virtues—such as savings, long-term investment, the postponement of gratification and discipline—that capitalism needs for its own survival.[17] Although Bell wrote about the contradictions of capitalism in the 1970s, his diagnosis also applies to investment bankers and American companies in the 1980s. The very same factors that have eroded the work ethic among the poor may also have weakened the commitment of some business and civic leaders to the kinds of long-term concern with quality and productivity that will enable them to hold off their Japanese rivals.

In order to boost productivity in American companies and thus raise the wages of the working poor, it is apparent that cultural changes must accompany economic reforms. As is often the case, economic incentives, whether cuts in the marginal tax rate or reductions in the capital gains tax, work best when they complement and reinforce an existing commitment by businesses to run productive and efficient firms. When those same incentives are used by anomic executives interested in short-term profits and conspicuous consumption, the very real danger exists that scarce capital may be squandered in ways that benefit neither the American economy nor the working poor. While there are numerous examples of American corporations that have painfully transformed themselves into productive and competitive firms, the original goal of Reagan Republicans to reinvigorate the corporate world and increase labor productivity has only been partially realized.

CONCLUSION

As we move farther into the 1990s, the American political system has two very clear options for dealing with the problem of poverty. While the desire of liberals to shield the poor from the demands of the marketplace is understandable and laudable, their concern may eventually prove to be self-defeating as well as politically harmful to the presidential aspirations of the Democratic party. With the international marketplace becoming increasingly competitive, all segments of society, including the poor, must adjust to a more demanding international marketplace. As manufacturing and service companies as well as blue- and white-collar workers alike try to adapt to this new environment, they are likely to become less and less sympathetic with a welfare state that does not demand equal sacrifices from all segments of society. The greater the extent to which liberalism becomes wedded to defending the status quo and the interest groups that make up the Democratic party, the greater the risk that it will be overtaken by events.

The fact that it is politically desirable as well as empirically possible to treat the actual causes of poverty does not necessarily mean that the political system will be motivated to start chipping away at the apparent causes of poverty. It remains unclear whether the political system currently has the willpower to adopt the cultural changes I have called civic conservatism. As a result there are contradictory signs as to whether the United States can realistically hope to fulfill Lyndon Johnson's dream of winning the war against poverty.

Until we can resocialize many of the poor and contain the growth of the underclass, life in our inner cities will remain as precarious and chaotic as ever. Fortunately, people are beginning to realize that we need to rebuild a common culture that stresses duties as well as rights, discipline as well as self-expression. In our efforts to be generous to our fellow humans, we must not lose sight of the fact that a large segment of the American population still favors the development of a welfare state that emphasizes responsibility, self-discipline, and civic virtue. As Michael Duneier has shown in his sensitive portrayal of the lives of working-class black men in *Slim's Table*, the working poor often share those same sentiments.[18] Many responsible and conscientious residents of the inner city feel isolated and alienated in their own communities because of the increasing amoral actions of the underclass and the indifference of politicians. Like Slim, the black working men and women of our inner cities have been the main victims of the fragmentation of traditional social values.

The recent decision of President Clinton to call for a new covenant between the government and the poor is a welcome sign that altering the welfare state may still be a real political possibility. Given the convoluted nature of poverty politics in this country, it would be ironic if Clinton's proposals for a "new covenant" managed to unite large numbers of liberals and conservatives behind a common welfare program. Clinton's emphasis on rewarding only those individuals who abide by the "rules of the game" embraces many of the same principles I have labeled "civic conservatism." But it remains to be seen if Clinton can really wean his party away from its libertarian view of public policy. While many of his fellow Democrats may reluctantly agree to vote for workfare, they may still harbor reservations about his efforts to alter the conduct of the underclass.

In fact, the future direction of social policy in America is anything but assured in light of the cross-currents presently buffeting public opinion. The cultural debates that have resonated in America during 1980s and 1990s have mimicked, albeit in muted fashion, the cultural ferment that marred the decades of the 1960s. While the period of the Vietnam War led to an angry rejection of the ethic of hard work and self-discipline, we can hope that the next decade may see a return to traditional values. But it may be easier to reject and abandon cultural norms than it is to reinstate them. Once groups abandon traditional values, they may be reluctant to embrace them again. Until the attitudes and policies of a whole array of institutions are dramatically changed, it is very likely that the problems of the underclass will remain as intractable as ever.

The fact that change is possible does not mean that it is probable. The danger thus exists that the country will become increasingly polarized. As the well-educated and affluent members of the middle class retreat to the isolation of their edge cities, the underclass may continue to destroy the fabric of community life within the inner city. This unfortunate result may occur because many fear that if government institutions teach the virtues of self-restraint to the public, the country will adopt an intolerant and authoritarian political system. A variety of political interests insist that by trying to make citizens virtuous, the state may find itself on the slippery slope of imposing a rigid and dogmatic moral code on its citizens. This attitude is especially prevalent among members of the "poverty industry," including government officials, civil rights activists, liberal interest groups, and policy analysts who are often wedded to existing policies and resentful of any suggestions that seem to criticize the poor. As Clinton may soon find out, too often they are more willing to live with the self-destructive actions of the underclass than to contemplate a more expansive role for public officials in regulating the private lives of the poor. That may be the ultimate irony of the government's efforts to fight poverty in the 1990s. While we may finally understand how to treat the actual causes of poverty, we may lack both the willpower and intellectual consensus necessary to act on that knowledge.

Appendix: The Controversy over the Government's Definition of Poverty

The government's official definition of poverty is based on Mollie Orshansky's notion that individuals need a certain level of income to purchase a nutritionally adequate diet. Despite the widespread use of Orshansky's definition, analysts from both the right and left have voiced a variety of complaints about her definition of the poor.

DETERMINING THE NEEDS OF THE POOR

The word "poor" means different things to different people. When statistics show that the poverty rate is at a certain level, does it mean that the poor (1) are financially desperate, facing starvation, malnutrition, and perhaps homelessness; (2) they are barely making ends meet, living an adequate but stark existence with few amenities or frills; or (3) they merely have a lower standard of living than their neighbors? While Orshansky's intent is unclear, most commentators have interpreted the official poverty figures as depicting the second scenario. That is, poverty in this country means an absolute sense of deprivation in which people have an austere but by no means desperate life-style. However, liberals and conservatives have attacked this interpretation on both normative and empirical grounds.

Many liberals believe that the official statistics grossly understate the severity of poverty. One of the key reasons for this assessment is their belief that poverty figures should be stated in relative rather than absolute terms. When Orshansky formulated her poverty index, she assumed that there was a fixed basket of goods and services that constituted the bare minimum for an adequate livelihood. Anyone who lacked sufficient income to purchase these items would be considered poor. But what constitutes an adequate income that one would need to purchase the necessities of life is a social judgment that reflects the customs and mores of a society at a particular point in time. While owning a car may be perceived as a luxury in Afghanistan, it may be a necessity for an able-bodied individual seeking gainful employment in a large, sprawling metropolitan area like Los Angeles or Dallas. Many critics on the left also take the argument one step further and contend that poverty should not be thought of as a level of income but as a way of life. In summing up this view, Peter Townsend says that "poverty . . . is the lack of resources necessary to permit participation in the activities, customs and diets commonly approved by society."[1] People are poor not only when their diet is inadequate but when they lack the resources necessary to share in the common culture of the country as a whole. Finally, liberals and Marxists often point out that if we do not employ a relative theory of deprivation, the income gap between the poor and the rest of society may grow unacceptably large. Even if the poor make major economic gains, the rest of society may see their economic situation improve at an even faster rate. The resulting disparities in the life-styles of upper-, middle-, and lower-income Americans may serve only to aggravate the poor's sense of alienation and exclusion from the mainstream of society.

To rectify this situation, the economist Victor Fuchs has proposed that poverty levels be tied to some socially agreed upon measure of economic well-being, such as median income.[2] He argues that whenever an individual earns less than one-half of the median income, that person should be classified as poor. As the country becomes more affluent, our conception of what it means to be poor will thus have to be revised upwardly. If we look at the last twenty years of fighting poverty in this country, we see that in a relative sense it has gotten worse. In 1964 Orshansky's official definition of poverty for a family of four equaled roughly 41 percent of the median family income while in 1991 the same figures had dropped to the high 30 percent range of median family income. Regardless of how well the poor were doing in an absolute sense, they had fallen further behind the rest of the country in a relative sense.

Despite its intuitive attractiveness, the adoption of a relative standard of poverty would not be without political costs. Many conservatives, as well as some main-line economists, believe the government would be opening up a Pandora's box of political problems if it sought to define poverty solely in relative terms. They believe that the insistence on a relative definition of poverty is really a surreptitious call for a significant redistribution of income.[3]

If poverty should be pegged to the median income, we have to ask what a fair percentage would be. Once we start to debate percentages, the political system is talking more about limiting disparities in income than in fighting poverty per se. The danger is that in expanding the welfare state in this fashion, Fuchs could very well jeopardize popular support for a more limited war on poverty. Many conservatives, who ideologically would endorse programs that help low-income people achieve upward mobility, often draw the line at more expansive redistributional efforts. The public also seems to share that sentiment. Numerous polls indicate that voters overwhelmingly favor programs that help the poor. However, that same public is extremely lukewarm to programs that would significantly equalize income in this country.

A second danger in adopting a relative standard of poverty is that it may hamper the ability of the government to achieve its goals, thereby eroding public support for programs targeted at the poor. By definition, a relative notion of poverty is a moving target that will not be easy to reduce. In defining its objectives in the most difficult way possible, the government almost guarantees that its efforts to fight poverty will be perceived as ineffective. In the 1970s, Daniel Bell, among others, argued that the American political system suffered from a legitimacy problem because it often could not deliver on its promises.[5] As the scope of government power expanded in the 1960s, officials often unrealistically raised public expectations they could not meet. By defining poverty in relative terms, the government would almost be stacking the deck against itself. For that reason alone, Robert Lampman has argued that the best way to monitor success in fighting poverty is to focus on a fixed target rather than one that is constantly changing.[6] The danger with unrealistic definitions of poverty is that they can easily invite frustration and cynicism about entitlement programs.

Finally, the more limited goal of eliminating the burdens of absolute poverty is a worthy goal in itself. As the percentage of the population living in poverty drops, substantial numbers of people will enjoy improved housing, nutrition, and medical care.[7]

Even if it were possible to resolve the relative absolute poverty debate, the controversy over identifying the poor would not be over. Many liberals insist that the official poverty definition is too stringent. If we use the three interpretations of poverty cited above, critics like H. R. Rodgers, Leonard Beeghley, and B. R. Schiller would argue that too many people who fall below the poverty line are having an extremely hard time surviving. The poor are not just people who are having difficulties making ends meet,[8] they are people whose economic prospects are so bleak that they cannot live with any degree of self-respect or dignity. Rodgers points out that the dollar amount Orshansky used to construct her poverty index was based on an economical food budget deemed sufficient to maintain individuals only through "temporary" or "emergency" times. The government's official definition of poverty thus appears to dramatically understate both the severity as well as the number of people suffering from absolute poverty. As Schiller aptly put it: "The line we have drawn separating the poor from the non-poor does not indicate what is enough—it only asserts with confidence what is too little."[10]

In addition, the government's official poverty figures fail to adjust the poverty threshold for the cost of living in different parts of the country. An income that might be adequate in Mississippi might be woefully inadequate in New York City.

Conservatives, on the other hand, often maintain that the official definition of poverty, which many liberals believe is too stringent, vastly overstates both the scope as well as the severity of the problem. The disparity in opinions about the official definition of poverty is so large that it is often hard to believe that the right and left are talking about the same poverty index. The economist Rose Friedman criticizes Orshansky for using the average budgets of all Americans rather than the actual budgets of low-income people to arrive at a poverty index.[11] Orshansky's index multiplies the amount of money needed to eat a nutritional diet by a factor of 3. That number was chosen because the average American family, which incidentally is not poor, spends roughly one-third of its income on food. But it is often the case that variations in expenditures by income or family size reflect systematic differences in taste. As Isabel Sawhill has noted, "larger families may spend more of their income on food or housing not just because they are larger but because people with children choose to spend more of their income on, say, backyard barbecues, and less on nightclubs."[12]

Besides assuming that tastes are constant among all families, Orshansky also failed to realize that there may be economies of scale in the purchase of certain goods. While the marginal cost of food may not drop significantly if you purchase additional supplies, the same proposition may not be true of housing or transportation. For example, the cost of a three bedroom house is the same whether a family has one or three children. To arbitrarily insist that the price of a nutritional diet must always be multiplied by three may give a misleading picture of how much it costs to properly feed and shelter a family.

Finally, in contrast to the data Orshansky relied on from the Department of Agriculture, evidence gathered by the Department of Labor in its consumer expenditure survey indicates that the country is increasingly spending a smaller and smaller percentage of its income on food. As the country has

Table A.1
Expenditures on Food and Nonalcoholic
Beverages (in percentages)

Household Income Level	1984	1989
Lowest fifth	35.2	38.6
Second fifth	22.1	22.3
Third fifth	15.6	16.3
Fourth fifth	12.6	13.1
Highest fifth	8.9	8.9
Average	18.8	19.8

Source: Figures for 1984 are from U.S. Department of Labor, "Consumer Expenditure Survey, 1984," *News* (June 22, 1986): 23, table 9. Figures for 1989 are from U.S. Department of Labor, "Consumer Expenditure Survey, 1989," *News* (November 30, 1990): 6, table 1.

become more affluent over the last thirty years, families have dramatically altered their consumption patterns (see table A.1).

In the 1960s the average family did spend around a third of its income on food, but by the 1980s that figure dropped below 20 percent. Because of these problems with the official poverty rate, Rose Friedman once calculated that Orshansky's index overstated the level of poverty by 100 percent: Orshansky calculated that the poverty rate was 20 percent in 1962, while Friedman found only 10 percent who fell below the poverty threshold point. Conservatives thus argue that the poverty multiplier is not objectively carved in stone. Depending on what assumptions one makes, the correct figure may fluctuate over time. As the above data clearly indicate, the belief that people will always spend a certain percentage of their income on food is just plain wrong.

CALCULATING THE RESOURCES OF THE POOR

The criticisms of the official poverty rate are not confined to the issue of needs alone. Not only has Orshansky's definition of basic necessities generated controversy, but so has her treatment of people's resources. Before we can tell how many indigents there actually are, we have to ask how many resources are available to low-income people to satisfy their needs. To answer this question, most researchers have looked at the poor's (1) earned income, (2) non-cash benefits, and/or (3) financial and tangible assets. The resulting discrepancy between the above measures and the official definition of need gives us some idea of the number of people who qualify as "poor."

In calculating the income of indigents, Orshansky has not always been sensitive to the policy implications of her results. If she had wanted to generate data on the ability of people to climb out of poverty on their own, she should have focused on their earned income. Given Lyndon Johnson's desire to solve the causes of poverty, his administration would undoubtedly have wanted to focus on pretransfer poverty. Orshansky based her official poverty rate on the total amount of cash income of a family and ignored the sources of that income. The official poverty rate consequently does not distinguish between those who earn their own income from those who receive government transfer payments. In order to know if the government is solving the causes of poverty rather than merely treating its effects, we need to look at pre-transfer as well as official poverty rates. This measurement of poverty never received much publicity until Charles Murray stressed it in his controversial book, *Losing Ground*.[13] What is ironic in this situation is that in the early 1960s the government adopted a measurement of poverty that was logically at odds with its stated policy objective. The goal of the war on poverty was to give people a hand rather than a handout. But the official definition of poverty the government haphazardly chose to adopt ignores the distinction between these alternative sources of income.

Besides commingling earned and unearned income, Orshansky's treatment of resources was also controversial because it focused on pretax income rather than net income. If we want to understand how much purchasing power the poor actually have, we should subtract their income and payroll taxes from their gross income. In times of rising taxes the Census Bureau's concern with pretax dollars seriously understates the number of people who are poor. To correct this problem Congress passed the 1986 Tax Reform Act, which, among other things, revised the personal exemptions and standard deductions of the IRS code so that the poor were exempted from all federal income tax liabilities and part of their payroll tax responsibilities. While these changes in the federal income tax have increased the disposable income of the poor, the dramatic rise in regressive taxes at the state level in the 1980s has had the opposite effect and curtailed the purchasing power of indigents. As long as the official poverty rate is calculated in pretax dollars, the actual income of indigents will rise and fall with the vagaries of state and federal tax laws.

To assess the ability of the poor to cope with their daily needs, we also have to look at their noncash benefits as well as their income. As the government has started to treat the consequences of poverty rather than its causes, it has dramatically increased the number of noncash benefits available to the poor. These items, which are commonly known as "relief in kind," include a long list of goods and services including food stamps, public housing, and free medical care. From 1970 to 1986 the value of these benefits has more than doubled in real terms. At present, over two-thirds of all relief given to the poor is made up of these noncash benefits.

Because Orshansky's official definition of resources ignores these benefits, her figures give us a misleading picture of how the poor are faring. The official poverty figures provide little insight into the main theme of this book: they do not tell us whether the causes of poverty are being corrected and if the consequences of poverty are being treated. To answer the former question we need to look at pretransfer rates, and to address the latter question we need to examine what is known as "net poverty rates." Net poverty rates, which have been calculated by a variety of economists, try to determine how many people are poor given their cash and noncash resources. At present, the most inclusive measures, which include food stamps, housing, and medical care, tend to reduce the number of people who are poor by about one-third. However, the question of how to value noncash benefits remains extremely controversial. At present the three most common approaches for valuing them are (1) by their market price, (2) worth to the recipient, or (3) what is known as the "poverty budget share." Market value merely calculates the worth of a service by what it would cost to buy it in the open market. But the people who participate in welfare programs might not evaluate such goods and services in a comparable fashion. For example, when housing, food stamps, and medical care are valued according to the second approach, which calculates noncash benefits by their worth to the beneficiaries rather than by their market value, net poverty rates fall by only 15 to 20 percent. The reason for this falloff in value is readily apparent. If the poor are given cash and allowed to spend it according to their own preferences, they would not necessarily purchase goods and services already offered by the government. When the government consequently insists on valuing noncash benefits by their market value, it is in effect overstating the benefits that accrue to a poor family.

To illustrate how complex this situation can be, we can look at medical care, which is the most expensive noncash benefit provided the poor. If the government calculates the medical benefits a family receives by the cost of purchasing those services in the marketplace, we would soon find ourselves in the paradoxical position of insisting that a family that had incurred serious illness had somehow become better off. Some analysts have proposed that we treat health care as an insurance program to get around this problem. If we knew what amounts consumers were willing to pay to enjoy a certain level of health care, we would have a more appropriate way of cashing out the value of medical treatment. Since almost all people have access to health care or receive subsidized health care, it is difficult to develop unbiased figures for this service.

The third alternative for attaching a dollar value to noncash benefits is to use what is known as a "poverty budget share" approach. In this case the government merely tries to calculate what the appropriate medical component of the poverty budget should be. If a poor family gets sick and runs up large medical bills, any sum above its budget share is not counted as additional disposable income.

At present, there is widespread disagreement as to which method is the best way to evaluate noncash benefits. In fact, this disagreement has led to a statistical standoff. Instead of publishing one set of net poverty figures, the Census Bureau publishes ten. The numbers vary according to which noncash benefits are included in family's income and how they are valued.

A related benefit that accrues to low-income individuals is the controversial issue of leisure time. When the government publishes its poverty rates, it provides no clues about the reasons that people became poor in the first place. Some may have a low income because they recently became disabled, or were laid off by their companies. Yet others may be poor because they have not spent much time investigating job prospects, reducing their potential for upward mobility. And if some people incur poverty voluntarily because they choose not to live up to their full potential and responsibilities, perhaps they should not be included in our poverty rates. Unfortunately, it is difficult if not impossible to determine by census data who is purposely consuming leisure and who is merely unable to find gainful employment.

Finally, in addition to income and noncash benefits, a third resource available to the poor is their tangible assets. However, like leisure time, tangible assets are a resource that the official definition of poverty chooses to ignore. This accounting oversight may cause the official figures to significantly overstate the scope of poverty. If people have accumulated savings, their actual income may be much higher than what is reported in survey data. Also, if people own a house or a durable good such as a car, they earn an imputed rate of return on that asset which does not show up on their income statements. Or put slightly differently, if they did not own a house or car, they would need to make a cash expenditure for housing and transportation. The crucial question is, what is the net worth of the average poor person? If low-income people have few assets, then the official poverty rate would not be seriously understating the resources at their disposal. While a variety of people have tried to calculate the wealth of the poor, there is a general consensus that the assets of the poor, especially among the elderly poor, are not insubstantial. One study, based on a 1983 survey of consumer finances, found that the mean net worth of the poor was around $30,000, that around 45 to 50 percent owned a car, and around 30 percent owned a house. While the median income of the poor is 17 percent of the average non-poor citizen, their mean net worth is 28 percent that of the non-poor.[14] These assets give the poor a level of purchasing power that we would not ordinarily see if we looked only at their reported income levels. In this sense the official government statistics on poverty that focus only on income may be seriously overstating both the relative and absolute number of people who are indigent.

It should also be noted that many conservatives believe that the figures used to calculate the official poverty rate may be based on faulty data. The income figures used by the Census Bureau to estimate the poverty population are basically self-reported. Even if individuals inadvertently overlook certain sources of income or wish to deliberately conceal part of it, the Census Bureau reports their claims at face value. Because the Census Bureau estimates that 10 percent of normal income and as much as 24 percent of welfare income goes unreported, the official poverty rates may be significantly overstating the number of America's poor.

Because of the above difficulties in identifying how many Americans are poor, the definition of "poor" is an issue that is far from resolved. While conservatives think the Census Bureau's figures vastly overstate the size of the poverty population, liberals insist that they severely understate it. Because the arguments from both the right and the left often seem convincing, there may be good theoretical reasons to believe that the objections and counterobjections partly cancel each other out. In any event, regardless of what reservations we may have about the accuracy of the official figures, the fact that they are widely used in all debates over poverty policy makes it practically impossible not to use them.

Notes

CHAPTER 1

1. Isabel V. Sawhill, "Poverty in the U.S.: Why Is It So Persistent?" *Journal of Economic Literature* 36 (September 1988): 1073–79.
2. Ibid., 1093.
3. Edward Banfield, *The Unheavenly City: The Nature and Future of Our Urban Crisis* (Boston: Little Brown, 1968).
4. Thomas Sowell, *Markets and Minorities* (New York: Basic Books, 1981).
5. Charles Murray, *Losing Ground* (New York: Basic Books, 1984).
6. Francis Fox Piven and Richard Cloward, *Regulating the Poor* (New York: Random House, 1971).
7. William Julius Wilson, *The Truly Disadvantaged: The Inner City, the Underclass, and Public Policy* (Chicago: University of Chicago Press, 1987).
8. Myron Magnet, *The Dream and the Nightmare* (New York: William Morrow, 1993).

CHAPTER 2

1. Sawhill, "Poverty in the U.S.," 1076.
2. Annual Report of the Council of Economic Advisors, January 1965, 163.
3. Michael Harrington, *The Other America: Poverty in the United States* (New York: Macmillan, 1963), 21.
4. See M. Elaine Burgess, "Poverty and Dependency: Some Selected Characteristics," *Journal of Social Issues* 21 (January 1965): 79–97; Robert Mugge, "Aid to Families with Dependent Children: Initial Findings of the 1961 Report on the Characteristics of AFDC Recipients," *Social Security Bulletin* 26 (March 1963): 3–15.
5. Greg Duncan, *Years of Poverty, Years of Plenty: The Changing Fortunes of American Workers and Families* (Ann Arbor: University of Michigan, Institute of Social Research, 1984).
6. Ibid., 40.
7. Ibid., 60–80.
8. Mary Jo Bane and David T. Ellwood, "The Dynamics of Dependence: The

Routes to Self Sufficiency," 1982. Supported by a U.S. Department of Health and Human Services grant, contract no. HHS-100-82-0038. Also Mary Jo Bane and David T. Ellwood, "Slipping into and out of Poverty: The Dynamics of Spells," *Journal of Human Resources* 21 (Winter 1986): 1–23.

9. This example is from *The Green Book,* Committee on Ways and Means, U.S. House of Representatives (Washington, D.C.: U.S. Government Printing Office, 1991), 640.

10. Bane and Ellwood, "Slipping into and out of Poverty."

11. Harrington, *The Other America.*

12. Daniel P. Moynihan, *The Negro Family: The Case for National Action* (Washington, D.C.: U.S. Department of Labor, Office of Family Planning and Research, 1965).

13. Ibid., 5–6.

14. Kenneth Clark, *Dark Ghetto: Dilemmas of Social Power* (New York: Harper and Row, 1965); E. Franklin Frazier, *The Negro Family in the United States* (Chicago: University of Chicago Press, 1939).

15. See Lee Rainwater and William Yancey, eds., *The Moynihan Report and the Politics of Controversy* (Cambridge: MIT Press, 1967).

16. James T. Patterson, *America's Struggle against Poverty, 1900–1985* (Cambridge: Harvard University Press, 1986).

17. Michael Katz, *In the Shadow of the Poorhouse: A Social History of Welfare in America* (New York: Basic Books, 1986), 277.

18. Ibid.

19. William Ryan, *Blaming the Victim* (New York: Pantheon Books, 1971).

20. Wilson, *The Truly Disadvantaged.*

21. Albert Camus, *The Stranger* (New York: Vintage International, 1988).

22. Erol Ricketts and Isabel V. Sawhill, "Defining and Measuring the Underclass," *Journal of Policy Analysis and Management* 7 (Winter 1988): 316–25.

23. Christopher Jencks and Paul E. Peterson, eds., *The Urban Underclass* (Washington, D.C.: Brookings Institution, 1991), 28–102.

24. Ibid., 29.

25. Sheldon Danziger, "Overview," *Focus* 12 (Spring 1989): 3; see also Frank Levy, "How Big is the American Underclass," Urban Institute Working Paper 0090-1 (September 1977).

26. Jencks and Peterson, *The Urban Underclass,* 30.

CHAPTER 3

1. Michael Harrington, *The New American Poverty* (New York: Penguin Books, 1984).

2. See Jacob Mincer, "Investment in Human Capital and Personal Income Distributions," *Journal of Political Economy* 66 (August 1958): 281–302.

3. Sowell, *Market and Minorities.*

4. Banfield, *The Unheavenly City.*

5. Lawrence Mead, *Beyond Entitlement: The Social Obligations of Citizenship* (New York: Free Press, 1986).

6. Gary Orfield and Carole Ashkinaze, *The Closing Door: Conservative Policy and Black Opportunity* (Chicago: University of Chicago Press, 1991).

7. See Rebecca M. Blank and Alan S. Blinder, "Macroeconomics, Income Distribution, and Poverty," 180–208, and David T. Ellwood and Lawrence H. Summers, "Poverty in America: Is Welfare the Answer or the Problem," 78–105, in *Fighting Poverty: What Works and What Doesn't,* ed. by Sheldon H. Danziger and Daniel H. Weinberg (Cambridge: Harvard University Press, 1986).

8. Peter Doeringer and Michael Piore, *Internal Labor Markets and Manpower Analysis* (Lexington, Mass.: Heath Publishers, 1971).

9. Bennett Harrison and Barry Bluestone, *The Great U-Turn: Corporate Restructuring and the Polarizing of America* (New York: Basic Books, 1988); Harrington, *The New American Poverty.*

10. Jon Elster, *Ulysses and the Sirens* (Cambridge: Cambridge University Press, 1979); Diego Gambetta, *Were They Pushed or Did They Jump?* (Cambridge: Cambridge University Press, 1987), 16–22.

11. Gambetta, *Were They Pushed,* 18–19.

12. Albert O. Hirschman, *Exit, Voice, and Loyalty: Responses to Decline in Firms, Organizations, and States* (Cambridge: Harvard University Press, 1970).

13. Ibid.

14. For the best introduction, see Michael R. Gottfredson and Travis Hirschi, *A General Theory of Crime* (Stanford: Stanford University Press, 1990), 85–122.

15. Gambetta, *Were They Pushed,* 16–22.

16. David Held, *Introduction to Critical Theory: Horkheimer to Habermas* (Berkeley and Los Angeles: University of California Press, 1980).

CHAPTER 4

1. Robert H. Haveman, ed., *A Decade of Federal Antipoverty Programs* (New York: Academic Press, 1977), 1–20.

2. See Mincer, "Investment in Human Capital," 281–302; Theodore W. Schultz, "Reflections on Investment in Man," *Journal of Political Economy* 70 (October 1962, supplement): 1–8; and Gary S. Becker, *Human Capital: A Theoretical and Empirical Analysis with Special References to Education* (New York: Columbia University Press for the National Bureau of Economic Research, 1964).

3. James Coleman et al., *Equality of Educational Opportunity* (Washington, D.C.: U.S. Government Printing Office, 1966).

4. Westinghouse Learning Corporation, *The Impact of Head Start: An Evaluation of the Effects of Head Start on Children's Cognitive and Affective Developments* (Washington, D.C.: Clearinghouse for Federal Scientific and Technical Information, June 1969). For a summary of the second evaluation of Head Start entitled the "The Head Start Evaluation, Synthesis and Utilization Project," see Douglas J. Besharov, "Giving the Juvenile Court a Preschool Education," in *From Children to Citizens,* ed. by James Q. Wilson and Glenn C. Loury (New York: Springer-Verlag, 1987).

5. J. Berrueta-Clement et al., *Changed Lives: The Effects of the Perry Preschool Program on Youths through Age 19* (Ypsilanti, Mich.: High/Scope Press, 1984).

6. Harvey A. Averch et al., *How Effective Is Schooling? A Critical Review of Research* (Englewood Cliffs, N.J.: Educational Technology Publications, 1974), 119; and Robert Taggart, A *Fisherman's Guide: An Assessment of Training and Remediation Strategies* (Kalamazoo, Mich.: W. E. Upjohn Institute for Employment Research, 1981).

7. Nathan Glazer, *The Limits of Social Policy* (Cambridge: Harvard University Press, 1988), 82.

8. Ken Auletta, *The Underclass* (New York: Random House, 1982), 226–28.

9. Eric A. Hanushek, "The Impact of Differential Expenditures on School Performance," *Educational Researcher* 45 (May 1989): 45.

10. Ray Marshall and Marc Tucker, *Thinking for a Living: Education and the Wealth of Nations* (New York: Basic Books, 1992), 66.

11. Henry Levin, "Economics of Investment in Educationally Disadvantaged Students," *American Economic Review, Papers and Proceedings* 79 (May 1989): 52.

12. See Samuel Bowles and Herbert Gintis, *Schooling in Capitalist America* (New York: Basic Books, 1976).

13. See Jerome Karabel, "Community College and Social Stratification," in *Power and Ideology in Education*, ed. by Jerome Karabel and A. H. Halsey (New York: Oxford University Press, 1977), 230–50.

14. Christopher Jencks, *Inequality: A Reassessment of the Effect of Family and Schooling in America* (New York: Basic Books, 1972), 131, 227, 228.

15. See Lester Thurow, "Education and Economic Equality," *The Public Interest* 35 (Summer 1972).

16. Nathan Caplan et al., *The Boat People and Achievement in America* (Ann Arbor, Mich.: University of Michigan Press, 1989), 149–80.

17. Jonathan Kozol, *Savage Inequalities: Children in America's Schools* (New York: Harper Perennial, 1992).

18. James Coleman, *Private and Public Schools* (Washington, D.C.: National Center for Education Statistics, 1981).

19. John Chubb and Terry Moe, *Politics, Markets, and American Schools* (Washington, D.C.: Brookings Institution, 1990).

20. Diane Ravitch, *The Troubled Crusade: American Education, 1945–1980* (New York: Basic Books, 1983).

21. Rita Kramer, *Ed School Follies: The Miseducation of America's Teachers* (New York: Free Press, 1991).

22. Diane Ravitch, "They're Not Learning How to Teach," *Wall Street Journal*, October 28, 1991, 19.

23. Gary S. Becker, "Why the Candidates Are Missing the Point on College Costs," *Business Week*, November 14, 1988, 42.

24. See McKinley L. Blackburn, David E. Bloom, and Richard B. Freeman, "The Declining Economic Position of Less Skilled American Men," in A *Future of Lousy Jobs? The Changing Structure of U.S. Wages*, ed. by Gary Burtless (Washington, D.C.: Brookings Institution, 1990).

25. Thomas Byrne Edsall and Mary D. Edsall, *Chain Reaction: The Impact of Race, Rights, and Taxes on American Politics* (New York: W. W. Norton, 1991), 249.

26. Marshall and Tucker, *Thinking for a Living*, 43.

27. Sawhill, "Poverty in the U.S.," 1073–79.

CHAPTER 5

1. Sowell, *Markets and Minorities*; Thomas Sowell, *Ethnic America* (New York: Basic Books, 1981); Thomas Sowell, *The Economics and Politics of Race: An International Perspective* (New York: William Morrow, 1983).

2. Michael Brown and Stephen Erie, "Blacks and the Legacy of the Great Society: The Economics and Political Impact of Federal Social Policy," *Public Policy* 29 (Summer 1981): 299–330.

3. Barry Chiseick, "An Analysis of the Earnings and Employment of Asian-American Men," *Journal of Labor Economics* 1 (April 1983).

4. *Survey of Minority-Owned Business Enterprises: Asian Americans, American Indians, and Other Minorities*, U.S. Department of Commerce, Bureau of the Census (Washington, D.C.: U.S. Government Printing Office, 1987), 2–5.

5. Joel Garreau, *Edge City* (New York: Doubleday, 1991), 146–47.

6. Ibid.

7. Ibid.

8. Robert Boyd, "Black and Asian Self Employment in Large Metropolitan Areas: A Comparative Analysis," *Social Problems* 37 (May 1990): 258.

9. Bart Landry, *The New Black Middle Class* (Berkeley and Los Angeles: University of California Press, 1987), 45.

10. *Survey of Minority-Owned Business Enterprises: Black*, U.S. Department of Commerce, Bureau of the Census (Washington, D.C.: U.S. Government Printing Office, 1987), 2–5.

11. As quoted by Landry, *The New Black Middle Class*, 46.

12. Ronald Takaki, *Strangers from a Different Shore: A History of Asian Americans* (Boston: Little, Brown, 1989), 92.

13. Harold Cruse, *Plural but Equal* (New York: William Morrow, 1987), 303–15.

14. Stanley Lieberson, *A Piece of the Pie* (Berkeley and Los Angeles: University of California Press, 1980), 365–66.

15. Sowell, *Ethnic America*, 219.

16. Lieberson, *A Piece of the Pie*, 365–66.

17. Takaki, *Strangers from a Different Shore*, 92.

18. Lieberson, *A Piece of the Pie*, 370–80.

19. Edna Bonacich and John Modell, *The Economic Basis of Ethnic Solidarity: Small Business in the Japanese American Community* (Berkeley and Los Angeles: University of California Press, 1980), 29–30; Ivan Light and Edna Bonacich, *Immigrant Entrepreneurs: Koreans in Los Angeles, 1965–1982* (Berkeley and Los Angeles: University of California Press, 1988).

20. Arthur Hertzberg, *The Jews in America* (New York: Simon and Schuster, 1989), 13.

21. Light and Bonacich, *Immigrant Entrepreneurs*, 119.

22. Harry Kitano, *Japanese Americans: The Evolution of a Subculture* (Englewood Cliffs, N.J.: Prentice Hall, 1976).

23. Lawrence E. Harrison, *Who Prospers: How Cultural Values Shape Economic and Political Success* (New York: Basic Books, 1991), 150–60.

24. Ivan Light, *Ethnic Enterprise in America: Business and Welfare among Chinese,*

Japanese, and Blacks (Berkeley and Los Angeles: University of California Press, 1972), 45–61.

25. See John Modell, *The Economics and Politics of Racial Accommodation* (Urbana: University of Illinois Press, 1977); Light and Bonacich, *Immigrant Entrepreneurs*; Light, *Ethnic Enterprise.*

26. Herbert Gutman, *The Black Family in Slavery and Freedom, 1750–1925* (New York: Pantheon Books, 1974).

27. E. Franklin Frazier, *Black Bourgeoisie* (Glencoe, Ill.: Free Press, 1957), 213–29.

28. *Survey of Minority-Owned Businesses: Black*, 2.

29. C. W. Mills, *White Collar* (New York: Oxford University Press, 1951).

30. Barry Stein, *Size, Efficiency, and Community Enterprise* (Cambridge, Mass.: Center for Community Economic Development, 1974).

31. Scott Fain, "Self-Employed Americans: Their Number Has Increased," *Monthly Labor Review* 103 (January 1980): 3–8.

32. David Birch, "Who Creates Jobs?" *The Public Interest* 65 (Fall 1981): 3–14.

33. Steven Erie, *Rainbow's End: Irish-Americans and the Dilemmas of Urban Machine Politics, 1840–1985* (Berkeley and Los Angeles: University of California Press, 1988).

34. Ibid.

35. Ibid., 89.

CHAPTER 6

1. Carol B. Stack, *All Our Kin* (New York: Harper and Row, 1970).

2. Sheppard Kellam, Margaret Ensminger, and R. Jay Turner, "Family Structure and the Mental Health of Children," *Archives of General Psychiatry* 34 (1977): 1012–22.

3. Moynihan, *The Negro Family.*

4. Andrew Billingsly, *Black Families in White America* (Englewood Cliffs, N.J.: Prentice Hall, 1968), 200.

5. Quoted in William Julius Wilson and Kathryn M. Neckerman, "Poverty and Family Structure," in *Fighting Poverty*, ed. by Danziger and Weinberg, 241.

6. Bane and Ellwood, "Slipping into and out of Poverty."

7. Martha Van Haitsma, "Attitudes, Social Context, and Labor Force Attachment: Blacks and Immigrant Mexicans in Chicago Poverty Areas," Urban Poverty and Family Life Conference, October 10–12, 1991, Chicago.

8. Barbara Dafoe Whitehead, "Dan Quayle Was Right," *Atlantic Monthly*, April 1993, 47.

9. Ibid.

10. Irwin Garfinkel and Sara S. McLanahan, *Single Mothers and Their Children* (Washington, D.C.: Urban Institute Press, 1986), 26–30. Also see Sara S. McLanahan, "Family Structure and the Reproduction of Poverty," *American Journal of of Sociology* 90 (1985): 873–901.

11. Garfinkel and McLanahan, *Single Mothers*, 30.

12. Whitehead, "Dan Quayle Was Right," 47.

13. Garfinkel and McLanahan, *Single Mothers.*

14. Duncan, *Years of Poverty, Years of Plenty*, 1–40.

15. Mary Jo Bane, "Household Composition and Poverty," in *Fighting Poverty*, ed. by Danziger and Weinberg, 209–29.
16. Ibid., 231.
17. McLanahan, "Family Structure and the Reproduction of Poverty."
18. Barbara Ehrenreich, *The Hearts of Men* (Garden City, N.Y.: Anchor Books, 1983).
19. Christopher Jencks, "Deadly Neighborhoods," *New Republic*, June 13, 1989, 20.
20. Gary S. Becker, E. M. Landes, and R. T. Michael, "An Economic Analysis of Marital Instability," *Monthly Labor Review* 85 (1977): 1141–87.
21. Richard A. Easterlin, *Birth and Fortune: The Impact of Numbers on Personal Welfare* (New York: Basic Books, 1980); also Robert Lerman, "Employment Opportunities of Young Men and Family Formation," *American Economic Review* 79 (May 1989): 64.
22. Moynihan, *The Negro Family*; also Frazier, *The Negro Family in the United States*.
23. Charles S. Johnson, *Shadow of the Plantation* (Chicago: University of Chicago Press, 1934).
24. Gutman, *The Black Family in Slavery and Freedom*.
25. Murray, *Losing Ground*.
26. As quoted in Glen Loury, "The Role of the Family: An Overview," Hearings before the Select Committee on Children, Youth, and Families, House of Representatives, 99th Congress, November 6, 1985.
27. Mary Jo Bane and David Ellwood, "Single Mothers and Their Living Arrangements," unpublished paper, Harvard University, 1984.
28. Garfinkel and McLanahan, *Single Mothers*.
29. Elliot Liebow, *Tally's Corner* (Boston: Little, Brown, 1967).
30. Wilson, *The Truly Disadvantaged*.
31. Saul Hoffman and John Holmes, "Husbands, Wives, and Divorce," in *Five Thousand American Families*, ed. by G. J. Duncan and J. Morgan, vol. 4 (Ann Arbor: University of Michigan Press, 1976).
32. Heather Ross and Isabel V. Sawhill, *Time of Transition* (Washington, D.C.: Urban Institute, 1975); Alan Cohen, "Economics, Marital Instability, and Race," Ph.D. diss., University of Wisconsin, 1979.
33. Mark Testa et al., "Ethnic Variation in Employment and Marriage among Inner City Fathers," *Annals of the American Academy of Political and Social Sciences* 503 (February 1989).
34. Dennis Hogan and Evelyn Kitagawa, "The Impact of Social Status, Family Structure, and Neighborhood on the Fertility of Black Adolescents," *American Journal of Sociology* 90 (January 1985).
35. Leon Dash, *When Children Want Children* (New York: William Morrow, 1989).
36. Clark, *Dark Ghetto*, 72.
37. Whitehead, "Dan Quayle Was Right," 47.
38. Ibid.
39. Ibid., 48.
40. "Child Support and Alimony," Current Population Reports Series P-23, no. 112 (Washington, D.C.: U.S. Government Printing Office, 1981).

CHAPTER 7

1. Richard B. Freeman, "Employment and Earnings of Disadvantaged Young Men in a Labor Shortage Economy," in *The Urban Underclass*, ed. by Jencks and Peterson, 103–22; Richard B. Freeman and Harry J. Holzer, *The Youth Employment Crisis* (Chicago: University of Chicago Press, 1986); Sar A. Levitan and Isaac Shapiro, *Working but Poor* (Baltimore: Johns Hopkins University Press, 1987); and David T. Ellwood, *Poor Support: Poverty in the American Family* (New York: Basic Books, 1988), 81–188.
2. Ellwood, *Poor Support.*
3. Freeman, "Employment and Earnings of Disadvantaged Young Men," in *The Urban Underclass*, ed. by Jencks and Peterson, 103–21.
4. Paul Osterman, "Gains from Growth? The Impact of Full Employment on Poverty in Boston," in *The Urban Underclass*, ed. by Jencks and Peterson, 122–34.
5. U.S. Bureau of the Census, "Money, Income and Poverty Status of Families in the U.S.," Current Population Reports Series P-60.
6. Lawrence Mead, *The New Politics of Poverty: The Nonworking Poor in America* (New York: Basic Books, 1992), 106.
7. See Christopher Jencks, *Rethinking Social Policy* (Cambridge: Harvard University Press, 1992), 255.
8. Frank Levy and Richard Michel, *The Economic Failure of American Families* (Washington, D. C.: Urban Institute, 1990), 18–22.
9. Ibid., 19.
10. This section of the book has been heavily influenced by Lawrence Mead's insightful discussion of the "Bad Jobs" problem in *The New Politics of Poverty*, 83–84.
11. Ellwood, *Poor Support*, 20.
12. Ellen Eliason Kisker et al., *The Child Care Challenge: What Parents Need and What Is Available in Three Metropolitan Areas* (Princeton, N.J.: Mathematical Policy Research, February 1989), 9; Irene Cox, "Families on Welfare in New York City," *Welfare in Review* 6 (March–April 1968); Harriet B. Presser and Wendy Baldwin, "Child Care As a Constraint on Employment: Prevalence, Correlates, and Bearing on the Work and Fertility Nexus," *American Journal of Sociology* 85 (March 1980); and Mead, *The New Politics of Poverty*, 121–22.
13. Mead, *The New Politics of Poverty*, 121–22.
14. Ibid., 169–70.
15. Ibid.
16. Ibid.
17. Ibid.
18. See Marilyn Krogh, "A History and Description of the Chicago Urban Poverty and Family Structure Study," paper presented at the Urban Poverty and Family Life Conference, October 10–12, 1991, Chicago. Available from the Center for the Study of Urban Inequality, University of Chicago.
19. Wilson, *The Truly Disadvantaged.*
20. See Robert Aponte, "Ethnicity and Male Employment in the Inner City: A Test of Two Theories," paper presented at the Urban Poverty and Family Life Conference, October 10–12, 1991, Chicago; and Martha Van Haitsma, "Atti-

tudes, Social Context and Labor Force Attachment: Blacks and Immigrant Mexicans in Chicago Poverty Areas," ibid.
21. Richard Taub, "Differing Conceptions of Honor and Orientations towards Work and Marriage among Low-Income African-Americans and Mexican-Americans," paper presented at the Urban Poverty and Family Life Conference, October 10-12, 1991, Chicago.
22. Ibid., 8.
23. Ibid.
24. Ibid., 13.
25. Sophie Pedder, "Social Isolation and the Labor Market: Black Americans in Chicago," paper presented at the Urban Poverty and Family Life Conference.
26. Ibid.
27. Ibid., 26.
28. Ibid.

CHAPTER 8

1. See Jencks, *Rethinking Social Policy*, 72–84.
2. "Overview of Entitlement Programs," in *The Green Book*, Committee on Ways and Means, U.S. House of Representative (Washington, D.C.: U.S. Government Printing Office, 1991), 597.
3. Robert Moffitt, "Incentive Effects of the U.S. Welfare System: A Review," *Journal of Economic Literature* 30 (March 1992): 9.
4. Robert Moffitt, "Work and the U.S. Welfare System: A Review," Institute of Research on Poverty, Special Report Series 46, University of Wisconsin at Madison, 1988, 25.
5. Sheldon Danziger and Peter Gottschalk, "The Poverty of Losing Ground," *Challenge*, May–June 1985, 34.
6. Moffitt, "Incentive Effects of the U.S. Welfare System," 11.
7. Ibid., 13.
8. Ibid., 17.
9. Ibid.
10. Ibid.
11. Sheldon Danziger, Robert Haveman, and Robert Plotnick, "How Income Transfers Affect Work, Savings and the Income Distribution: A Critical Review," *Journal of Economic Literature* 19 (September 1982).
12. Ibid.
13. Moffitt, "Incentive Effects of the U.S. Welfare System."
14. Arthur Okun, *Equality and Efficiency: The Big Tradeoff* (Washington, D.C.: Brookings Institution, 1975).
15. Murray, *Losing Ground*, 157–61.
16. Charles Murray, "Have the Poor Been Losing Ground?" *Political Science Quarterly* 100 (Fall 1985): 443.
17. Mickey Kaus, *The End of Equality* (New York: Basic Books, 1992), 119.
18. John Kasarda, "Urban Change and Minority Opportunities," in *The New Urban Reality*, ed. by Paul E. Peterson (Washington, D.C.: Brookings Institution, 1985), 56–90.

19. Kaus, *The End of Equality*, 120.
20. Auletta, *The Underclass*.
21. Ibid., 41.
22. See Marta Tienda, "Welfare and Work in Chicago's Inner City," *American Economic Review* 80 (May 1990): 373; and Marta Tienda and Haya Stier, "Intergenerational Continuity of Welfare Dependence: Ethnic and Neighborhood Comparisons," paper presented at the Urban Poverty and Family Life Conference, October 10–12, 1991, Chicago.
23. Tienda, "Welfare and Work in Chicago's Inner City."
24. Richard D. Coe and Greg J. Duncan, "Welfare: Promoting Poverty or Progress?" *Wall Street Journal*, May 15, 1985, 19.
25. Tienda, "Welfare and Work in Chicago's Inner City."
26. Murray, *Losing Ground*, 227.
27. Ellwood, *Poor Support*.

CHAPTER 9

1. Emile Durkheim, *Suicide* (New York: Free Press, 1951).
2. Ibid.
3. My whole discussion on the importance of culture and the role played by various institutions in socializing workers draws heavily on the seminal work of James Q. Wilson and Richard J. Herrnstein, *Crime and Human Nature* (New York: Simon and Schuster, 1985), 430–37.
4. Ibid., 432.
5. William Wilson, *The City Beautiful Movement* (Baltimore: Johns Hopkins University Press, 1989), 75–99.
6. Daniel Bell, *The Cultural Contradictions of Capitalism* (New York: Basic Books, 1976), 3–175. The quote is from E. J. Dionne, Jr., *Why Americans Hate Politics* (New York: Simon and Schuster, 1991), 70.
7. Magnet, *The Dream*.
8. I am heavily indebted to Richard Taub for this idea. See his "Differing Conceptions of Honor," 2.
9. James Q. Wilson, *On Character* (Washington, D.C.: AEI Press, 1991), 22.
10. Theodore J. Lowi, *The End of Liberalism* (New York: W. W. Norton, 1969).
11. Murray, *Losing Ground*.
12. Mead, *Beyond Entitlement*, 54–61.
13. Garreau, *Edge City*.
14. Nicholas Lemann, *The Promised Land: The Great Black Migration and How It Changed America* (New York: Alfred A. Knopf, 1991).
15. Marc Mauer, *Young Black Men and the Criminal Justice System: A Growing National Problem* (Washington, D.C.: The Sentencing Project, 1991).
16. Richard B. Freeman and Harry J. Holzer, *The Black Youth Employment Crisis: Summary of Findings* (Chicago: University of Chicago Press, 1986), 3–21.
17. Samuel Freedman, *Upon This Rock: The Miracles of a Black Church* (New York: Harper Collins, 1993).
18. C. Eric Lincoln and Lawrence H. Mamiya, *The Black Church in the African American Experience* (Durham, N.C.: Duke University Press, 1990).

19. Elijah Anderson, *Streetwise: Race, Class, and Change in Urban Communities* (Chicago: University of Chicago Press, 1990), 59.
20. Wilson, *The Truly Disadvantaged.*
21. Mitchell Duneier, *Slim's Table: Race, Respectability, and Masculinity* (Chicago: University of Chicago Press, 1992).
22. Ibid., 131.
23. Mead, *Beyond Entitlement*, 22.
24. Jencks and Peterson, *The Urban Underclass*, 28–101; also Jencks, *Rethinking Social Policy.*
25. Bowles and Gintis, *Schooling in Capitalist America.*
26. Dennis Wrong, "The Over Socialized Conception of Man in Modern Sociology," *American Sociological Review* 26 (April 1961): 183–93.
27. See William V. Shannon, *The American Irish* (Amherst: University of Massachusetts Press, 1963), 250–54, for an insightful discussion of Studs Lonigan.
28. See William Julius Wilson, "Public Policy Research and *The Truly Disadvantaged*," in *The Urban Underclass*, ed. by Jencks and Peterson, 460–83.
29. Lemann, *The Promised Land.*
30. David Whitman, "The Migrants' Tale and Ghetto Culture," *Public Interest* 105 (Fall 1991): 114–21.
31. See Wilson, *The Truly Disadvantaged.*
32. Ibid.
33. Ibid., 60.
34. Duneier, *Slim's Table*, 127.
35. Robert K. Merton, "Social Structure and Anomie," *American Sociological Review* 3 (1938): 672–82.
36. Ibid., 680.
37. Wilson, *Crime and Human Nature*, 407–39.
38. Wilson, *On Character*, 27.
39. Ibid., 27–28.
40. P. J. Cook and G. A. Zarkin, "Crime and the Business Cycle," *Journal of Legal Studies* 14 (Fall 1985): 115–28; and James Q. Wilson and P. J. Cook, "Unemployment and Crime: What Is the Connection?" *Public Interest* 79 (Spring 1985): 3–8.
41. P. C. Sagi and C. F. Wellford, "Age Composition and Patterns of Change in Criminal Statistics," *Journal of Criminal Law, Criminology, and Police Science* 59 (1968): 29–36; and Theodore N. Ferdinand, "Demographic Shifts and Criminality," *American Journal of Sociology* 73 (1970): 84–99.
42. Liebow, *Tally's Corner.*
43. Douglas G. Glasgow, *The Black Underclass: Poverty, Unemployment, and Entrapment of Ghetto Youth* (New York: Vintage Books, 1981).
44. Ibid.
45. Ibid., 159.

CHAPTER 10

1. See Sowell, *Markets and Minorities*, 19–33.
2. Gunnar Myrdal, Richard Sterner, and Arnold Rose, *An American Dilemma:*

The Negro Problem and Modern Democracy (New York: Harper & Brothers, 1944); see also David Southern, *Gunnar Myrdal and Black-White Relations* (Baton Rouge: Louisiana State University Press, 1987).

3. George M. Frederickson, *The Arrogance of Race* (Middletown, Conn.: Wesleyan University Press, 1988), 5.

4. Ibid.

5. William Julius Wilson, *The Declining Significance of Race* (Chicago: University of Chicago Press, 1978), 4.

6. Ibid., 5.

7. Sowell, *Markets and Minorities*, 27–33.

8. See Joleen Kirschenman and Kathryn M. Neckerman, "We'd Love to Hire Them, But . . . ," in *The Urban Underclass*, ed. by Jencks and Peterson, 203–32.

9. See Christopher Jencks, "Discrimination and Thomas Sowell," *New York Review of Books* 30 (February 1983).

10. M. Corcoran and G. Duncan, "Work History, Labor Force Attachment, and Earning Differences between the Races and Sexes," *Journal of Human Resources* 14 (Winter 1979): 1–20; also Thomas Boston, *Race, Class, and Conservatism* (Boston: Unwin Hyman, 1988), 58–72.

11. Auletta, *The Underclass*, 260.

12. These calculations are based on an excellent review of black men by Philip Moss and Chris Tilly entitled *Why Black Men Are Doing Worse in the Labor Market: A Review of Supply-Side and Demand-Side Explanations* (New York: Social Science Research Council, 1991).

13. This concept of limited discrimination is from Jencks's extremely perceptive argument in "Discrimination and Thomas Sowell," 75.

14. Jencks, "Discrimination and Thomas Sowell." The example of Jewish and black attorneys is taken from Jencks's article on Thomas Sowell. Given the insightful nature of his monograph on Sowell, the Jencks article on discrimination deserves a wide audience among the academic community.

15. Wilson, *The Truly Disadvantaged*, 11.

16. Ibid.

17. *Child Support and Alimony*, Current Population Reports Series P-23, no. 112 (Washington, D.C.: U.S. Government Printing Office, 1981).

18. Jesse Jackson, "Keeping Silent on Thugs Hurts Black Community," *Florida Times-Union*, October 11, 1993, A-15.

19. The data are from Christopher Jencks, "Special Treatment for Blacks," *New York Review of Books* 30 (March 1983).

20. Ibid.

21. C. Vann Woodward, *The Strange Career of Jim Crow* (New York: Oxford University Press, 1957).

22. Howard Schuman, Charlotte Steeh, and Lawrence Bobo, *Racial Attitudes in America: Trends and Interpretations* (Cambridge: Harvard University Press, 1985), 191.

CHAPTER 11

1. Danziger and Gottschalk, "The Poverty of Losing Ground."
2. See John E. Schwarz, letter to the editor, *Wilson Quarterly* 9 (Spring 1985): 172–73. For a fuller discussion of this topic, see his *America's Hidden Success: A Reassessment of Twenty Years of Public Policy* (New York: W. W. Norton, 1983).
3. Frank Levy, "Poverty and Economic Growth" (University of Maryland, College Park: Maryland School of Public Affairs), 1988.
4. Rebecca M. Blank, *Why Were Poverty Rates So High in the 1980s?* Working Paper No. 3878 (Cambridge, Mass.: National Bureau of Economic Research, 1991); see also David M. Cutler and Lawrence F. Katz, "Macroeconomic Performance and the Disadvantaged," in *Brookings Papers on Economic Activity* 2 (Washington, D.C.: Brookings Institution, 1991), 62–126.
5. Elijah Anderson, *A Place on the Corner* (Chicago: University of Chicago Press, 1978); William Julius Wilson, "Poverty, Joblessness, and Family Structure in the Inner City: A Comparative Perspective," paper presented at the Urban Poverty and Family Life Conference, October 10–12, 1991, Chicago.
6. Duneier, *Slim's Table*.
7. Ibid., 65.
8. Ibid., 65–70, 161–62.
9. Ibid., 66.
10. Ibid.
11. Ibid., 157.
12. Ibid., 96.
13. Ibid., 159.
14. Garreau, *Edge City*.
15. Duneier, *Slim's Table*, 100.
16. Ibid.
17. Ibid., 158.
18. Rebecca M. Blank and Alan S. Blinder, "Macroeconomics, Income Distribution, and Poverty," in *Fighting Poverty*, ed. by Danziger and Weinberg, 181.
19. Ibid., 207.
20. Ibid., 181.
21. Ibid., 207.
22. Blank, *Why Were Poverty Rates So High*, 1.
23. Ibid., 6.
24. Ibid.
25. Ibid.
26. Ibid., 3.
27. William Julius Wilson, "Social Policy and Minority Groups," in *Divided Opportunities: Minorities, Poverty, and Social Policy*, ed. by Gary D. Sandefur and Marta Tienda (New York: Plenum Press, 1988), 242; and John N. Kasarda, "Jobs, Migration, and Emerging Urban Mismatches," in *Urban Change and Poverty*, ed. by Michael G. H. McGeary and Laurence E. Lynn, Jr. (Washington, D.C.: Academy Press, 1988), 148–98.
28. Blank, *Why Were Poverty Rates So High*, 9.

29. Kasarda, "Jobs, Migration, and Emerging Urban Mismatches," 149.
30. Ibid.
31. Ibid.
32. Paul Jargowsky, "Ghetto Poverty among Blacks in the 1980's," unpublished manuscript, 1993.
33. Blank, *Why Were Poverty Rates So High*, table 6.
34. John F. Kain, "Housing Segregation, Negro Employment, and Metropolitan Decentralization," *Quarterly Journal of Economics* 82 (May 1968): 175–97; and Kasarda, "Jobs, Migration, and Emerging Urban Mismatches"; and Wilson, "Social Policy and Minority Groups."
35. Kasarda, "Jobs, Migration, and Emerging Urban Mismatches," 168.
36. Ibid.
37. Wilson, "Social Policy and Minority Groups," 242.
38. Joseph D. Mooney, "Housing Segregation, Negro Employment, and Metropolitan Decentralization: An Alternative Perspective," *Quarterly Journal of Economics* 83 (1969): 299–311; and John E. Farley, "Disproportionate Black and Hispanic Unemployment in U.S. Metropolitan Areas," *American Journal of Economics and Sociology* 46 (1987): 129–50.
39. David T. Ellwood, "The Spatial Mismatch Hypothesis: Are There Teen-Age Jobs Missing in the Ghetto," in *The Black Youth Employment Crisis*, ed. by Freeman and Holzer.
40. Jonathan Leonard, "The Interaction of Residential Segregation and Employment Discrimination," *Journal of Urban Economics* 21 (1987): 323–46; and Peter Hutchinson, "The Effects of Accessibility and Segregation on the Employment of the Urban Poor," in *Patterns of Racial Discrimination*, ed. by George M. Von Furstenberg, Bennett Harrison, and Ann R. Horowitz (Lexington, Mass.: Lexington Books, 1974).
41. See Aponte, "Ethnicity and Male Employment in the Inner City," tables 1 and 4.
42. William S. Robinson, "Ecological Correlations and the Behavior of Individuals," *American Sociological Review* 15 (1950): 351–57.
43. Marta Tienda and Haya Stier, "Makin' a Livin': Color and Opportunity in the Inner City," paper presented at the Urban Poverty and Family Life Conference, October 10–12, 1991, Chicago.
44. Aponte, "Ethnicity and Male Employment in the Inner City," tables 1 and 4.
45. Ibid., table 2.
46. McLanahan, "Family Structure and the Reproduction of Poverty," 873–901.
47. Kasarda, "Jobs, Migration, and Emerging Urban Mismatches," 190.
48. Aponte, "Ethnicity and Male Employment in the Inner City," 41.
49. Kirschenman and Neckerman, "We'd Love to Hire Them, But . . . ," 208.
50. Deirdre Alexia Royster, "Public Training—Help or Hindrance? An Exploration of Employers' Perceptions of the Publicly-Trained," paper presented at the Urban Poverty and Family Life Conference, October 10–12, 1991, Chicago.
51. David Whitman, "What Keeps the Poor Poor?" *U.S. News and World Report*, October 21, 1991, 44.
52. Kasarda, "Jobs, Migration, and Emerging Urban Mismatches," 191.
53. Mickey Kaus, "False Hopes for the Cities?" *Newsweek*, October 19, 1992, 35.

54. Kasarda in "Jobs, Migration, and Emerging Mismatches" discusses a variety of other proposals to facilitate mobility.

CHAPTER 12

1. Peter M. Blau and Otis Dudley Duncan, *The American Occupational Structure* (New York: Wiley, 1967). Also Robert Hauser et al., "Structural Changes in Occupational Mobility among Men in the United States," *American Sociological Review* 40 (October 1975): 585–98.
2. Doeringer and Piore, *Internal Labor Markets and Manpower Analysis.*
3. Ibid.
4. Duncan, *Years of Poverty.*
5. William T. Dickens and Lawrence F. Katz, "Inter-Industry Wage Differences and Industry Characteristics," *Unemployment and the Structure of Labor Markets,* ed. by Kevin Lang and Jonathan S. Leonard (New York: Basil Blackwell, 1987), 84.
6. Doeringer and Piore, *Internal Labor Markets,* 178.
7. Blau and Duncan, *The American Occupational Structure.*
8. Harrison and Bluestone, *The Great U-Turn.*
9. Joseph Schumpeter, *The Theory of Economic Development* (Cambridge: Harvard University Press, 1936).
10. Harrison and Bluestone, *The Great U-Turn,* 39.
11. Ibid., 27.
12. Blackburn, Bloom, and Freeman, "The Declining Economic Position of Less Skilled American Men," in *A Future of Lousy Jobs?* ed. by Burtless, 31–67.
13. William T. Dickens and Kevin Lang, "Where Have All the Good Jobs Gone? Deindustrialization and Labor Market Segmentation," in *Unemployment and the Structure of Labor Markets,* ed. by Lang and Leonard, 101.
14. See Lawrence Mishel and Ruy A. Teixeira, *The Myth of the Coming Labor Shortage: Jobs, Skills, and Incomes of America's Workforce 2000* (Washington, D.C.: Economic Policy Institute, 1991), 28–40.
15. Stan Davis, *Future Perfect* (Reading, Mass.: Addison-Wesley, 1987), 157.
16. See B. Joseph Pine, *Mass Customization: The New Frontier in Business Competition* (Boston: Harvard Business School Press, 1993).
17. James P. Womack, Daniel T. Jones, and Daniel Roos, *The Machine That Changed the World* (New York: Rawson Associates, 1990).
18. Pine, *Mass Customization,* 48.
19. W. B. Johnston and A. E. Parker, *Workforce 2000: Work and Workers for the 21st Century* (Indianapolis, Ind.: Hudson Institute, 1987).
20. Chinhui Juhn, Kevin Murphy, and Robert Topel, "Why Has the Natural Rate of Unemployment Increased over Time?" *Brookings Papers on Economic Activity* 2 (Washington, D.C.: Brookings Institution, 1991), 75–133.
21. Charles L. Schultze, *Memos to the President: A Guide through Macroeconomics for the Busy Policymaker* (Washington, D.C.: Brookings Institution, 1993), 295.
22. L. Katz and K. M. Murphy, "Changes in Relative Wages, 1963–1987: Supply and Demand Factors," unpublished manuscript, April 1990, as cited in Mishel and Teixeira, *The Myth of the Coming Labor Shortage.*

23. See Kaus, *The End of Equality,* for an excellent discussion of this topic.
24. Ibid., 65.
25. Thurow, "Education and Economic Equality."
26. Franklin Toker, *Pittsburgh: An Urban Portrait* (University Park: Pennsylvania State University Press, 1986), 79–131.
27. Ibid.

CHAPTER 13

1. William J. Baumol, Sue Anne Bately Blackman, and Edward N. Wolff, *Productivity and American Leadership: The Long View* (Cambridge: MIT Press, 1989), 65–84.
2. Ibid., 15.
3. Schultze, *Memos to the President,* 291.
4. John Bishop, "Is the Test Score Decline Responsible for the Productivity Growth Decline?," *American Economic Review* 79 (March 1989): 178–97.
5. Robert M. Solow, "Technical Change and the Aggregate Production Function," *Review of Economics and Statistics* 39 (August 1957): 312–20; and Edward F. Denison, *Trends in American Economic Growth, 1929–82* (Washington, D.C.: Brookings Institution, 1985).
6. See Schultze, *Memos to the President,* 241.
7. J. Bradford De Long and Lawrence H. Summers, "Equipment Investment and Economic Growth: How Strong Is the Nexus?" in *Brookings Papers on Economic Activity* 2 (Washington, D.C.: Brookings Institution, 1992), 157–99.
8. Evsey D. Domar, *Essays in the Theory of Economic Growth* (New York: Oxford University Press, 1957).
9. John F. Walker and Harold G. Vatter, "Why Has the United States Operated below Potential since World War II," *Journal of Post-Keynesian Economics* (Spring 1989): 326.

CHAPTER 14

1. Piven and Cloward, *Regulating the Poor;* and Michael Katz, *The Undeserving Poor: From the War on Poverty to the War on Welfare* (New York: Pantheon Books, 1991); also Katz, *In the Shadow of the Poorhouse.*
2. Saul David Alinsky, *Rules for Radicals: A Practical Primer for Realistic Radicals* (New York: Vintage Books, 1971). See also William Kelso, *American Democratic Theory: Pluralism and Its Critics* (Westport, Conn.: Greenwood Press, 1978), 25–34.
3. Gertrude Himmelfarb, *The Idea of Poverty: England in the Early Industrial Age* (New York: Vintage Books, 1985), 392.
4. Ibid.
5. Hannah Arendt, *The Human Condition* (Chicago: University of Chicago Press, 1958), 79.
6. Himmelfarb, *The Idea of Poverty,* 390.
7. Ibid., 391.

8. Piven and Cloward, *Regulating the Poor*; and Katz, *The Underserving Poor.*
9. Katz, *The Underserving Poor*, 165.
10. Piven and Cloward, *Regulating the Poor*, 285–349.
11. Harrison and Bluestone, *The Great U-Turn*, 38.
12. See Robert J. Gordon, *Macroeconomics* (Boston: Little, Brown, 1981), 164.
13. Katz, *The Undeserving Poor*, 163.
14. Ibid., 164.
15. Ibid.
16. Piven and Cloward, *Regulating the Poor*, 123.
17. Ibid., 147.
18. See Kelso, *American Democratic Theory*, 25–34.

CHAPTER 15

1. Greg J. Duncan, Timothy M. Speeding, and William Rodgers, "Wither the Middle Class? A Dynamic View," paper prepared for the Levy Institute Conference on Income Inequality, Bard College, June 18–20, 1991.

CHAPTER 16

1. Lester Thurow, *Head to Head: The Coming Economic Battle among Japan, Europe, and America* (New York: William Morrow, 1992).
2. Andrew Hacker, *Two Nations: Black and White, Separate, Hostile, Unequal* (New York: Charles Scribner's Sons, 1992), 171–72.
3. E. J. Dionne, Jr. *Why Americans Hate Politics* (New York: Simon & Schuster, 1992), 14.
4. Ibid., 324.
5. See chapter 9, table 9.1.
6. Kelso, *American Democratic Theory*, 16.
7. Thomas Byrne Edsall and Mary D. Edsall, *Chain Reaction*, 16.
8. Dionne, *Why Americans Hate Politics*, 74.
9. See Theda Skocpol, "Targeting within Universalism: Politically Viable Policies to Combat Poverty in the United States," in *The Urban Underclass*, ed. by Jencks and Peterson, 411–35. Also Wilson, *The Truly Disadvantaged.*
10. Skocpol, "Targeting within Universalism," 413.
11. Sowell, *Market and Minorities*; Murray, *Losing Ground*; Mead, *Beyond Entitlement.*
12. Mead, *Beyond Entitlement*, 241–55.
13. Coleman, *Private and Public Schools*; Chubb and Moe, *Politics, Markets, and American Schools.*
14. Harrison and Bluestone, *The Great U-Turn*, 144.
15. Michael Porter, "Capital Choices: Changing the Way America Invests in Industry," report from the Harvard Business School, 1992.
16. Ibid.
17. Bell, *The Cultural Contradictions of Capitalism.*
18. Duneier, *Slim's Table*, 83.

APPENDIX

1. Quoted in Harrington, *The New American Poverty*, 74.
2. Victor Fuchs, "Redefining Poverty and Redistributing Income," *The Public Interest* 8 (Summer 1967): 88–95.
3. See Gordon Tullock, *Economics of Income Redistribution* (Boston: Kluwer Nijhoff, 1983), 1–20. Also Gordon Tullock, *Welfare for the Well-To-Do* (Dallas: Fisher Institute, 1983).
4. James R. Kluegel and Eliot R. Smith, *Beliefs about Inequality* (New York: Aldine De Gruyter, 1986), 106–7.
5. Daniel Bell, *The Coming of Post-Industrial Society* (New York: Basic Books, 1978).
6. Robert Lampman, *Ends and Means of Reducing Income Poverty* (New York: Academic Press, 1971); also Robert Lampman, *Social Welfare Spending: Accounting for Changes from 1950 to 1978* (New York: Academic Press, 1984).
7. Sawhill, "Poverty in the U.S," 1076.
8. H. R. Rodgers, *Poverty amid Plenty* (Reading, Mass.: Addison-Wesley, 1979); H. R. Rodgers, *The Cost of Human Neglect* (Armonk, N.Y.: M. E. Sharp, 1982); Leonard Beeghley, *Living Poorly in America* (New York: Praeger, 1983); B. R. Schiller, *The Economics of Poverty and Discrimination* (Englewood Cliffs, N.J: Prentice Hall, 1976).
9. H. R. Rodgers, "Hiding versus Ending Poverty," *Politics and Society* 8 (Fall 1978): 253–66.
10. Schiller, *The Economics of Poverty and Discrimination*, 21.
11. Rose Friedman, *Poverty: Definition and Perspective* (Washington, D.C.: American Enterprise Institute, 1965).
12. Sawhill, "Poverty in the U.S.," 1077.
13. Murray, *Losing Ground*, 65.
14. Robert Avery, Gregory Elliehausen, and Glen Canner, "Survey of Consumer Finances" (1983), *Federal Reserve Bulletin* 70 (Sept. 1984): 679–92. Also see Sawhill, "Poverty in the U.S.," 1079.

Index